Ultra-fast ASP.NET

Building Ultra-fast and Ultra-scalable Web Sites Using ASP.NET and SQL Server

Richard Kiessig

Ultra-fast ASP.NET

ISBN-13 (pbk): 978-1-4302-2383-2

ISBN-13 (electronic): 978-1-4302-2384-9

Printed and bound in the United States of America 9 8 7 6 5 4 3 2 1

Lead Editor: Matthew Moodie
Technical Reviewer:
Editorial Board: Clay Andres, Steve Anglin, Mark Beckner, Ewan Buckingham, Tony Campbell, Gary Cornell, Jonathan Gennick, Michelle Lowman, Matthew Moodie, Jeffrey Pepper, Frank Pohlmann, Ben Renow-Clarke, Dominic Shakeshaft, Matt Wade, Tom Welsh
Copy Editors: Kim Wimpsett and Tiffany Taylor
Production Assistance: Patrick Cunningham
Indexer: Becky Hornyak
Artist: April Milne

Distributed to the book trade worldwide by Springer-Verlag New York, Inc., 233 Spring Street, 6th Floor, New York, NY 10013. Phone 1-800-SPRINGER, fax 201-348-4505, e-mail orders-ny@springer-sbm.com, or visit http://www.springeronline.com.

For information on translations, please e-mail info@apress.com, or visit http://www.apress.com.

Apress and friends of ED books may be purchased in bulk for academic, corporate, or promotional use. eBook versions and licenses are also available for most titles. For more information, reference our Special Bulk Sales–eBook Licensing web page at http://www.apress.com/info/bulksales.

The source code for this book is available to readers at http://www.apress.com.

Contents at a Glance

Contents

About the Author

After graduating from UC Santa Barbara with a BA in Mathematics in 1979, I went to work at the Rand Corporation, where I continued my involvement with Unix, C, and the Internet. During the 1980s, I moved to Silicon Valley, where I specialized in low-level operating systems work, performance tuning, and network-oriented applications. I wrote a Unix-like OS from scratch, including a high-performance filesystem. I developed an XNS-based network stack and helped architect Intel's first port of Unix to the x86. I also wrote several 3-D scientific animation systems and a gate array placement package.

In the early 1990s, I wrote a custom real-time OS that was used in the US Navy's F-18 aircraft. I developed real-time applications that were used in spacecraft and associated ground support systems, including a system called the Stellar Compass that measures vehicle attitude using digital images of stars. That software has flown to the Moon, to Mars three times, and to a comet and back. I was also the principal architect and designer of the ground system and various flight software components for one of the world's first commercial imaging satellites.

I was very enthusiastic about Java when I first heard about it. One of the first large-scale things I developed with it was an audio conferencing system. After that, I used it to develop a custom high-performance application server. I helped to architect and build several large-scale Java-based data-intensive web sites and web applications, including one that was designed to be deployed to and used by 20 million set-top boxes to provide Internet over TV. My last Java-based project was building a document-management-oriented filesystem; I am the primary inventor of several related patents. Multiple financial institutions are now using the system to help address risk-management issues.

I went to work for Microsoft in late 1999. My first project there was to develop a comprehensive architecture to deliver MSN content via TV-oriented middleware platforms such as WebTV using C#, ASP.NET, and SQL Server. A few years later, after completing development of the initial system, I moved to the Microsoft Technology Center, where I began working with and advising some of Microsoft's largest customers regarding the .NET- and SQL Server–oriented aspects of their system architectures.

The common threads that bind my career together include a focus on performance and reliability. The software development process is another long-time interest of mine, because I've seen first-hand how much of an impact it can have on the success or failure of a project.

In December 2006, my family and I left the intensity of Silicon Valley and moved to beautiful New Zealand, where we currently live. My hobbies include ham radio (callsign ZL2HAM) and photography.

About the Technical Reviewer

■Simon Taylor is Head of Engineering at Trigger Software in Cheltenham, UK where he is involved in projects that make use of technologies including Java, Flex and his main passion .Net. Simon started professional life as a C developer on Unix platforms after graduating from the University of Manchester with a BSc in Computer Science. From there Simon moved onto developing with Java and finally .Net 4 years ago. This year he has become more active in the .Net community regularly attending local user group meetings and setting up a blog at http://www.sharpcoder.co.uk.

Introduction

The time that I spent working at Microsoft was an unexpectedly transforming experience. The first half of my career regularly put me and the companies I worked with in competition with Microsoft, and I was often surrounded by anti-Microsoft stories and propaganda. However, when I heard about .NET, I decided I wanted to know more and that the best way to do that was to learn at the source.

As I got into the technology and the company, what I found was more than a little surprising. The .NET Framework, the C# language, ASP.NET, and SQL Server are sophisticated and technically beautiful achievements. After working with Java for several years, which also has a definite elegance, it was refreshing and empowering to use a well-integrated *platform*, where everything (mostly) worked together seamlessly. At a technical level, I found that I usually agreed with the decisions and tradeoffs the platform developers made, and that the resulting system helped to substantially improve my productivity as a developer. I also found the Microsoft engineering teams to be wonderfully bright, creative, and—perhaps most surprising of all to me as a former outsider—sincerely interested in solving customer problems.

My enthusiasm for the technology helped carry me into a customer-facing position as a solutions architect at the Microsoft Technology Center in Silicon Valley. Being exposed in-depth to customer issues was another eye-opening experience. First, I could see first hand the remarkably positive impact of Microsoft technologies on many people and companies. Second, I could also see the intense frustration and poor results that some people were having. This book is, in part, a response to some of those frustrations.

My perspective is that ASP.NET and SQL Server have tremendous potential. However, key aspects of the technologies are not obvious. I've talked with many developers and managers who sense the potential but who have had extreme difficulty when it comes to the implementation. Unfortunately, realizing the technology's full potential requires more up-front effort than some alternative approaches; it's a rich environment, and to appreciate it fully requires a certain perspective. One of my goals for this book is to help remove some of the fog that may be masking the end-to-end vision of the technology and to help you see the beauty and the full potential of ASP.NET and SQL Server.

Another reason I wrote this book is that I am frustrated constantly by how slow some sites are, and I'm hoping you will be able to use the information here to help change that. The Web has amazing possibilities, well beyond even the fantastic level it's reached already—but they can be realized only if performance is good. Slow sites are a turn-off for everyone.

My connection to the Internet today uses a 3+Mbps DSL line, and each of the four cores in my desktop CPU runs at nearly 3GHz; that's astonishingly fast compared to what was possible just a few years ago. Even with all that speed and power, many web sites still take a long time to load—sometimes a minute or more per page—and my local network and CPU are almost idle during that time. As software professionals, that should concern us. I find it almost embarrassing. I want to be proud of not just my own work but also of my profession's. Let's make our sites not just fast, but *ultra-fast*.

Who This Book Is For

The first two and last two chapters in this book provide information that will be useful to all web developers, regardless of which underlying technology you use. The middle seven chapters will interest intermediate to advanced architects and developers who are designing, building or maintaining web sites using ASP.NET and SQL Server. Experienced web developers who have recently moved from Java or PHP to .NET will also find lots of valuable and interesting information here.

This book will be useful for non-developers who have a technical interest in what makes a web site fast. In particular, if you're involved with web site operations, testing, or management, you will discover many of the principals and issues that your development teams should be addressing, along with demonstrations that help drive the points home.

Contacting the Author

You can reach me at `rick@12titans.net`. Please visit my web site at `http://www.12titans.net/`.

I would love to hear about your experiences with the ultra-fast approach.

Techniques to improve performance and scalability are constantly evolving, along with the underlying technology. I am very interested in hearing about any techniques I haven't covered here that you find to be effective.

Please let me know if you find any errors in the text or the code samples, or tweaks that can make them even better.

Acknowledgments

I would like to thank the wonderful team at Apress: Ewan Buckingham for his early support and encouragement; Matthew Moodie for help with the overall structure and flow; Simon Taylor for technical reviews, including double-checking the code samples; Anita Castro for project management; and Kim Wimpsett and Tiffany Taylor for copy editing.

I would also like to thank Phil de Joux for his feedback

CHAPTER 1

■ ■ ■

Principles and Method

Modern large-scale web sites are amazingly complex feats of engineering. Partly as a result of this, many sites run into significant performance and scalability problems as they grow. In fact, it's not unusual for large sites to be reengineered almost from scratch at some point in order to handle their growth. Fortunately, consistently following a few basic principles can make sites faster while they're still small and can also minimize the problems you will encounter as they grow.

This book will explore those principles and help you understand how and why you should apply them.

I'm basing the ideas presented here on my work developing network-oriented software over the past 30 years. I started working with the Internet in 1974 and with Unix and C in 1979 and later moved to C++ and then Java and C#. I learned about ASP.NET and SQL Server in depth while working at Microsoft, where I helped architect and develop a large-scale web site for MSN TV. I polished that knowledge over the next few years while I was an architect at the Microsoft Technology Center (MTC) in Silicon Valley. During that time, I helped run two- to three-day architectural design sessions once or twice each week for some of Microsoft's largest and most sophisticated customers. Other MTC architects and I would work to first understand customer issues and problems and then help architect solutions that would address them.

It didn't take long before I discovered that a lot of people had the same questions, many of which were focused around performance and scalability. For example:

- "How can we make our HTML display faster?" (Chapter 2)

- "What's the best way to do caching?" (Chapter 3)

- "How can we use IIS to make our site faster?" (Chapter 4)

- "How should we handle session state?" (Chapter 5)

- "How can we improve our ASP.NET code?" (Chapters 5 to 7)

- "Why is our database slow?" (Chapters 8 and 9)

- "How can we optimize our infrastructure and operations?" (Chapter 10)

- "Where do we start?" (Chapter 11)

One of the themes of this book is to present high-impact solutions to issues like these.

1

One aspect of the approach I've taken is to look at a web site not just as an application running on a remote server but rather as a distributed collection of components that need to work well together as a system.

In this chapter, I'll start with a description of performance and scalability, along with what I mean by *ultra-fast* and *ultra-scalable*. Then I'll present a high-level overview of the end-to-end process that's involved in generating a web page, and I'll describe the core principles upon which I base this approach to performance. I'll conclude with a description of the environment and tools that I used in developing the examples that I present later in the book.

The Difference Between Performance and Scalability

Whenever someone tells me that they want their system to be fast, the first question I ask is, "What do you mean by *fast*?" A typical answer might be "It needs to support thousands of users." A site can be slow and still support thousands of users. In fact, some large sites are very slow.

Scalability and performance are distinctly different. In the context of this book, when I talk about improving a site's performance, what I mean is decreasing the time it takes for a particular page to load or for a particular user-visible action to complete. What a single user sees while sitting at their computer is "performance."

Scalability, on the other hand, has to do with how many users a site can support. A scalable site is one that can easily support additional users by adding more hardware and network bandwidth (no significant software changes), with little or no difference in overall performance. If adding more users causes the site to slow down significantly and adding more hardware or bandwidth won't solve the problem, then the site has reached its scalability threshold. One of the goals in designing for scalability is to increase that threshold; it will never go away.

Why *Ultra-fast* and *Ultra-scalable*?

Speed and scalability should apply to more than just your web servers. Many aspects of web development can and should be fast and scalable. All of your code should be fast, whether it runs at the client, in the web tier, or in the data tier. All of your pages should be fast, not just a few of them. Your changes, fixes, and deployments should also be fast.

A definite synergy happens when you apply speed and scalability deeply in a project. Not only will your customers and users be happier, but engineers too will be happier and will feel more challenged. Surprisingly, less hardware is often required, and quality assurance and operations teams can often be smaller. That's what I mean by *ultra-fast* and *ultra-scalable*. (I will often refer to it as just *ultra-fast* for short, even though scalability is always implied.)

The ultra-fast approach is very different from an impulsive, "do-it-now" type of programming. The architectural problems that inevitably arise when you don't approach development in a methodical way tend to significantly offset whatever short-term benefits you might realize from taking shortcuts. Most large-scale software development projects are marathons, not sprints; advance planning and preparation pay huge long-term benefits.

I've summarized the goals of the ultra-fast and ultra-scalable approach in Table 1-1.

Table 1-1. Goals of the Ultra-fast and Ultra-scalable Approach

Component	Ultra-fast and Ultra-scalable Goals
Pages	Every page is scalable and fast under load.
Tiers	All tiers are scalable and fast under load.
Agility	You can respond quickly to changing business needs, and you can readily maintain performance and scalability in the event of changes.
Maintainability	You can quickly find and fix performance-related bugs.
Operations	You can quickly deploy and grow your sites. Capacity planning is straightforward and reliable.
Hardware	Your servers are well utilized under load; fewer machines are required.

Building a fast and scalable web site has some high-level similarities to building a race car. You need to engineer and design the core performance aspects from the beginning in order for them to be effective. In racing, you need to decide what class or league you want to race in. Is it going to be Formula One, stock car, rallying, dragster, or maybe just kart? If you build a car for kart, not only will you be unable to compete in Formula One, but you will have to throw the whole design away and start again if you decide you want to change to a new class. With web sites, building a site for just yourself and your friends is of course completely different from building eBay or Yahoo. A design that works for one would be completely inappropriate for the other.

A top-end race car doesn't just go fast. You can also do things like change its wheels quickly, fill it with fuel quickly, and even quickly swap out the engine for a new one. In that way, race cars are fast in multiple dimensions. Your web site should also be fast in multiple dimensions.

In the same way that it's a bad idea to design a race car to go fast without considering safety, it is also not a good idea to design a high-performance web site without keeping security in mind. In the chapters that follow, I will therefore make an occasional brief diversion into security in areas where there is significant overlap with performance, such as with cookies in Chapter 3.

Optimization

As many industry experts have rightly pointed out, optimization can be a deadly trap and time-waster. The key to building high-performance web sites is engineering them so that optimization is not required to get decent results. However, as with racing, if you want to compete with the best, then you need to integrate measuring, adjusting, tuning, tweaking, and innovating into your development process. There's always something you can do better, provided you have the time, money, and motivation to do so.

The real trick is knowing where to look for performance and scalability problems and what kinds of changes are likely to have the biggest impact. Comparing the weight of wheel lugs to one another is probably a waste of time, but getting the engine mixture just right can win the race. Improving the efficiency of an infrequently called function won't improve the scalability of your site; switching to using asynchronous pages will.

I don't mean that small things aren't important. In fact, many small problems can quickly add up to be a big problem. However, when you're prioritizing tasks and allocating time to them, be sure to focus on the high-impact tasks first. Putting a high polish on a race car is nice and might help it go a little faster, but if the transmission is no good, you should focus your efforts there first. Polishing some internal API just how you want it might be nice, but eliminating round-trips should be a much higher priority.

Process

Ultra-fast is a state of mind—a process. It begins with the architecture and the design, and it flows into all aspects of the system, from development to testing to deployment, maintenance, upgrades, and optimization. However, as with building a race car or any other complex project, there is usually a sense of urgency and a desire to get something done quickly that's "good enough." Understanding where the big impact points are is a critical part of being able to do that effectively, while still meeting your business goals. The approach I've taken in this book is to focus on the things you *should* do, rather than to explore everything that you *could* do. The goal is to help you focus on high-impact areas and to avoid getting lost in the weeds in the process.

I've worked with many software teams that have had difficulty getting management approval to work on performance. Often these same teams run into performance crises, and those crises sometimes lead to redesigning their sites from scratch. Management tends to focus inevitably on features, as long as performance is "good enough." The problem is that performance is only good enough *until it isn't*—and that's when a crisis happens. In my experience, you can often avoid this slippery slope by not selling performance to management as a feature. It's *not* a feature, any more than security or quality are features. Performance and the other aspects of the ultra-fast approach are an integral part of the application; *they permeate every feature*. If you're building a race car, making it go fast isn't an extra feature that you can add at the end; it is part of the architecture, and you build it into every component and every procedure.

There's no magic here. These are the keys to making this work:

- Developing a deep understanding of the full end-to-end system

- Building a solid architecture

- Focusing effort on high-impact areas, and knowing what's safe to ignore or defer

- Understanding that a little extra up-front effort will have big benefits in the long term

- Using the right software development process and tools

You might have heard about something called the "eight-second rule" for web performance. It's a human-factors-derived guideline that says if a page takes longer than eight seconds to load, there's a good chance users won't wait and will click away to another page or site. Rather than focusing on rules like that, this book takes a completely different approach. Instead of targeting artificial performance metrics, the idea is to *focus first on the architecture*. That puts you in the right "league." Then, build your site using a set of well-grounded guidelines. With the foundation in place, you shouldn't need to spend a lot of effort on optimization. The idea is to set your sights high from the beginning by applying some high-end design techniques. You want to avoid building a racer for kart and then have to throw it away when your key competitors move up to Formula One before you do.

The Full Experience

Performance should encompass the full user experience. For example, the time to load the full page is only one aspect of the overall user experience; perceived performance is even more important. If the useful content appears "instantly" and then some ads show up ten seconds later, most users won't complain, and many won't even notice. However, if you display the page in the opposite order, with the slow ads first and the content afterward, you might risk losing many of your users, even though the total page load time is the same.

Web sites that one person builds and maintains can benefit from this approach as much as larger web sites can (imagine a kart racer with some Formula One parts). A fast site will attract more traffic and more return visitors than a slow one. You might be able to get along with a smaller server or a less expensive hosting plan. Your users might visit more pages.

As an example of what's possible with ASP.NET and SQL Server when you focus on architecture and performance, *one* software developer by himself built the site plentyoffish.com, and it is now one of the highest-traffic sites in Canada. The site serves more than 45 million visitors per month, with 1.2 billion page views per month, or 500 to 600 pages per second. Yet it only uses *three* load-balanced web servers, with dual quad-core CPUs and 8GB RAM, plus a few database servers, along with a content distribution network (CDN). The CPUs on the web servers average 30 percent busy. I don't know any details about the internals of that site, but after looking at the HTML it generates, I'm confident that you can use the techniques I'm providing in this book to produce a comparable site that's even faster.

Unfortunately, there's no free lunch: building an ultra-fast site does take more thought and planning than a quick-and-dirty approach. It also takes more development effort, although usually only in the beginning. Over the long run, maintenance and development costs can actually be significantly less, and you should be able to avoid any costly ground-up rewrites. In the end, I hope you'll agree that the benefits are worth the effort.

End-to-End Web Page Processing

A common way to think about the Web is that there is a browser on one end of a network connection and a web server with a database on the other end, as in Figure 1-1.

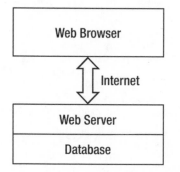

Figure 1-1. Simplified web architecture model

The simplified model is easy to explain and understand, and it works fine up to a point. However, quite a few other components are actually involved, and many of them can have an impact on performance and scalability. Figure 1-2 shows some of them for web sites based on ASP.NET and SQL Server.

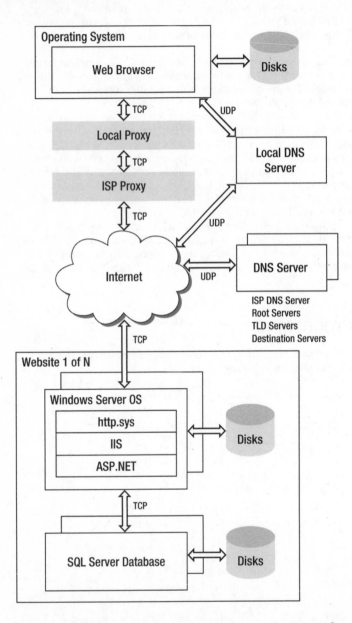

Figure 1-2. Web architecture components that can impact performance

All of the components in Figure 1-2 can introduce delay into the time it takes to load a page, but that delay is manageable to some degree. Additional infrastructure-oriented components such as routers, load balancers, and firewalls aren't included because the delay they introduce is generally not manageable.

In the following list, I've summarized the process of loading a web page. Each of these steps offers opportunities for optimization that I'll discuss in detail later in the book:

1. First, the browser looks in its local cache to see whether it already has a copy of the page. See Chapter 2.

2. If the page isn't in the local cache, then the browser looks up the IP address of the web server using DNS. Both the browser and the operating system have their own DNS caches to store the results of previous queries. If the address isn't already known or if the cache entry has timed out, then a nearby DNS server is usually consulted next (it's often in a local router, for example). See Chapter 10.

3. Next, the browser opens a network connection to the web server. In some cases, the connection might be directed to a proxy server. This can be either a visible proxy or a transparent one. A visible proxy is one that a user configures by name. They are sometimes used at large companies, for example, to help improve web performance for their employees or sometimes for security or filtering purposes. A transparent proxy is one that doesn't have to be configured. It intercepts all outgoing TCP connections on port 80 (HTTP), regardless of local client settings. If the local proxy doesn't have the desired content, then the HTTP request is forwarded to the target web server. See Chapters 2 and 3.

4. Some ISPs also use proxies to help improve performance for their customers and to reduce the bandwidth they use. As with the local proxy, if the content isn't available in the ISP proxy cache, then the request is forwarded along. See Chapter 3.

5. The next stop is a web server at the destination site. A large site will have a number of load-balanced web servers, any of which will be able to accept and process incoming requests. Each machine will have its own local disk and separate caches at the operating system driver level (`http.sys`), in Internet Information Services (IIS), and in ASP.NET. See Chapters 3 through 7.

6. If the requested page needs data from the database, then the web server will open a connection to one or more of those servers. It can then issue queries for the data it needs. The data might reside in RAM cache in the database, or it might need to be read in from disk. See Chapters 8 and 9.

7. When the web server has the data it needs, it dynamically creates the requested page and sends it back to the user. If the results have appropriate HTTP response headers, they can be cached in multiple locations. See Chapters 3 and 4.

8. When the response arrives at the client, the browser parses it and renders it to the screen. See Chapter 2.

Overview of Principles

The first and most important rule of building a high-performance site is that performance starts with the application itself. If you have a page with a loop counting to a gazillion, for example, nothing I'm describing will help.

Performance Principles

With the assumption of a sound implementation, the following are some high-impact core architectural principles for performance and scalability:

- **Focus on perceived performance.** Users are happier if they quickly see a response after they click. It's even better if what they see first is the information they're most interested in. See Chapter 2.

- **Minimize blocking calls.** ASP.NET provides only a limited number of worker threads to process web page requests. If they are all blocked waiting for long-running tasks, the runtime will queue up new incoming HTTP requests instead of executing them right away, and your web server throughput will decline dramatically. You could have a long queue of requests waiting to be processed, while your server's CPU utilization was very low. Minimizing the time worker threads are blocked is a cornerstone of building a scalable site. You can do that using features such as asynchronous pages, async `HttpModules`, async I/O, async database requests, background worker threads, and Service Broker. Maximizing asynchronous activity in the browser is a key aspect of reducing browser page load times because it allows the browser to do multiple things at the same time. See Chapters 2 and Chapters 5 through 8.

- **Reduce round-trips.** Every round-trip is expensive. "Chattiness" is one of the most common killers of good site performance. You can eliminate round-trips between the client and the web server and between the web server and the database by caching, combining requests (batching), combining source files or data, combining responses (multiple result sets), working with sets of data, and other similar techniques. See Chapters 2 through 8.

- **Cache at all tiers.** Caching is important at most steps of the page request process. You should leverage the browser's cache, cookies, on-page data (hidden fields or `ViewState`), proxies, the Windows kernel cache (`http.sys`), the IIS cache, the ASP.NET application cache, page and fragment output caching, the ASP.NET cache object, server-side per-request caching, database dependency caching, distributed caching, and caching in RAM at the database. See Chapters 3 and 8.

- **Optimize disk I/O management.** Disks are physical devices; they have platters that spin and read/write heads that move back and forth. Rotation and head movement (disk seeks) take time. Disks work much faster when you manage I/O to avoid excessive seeks. The difference in performance between sequential I/O and random I/O can easily be 40 to 1 or more. This is particularly important on database servers, where the database log is written sequentially. Proper hardware selection and configuration plays a big role here, too, including choosing the type and number of drives, using the best RAID level, using the right number of logical drives or LUNs, and so on. See Chapters 8 and 10.

Secondary Techniques

You can often apply a number of secondary techniques easily and quickly that will help improve system-level performance and scalability. As with most of the techniques described here, it's easier to apply them effectively when you design them into your web site from the beginning. As with security and quality requirements, the later in the development process that you address performance and scalability requirements, the more difficult the problems tend to be. I've summarized a few examples of these techniques in the following list:

- **Understand browser behavior.** By understanding the way that the browser loads a web page, you can optimize HTML and HTTP to reduce download time and improve both total rendering speed and perceived speed. See Chapter 2.

- **Avoid full page loads by using Ajax, Silverlight, and plain JavaScript.** You can use client-side field validation and other types of request gating with JavaScript to completely avoid some page requests. You can use Ajax and Silverlight to request small amounts of data that can be dynamically inserted into the page or into a rich user interface. See Chapter 2.

- **Avoid synchronous database writes on every request.** Heavy database writes are a common cause of scalability problems. Incorrect use of session state is a frequent source of problems in this area, since it has to be both read and written (and deserialized and reserialized) with every request. You may be able to use cookies to reduce or eliminate the need for server-side session state storage. See Chapters 5 and 8.

- **Monitoring and instrumentation.** As your site grows in terms of both content and users, instrumentation can provide valuable insights into performance and scalability issues, while also helping to improve agility and maintainability. You can time off-box calls and compare the results against performance thresholds. You can use Windows performance counters to expose those measurements to a rich set of tools. Centralized monitoring can provide trend analysis to support capacity planning and to help identify problems early. See Chapter 10.

- **Understand how SQL Server manages memory.** For example, when a T-SQL command modifies a database, the server does a synchronous (and sequential) write to the database log. Only after the write has finished will the server return to the requestor. The modified data pages are still in memory. They will stay there until SQL Server needs the memory for other requests; they will be written to the data file by the background lazy writer thread. This means that SQL Server can process subsequent read requests for the same data quickly from cache. It also means that the speed of the log disk has a direct impact on your database's write throughput. See Chapter 8.

- **Effective use of partitioning at the data tier.** One of the keys to addressing database scalability is to partition your data. You might replicate read-only data to a group of load-balanced servers running SQL Express, or you might partition writable data among several severs based on a particular key. You might split up data in a single large table into multiple partitions to avoid performance problems when the data is pruned or archived. See Chapter 8.

I will discuss these and other similar techniques at length in the chapters ahead.

What this book is not about is low-level code optimization; my focus here is mostly on architecture and process and partly on approach.

Environment and Tools Used in This Book

Although cross-browser compatibility is important, in keeping with the point I made earlier about focusing on the high-impact aspects of your system, I've found that focusing development and tuning efforts on the browsers that comprise the top 90 percent or so in use will bring most of the rest for free. You should be able to manage whatever quirkiness might be left afterward on an exception basis, unless you're building a site specifically oriented toward one of the minority browsers.

I also don't consider the case of browsers without JavaScript or cookies enabled to be realistic anymore. Without those features, the Web becomes a fairly barren place, so I think of them as being a given for real users; search engines and other bots are an entirely different story, of course.

As of June 2009, the most popular browsers according to w3schools.com were Firefox with 47 percent and Internet Explorer with 41 percent of the market. The remaining 11 percent was split between Chrome, Safari, Opera, and others. They also report that 95 percent of all browsers have JavaScript enabled. I would wager that a significant fraction of the remaining 5 percent are bots masquerading as browsers.

Software Tools and Versions

The specific tools that I've used for the code examples and figures are listed in Table 1-2, including a rough indication of cost. A single $ indicates a price under US$100, $$ is between US$100 and US$1,000, and $$$ is more than US$1,000.

Table 1-2. *Software Tools and Versions*

Software	Version	Cost
Adobe Photoshop	CS3	$$
Contig	1.55	Free download
Expression Web	12.0.6211.1000 SP1	$$
Fiddler Web Debugger	2.2.0.0	Free download
Firebug	1.4.0	Free download (Firefox plug-in)
Firefox	3.0.5	Free download
Internet Explorer	7 and 8	Free download
Log Parser	2.2	Free download
.NET Framework	3.5 SP1 and 4.0 beta 1	Free download

Software	Version	Cost
Office	Ultimate 2007	$$
Silverlight	2 and 3	Free download
Silverlight Projects	2008	Free download
SQL Server	Developer 2008	$
SQL Server	Standard and Enterprise 2008	$$$
SQL Server Feature Pack	October 2008	Free download
System Center Operations Manager	2007 R2	$$
Visual Studio Team Suite	2008 SP1	$$$
Team System Database Edition	2008 GDR	Free upgrade to Team Suite
Web Deployment Projects	2008	Free download
Windows Server	Standard 2008	$$
Windows Vista	Ultimate SP1	$$
Wireshark	1.0.5	Free download
YSlow	2.0.0b4	Free download (Firefox plug-in)

Although I'm using Visual Studio Team Suite, most of the code that I discuss and demonstrate will also work in Visual Studio Web Express, which is a free download.

Terminology

See the glossary for definitions of business intelligence (BI)–specific terminology.

Typographic Conventions

I am using the following typographic conventions:

- *Italics*: Term definitions and emphasis
- **Bold**: Text as you would see it on the screen
- `Monospace`: Code, URLs, file names, and other text as you would type it

Author's Web Site

My web site at `http://www.12titans.net/` has online versions of many of the web pages used as samples or demonstrations, along with code downloads and links to related resources.

Summary

In this chapter, I covered the following:

- Performance relates to how quickly something happens from your end user's perspective, while scalability involves how many users your site can support and how easily it can support more.

- *Ultra-fast* and *Ultra-scalable* include more than just the current performance of your web site. You should apply speed and scalability principles at all tiers in your architecture. Your site should also be agile, with instrumentation and monitoring that allow you to identify problems quickly.

- Processing a request for a web page involves a number of discrete steps, many of which present opportunities for performance improvements.

- You should apply a handful of key performance and scalability principles throughout your site: focus on perceived performance, minimize blocking calls, reduce round-trips, cache at all tiers, and optimize disk I/O management.

In the next chapter, I'll cover the client-side processing of a web page, including how you can improve the performance of your site by structuring your content so that a browser can download and display it quickly.

■ ■ ■

CHAPTER 2

Client Performance

The process of displaying a web page involves distributed computing. A browser on the client PC requests and parses the HTML, JavaScript, CSS, images, and other objects on a page, while one or more servers generate and deliver dynamic and static content. Building a fast *system*, therefore, requires both the browser and the server to be fast, as well as the network and other components in between. One way to think about it is that the server is really sending one or more programs to the browser in the form of HTML (which is after all, Hypertext Markup *Language*) and Java*Script*. The browser then has to parse and execute those programs and render the results to the screen.

For existing sites, I've found that optimizing the output of your web site so that it runs faster on the client can often produce larger user-visible performance improvements than making your server-side code run faster. It is therefore a good place to start on the road to building an ultra-fast site.

Particularly on the browser side of the performance equation, many small improvements can quickly add up to a large one. Slow sites are often the result of the "death of 1,000 cuts" syndrome. A few extra characters here or there don't matter. However, many small transgressions can quickly add up to make the difference between a slow site and a fast one, or between a fast site and an ultra-fast one. Another way to think about it is that it's often a lot easier to save a handful of bytes in 100 places than 100 bytes in a handful of places.

Imagine building a house. A little neglect here or there won't compromise the quality of the final product. However, if the attitude becomes pervasive, it doesn't take long before the whole structure suffers as a result. In fact, at some point, repairs are impossible, and you have to tear down the house and build again from scratch to get it right. A similar thing happens with many aspects of software, including performance and scalability.

In this chapter, I will cover the following:

- Browser page processing

- Browser caching

- Network optimizations

- Script include file handling

- Download less

- Using JavaScript to gate page requests

- Using JavaScript to reduce HTML size

- Upload less

- CSS optimizations

- Image sprites and clustering

- Leveraging DHTML

- Using Silverlight

- Improving rendering speed

- Precaching

- Table-less layout using CSS

- Optimizing JavaScript performance

The example files for this chapter are available online at www.12titans.net and in the download that's available from www.apress.com.

Browser Page Processing

When a browser loads a page, it's not a batch process. Users don't close their eyes after they enter a URL and open them again when the browser has finished loading the page. Browsers do what they can to overlap activity on multiple network connections with page parsing and rendering to the screen. The steps browsers follow are often extremely visible to users and can have a significant impact on both perceived performance and total page load time.

Network Connections and the Initial HTTP Request

To retrieve a web page, browsers start with a URL. The browser determines the IP address of the server using DNS. Then, using HTTP over TCP, the browser connects to the server and requests the content associated with the URL. The browser parses the response and renders it to the screen in parallel with the ongoing network activity, queuing and requesting content from other URLs in parallel as it goes.

Rather than getting too sidetracked with the variations from one browser to another, my focus here will mostly be on Internet Explorer 7 (IE7, or just IE), partly because it's the browser that I understand best. Other browsers work similarly, although there are definite differences from one implementation to another. With Firefox, users can set parameters that change some of the details of how it processes pages, so the page load experience may not be 100 percent identical from one user to another, even when they're using the same browser.

Figure 2-1 shows the TCP networking aspect of connecting to a remote server and requesting a URL with HTTP.

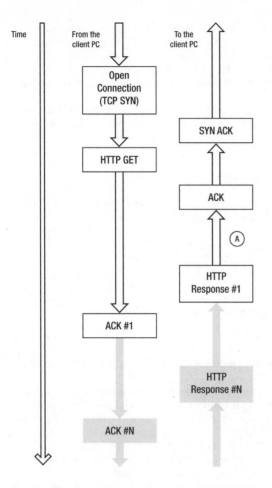

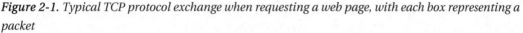

Figure 2-1. *Typical TCP protocol exchange when requesting a web page, with each box representing a packet*

The browser asks the server to open a connection by sending a TCP SYN packet. The server responds by acknowledging the SYN, at which point the connection is open.

The browser then sends an HTTP GET, which includes the requested URL, cookies, and other details. After a while, the server ACKs that packet, and during the time marked as A in Figure 2-1, it generates a response.

Then the server sends the response and the client ACKs it. How often the ACKs are required is determined by the size of the TCP "window," which is a big factor in achievable network speeds.

You can see that the response to the browser's request doesn't arrive all at once. There are gaps of time between when the client sends a packet and when the server responds, as well as in between successive packets.

Horizontal zones such as area A in Figure 2-1 where there are no boxes containing packets indicate that the network is idle during those times. Using multiple simultaneous connections can help minimize that idle time and thereby minimize total page load time.

The maximum packet size varies from 500 to 1,500 bytes depending on the network *maximum transmission unit* (MTU).). The first data packet from the server includes the HTTP response header, usually along with some HTML, depending on the size of the header. Because of the way that the TCP network protocol works (a feature called *slow start*), there can be a relatively long delay between when the first data packet arrives and when the next one does while the network connection ramps up to full speed.

The SYN and SYN ACK packets along with TCP slow-start combine to make opening a network connection a relatively time-consuming process. It is therefore something that we would like to avoid doing too much.

Page Parsing and New Resource Requests

While IE is waiting for a packet of data, it parses what it already has and looks for any new HTTP requests that it might be able to start in parallel. It will open up to two connections to each server.

The timeline shown here illustrates how IE handles a page where an `<img>` tag is located in the middle of a bunch of text (see `file01.htm`).

The horizontal axis is time, and each row corresponds to a different request made by the browser. The top row shows the time needed to resolve the IP address of the server using DNS.

The second row shows the time to read the main page. The section on the left is the time to connect to the server (the SYN and SYN ACK). It starts right after the IP address has been resolved. The middle section is the time to send the initial HTTP `GET` request and to receive the initial HTTP response, and the section on the right is the time for the rest of response to arrive.

The bottom row is the time to retrieve the image, with connect time on the left and time to request and then receive the initial response on the right. Since the image is small, all of the image data is included in the same packet as the HTTP response, so the third section is not present.

IE doesn't open the second connection to the server to request the image until about halfway through the time that it takes to receive the HTML. That's because it is parsing the HTML as it arrives, and since the `<img>` tag is located some distance from the beginning, IE doesn't see it until after several packets of data have arrived.

The next timeline shows what happens when the `<img>` tag is located close to the beginning of the file so that it's in the first packet of data received by IE (see `file02.htm`):

The first two rows are roughly the same. Now the request for the image starts shortly after the first packet of HTML arrives. As a result, it takes less total time to retrieve the page and the image; the entire image arrives shortly after the last of the HTML does.

To leverage this aspect of how IE processes a page, you should put one or more requests for objects near the top of your HTML. Since the size of the HTTP response headers can vary and since the maximum size of packets is about 1,500 bytes, I've found that putting the requests in the first 500 bytes of your HTML is a good rule of thumb.

Page Resource Order and Reordering

IE retrieves all resources requested in the <head> section of the HTML before it starts rendering the <body>. Since the <head> section can't contain any tags that will cause the browser to draw content on the screen, users will see nothing until it has downloaded all resources in the <head> section. If you place the requests in the <body> section instead, then page rendering and downloading resources can happen in parallel. You should move as many resource requests as you can from the <head> section into the <body> of your HTML.

■ **Note** The HTML specification calls for <link> and <style> tags (for CSS) to be in the <head> section, although browsers don't enforce that limitation.

As HTML parsing continues, resources that the page references, including images, are queued for retrieval in the order IE encounters them. IE will request an image near the top of the file before other resources from the same domain. This means that you should *make the position of objects on the page independent from object download order*. For example, if you have a large image banner or logo at the top of your page, although it may be important for site aesthetics or branding, it may not be the first thing that users will want to see, but if it's at the top of the HTML, it will be the first thing downloaded by the browser.

You can use JavaScript and CSS to achieve out-of-order object loading. For example, you can reserve the space on the page with an <img> tag and request the image associated with that tag earlier or later in the file using script. That way, you can call the script according to when users should see the image. Here's an example of late loading:

```
<img id="myimg" width="50" height="50" />
. . .
<script type="text/javascript">
document.getElementById("myimg").src = "myimage.jpg";
</script>
```

The <img> tag only has the width, the height, and an ID. Script later in the file then sets the src attribute, which will cause the browser to queue the download.

■ **Note** As a best practice, you should always specify the width and height for your images, using either properties or CSS. Doing so helps minimize the time it takes the browser to render the page.

For early loading:

```
<script type="text/javascript">
var myimg = new Image();
myimg.src = "myimage.jpg";
</script>
. . .
<img src="myimage.jpg" width="50" height="50" />
```

Allocate an Image object, and set its src attribute to the desired filename. That will cause the browser to queue the image for downloading. Then, in the <img> tag, just use the same filename again. Since the browser should cache the image, it will be downloaded only once.

You should use late loading for images that the user wouldn't consider important or that are below the fold where they can't be seen. You should use early loading for images that are important to the user and that are above the fold.

Browser Caching

The browser cache is case-sensitive. Since the Windows NTFS filesystem and IIS URL handling are not (unlike Unix/Linux with Apache), this can result in the browser downloading the same object more than once if you don't use consistent case for URLs that refer to the same object. Browsers use a direct string comparison to determine whether two URLs refer to the same object. For example, the following code would cause the browser to download the same image twice, even if it was cacheable:

```
<img src="myimage.jpg" width="50" height="50" />
<img src="myimage.JPG" width="50" height="50" />
```

One approach to addressing this issue is to adopt a policy of having your URLs be entirely in lowercase.

For dynamic content, it might also make sense to check for mixed-case incoming URLs in an ASP.NET HttpModule. You could increment a performance counter to provide an indication of how often the server encounters such URLs, or you could write the URL and its referrer to a log, or perhaps issue a permanent redirect to the lowercase URL (this is an extreme response; see the discussion later about redirects). We will cover HttpModules in Chapter 7.

Since the browser cache associates a particular URL with some content, for best performance you should always reference identical content with identical URLs. If you are running several sites, you can improve performance by using a shared domain for common static content. For example, if you're running both www.12titans.net and www.apress.com and there's a good chance that visitors to one site will also visit the other, then you might want to have a third domain, such as s1.12titansapress.net, that both sites can use for common static content.

If several developers are working on the site, they should take care to share and reuse content, rather than duplicating it on a page-by-page, developer-by-developer, or even project-by-project basis. Make sure that your site doesn't have multiple copies of the same file.

A similar strategy also applies to your domain name. If you have several different domains that refer to the same site, you can improve client-side caching if you reference them consistently and help users do the same. For example, you might redirect all references from domains like 12titans.net and www.12titans.com to www.12titans.net instead, as opposed to serving identical content from all three domains. Otherwise, a user who visited the site first with one domain name and then with another would need to download all cacheable content twice instead of only once. Keep in mind that you can't control how others link to your site. You might be consistent on your site about using www, but another site could link to you without it.

Merging identical domains also helps with search engine optimization. It's possible that search engines will exclude or otherwise penalize your site if they see many copies of identical content.

Network Optimizations

When IE doesn't find images and other resources in its cache, it places requests to retrieve them in queues that it services with a maximum of two connections per domain, as per the HTTP 1.1 specification.

■ **Note** Browsers don't look at the IP address of a domain when determining whether to open a new connection; they do a direct string comparison of the domain names.

Consider the following page (see `file03.htm`):

```
<img src="q1.gif" height="16" width="16" />
<img src="q2.gif" height="16" width="16" />
<img src="q3.gif" height="16" width="16" />
<img src="q4.gif" height="16" width="16" />
<img src="q5.gif" height="16" width="16" />
<img src="q6.gif" height="16" width="16" />
<img src="q7.gif" height="16" width="16" />
<img src="q8.gif" height="16" width="16" />
<img src="q9.gif" height="16" width="16" />
<img src="q10.gif" height="16" width="16" />
```

There are ten images, all loaded from the same domain as the page (the "host" domain). Here's a timeline that shows how IE loads the page:

The first row shows the time to open the connection and read the HTML. The next row shows the first image being requested, using the same connection as the first request. The third row shows IE requesting the second image at the same time as the first. However, it needs to open a second connection, which is indicated by the area on the left side of the row. After that, IE keeps both connections active. As each image completes, a new transfer is started; the beginning of each row corresponds to the end of the one two rows before.

Now, let's change the HTML so that only two images are requested from each of five different subdomains (see file04.htm):

```
<img src="q1.gif" height="16" width="16" />
<img src="q2.gif" height="16" width="16" />
<img src="http://s1.12titans.net/samples/ch02/q3.gif" height="16" width="16" />
<img src="http://s1.12titans.net/samples/ch02/q4.gif" height="16" width="16" />
<img src="http://s2.12titans.net/samples/ch02/q5.gif" height="16" width="16" />
<img src="http://s2.12titans.net/samples/ch02/q6.gif" height="16" width="16" />
<img src="http://s3.12titans.net/samples/ch02/q7.gif" height="16" width="16" />
<img src="http://s3.12titans.net/samples/ch02/q8.gif" height="16" width="16" />
<img src="http://s4.12titans.net/samples/ch02/q9.gif" height="16" width="16" />
<img src="http://s4.12titans.net/samples/ch02/q10.gif" height="16" width="16" />
```

Here's the resulting timeline:

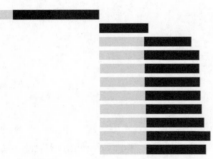

The HTML takes about the same amount of time to load, as does the first image. However, now IE requests all of the other images at the same time. Notice that there is significant overhead in opening the connections. Opening ten connections and reusing only one of them is not particularly efficient; even so, this page loads in about half the time as the original (1.92 seconds vs. 1.00 seconds).

IE behaves very differently when it uses a visible proxy. For example, loading this same page when Fiddler is active results in the following timeline:

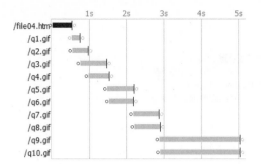

IE loads the images two at a time, just like when they all came from the same domain.

With an invisible proxy, IE can't tell that it's not directly connected to multiple remote servers, so it behaves as if it was. In fact, my ISP uses an invisible proxy, so the results you see here reflect that.

You can take advantage of parallel object downloads by strategically using several different domains for your content. Because it takes a little while to open a new TCP connection and the browser limits the maximum number of simultaneous connections, a good rule of thumb is to load your content from at least two and no more than four domains. You might want to have several domain aliases for your site. That allows you to optimize download parallelism by simply adjusting the domain names in your pages, without having to manage which content is in which domain.

Script Include File Handling

IE serializes JavaScript `<script>` resource requests with requests that follow them. If you have several `<script>` include files in a row in your HTML, IE will retrieve each one before the next. No new resource requests (such as for images) will be started once a script request has begun. For example, consider the following page (see `file05.htm`):

```
<script type="text/javascript" src="script.js">
</script>
<script type="text/javascript" src="http://s1.12titans.net/samples/ch02/script.js">
</script>
<img src="q1.gif" height="16" width="16" />
<img src="q2.gif" height="16" width="16" />
<img src="http://s1.12titans.net/samples/ch02/q3.gif" height="16" width="16" />
<img src="http://s1.12titans.net/samples/ch02/q4.gif" height="16" width="16" />
```

The page references two JavaScript files. One is from the same domain as the HTML page, and the other is from a different domain. Four images come next, two from the host domain and two from the same domain as the script file. Here's the resulting timeline:

Here's what happens:

1. The browser opens a connection to the host domain and transfers the HTML file.

2. The first script file is loaded over the original connection.

3. The browser opens a new connection to the s1.12titans.net domain and loads the second script file.

4. The four images are loaded. The first one uses the already-open connection to the host domain. The second one opens a new connection to the host domain. The third one uses the already-open connection to the s1 domain. The fourth one opens a second connection to the s1 domain.

You can see that IE serialized both of the <script> requests, in spite of the fact that they are from separate domains. None of the images were loaded until both script files had been processed.

Increase Parallelism by Queuing Resources Before Scripts

If resources are already in the queue before IE encounters <script> requests, then the script will be loaded in parallel with them, as though it was an image. You can reduce the total load time of the previous example by moving some of the images into a different subdomain and moving the <script> tags after them (see file05a.htm):

```
<img src="q1.gif" height="16" width="16" />
<img src="http://s1.12titans.net/samples/ch02/q2.gif" height="16" width="16" />
<img src="http://s2.12titans.net/samples/ch02/q3.gif" height="16" width="16" />
<img src="http://s2.12titans.net/samples/ch02/q4.gif" height="16" width="16" />
<script type="text/javascript" src="script.js">
</script>
<script type="text/javascript" src="http://s1.12titans.net/samples/ch02/script.js">
</script>
```

Here's the resulting timeline:

As before, first the HTML file is loaded. Next, all four images are loaded in parallel, along with the first script file. The first one uses the already-open connection, while the others require new connections. IE starts to load the second script file after the first one completes.

Since objects that are already queued don't interfere with the transfer of scripts and since IE stops rendering the page while script transfers are in progress, you should place `<script>` tags as late in your HTML as you can. If you need the script files early in your HTML, load one or more images first to increase network parallelism.

Minimize the Number of Script Files

To reduce round-trips, it's important to have as few script files as possible. You can do this by using one or more of the following techniques:

- Combine them together statically (such as with an editor)
- Combine them together dynamically, either:
  - As a compile post-processing step or
  - Programmatically (on-demand) when the browser requests the script
- Avoid `document.write()` if you can, and use `innerHTML` or direct DOM manipulation instead
- If you can't avoid `document.write()` (such as with scripts from third-parties), then instead of using multiple `<script>` files for each output location in your HTML, either:
  - Use absolute positioning to invoke the script late in the file, or
  - Invoke the script in a hidden `<div>`, and then move the contents of the `<div>` into its desired location by manipulating the DOM

Avoiding document.write()

Here's a script that contains an inline `document.write()` (see `img1.js`):

```
document.write('<img src="q1.gif" height="16" width="16" />');
```

The script file is included in `file06.htm`:

```
<div>
<script type="text/javascript" src="img1.js"></script>
</div>
```

Here's an alternative approach (see `img2.js`):

```
var qimg = '<img src="q1.gif" height="16" width="16" />';
```

The script is included in `file07.htm`:

```
<style type="text/css">
#exd{height:16px;width:16px}
</style>
<div id="exd">
</div>
<script type="text/javascript" src="img2.js"></script>
<script type="text/javascript">
document.getElementById('exd').innerHTML = qimg;
</script>
```

Instead of using `document.write()`, we use a variable in the include file to hold the desired HTML and then add it to the `<div>` using `innerHTML`. We assign the `<div>` tag a `width` and `height` to match the image to avoid HTML page relayouts when its contents are updated.

Here's another approach (see `img3.js`):

```
function putimg(qdiv) {
    var myim = new Image(16, 16);
    myim.src = "q1.gif";
    qdiv.appendChild(myim);
}
```

The script is included in `file08.htm`:

```
<style type="text/css">
#exd{height:16px;width:16px}
</style>
<div id="exd">
</div>
<script type="text/javascript" src="img3.js"></script>
<script type="text/javascript">
putimg(document.getElementById('exd'));
</script>
```

This time, we use a function to create an `Image` object and append it as a child of the DOM node of the `<div>`.

Reordering Script That You Can't Modify

Let's say that you have an image at the top of your page that's inserted by a script that you don't have control over, followed by some text (see `file09.htm`):

```
<div>
<script type="text/javascript" src="img1.js"></script>
</div>
<div>
Lorem Ipsum
</div>
```

To move the script to the end of the HTML, you can assign absolute positions to both of the `<div>` tags and then reverse their order (see `file10.htm`):

```
<style type="text/css">
.content,.banner{position:absolute; left:10px}
.content{top:40px}
.banner{top:10px}
</style>
<div class="content">
Lorem Ipsum
</div>
<div class="banner">
<script type="text/javascript" src="img1.js"></script>
</div>
```

Alternatively, you can call the script in a hidden `<div>` and then move that DOM node into position (see `file11.htm`):

```
<style type="text/css">
.temp{display:none}
#banner{height:20px;width:16px}
</style>
<div id="banner">
</div>
<div>
Lorem ipsum
</div>
<div class="temp">
<div id="mystuff">
<script type="text/javascript" src="img1.js"></script>
</div>
</div>
<script type="text/javascript">
var ba = document.getElementById('banner');
var ms = document.getElementById('mystuff');
if ((ba != null) && (ms != null))
    ba.appendChild(ms);
</script>
```

■ **Note** appendChild() unlinks the argument node (ms) before appending it as a child of the source (ba).

Requesting Objects After the Rest of the Page

You can combine use of the page onload handler with the late image load technique to make very late requests, after everything else on the page. Rollover images are an example, since they don't need to be displayed when the page is initially rendered, but if they are eventually used, the user experience will be much better if they are already in the browser's cache (image sprites or transparency variations are generally a better solutions for rollover images; see the sections "Image Sprites and Clustering" and "Use Transparency as an Alternative to Rollover Images" for details). Large, low-priority images, or images that are below the fold are other possibilities. Here's an example (see file12.htm):

```
<body onload="lateimage()">
<img id="slow" height="16" width="16" />
<div>
Lorem ipsum
</div>
<script type="text/javascript">
function lateimage() {
    document.getElementById('slow').src = "big.jpg";
}
</script>
```

An <img> tag with an id, height, and width, but without src, is a placeholder for the image. Then the <body> onload handler sets the src of the <img> tag to be the path to the image, which causes the browser to load the image.

Script Defer

Using <script defer="true"> can sometimes help improve the performance of a page by delaying the point at which the browser parses and executes the associated script until after the page has loaded. Unfortunately, it's often not a very practical option. The biggest issue is that since other scripts on the page execute as the page loads, it might not be able to access any script in the deferred file when you need it. Another complication is that deferred scripts can't call document.write() since they are run after the page load is complete.

Server-Side Alternatives to Script

There are of course places where using client-side script is the right and best solution. However, there are also situations where the server can help. Generating browser-specific HTML, JavaScript, or CSS are typical examples; it's much easier and better to handle that on the server than with client-side JavaScript. With the User-Agent HTTP header, the server knows which browser the user is running. ASP.NET provides several very powerful mechanisms for generating browser-specific code. I'll cover them in detail in Chapter 6.

Download Less

Every byte of content consumes resources. The server statically or dynamically generates each byte and sends it over the network to the browser, which then has to process everything it receives. Assuming no changes in the core logic that creates the page, every byte you save will reduce the time it takes the browser to download and display the resulting page. The following sections describe several techniques to accomplish this.

Reduce the Number of Resources per Page

Eliminate "spacer" GIFs, and use CSS instead. Since today's browsers have good CSS support, there should no longer be a reason to use spacers, yet it's surprising how prevalent they are. Using margin and padding should serve the same purpose.

You should replace "text images" (images with words on them) with CSS and text. The result will be much smaller and easier to maintain (you won't need graphics programs to make changes). You can more easily support localization that way, too. Apply gradients using background images, and use absolute positioning when needed for fine-grained control over text placement.

For example, consider the following HTML, which overlays an image with a transparent background onto a gradient (see file13.htm):

```
<style type="text/css">
.hdr{border:1px solid #000;height:40px;background:url(top-grad.gif)}
.logo{height:40px;width:250px;float:left}
</style>
<div class="hdr">
<img class="logo" src="logo.png" />
</div>
```

The result looks like this:

12 Titans

You can achieve the same result on client machines that have the Lucida Handwriting font installed by using the following code instead (see file14.htm):

```
<style type="text/css">
.hdr{border:1px solid #000;height:40px;background:url(top-grad.gif)}
.txtlogo{font-family:lucida handwriting,cursive;
    font-size:32px;color:#fff;padding:3px}
.txtlogo span{color:yellow}
</style>
<div class="hdr">
<span class="txtlogo"><span>12</span> Titans</span>
</div>
```

The `.txtlogo span` CSS selector says to apply `color:yellow` for `<span>` tags that follow a `txtlogo` class assignment. That way, you can avoid specifying a separate class or ID on the `<span>` tag.

Although I'm still using the gradient image, I've replaced the logo image with text plus CSS formatting, which saves a round-trip. On machines that don't have the right font, the browser will use the standard `cursive` font as a fallback.

In cases where the exact look of the text is important, such as for branding reasons, you can replace the text with an image in the page `onload` handler (see `file15.htm`):

```
<body onload="getlogo()">
<style type="text/css">
.hdr{border:1px solid #000;height:40px;background:url(top-grad.gif)}
#txtlogo{font-family:lucida handwriting,cursive;
    font-size:32px;color:#fff;padding:3px}
#txtlogo span{color:yellow}
</style>
<div class="hdr">
<span id="txtlogo"><span>12</span> Titanx</span>
</div>
<script type="text/javascript">
var limg;
function getlogo() {
    limg = new Image(250, 40);
    limg.onload = gotlogo;
    limg.src = "logo.png";
}
function gotlogo() {
    var logo = document.getElementById("txtlogo");
    logo.parentNode.replaceChild(limg, logo);
}
</script>
```

The page `onload` handler creates a new `Image` object and sets the `onload` handler for the image to the `gotlogo()` function. After the browser loads the image, `gotlogo()` uses it to replace the `<span>` tag containing the text. I've changed the last letter of the text so that you can more easily see when the image loads in case you have the Lucida Handwriting font installed. Of course, the larger the image is and the more objects there are on the page, the more noticeable the effects.

Minify Your HTML, CSS, and JavaScript

Minimize the size of your HTML, CSS, and JavaScript by removing extra spaces, tabs, newlines, and comments. I'm always surprised when I look at the generated HTML for a site and see lots of comments. The browser can't use them, so they shouldn't be there. One way to avoid sending comments in your `.aspx` files to clients is to enclose them in a `<% %>` code block. Here's an example:

```
<% // this is a comment that won't be sent to the browser %>
```

That tells the compiler to insert the contents of the brackets into the source code that it generates for the page, but not in the generated HTML. Since it's part of the source code, the double slash just defines a C#-style comment.

For static files, you can remove comments as a post-compile step or as part of the installation and deployment process.

For JavaScript, the `jsmin` tool by Douglas Crockford is available online as a free download from this location:

```
http://www.crockford.com/javascript/jsmin.html
```

`jsmin` removes comments and unnecessary whitespace and from script files. The behavior of the resulting file doesn't change, but it will be much smaller (often as little as half the original size).

To use `jsmin` with Visual Studio, first download the software and install `jsmin.exe` in your path (or perhaps in `C:\windows\system32`).

The standard web site projects in Visual Studio don't support post-build actions. Fortunately, though, Microsoft provides an optional Web Deployment Projects add-in that supports that capability. You can download the current version from

```
http://www.microsoft.com/downloads/
    details.aspx?FamilyId=OAA30AE8-C73B-4BDD-BB1B-FE697256C459&displaylang=en
```

After installing the add-in, right-click your web site project, and select **Add Web Deployment Project**, as in Figure 2-2. Call the new project `DeployWeb`.

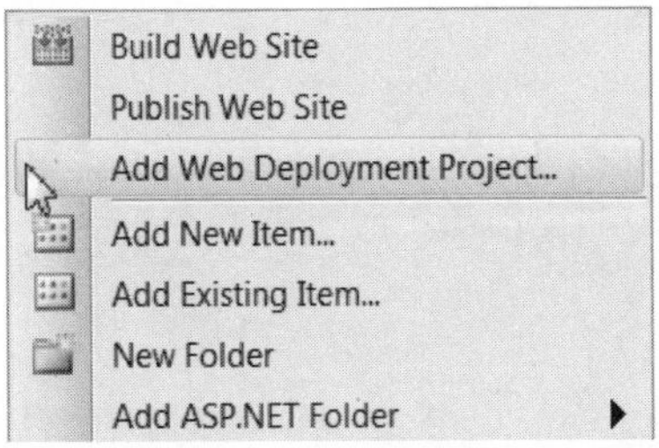

Figure 2-2. *Adding a Web Deployment project in Visual Studio*

Next, right-click the `DeployWeb` project, and select **Open Project File**. At the end of the file (before the `</Project>` tag), add a post-build step that invokes `jsmin` with the standard input set to the original file and the standard output set to the corresponding file in the build output folder. Something like this:

```
<Target Name="AfterBuild">
  <Exec Command="jsmin &lt; ..\Sample\page.js &gt; $(OutputPath)\page.js" />
</Target>
```

■ **Note** The less-than and greater-than signs for standard input and output need to be escaped in order for them to be valid XML. Be sure to put the command all on one line.

You will need to invoke `jsmin` once for each JavaScript file in your project.

After saving the project file, right-click the `DeployWeb` project, and select **Build**. That will create a precompiled version of your project in `DeployWeb\Debug`, with all your web pages merged into a single DLL. The `.aspx` pages will remain as placeholders, but without the code-behind. You can deploy that folder to your staging environment and use it to avoid the startup delay that otherwise happens when your pages are compiled after they are referenced for the first time.

You can also use this process to run other static minifiers, such as ShrinkSafe (part of the Dojo Toolkit) for JavaScript or the Java-based YUI Compressor from Yahoo, which minifies both JavaScript and CSS.

For dynamically generated files, you can minify the output as a post-processing step after it is generated by filtering whitespace. I'll cover the details in Chapter 7.

Maximize Compressibility

Since lowercase appears more frequently than uppercase, it also compresses better (the bit patterns of lowercase letters help too). You should therefore use lowercase in your text files as much as possible to maximize their compressibility. For example, in your HTML, `<img src="myimage.jpg" />` is much better than `<IMG SRC="myimage.JPG" />`. In addition to improving server-side compression, this also helps in cases where a client accesses the Internet over dial-up with a modem that has compression enabled, as most of them do.

I will cover server-side compression in Chapter 4.

Image Optimization

Images often consume a larger fraction of total site bandwidth than HTML does. Aggressively managing the size of your images is important for the same reasons as optimizing HTML size: every byte you can save is a byte that the browser doesn't have to download and process.

Minimize the Number of Images on Your Pages

The first step in image optimization should be to think about whether you need the image at all. I personally prefer the Zen aesthetic of simple, uncluttered sites that avoid a large number of images. Reducing the number of images can have a big impact on site performance, since it also eliminates the associated round-trips.

As an alternative to images, consider using CSS to define backgrounds or section dividers. Varying border thickness and color can sometimes be used to good effect.

After you've eliminated as many images as you can, the next step is to make the remaining ones as small as you can.

I am not suggesting that your site needs to look bad and have no images or only a few tiny ones in order to achieve good performance. Rather, the idea is to look carefully at what your requirements really are and create your images in line with those requirements. Do you *really need* 50 or more images on your home page? Do you really need an 800 × 600-pixel background? Do you really need top image quality for your tiny thumbnails?

Use Transparency as an Alternative to Rollover Images

Varying object opacity using CSS is another option. You can use transparency stylistically or as an alternative to a separate rollover image. For example, the following CSS works on all modern browsers (see file16.htm):

```
<style type="text/css">
.hov:hover img{-ms-filter:"progid:DXImageTransform.Microsoft.Alpha(Opacity=60)";
    filter:alpha(opacity=60);opacity:0.6}
</style>
<a class="hov" href="#">
<img src="images/right.png" height="56" width="56" border="0" />
</a>
```

When you mouse over the image, the :hover style will alter its opacity.

Optimize Background Images

For background images, be sure to take advantage of the browser's ability to duplicate a single image through tiling. The background gradient image used earlier in file14.htm is 1-pixel wide and the height of the containing <div>. The browser then copies it as needed to tile the background.

For IE only, you can replace a simple gradient background with CSS. Here's an example (see file17.htm):

```
<style type="text/css">
.hdr{border:1px solid #000;height:40px;background-color:#0052ce;
-ms-filter:"progid:DXImageTransform.Microsoft.Alpha
(opacity=78,finishopacity=100,style=1,starty=0,finishy=100,startx=0,finishx=0)";
filter:alpha
(opacity=78,finishopacity=100,style=1,starty=0,finishy=100,startx=0,finishx=0)}
.txtlogo{font-family:lucida handwriting,cursive;font-size:32px;
color:#fff;padding:3px}
.txtlogo span{color:yellow}
</style>
<div class="hdr">
<span class="txtlogo"><span>12</span> Titans</span>
</div>
```

The result is very close to file13.htm shown earlier, but now with no images instead of two.

Firefox doesn't have a similar linear opacity filter, so on the server you should dynamically generate alternative code. In this case, we can start with a solid background and then load a gradient image in the onload handler (see file18.htm):

```
<body onload="getgrad()">
<style type="text/css">
#hdr{border:1px solid #000;height:40px;background-color:#0052ce}
.txtlogo{font-family:lucida handwriting,cursive;font-size:32px;
color:#fff;padding:3px}
.txtlogo span{color:yellow}
</style>
```

31

```
<div id="hdr">
<span class="txtlogo"><span>12</span> Titans</span>
</div>
<script type="text/javascript">
function getgrad() {
    var h = document.getElementById("hdr");
    h.style.backgroundImage = "url(top-grad.gif)";
}
</script>
</body>
```

This code also works in IE of course, but the version in `file17.htm` is faster since it doesn't require an image to be loaded.

Choose the Right Image Format

Images with only a few colors or that require consistent and smooth gradients or sharp edges should use a lossless format. In those cases, you should in general prefer PNG or GIF to BMP. PNG files tend to be smaller, and the format supports alpha channels for variable transparency (blending) as well as gamma correction and progressive display (interlacing), which the other lossless formats do not support.

For larger PNG files, encoding them with progressive display is desirable, in keeping with our principle for focusing on perceived performance. A page doesn't feel as slow when the browser progressively renders large images.

Although PNGs tend to be smaller than GIFs, that isn't always the case. It's worthwhile to compare the sizes when making a choice. Notice in the previous examples that small background gradient image I used was a GIF, for example, since it was smaller than the equivalent PNG.

In addition, unfortunately IE6 does not support PNG alpha channels, although IE7 and Firefox do. Therefore, if you're using transparency, as with the logo image in the `file15.htm` example shown earlier and if support for IE6 is important, then GIFs are the right choice there too, although GIFs can only do 100 percent transparency and not alpha blending.

Use the minimum bit depth that you really need. An 8-bit image will be one-third the size of a 24-bit image. The fewer colors your image needs, the lower the bit depth can be. Sometimes you can apply dithering that will make a lower-bit depth image more acceptable than it would be otherwise.

Most photographs should be JPG files.

Optimize Image Compression and Dimensions

Check to see whether you can increase the level of compression for JPG files. Higher-compression ratios result in a loss of quality, particularly for edge definition. In fact, some image-editing software, including Adobe Photoshop, refers to the degree of image compression as *quality*. With many images, though, the difference in quality isn't very noticeable for small to moderate changes in compression, and the resulting decrease in file size can be considerable. If higher levels of compression won't work for all images, perhaps they will for some, such as small thumbnails. In keeping with one of the themes of this chapter, even small changes are worthwhile.

If the image has an empty border area or other unnecessary details, you should crop it as much as you can without sacrificing useful content. Use CSS instead for borders and margins.

Some very good tools are available to help simplify image optimization. For example, Adobe Photoshop has a Save for Web feature that makes it easy to compare several different approaches. The control panel for optimizing images is shown in Figure 2-3, in JPG mode.

Figure 2-3. Adobe Photoshop CS3's Save for Web control panel for optimizing images

You can change the quality setting to adjust the amount of compression, enable or disable progressive rendering, apply a blur to the image to help reduce artifacts, and resize the image. Photoshop shows the impact of the changes in either two or four images to the left of the control panel, including how large the image is, so you can readily compare them to one another and to the original. You can also select and evaluate formats other than JPG, including GIF and PNG.

When to Use Image Slicing

Image *slicing* takes a large image and splits it up into multiple smaller images. You might use this approach to apply links or script or CSS to just part of the image, rather than the whole thing. However, the resulting multiple round-trips can have a significant performance impact, particularly when the images are relatively small. Even though the first image arrives before the full one would have, the round-trip overhead can give the page a slow feeling.

For large images, though, slices can improve perceived performance. If you spread them among multiple domains, the resulting overlap of network accesses can also reduce total page load time. Therefore, we sometimes have a choice between two of our guiding principles: improving perceived performance and reducing round-trips. In general, you should prefer perceived performance; that's what really counts in the end.

A reasonable rule of thumb for deciding whether perceived performance would benefit from slicing is to watch a page load with a network speed similar to what your users will see. If a single image takes more than a few seconds, if it feels much slower than the rest of the page, or if it's something that your users will be waiting for, then you might consider slicing it. You should not slice images that take less than about a second that users won't care about or that are loaded below the fold where they can't even be seen. In fact, those images are candidates to be combined together using image sprites or clustering, as described later in this chapter.

You can use Photoshop to slice your images, with the slicing tool in the default toolbar. Simply use the tool to draw a rectangle around each area that you'd like to have a separate slice. Then in **Save for Web**, when you save the result, each slice will be saved as a separate image. Each slice can have a different format or a different level of optimization.

Since slicing is commonly used for menus, don't forget that CSS-based text is a much better alternative, as I described earlier.

Client-Side Image Maps

In cases where adding multiple links to a large image is your main motivation for slicing, you should use client-side image maps instead. Here's an example:

```
<img src="images/bigimage.png" height="50" width="200" usemap="#mymap" />
<map name="mymap">
    <area shape="rect" coords="0,0,50,50" href="one.aspx" alt="One" />
    <area shape="rect" coords="50,0,100,50" href="two.aspx" alt="Two" />
    <area shape="circ" coords="150,25,25" href="three.aspx" alt="Three" />
</map>
```

The image will have three zones: two rectangular in shape and one circular. Hovering over the zones will show the corresponding `alt` string, along with the destination URL in the browser's status bar. Clicking the zone will cause the browser to navigate to the destination URL, just like with an `<a>` tag.

Specify Image Size Attributes

You should specify an image's native size or larger in the `<img>` tag's `height` and `width` attributes. If you would like the image to be displayed at a smaller size, then it's better to resize the image on the server and avoid downloading the extra bits. In addition, the resizing algorithms used by an application like Photoshop will generally result in a much better-looking image than whatever the browser happens to do.

Enlarging an image by specifying a larger-than-actual size is generally not useful and requires the browser to do extra work that could otherwise be avoided. If you need a little extra filler, try using a larger border or a CSS-based background color.

You can also resize images dynamically on the server. See Chapter 6 for details.

Web Site Icon File

When the browser finishes loading the first page it sees from your site, it will request a file called `favicon.ico`. If the file is present, the browser will display it in its address bar, to the left of URLs from your site. You should make sure that the file is present on your site. If it's not there, the browser will rerequest it every so often, resulting in round-trips and "file not found" errors that you could avoid by returning the file the first time it's requested. The file must be a 16 × 16-pixel image in ICO format (which is not the same as JPG, GIF, or PNG).

You can specify an alternate name for the icon file with a `<link>` tag in your HTML. Here's an example:

```
<link rel="shortcut icon" href="/myicon.ico" type="image/x-icon" />
```

However, since this approach requires adding extra text to all your pages, you should avoid it if you can.

Most static content can be versioned by changing the name of the files (or the folders they're in). Since you should keep the name `favicon.ico`, you will have to rely on the content expiring from the browser cache in the event you want to update the icon. That means unlike with normal images and static content, `favicon.ico` should be marked with a relatively near-term cache expiration date, perhaps a month or so.

General HTML, CSS, and JavaScript Optimization

Here are a few general things you can do to clean up your pages:

- Check for and remove redundant tags. For example, if you have two `<span>` tags right next to each other, you can merge them.

- Remove `<meta refresh>` tags. Automatic page updates might at first seem appealing in some cases, but think about the situation where a user walks away from their PC or goes to another tab in their browser. If the updates continue, as they would with `<meta refresh>`, you are just wasting client and server resources.

- Remove empty content tags.

- Remove extraneous tags from automated content generators.

- Minimize the length of your `alt` text.

- Remove comments and extra whitespace.

- Remove unused CSS.

- Use self-closing tags, such as `<img />`, instead of `<img></img>` (the only place I don't like to do that is with `</script>`, where I've run into browser bugs).

- Remove unused JavaScript. When you're using JavaScript libraries, it's particularly easy to accumulate a large number of functions that are never used.

Using an HTML Optimizer

Microsoft's Expression Web has a very handy **Optimize HTML** command, as in Figure 2-4. It can also remove unused CSS classes.

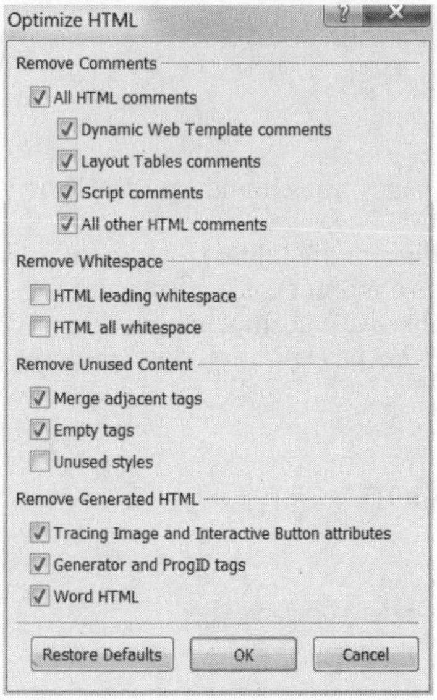

Figure 2-4. *The Optimize HTML menu for single files in Expression Web*

You can optimize an entire web site as part of the publishing process, as in Figure 2-5.

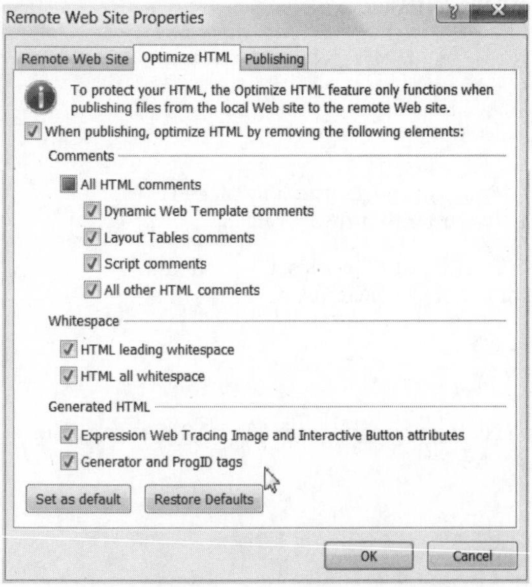

Figure 2-5. *Optimize HTML while publishing your web site from Expression Web*

Avoid Optimization Techniques That Violate the HTML Standards

You may hear about optimization techniques that can reduce the size of your HTML by violating various aspects of the HTML standards. I don't recommend using them, for several reasons:

- Some tools can help find different types of bugs in your HTML, or identify accessibility issues, and so on. The HTML parsers used by those tools are not always as "friendly" as the parsers used by browsers, so HTML that violates the standard has a higher probability of not being properly understood.

- You might want to store your content in a database or use a local search engine of some kind. The more standard your code is, the better the odds are that it will integrate with those applications quickly, smoothly, and effectively.

- There are a couple of obscure browser bugs with nonstandard HTML. It's difficult to expect one browser to behave the same as others when it comes to bugs.

- In addition to being "browser-friendly," you should also want your site to be search-engine friendly. The parsers used by a large search engine like Google might understand your nonstandard code, but other search engines might not. The situation might be compounded if you use a `<!DOCTYPE>` that declares conformance with a particular version of the standard, and then you violate that standard.

In fact, it's a good practice to run your pages through a well-known HTML validation service periodically, such as the one offered by W3C at `http://validator.w3.org/`.

Eliminating CSS Round-Trips for the First Page View

Client-side caching of CSS include files will reduce the load time for a page the second time a user sees it (known as *PLT2*), since the browser won't need to request the cached content again from the server. However, since loading an include file requires a round-trip and since that round-trip increases the time to load the page the first time a users sees it (*PLT1*), it is sometimes worth considering an optimization that can help mitigate the increase to PLT1 while not sacrificing PLT2. The algorithm works as follows:

- The first time the browser requests a particular page, include the CSS with the HTML using a `<style>` tag instead of using `<link>`.

- In the page `onload` handler, dynamically insert a `<link>` tag into the DOM that references the CSS file. That will cause the browser to load the file from the server, but it won't slow down the rendering of the page.

- Set a cookie in the HTTP response headers for the CSS file. The response should be marked with a far-future cache expiration date, and it should be publically cacheable so that it can be stored in proxies (even though some proxies won't cache responses that include `Set-Cookie`).

- For the second and subsequent requests of pages that use the CSS file, which you can identify because the cookie is set, generate a `<link>` tag on the page instead of embedding the CSS. The CSS file will be loaded from the browser's cache, so an extra round-trip won't be required.

- Here's an example of how to load a CSS file from the page onload handler (see file19.htm):

```
<body onload="getcss()">
<style type="text/css">
.hdr{border:1px solid #000;height:40px;background:url(images/top-grad.gif)}
.logo{height:40px;width:250px;float:left}
</style>
<div class="hdr">
<img class="logo" src="logo.png" />
</div>
<script type="text/javascript">
function getcss() {
    var h = document.getElementsByTagName('head');
    var l = document.createElement('link');
    l.type = 'text/css';
    l.rel = 'stylesheet';
    l.href = 'css/file19.css';
    h[0].appendChild(l);
}
</script>
</body>
```

With the embedded <style> section, the browser will render the page correctly before the CSS include file is loaded.

The CSS file contains the same information as in the <style> tag, except the path to the referenced image is relative to the folder containing the CSS, rather than relative to the folder containing the HTML:

```
.hdr{border:1px solid #000;height:40px;background:url(../images/top-grad.gif)}
.logo{height:40px;width:250px;float:left}
```

You can manage path name differences either by applying regular expressions when you merge the files (and caching the results) or by using dynamically generated CSS.

You can set the cookie for the CSS file using a Set-Cookie HTTP header that you configure from IIS Manager. First, select the file in the **Content View**, then switch to **Features View**, double-click **HTTP Response Headers**, and select **Add** from the panel on the right. See Figure 2-6.

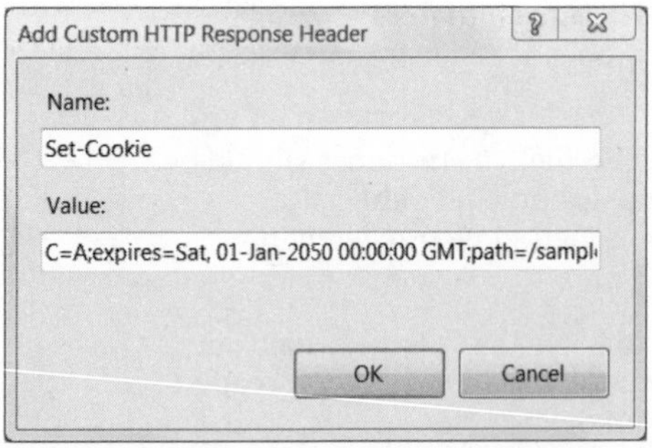

Figure 2-6. Using the Add Custom HTTP Response Header in IIS Manager to set a cookie

In this case, I'm setting a cookie called C to a value of A, with a far-future expiration date. The path is set to the folder containing the active content (/samples/ch02) so that the cookie is uploaded to the server only when it's needed.

Alternatively, you can accomplish the same thing by creating a new web.config file in the same folder as the CSS file (the IIS Manager GUI creates this same file):

```
<?xml version="1.0" encoding="utf-8"?>
<configuration>
    <location path="file19.css">
        <system.webServer>
            <httpProtocol>
                <customHeaders>
                    <add name="Set-Cookie"
value="C=A;expires=Sat, 01-Jan-2050 00:00:00 GMT;path=/samples/ch02/" />
                </customHeaders>
            </httpProtocol>
        </system.webServer>
    </location>
</configuration>
```

This approach is particularly useful for the pages that users see when they first come to your site, where PLT1 is especially important, such as the home page. The disadvantages are that extra work is required on the cache management side, since there would be different versions of the page depending on whether the cookie is set, and that every page after the first one will have the cookie included with it. However, since many of the page views on an average site tend to originate from browsers that have empty caches and since the cookie is very small, it can be a reasonable trade-off.

In some cases, it might be advisable to *always* generate the CSS inline and cause the include file to be loaded with script on the entry page, rather than doing so dynamically or using the cookie approach. That would allow you to mark the page as publically cacheable so that it can be cached by proxies and http.sys, and the home page would always have a fast PLT1. Interior pages would have a slightly slower PLT1 since they would have to load the CSS file, but their PLT2 would not be affected.

Using JavaScript to Gate Page Requests

You shouldn't allow users to submit a web form until they have completed all the required fields. You should also validate fields on the client before submitting the form. In addition to reducing the load on the server by preventing invalid submits, this approach has the advantage of providing more immediate user feedback, which improves perceived performance.

You can use a similar approach with links. For example, you might want to wait a few seconds after a page loads before enabling a link that refreshes the current page.

Submit Buttons

Here's an example that doesn't enable the submit button until the entered text is at least three characters long (see file23.htm):

```
<form>
<input id="par" name="par" width="150" onkeyup="check(this)" />
<input id="sub" type="submit" value="OK" />
</form>
<script type="text/javascript">
var s = document.getElementById('sub');
s.disabled = true;
function check(v) {
    s.disabled = v.value.length < 3;
}
</script>
```

It's important to revalidate data on the server since it is possible for hackers to bypass the script checks on the page. In fact, it's a good idea to log requests where invalid fields are detected on the server that should have been prevented by client-side script. In addition to being an indication of potential bugs in client or server code, they could also be indications of a security threat.

JavaScript can also be used to avoid submitting a form if the selected parameters are the same as the ones that were used to generate the page. For example, you can prevent users from rerequesting a page if a selected sort key on a table is the same as the current one or if they are requesting the same page again (unless the content might have changed).

Links

Here's an example that waits five seconds before enabling a Refresh link (see file20.htm):

```
<a id="ref" dhref="file20.htm"></a>
<script type="text/javascript">
var r = document.getElementById("ref");
r.style.color = "gray";
r.style.textDecoration = "underline";
var sec = 5;
enableLink();
function enableLink() {
    if (sec > 0) {
        r.innerHTML = "Refresh available in " + sec + " seconds";
        setTimeout("enableLink()", 1000);
    } else {
        r.innerHTML = "Refresh";
        r.style.color = "black";
        r.href = r.dhref;
    }
    sec--;
}
</script>
```

You temporarily store the destination URL in a new property called dhref, and use setTimeout() to have the JavaScript runtime call you back once a second to provide user feedback. Without some user feedback, a disabled link on its own might be confusing. The first parameter to setTimeout() is the function name to call, and the second is the time interval in milliseconds. After five seconds, you activate the link by setting the `href` property from the temporary `dhref`. This approach also helps prevent the cursor from changing to indicate that it's on a valid link when you hover over the text.

To prevent the link from being disabled again if the user hits the back button in their browser to come back to this page from another one, you would need to record some state information on the client by setting a cookie from script. You should configure the cookie to expire quickly, probably after just a few minutes. It should have a `path` set on it, so that it's only attached to the minimum number of URLs possible. The script could then check for the presence of the cookie. If it's there, then the link can be enabled immediately.

You can also disable a link after a user clicks it to prevent them from clicking twice. Here's an example that disables the link after a click, and then waits three seconds before navigating to the destination page, to give you a chance to see the disabled link (see `file21.htm`):

```
<a id="some" href="file19.htm" onclick="disableMe(this);return false;">Go somewhere</a>
<script type="text/javascript">
var v;
function disableMe(val) {
    v = val;
    v.style.color = "gray";
    v.style.textDecoration = "underline";
    v.dhref = v.href;
    v.removeAttribute("href");
    setTimeout("goSome()", 3000);
}
function goSome() {
    window.location.href = v.dhref;
}
</script>
```

Since you start with a valid link in the `<a>` tag, when the user clicks, you move the destination URL from the `href` property to `dhref` and change the `color` and `textDecoration` style of the link text. Removing the `href` property prevents the browser from changing the cursor to indicate that the text is a valid link. Then you use `setTimeout()` to call a function after three seconds that will cause the browser to go to the new page.

Using JavaScript to Reduce HTML Size

You can generate frequently repeating HTML on the client and thereby decrease the size of the downloaded file. A secondary benefit is that it can effectively remove keywords from the page that you would rather not have indexed by search engines.

Generate Repetitive HTML

For example, if you have a drop-down box with a list of all the countries in the world or with all of the states in the United States, the JavaScript to generate them will be much smaller than the pure HTML would be.

Consider this XHTML:

```
<select>
<option value='AF'>Afghanistan</option>
<option value='AL'>Albania</option>
<option value='DZ'>Algeria</option>
<option value='US' selected>United States</option>
</select>
```

To create the same thing using JavaScript, put the following code in an include file (see `file24.js`):

```
var countryList = "AF,Afghanistan,AL,Albania,DZ,Algeria,US,United States";
function DisplayCountries(selected) {
  var countries = countryList.split(",");
  var count = countries.length;
  var i = 0;
  document.write('<select>');
  while(i < count) {
    document.write('<option value="');
    document.write(countries[i]);
    document.write('"');
    document.write(countries[i] == selected ? ' selected' : "");
    document.write(">");
    document.write(countries[i+1]);
    document.write('</option>');
    i=i+2;
  }
  document.write('</select>');
}
```

Then include the file and call the function from where you want the option list to appear in your HTML (see `file24.htm`):

```
<script type="text/javascript" src="file24.js"></script>
<script type="text/javascript">
DisplayCountries("US");
</script>
```

Of course, in a real application, the list of countries would be much longer. If the drop-down menu is used on multiple pages or on pages that can't be cached, putting the JavaScript to generate it in an include file helps further because the script file *can* be cached. For a long list of items, the script will be shorter than the HTML, so if you're already loading another script file into which the code can be placed, both PLT1 and PLT2 will be decreased.

■ **Note** Using script to generate HTML will result in the related text not being accessible to search engines. That can be a good thing, as mentioned earlier, in the event that you have text on your page that isn't relevant to your content. However, if it hides important content, keywords, or links, the trade-off for performance probably isn't worth it.

Add Repetitive Text to Your Tags

Another way to make your HTML shorter with script is to use it to add, append, or prepend repetitive text to your tags. Sometimes this can improve search engine friendliness too.

For example, let's say that you have a long query string parameter that you'd like to attach to a bunch of links on your page, such as a tracking ID of some kind. Rather than attaching it in the HTML directly, where it increases the length of the file and possibly confuses search engines, it can be done by manipulating the DOM. That way, search engines would see the bare URL, but users would see one that was properly tailored for them.

For example (see file25.htm):

```
<a id="lk" href="file25.htm">My Link</a>
<script type="text/javascript">
var l = document.getElementById('lk');
l.href += "?trk=90283109830192830923193800023744793939";
</script>
```

You can also use this approach to generate URLs that have common prefixes, rather than hard-coding them in your HTML.

Upload Less

For every HTTP request, the browser sends a bunch of information to the server. Here's an example request for http://www.apress.com/ using IE7 on my desktop PC:

```
GET / HTTP/1.1
Accept: image/gif, image/x-xbitmap, image/jpeg,
  application/x-ms-application, application/vnd.ms-xpsdocument,
  application/xaml+xml, application/x-ms-xbap, application/x-shockwave-flash,
  application/vnd.ms-excel, application/vnd.ms-powerpoint, application/msword,
  image/pjpeg, */*
Referer: http://www.apress.com/
Accept-Language: en-us
UA-CPU: x86
Accept-Encoding: gzip, deflate
User-Agent: Mozilla/4.0 (compatible; MSIE 7.0; Windows NT 6.0; SLCC1;
  .NET CLR 2.0.50727; Media Center PC 5.0; InfoPath.2;
  .NET CLR 3.5.21022; .NET CLR 1.1.4322; .NET CLR 3.5.30428;
  MS-RTC LM 8; .NET CLR 3.5.30729; .NET CLR 3.0.30618;
  OfficeLiveConnector.1.3; OfficeLivePatch.0.0)
```

```
Host: www.apress.com
Connection: Keep-Alive
Cookie: PHPSESSID=5e90ca5a6a085b1b5523c7010e0ed535;
  utma=26350701.1344204143.1233497415.1233497415.1233497415.1;
  utmc=26350701;
  utmz=26350701.1233497415.1.1.utmccn=(direct)|utmcsr=(direct)|utmcmd=(none)
```

You can tell a few things about my machine from these headers. The `Accept` header indicates a number of different applications that I have installed. The `UA-CPU` header tells you that I'm running on an x86 processor. The `User-Agent` string tells you which browser I'm using (`MSIE 7.0`), which operating system I'm using (`Windows NT 6.0`, otherwise known as Vista), that I have several different versions of the .NET Framework installed, and so on. Several cookies are also included.

Most of this information other than the full `Accept` header is sent to the server with every request on a page, including every image, JavaScript file, and CSS file. That process takes time. Excluding most of the `Accept` header (the browser just sends */* for most requests), for the previous example, which includes the shortest-possible URL (the / after `GET`), there are about 620 bytes. A typical DSL connection with a 128Kbps uplink can upload text at about 10.2KB/sec. That's about 61ms per requested URL. For a page with 16 objects on it, that would be about 976ms, or close to one second *just for the browser to send the HTTP requests*. A typical 56Kbps dial-up connection might actually connect at 44Kbps, which would be about 3.5KB/sec throughput, or 2.8 seconds just to send the HTTP requests.

These numbers are useful for two reasons. First, they add to the importance of reducing the number of HTTP requests that the browser needs to make per page. Even if the responses have nothing in them, the time to send the requests can, by itself, make a big difference in performance. Second, they help emphasize that reducing the amount of data uploaded is important. Unfortunately, working from the server side, you don't have a way to alter things like the client's `User-Agent` string, or most of the other headers. The two that you do have control over, though, are cookies and the URL.

When the server asks the browser to set a cookie, it does so by sending a `Set-Cookie` header in the HTTP response. Here's an example:

```
Set-Cookie: ads=TW.Ads.8cb5307a6a45c34;
  expires=Tue, 03-Feb-2009 12:41:30 GMT;
  path=/pages; HttpOnly
```

The header includes the `name=value` pair for the cookie, along with an optional expiration time, `path`, `domain` name, and property keywords. The HTTP specification allows for up to a maximum of 20 cookies per domain, each of which can be at most 4KB long.

The cookies in the HTTP response shown earlier are about 200 bytes long all together. If they were 9KB long, which is well within the limits of the standard, the total upload time per request would increase by a factor of ten, to 610ms per request, or an astounding 28 seconds for a page that references 16 objects.

Most objects on a page, and in particular most static objects, rarely need cookies. Cookies are generally used to store some state information, such as who you are (either by name or by session), that you have previously logged on or accepted some site-specific terms and conditions, and so on. The server can then examine the cookie as part of processing the request, and it can take some action based on what it finds. Perhaps the page is rendered differently, or it might direct you to a logon page if the cookie shows that you're not already logged on. By definition, those types of actions are only taken for dynamic content.

Static content does not involve any programmatic decision making; the server is presented with the URL, and the content is delivered. Since the server doesn't usually look at cookies that are associated with static content, you should be careful to not associate cookies with those files, to save the client from having to send them back. One exception is when the receipt of a particular static file should trigger a later action by the server on the dynamic side, such as with the CSS example earlier.

One way you can decrease the time browsers spend uploading cookies is by using the cookie `path` property. The `path` tells the browser to send that cookie only when the first part of the requested URL starts with the `path` string, which is case-sensitive. In the earlier example, the browser will send the cookie back to the server only when the URL starts with `/pages`, which includes both `/pages/page.aspx` and `/pagesmore/stuff.aspx`. If it's not explicitly set, the default cookie `path` is the root, which means that the cookie will be attached to all URLs in the domain of the site that set it.

With the earlier HTTP response example, if you eliminated cookies from the 16 static objects on the page, that would reduce upload time by about $200 / 620 = 32\%$.

I recommend putting all your dynamic content under a single top-level folder, such as `/pages`. Static content should be placed in a separate folder, such as `/static`. With that layout, cookie paths can be set either on `/pages/` or on specific subfolders.

Another approach to avoiding this problem is to put all your static content into one or more different subdomains. You might have `s1.12titans.net`, `s2.12titans.net`, and `www.12titans.net`, for example. That would allow you to set cookies at the root of your main site (perhaps accidentally) without causing an adverse impact on the performance of static files. In the "Network Optimizations" section earlier in this chapter, I covered using separate subdomains to help improve download performance through the use of multiple simultaneous network connections.

Cookie names and their associated values should be kept as short as possible. There's no need to use a really long name for a cookie when one or two letters will work just fine. I suggest using two character names in most cases. Cookie values should be abbreviated, encoded, and possibly compressed to keep them short.

■ **Note** When HTTP compression is enabled, only the body of the response is compressed, not the headers, which includes cookies. If cookies are long enough to benefit from compression, you will need to do it programmatically.

You can also merge multiple cookies into one, perhaps using a comma character as a field separator. Minimizing the number of cookies is also important because browsers allow only up to 20 cookies per domain. If you create too many cookies, the browser will silently ignore them.

CSS Optimizations

In your HTML, one of the first and easiest CSS optimizations is to replace any `style` properties with CSS classes or ID tags. For example, instead of this:

```
<div style="display:none; width:250px; z-index:1000;
  background-color:red; border:3px solid #C63; padding:0">
```

pull the style information out, assign it to a new class name, and put it in your CSS file:

```
.info { display:none; width:250px; z-index:1000; background-color:red;
  border:3px solid #C63; padding:0 }
```

Then remove the style property from the `<div>` and replace it with the new `class`:

```
<div class="info">
```

Even though that doesn't reduce the total amount of text, there are several advantages of moving the style information into a static include file:

- It makes it easier to change the style of your pages consistently on a site-wide basis.

- It simplifies the process of dynamically switching to a different style, perhaps using ASP.NET themes.

- It helps facilitate parallel development, where a web designer might work only with the CSS to establish the look of the pages, while a programmer works on the associated HTML at the same time.

- The CSS include file can be cached on the client so that when it's requested for other pages on your site, it doesn't have to be downloaded again.

While you're factoring the style information out of your HTML, be sure to watch for duplicates. You can share common elements of each class by listing more than one class name before the definition, separated by commas. For example, instead of this:

```
.one { background-color:red; border:3px solid #C63; padding:0 }
.two { background-color:red; border:3px solid #C63; padding:0; color:white }
```

do this:

```
.one,.two { background-color:red; border:3px solid #C63; padding:0 }
.two { color:white }
```

You list the common `background-color`, `border`, and `padding` values once and attach them to both classes. The `color` property that's unique to the `two` class is then listed separately.

Some CSS properties can be inherited from parent tags by child tags. Inherited page-wide defaults should be set on the `body` selector so that they don't have to be duplicated for every style. This is particularly useful for things like fonts and color properties.

Although many CSS properties are inherited, not all of them are. The following CSS properties can be inherited:

- `background` and related properties (only in CSS 2+)

- `color`

- `font` and related properties

- `letter-spacing`

- `line-height`

- `list-style` and related properties

- `text-align`

- `text-indent`

- text-transform
- visibility
- white-space
- word-spacing

The following properties don't inherit:

- border and related properties
- display
- float
- clear
- height
- width
- margin and related properties
- min and max-height and width
- outline
- overflow
- padding and related properties
- text-decoration
- vertical-align
- z-index

As an example of inheritance, don't do this:

```
h1 {color: blue}
h1.name {color: blue; font-style: italic}
```

Do this instead:

```
h1 {color: blue}
h1.name {font-style: italic}
```

The color attribute is inherited by h1.name from the h1 entry.

Here are a few more easy optimizations:

- When you specify zero pixels, the px unit specifier isn't required.

- Whitespace is not required before or after braces, colons, or semicolons in a CSS specification.

- When specifying the same value for the top, right, bottom, and left margins or padding, you only need to list the value once, not four times.

- Use three-digit hex color codes instead of the six-digit version when you can. A three-digit code is equivalent to a six-digit that has each digit twice. For example, #0a9 is the same as #00aa99.

- Use hex color codes instead of their rgb() equivalents. The following standard colors have three-digit equivalents that are shorter than their names: black (#000), fuchsia (#f0f), white (#fff), and yellow (#ff0).

- Use the text version of color names instead of the numeric version, when they're the same length or shorter. If the color name has four or fewer characters, you should always use it. You should only use color names with between five and seven characters if they don't have a three-digit hex code.

- Use CSS shorthand when possible. For example, instead of using four different values for margin-top, margin-right, margin-bottom, and margin-left, you can list them in a single margin style.

- A semicolon is not required at the end of a CSS property list. It is only needed in between properties.

- To demonstrate several of these suggestions, consider this CSS:

```
body
{
    margin-top: 0px;
    margin-right: 1px;
    margin-bottom: 2px;
    margin-left: 3px;
    position: absolute;
    top: 0px;
    left: 0px;
    right: 0px;
    bottom: 0px;
    background-color: #00ffff;
}
table
{
    padding: 0px 0px 0px 0px;
    margin: 0px 0px 0px 0px;
    border-collapse: collapse;
}
```

```
tr
{
  padding: 0px 0px 0px 0px;
  margin: 0px 0px 0px 0px;
}
td
{
  padding: 0px 0px 0px 0px;
  margin: 0px 0px 0px 0px;
}
```

That can be optimized into the following, which is exactly equivalent:

```
body{margin:0 1px 2px 3px;background-color:#0ff}
table{border-collapse:collapse}
table,tr,td{padding:0;margin:0}
```

The fact that styles can cascade (as in *Cascading* Style Sheets) can also be used to make your CSS smaller.

If you wanted to set the padding for **td** elements to be **2px**, one approach would be as follows:

```
table,tr{padding:0;margin:0}
td{padding:2px;margin:0}
```

However, you can shorten the CSS by allowing the format to cascade from one selector to another:

```
table,tr,td{padding:0;margin:0}
td{padding:2px}
```

The first **td** setting of **padding:0** is overridden by the next line, which sets it to **2px**.

Image Sprites and Clustering

One way to reduce the number of round-trips required to retrieve images on a page is to combine multiple images into a single file and then to use CSS to display them individually. The resulting file usually loads faster since it avoids round-trips and the associated upload overhead; the smaller the files are, the larger the improvement. One way to do this is using a technique called *image sprites*.

The first step in implementing sprites is to combine your images into a single file. You can do this in an image editor, or you can use an online generator (search the Web for *CSS sprite generator* to see several possibilities). If the images are close to the same size, one way to arrange them is in a single column, with all the left edges on the left side. As you're making the file, record the X and Y coordinates of the upper-left corner of each embedded image, along with its size. A more complex layout might be needed if there is a large variation in images sizes. You should arrange them so that the amount of empty space in the aggregated image is minimized in order to help minimize the final size of the file. See Figure 2-7 for an example.

Figure 2-7. Sample image sprite

The next step is to create the CSS to display the desired image. The first style you need is one that sets the background to the new composite image and sets the image size as a clipping rectangle. In the example, all of the images are 56 × 56 pixels in size, so the `height` and `width` CSS properties are set accordingly, and anything beyond that size will be clipped:

```
.sp { background: url(csg.png); height:56px; width:56px; display: block }
```

The `display: block` property is needed for Firefox in order for it to accept a `height` and `width` on nonblock elements such as an `<a>` tag.

Next, create one selector for each image that specifies how the background image should be positioned inside the clipping rectangle. In the example, the images are all on the left side, so their X offsets are zero. Images are normally aligned so that their upper-left corner is in the upper-left of the target location. You can move the image up within the clipping rectangle defined above by specifying a negative Y coordinate. The clipping rectangle will hide the rest of the image.

In the example, the images are separated by 1 pixel. To display the first image, we need to move the composite up by 1 pixel. The image is 56 pixels tall, and there's another 1 pixel between it and the next image, so to see the next one, you need to move the composite up by 58 pixels, and so on for the rest of the images. See Figure 2-8.

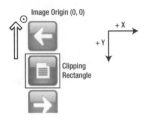

Figure 2-8. Move the image up within the clipping rectangle by applying a negative offset.

In addition to the X and Y offsets, each image should be given a `:hover` selector if it should be displayed when the mouse hovers over the original. This has the added advantage of replacing any JavaScript that might have otherwise been used for the same purpose. `float: left` is included for Firefox in order to get the block elements to line up horizontally instead of vertically. The resulting CSS for the example is shown here:

```
:hover.sprite-left { background-position: 0 -1px }
.sprite-notes { background-position: 0 -58px }
:hover.sprite-right { background-position: 0 -115px }
.sprite-right { float:left; background-position: 0 -172px }
.sprite-left { float:left; background-position: 0 -229px }
.sprite-notes-p { background-position: 0 -286px }
```

Finally, you can apply the CSS to your HTML. The class that assigns the background image and sets the size of the clipping rectangle should be set first, followed by the class that properly positions the image within that rectangle. The classes will work with several different HTML tags, including `<span>`, `<div>`, and `<a>`. Ironically, one of the tags they should not be used on is `<img>`, since the CSS doesn't replace the image `src` property, even if it's not used. Here are a few examples:

```
<span class="sp sprite-notes"></span>
<div class="sp sprite-notes-p"></div>
<a class="sp sprite-left" href="#"></a>
<a class="sp sprite-right" href="#"></a>
```

Notice that the `sp` class is applied first, followed by a space and the other class. This is a general technique that you can use to apply one class and then another. The resulting page is shown in Figure 2-9 (also see `file26.htm`):

Figure 2-9. Web page with CSS sprite images

When you hover over the left and right arrows, the images will be replaced, as per the :hover directive.

CSS images are loaded from paths relative to the CSS file. If your CSS is in an include file that's located in an ASP.NET theme, there may be cases where using an <img> tag is preferable so that the images can be more easily managed outside the theme system. In that event, you can use a slightly different technique, where an outer <div> sets the size of the clipping rectangle, and CSS on the <img> tag is used to position the image, but this time using relative positioning. Here's an example (see file27.htm):

```
<style>
.clu { position:relative; height:56px; width:56px; overflow:hidden }
.clu-notes { position:relative; top:-58px }
</style>
<div class="clu">
<img class="clu-notes" src="csg.png" width="56" height="343" border="0" />
</div>
```

Although this approach still uses composite images, I call it *image clustering* to differentiate it from the other technique.

Leveraging DHTML

You can make some types of page changes entirely on the client to avoid a server round-trip. For example:

- Show and hide parts of the page. For example, you can set the CSS property display: none with script.

- Show the current time using script, rather than setting it on the server. If the current time is the only thing on a page that changes regularly, that might also allow you to cache the page longer than you could otherwise.

- Apply user-configured UI customizations. You can use script to set or change fonts and colors, for example, or to position content blocks.

- Leverage event-based actions, such as timers, mouse movement, key presses, and so on. For example, you can allow a large image to be dragged within a clipping window, rather than panning it on the server.

Using Ajax

Normally, when you click a link to go to a new page, the browser does either an HTTP GET or POST, and the server responds with an entirely new page. This is also true for ASP.NET postbacks, which are just a specialized form of POST.

It's possible to submit a request to the server without leaving the current page and without causing the response to be loaded as a new page. This technique is called Ajax, short for *Asynchronous JavaScript and XML*, although the name is actually a misnomer, since the core mechanism has nothing to do with XML. Ajax has the following high-level features:

- It can retrieve arbitrary text from the server without requiring the page to reload.

- It facilitates fast partial-page updates or refreshes.

- It supports synchronous and asynchronous requests.

- It is supported on all modern browsers.

You might use Ajax to retrieve HTML fragments from the server and insert them directly into the page. You can also parse text that the server returns and use the results to update the page, or the server can generate JavaScript that the browser executes.

The enabling technology behind Ajax is the XmlHttp control, which allows you to submit an HTTP request and receive the response without leaving the page.

Here's an example that builds on the earlier image sprite code (see file28.htm):

```
<title>Chapter 2: File 28</title>
<style type="text/css">
.sp { background:url(csg.png); height:56px; width:56px; display:block }
.sprite-right { position:absolute; top:10; left:10; background-position:0 -172px }
</style>
</head>
<body>
<a class="sp sprite-right" href="#" onclick="move(this)"></a>
<script type="text/javascript">
var req = null;
var im = null;
function move(obj) {
    im = obj;
    req = getreq();
    if (req != null) {
        try {
            req.onreadystatechange = done;
            req.open("GET", "ajax1.aspx", true);
            req.send(null);
        } catch (e) {
            return null;
        }
    }
}
function getreq() {
    if (window.XMLHttpRequest) {
        req = new XMLHttpRequest();
    } else if (window.ActiveXObject) {
        req = new ActiveXObject("Microsoft.XMLHTTP");
    }
    return req;
}
```

```
function done() {
    if ((req.readyState == 4) && (req.status == 200)) {
        var resp = req.responseText.split(":");
        im.style.top = resp[0] + "px";
        im.style.left = resp[1] + "px";
    }
}
</script>
```

Each time you click the image, you use the XmlHttp control to request the ajax1.aspx page, which returns a pair of random numbers separated by a colon. The response is parsed with script and used to move the image to a random location on the screen.

The HTML is mostly the same as before; there's an <a> tag with a CSS class that assigns a background image and position, along with an appropriate size. The function move() is called when you click the image.

1. First, move() calls getreq() to get a reference to an XmlHttp object in a browser-independent way.

2. Next, it sets onreadystatechange on the returned XmlHttp object to the function that should be called when the request returns or fails.

3. Then it calls open() to set the parameters for a request to the server to GET ajax1.aspx. The third parameter is set to true to indicate that the call should be made asynchronously.

4. Then send() is called to start the request.

5. After send() returns, the done() function is called:

    a. The readyState property indicates the state of the call, and a value of 4 means that it completed successfully.

    b. The status field is the HTTP status code, where 200 means that the request was processed successfully, 404 would be Not Found, and so on.

    c. The body of the response is located in the XmlHttp object's responseText property, which you split into two fields with the string split function.

    d. The resulting values are parsed as integers and then used to set the absolute position top and left style properties of the <a> tag.

The server code for ajax1.aspx generates two random integers between 0 and 500 (see ajax1.aspx):

```
<script runat="server" language="C#">
Random random = new Random();
</script>
<%= random.Next(500) %>:<%= random.Next(500) %>
<% Response.Cache.SetCacheability(HttpCacheability.NoCache); %>
```

The response is marked not cacheable to ensure that the client receives a different pair of values for each request.

A number of powerful and flexible Ajax framework libraries are available. I happen to like jQuery, although it's only one option. There are certainly times when a very lightweight do-it-yourself approach as I've demonstrated here is appropriate, but most projects would benefit from adopting a library to help simplify and streamline your code.

Using Silverlight

Silverlight allows you to embed an application that uses a trimmed-down version of the .NET Framework into a web page. The application can display text or graphics in a window on the page and interact with the user in the same way as a desktop application. It can also use web services and interact with the page DOM and JavaScript. You can write Silverlight applications in any .NET language.

Users will need a one-time download of the Silverlight runtime before they can run your application. Fortunately, the download is small (under 5MB). Silverlight is compatible with most browsers, including IE, Firefox, Opera, Chrome, and Safari on both PCs and Macs. The concept is similar to a Java applet or Adobe Flash, which also require browser plug-ins.

Although Silverlight isn't as widely available as Flash or JavaScript, it seems to be gaining acceptance rapidly from both users and web developers. As of mid-2009, according to Microsoft, Silverlight was available on about 30 percent of all PCs worldwide. At the MIX09 conference, Microsoft reported that there were 350+ million installations, 300,000+ developers, 200+ partners in 30+ countries, and tens of thousands of sites with Silverlight applications on them, including large ones such as Netflix, eBay, and NBC. Microsoft is apparently not planning to push the Silverlight runtime to clients using Windows Update. However, once users have installed the runtime, they can get subsequent updates that way.

The advantage of Silverlight for ASP.NET developers is that since the apps are written in a compiled and type-safe language, they can be faster to develop, easier to maintain, and more reliable than the equivalent code written in JavaScript and DHTML.

One of the many cool things you can do with Silverlight that's not possible with JavaScript is that you can save application data on the user's local disk and share that data between different browsers. I will cover that in more detail in Chapter 3.

Silverlight applications can have a desktop application–style GUI and even 3D graphics. You build the UI using a trimmed-down version of the XAML-based Windows Presentation Foundation (WPF), which includes support for embedded video and complex animation.

Silverlight applications have full access to the page DOM and to cookies. Code within the application can both call out to and be called by JavaScript. There is an object sharing model that helps simplify those interfaces. In cases where complex script might otherwise be required, performing those functions in a Silverlight application instead can considerably simplify development and maintenance.

Silverlight isn't intended to be a replacement for a typical HTML page. However, if you have a site that requires or would benefit from a lot of interactivity or if you have a lot of script that would benefit from being written in a .NET language, then it's is definitely worth considering.

Building HTML Controls

As an example, let's implement a technique similar to the one used earlier to generate a drop-down list using JavaScript, except this time I'll show how to do it with Silverlight instead.

To create a Silverlight application, you will need to download and install the Silverlight SDK. Here's a link:

`http://silverlight.net/GetStarted/`

After installing the SDK, add a Silverlight project to your solution. Right-click the solution in Solution Explorer, and select **Add ➤ New Project**. Then select **Visual C#** in the left panel and **Silverlight Application** on the right side. Call the project `CountryList`, and click **OK**.

Next, Visual Studio will bring up the **New Silverlight Application** dialog, as in Figure 2-10. Accept the defaults, as shown, to link the application into an existing web site in your solution.

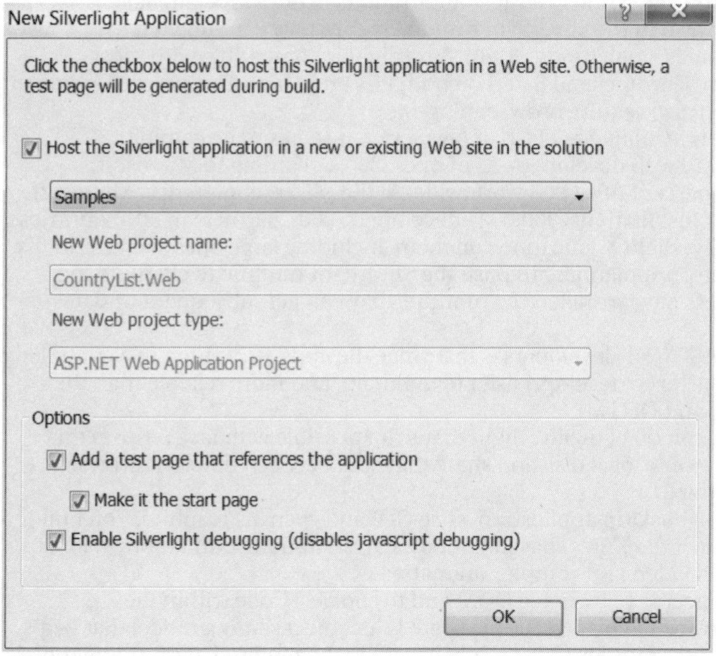

Figure 2-10. Adding a Silverlight application in Visual Studio

This application won't have a UI of its own in this case, so edit `MainPage.xaml` to set `d:DesignWidth` and `d:DesignHeight` to zero, and remove the default `<Grid>` control:

```
<UserControl x:Class="CountryList.MainPage"
    xmlns="http://schemas.microsoft.com/winfx/2006/xaml/presentation"
    xmlns:x="http://schemas.microsoft.com/winfx/2006/xaml"
    xmlns:d="http://schemas.microsoft.com/expression/blend/2008"
    xmlns:mc="http://schemas.openxmlformats.org/markup-compatibility/2006"
    mc:Ignorable="d" d:DesignWidth="0" d:DesignHeight="0">
</UserControl>
```

Next, edit MainPage.xaml.cs as follows:

```
using System.Text;
using System.Windows;
using System.Windows.Browser;
using System.Windows.Controls;

namespace CountryList
{
    public partial class MainPage : UserControl
    {
        private string[] countries =
        { "AF", "Afghanistan", "AL", "Albania", "DZ", "Algeria", "US", "United States" };

        public MainPage()
        {
            this.Loaded += new RoutedEventHandler(Page_Loaded);
            InitializeComponent();
        }

        private void Page_Loaded(object sender, RoutedEventArgs e)
        {
            HtmlElement div = HtmlPage.Document.GetElementById("putCountriesHere");
            if (div != null)
            {
                string selected = (string)div.GetProperty("innerHTML");
                StringBuilder sb = new StringBuilder();
                sb.Append("<select>");
                for (int i = 0; i < countries.Length; i += 2)
                {
                    sb.Append("<option value=\"");
                    sb.Append(countries[i]);
                    sb.Append("\"");
                    if (countries[i] == selected)
                        sb.Append(" selected");
                    sb.Append(">");
                    sb.Append(countries[i + 1]);
                    sb.Append("</option>");
                }
                sb.Append("</select>");
                div.SetProperty("innerHTML", sb.ToString());
            }
        }
    }
}
```

The code adds the Page_Loaded method as an event handler for the Loaded event.

When the event fires, it looks to see whether a node in the HTML DOM exists with the putCountriesHere ID. If it does, you retrieve the innerHTML property of that node and use it to determine which element in the drop-down to select. You then assemble the generated HTML using StringBuilder, with logic that mirrors the earlier JavaScript, and write the results to the innerHTML property of the target object.

Next, edit the CountryListTestPage.html file that Visual Studio autogenerated in your web site to hold the Silverlight control. Right before the <form> tag, add the following:

```
<div id="putCountriesHere">US</div>
```

The id is the one that you're looking for from Silverlight, and the US text inside the <div> is the country you want to have selected in the drop-down box.

When you compile the project and display the test page in a browser, you will see the drop-down box with **United States** selected.

This particular example isn't too compelling on its own based on performance alone, because it replaces a small amount of HTML with a Silverlight application that's 5KB in size. However, if you already have a Silverlight app on the page for other reasons, the incremental size difference might be worth it, particularly if the page itself wasn't cacheable and if you can use the code on several pages. The more HTML and JavaScript you can replace, the better.

Calling into Silverlight from JavaScript

In addition to writing into the DOM from Silverlight as described earlier, it's also possible to call into Silverlight from script. You can use both approaches to help move some of your script into Silverlight's compiled and type-safe environment. In general, compiled code should be smaller and faster than script.

Let's extend the previous example by displaying the browser's **User-Agent** string below the generated option box. First, register the MainPage object with the Silverlight runtime as an object that JavaScript is allowed to access by adding the following line at the beginning of the constructor:

```
HtmlPage.RegisterScriptableObject("Page", this);
```

Next, add the following method to the MainPage class:

```
[ScriptableMember]
public string BrowserType()
{
    return HtmlPage.BrowserInformation.UserAgent;
}
```

The ScriptableMember attribute tells the runtime that JavaScript is allowed to access this method.

Next, add the following <div> block to the test HTML file, below the earlier one for the drop-down box:

```
<div id="useragent"></div>
```

This <div> will hold the results. You use the id attribute to find it from script.

Add the following <script> block at the end of the page, above </body>:

```
<script type="text/javascript">
function getagent(sender) {
    var dest = document.getElementById("useragent");
    if (dest != null) {
```

```
        try {
            dest.innerHTML = sender.getHost().content.Page.BrowserType();
        } catch (e) {
            dest.innerHTML = "Error";
        }
    }
}
</script>
```

The script uses getElementById() to find the <div> target. If the target is present, then the function calls the Silverlight control and stores the result in the target. If the control throws an Exception, an error message is displayed.

Note that the first part of the name of the function in Silverlight consists of sender.getHost().content, where sender is passed as an argument to the handler. The last part is constructed by adding the string you passed to RegisterScriptableObject (Page), followed by the name of the method itself (BrowserType).

Add the following parameter for the Silverlight <object>, which will call the script after the Silverlight control loads:

```
<param name="onLoad" value="getagent" />
```

After making the changes, rebuild the web site to compile the application and to pull the new .xap file into your web site, and then run the test page to see the results.

Other Ways to Use Silverlight to Improve Performance

Here are a few examples of other things you can do with Silverlight to improve the performance of your site:

- Use Silverlight as either a replacement for Ajax or a supplement to it.

- Implement forms entirely in Silverlight. Improve error checking, and provide feedback that is more dynamic, resulting in fewer round-trips.

- Implement dynamic charts, graphs, and images; support frequently updating images.

- Implement dynamic tables or grids, including features like client-side sorting.

- Reduce page weight by eliminating complex tables. Provide lightweight updates when data changes.

- Replace script functions with managed code. Use the bidirectional script and DOM interface to reduce page weight.

Silverlight can also improve performance by reducing the amount of data retrieved from the server and by eliminating page refreshes in certain cases. For example, instead of requesting an entirely new page when a live chart or a graph is updated, the application can request just the new data and create the graphics on the client instead of on the server. For sites that deal with large collections of items, such as e-mail messages or images in a gallery, the application might display just a few items at first to minimize startup time and then request more as needed, without going to a new page.

You can offload the generation of certain types of pages (or parts of pages) from the server into Silverlight. For example, consider a product catalog. Rather than sending a separate web page to the client for each product, you would only need to send the core content and any related images, which Silverlight could then assemble, format, and display.

A Silverlight application can use web requests or web services. With the right policy files in place, Silverlight can make cross-domain web service calls, which are only awkwardly possible in Ajax by using frames (for security reasons).

Something to be aware of with Silverlight is that any content that the application displays isn't directly visible to search engines, since they won't execute the app or any associated script. That can be good when you have content that you don't particularly want a search engine to see, such as a registration form. Of course, there are also cases when you do want the content to be visible. It's possible to work around this problem in part by generating an alternate version of the page when you detect a search engine's `User-Agent` string in a request. Even though most search engines don't endorse sending them content different from what you send to regular users, it may be appropriate in cases like this, when your goal is clarification. The alternate content might just be descriptive text, or it could be an extract of your `.xaml` and text resource files, which you might generate dynamically, perhaps using XSLT transforms.

Improving Rendering Speed

The browser doesn't start rendering `<table>` tags until it knows the sizes of all resources contained in the table. For example, if you have an image in a `<table>` and don't specify its size in the `<img>` tag, then the browser has to retrieve the image before it can start rendering. If you include the size, then the browser can continue rendering the table while it's waiting for the image to load.

Using the `<col>` tag with a `width` property can also help improve table rendering speed, particularly for large or complex tables. Here's an example:

```
<table>
<col width="400" />
<col width="300" />
<tr>
<td>
This column will be 400 pixels wide
</td>
<td>
This one will be 300 pixels wide
</td>
</tr>
</table>
```

You can also associate a CSS class with a `<col>` tag. All major browsers support the `<col>` tag.

Be sure to include a `<!DOCTYPE>` tag as the first line of your HTML. `<!DOCTYPE>` tells the browser which "dialect" of HTML you're using on the page, such as whether it's old-and-quirky HTML, nice-and-shiny XHTML free of deprecated elements, or something in between. Knowing that information helps the browser render the page more quickly, because it doesn't need to spend time guessing which dialect it's looking at. I recommend the in-between variety, also known as `Transitional`, which is the same one that Visual Studio sets by default when you create a new `.aspx` page. It allows deprecated HTML elements like `<font>`, although framesets are not allowed:

```
<!DOCTYPE html PUBLIC "-//W3C//DTD XHTML 1.0 Transitional//EN"
    "http://www.w3.org/TR/xhtml1/DTD/xhtml1-transitional.dtd">
```

The `Strict` `<!DOCTYPE>` doesn't allow deprecated elements such as `<font>`:

```
<!DOCTYPE html PUBLIC "-//W3C//DTD XHTML 1.0 Strict//EN"
    "http://www.w3.org/TR/xhtml1/DTD/xhtml1-strict.dtd">
```

Both `Transitional` and `Strict` require your markup to be well-formed XML, so remember to close all your tags and to use quotes on attributes, such as:

```
<img src="myimage.jpg" />
```

Since "bare" ampersands are illegal in XML, you should escape them in URLs with `&amp;`. Here's an example:

```
<a href="page.aspx?a=1&amp;b=2">My page</a>
```

For static content, you should specify the character set you're using with a `<meta charset>` tag. If you don't, the browser tries to guess it. Not only do you risk having the browser guess incorrectly, but the process of guessing takes time.

Here's how to specify UTF-8 encoding:

```
<meta http-equiv="Content-type" content="text/html; charset=utf-8">
```

Omitting the tag can also result in security issues. For example, the string `<script>alert()</script>` can be encoded in the UTF-7 character set as `+ADw-script+AD4-alert()+ADw-/script+AD4-`. If the browser incorrectly guesses that a page is UTF-7 encoded when it's actually UTF-8, it might allow a hacker to inject script. For that reason, even static error pages should include `<meta charset>`.

Be sure to include the tag early in your HTML, before `<title>`.

As a shorter alternative, you can also inform the browser about the content type of your page by using the `Content-Type` HTTP header. For dynamic pages, the ASP.NET runtime adds the `Content-Type` header for you automatically by default.

Precaching

In cases where you can anticipate the next page on your site that a user is likely to visit, you can use JavaScript to precache objects used by that page. When the user goes there, the page will load more quickly, since some of the objects it uses will already be in cache on the client. The user shouldn't notice precaching, since it happens after the current page finishes loading, when the network would have been idle otherwise.

Using Fiddler can be very useful here to help you figure out the objects used by the most common destination pages after the current one.

Precaching Images

One approach is to precache images using the page's `onload` handler. Here's an example:

```
<body onload="preload()">
. . .
<script type="text/javascript">
function preload() {
    var pre = new Image(0,0);
    pre.src = "http://s1.12titans.net/static/next1.jpg";
    var prx = new Image(0,0);
    prx.src = "http://s2.12titans.net/static/next2.jpg";
}
</script>
</body>
```

The `onload` handler creates a new `Image` object and then sets its `src` property. That will cause the image to be downloaded and cached so that it is available immediately on any following page that might need it. The zero width and height specified in the constructor minimizes the work the browser has to do after it finishes retrieving the image. Images that you request in this way are placed into the same queue that the browser uses when loading the rest of page, so the same rules apply: multiple images should be spread across multiple domains so that they can be requested and downloaded in parallel.

When deciding which images to precache, you should take into account what will be most helpful to users. Good choices might include things like a composite sprite image or images that are needed for navigation. Images above the fold are generally more important than those below the fold, since the latter can't even be seen when the page first loads.

Precaching CSS and JavaScript

You can also precache CSS and JavaScript. Precaching script can have a bigger impact than images because of the negative effects that loading them can have on page performance.

In case you might be tempted, it's not possible to use an `Image` object to precache CSS or JavaScript. The file will be downloaded if you set it as the `src` property. However, because the MIME type of the response is not an image, IE simply discards the result.

One solution is to use Ajax. However, this approach is not ideal because it doesn't allow content to be downloaded from domains other than the one associated with the containing page. Building on the earlier example:

```
<body onload="preload()">
. . .
<script type="text/javascript">
function preload()
{
    var req = getreq();
    if (req != null) {
        req.open("GET", "/static/next.js", true);
        req.send(null);
    }
    var rex = getreq();
    if (rex != null) {
```

```
        rex.open("GET", "/static/next.css", true);
        rex.send(null);
    }
}
</script>
</body>
```

Notice that the third parameter to the `open()` function is true. That means the request is made asynchronously, so the browser doesn't wait for the first request to finish before it starts the second one, subject to limits on the maximum number of simultaneous connections.

However, if your scripts and CSS reside on several different domains, as I'm advocating, then a different approach is required. You can dynamically create `<script>` elements. Unfortunately, this has the side effect that the script is parsed and executed, so you need to be careful to only reference code that doesn't cause any undesirable side effects. Here's an example:

```
<body onload="preload()">
. . .
<script type="text/javascript">
function preload() {
    var scr = document.createElement("script");
    scr.src = "http://s1.12titans.net/ch02/next.js";
}
</script>
</body>
```

Note that the `<script>` element does not have to be inserted into the DOM; the file will still be downloaded and placed in the browser's cache.

You can use a similar technique for CSS:

```
<body onload="preload()">
. . .
<script type="text/javascript">
function preload() {
    var lnk = document.createElement("link");
    lnk.rel = "stylesheet";
    lnk.type = "text/css";
    lnk.href = "http://s1.12titans.net/ch02/next.css";
    document.getElementsByTagName('head')[0].appendChild(lnk);
}
</script>
</body>
```

However, unlike with `<script>`, the dynamic `<link>` tag *does* need to be added to the DOM in order for the file to be downloaded. Unfortunately, the result is that the CSS in the downloaded file will be applied to the current page, so it's important to make sure it doesn't cause any problems (such as conflicting selectors) before using this technique.

Tableless Layout Using CSS

There's a long-standing debate among web designers about the desirability of using CSS for layout instead of tables. Those in favor of that approach cite things like "purity of semantics" and "separation of concern" between content and style. Those opposed believe that using tables is easier to learn and implement. My recommendation is somewhere in between. I generally prefer CSS, but I also think there are times when tables can be a perfectly good solution.

From a performance perspective, CSS-based layouts tend to be much faster than their table-based equivalents. Equally important, though, is that by using CSS, you can place content in your HTML in the order of importance to your users. Since the browser renders content in the order it's encountered, you can make it so that users will see the most important content first, regardless of its location on the screen, which also improves *perceived* performance.

An additional benefit is that because one of the algorithms used by search engines ranks pages by how far away keywords are from the beginning of a file, moving your main content closer to the beginning can help improve the rank of your page. In addition, pages designed this way often look better on a wider range of devices, such as small-screen mobiles.

The area where this has the most impact is for the high-level arrangement of sections on a page; it's definitely worth the effort to avoid enclosing most of your page in a single large table. With a typical page that has a large navigation column on the left side of the page, if you use a table for the layout, that column will come first in the HTML, before your main content. By using CSS, you can avoid that requirement and have your content first instead.

The most powerful way to do this is with absolute positioning. Unfortunately, the downside is that the resulting layout isn't flexible in some ways. For example, the size of a top header section might be fixed, so extra-long text might not fit without some additional coding. Moving things around on the page can also be a little complicated, because adjusting the position of one item doesn't automatically change the position of others. However, the idea here is to set this up as a template (probably using an ASP.NET master page, as I discuss in Chapter 6) so that it has to be done only once or a small number of times for your site, and not for every page.

Here are the key concepts for doing tableless layout using CSS with absolute positioning:

- `<div>` is your friend.

- You can apply absolute positioning to as few as one or two edges. The other boundaries of the `<div>` can be set using `width` or `margin`.

- You can position edges using either percentages or pixels.

- You can specify widths as either percentages or pixels.

One disadvantage of using absolute positioning for a multicolumn page layout is that it's difficult to properly position a footer. Since there isn't a single container around all the columns, footers require some tricks that are beyond the scope of this book.

Here's the CSS for an example layout:

```
<style type="text/css">
.hdr,.lft,.rgt,.ctr{position:absolute;top:90px;border:1px solid #000;padding:10px}
.hdr {
top: 10px;
left: 10px;
right: 10px;
height: 55px
}
```

```
.lft {
left: 10px;
width: 120px
}
.rgt {
right: 10px;
width: 160px
}
.ctr {
left: 155px;
right: 195px;
padding: 1em
}
h1,h2{margin:0}
</style>
```

You can use separate classes for the header (`hdr`), left (`lft`), right (`rgt`), and center (`ctr`) content areas. All of the classes have absolute positioning set, along with a default position of 90 pixels from the top of the page, a 1-pixel-wide black `margin` and 10 pixels of `padding`. Each class then sets its specific location with offsets relative to the edges of the page, using the `left` or `right` properties. The `hdr` class also overrides the `top` property, and the `ctr` class overrides `padding`. The `margin` for the `<h1>` and `<h2>` tags is set to zero to make the page look more consistent across browsers.

Notice that the `rgt` and `lft` columns have their width determined explicitly, using the `width` property. However, the `ctr` column binds its left and right edges to the edges of the page using absolute positioning. The result is that if the page is resized, the size of that column will also change. This is sometimes called a *liquid* layout.

The position of the outer edges of the two outer columns is straightforward: the `<div>` is placed a certain distance from the respective edge and assigned a `width`.

The exact location of the upper edge and both edges of the center area takes a little math. The total width of a `<div>` is determined by adding the content width (the value of the width property) to the left and right padding and to the width of the left and right margins and borders. Using the left side as an example: `10` (position from left side of the page) + `120` (content width) + `10` (left padding) + `10` (right padding) + `0` (left and right margins) + `1` (left border) + `1` (right border) = `152`. In the example, I've specified a 3-pixel space between the each area of the page so that the borders can be clearly seen, which puts the left offset of the center area at `152 + 3 = 155` pixels. The same process is repeated for the other areas.

With the CSS in place, the HTML consists of wrapping the four sections of the page in separate `<div>` tags and attaching the appropriate class to each:

```
<body>
<div class="hdr">
<h1>Page Header</h1>
</div>
<div class="ctr">
<h2>Heading</h2>
<p>Lorem ipsum dolor sit amet, consectetur adipiscing elit.
Donec vehicula. Praesent sed erat. Integer suscipit pede
laoreet tortor. Aenean pulvinar, lectus malesuada ullamcorper
sollicitudin, lectus orci vehicula augue, vel ultricies eros
urna eget nulla. Suspendisse ac nisl.</p>
</div>
```

```
<div class="lft">
<p>Aenean tempus ultrices turpis. Aenean mollis.
Ut vestibulum suscipit pede. Vestibulum commodo odio
eget arcu.</p>
</div>
<div class="rgt">
<p>Suspendisse imperdiet ligula imperdiet purus. Suspendisse
potenti. Aliquam id diam id lorem tristique malesuada.</p>
</div>
</body>
```

Notice that the center (main) content comes before the left and right columns, which was one of our goals. See Figure 2-11.

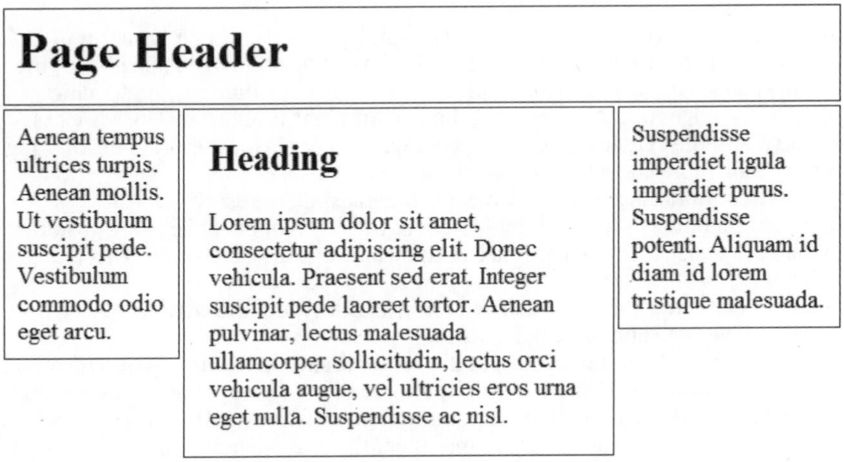

Figure 2-11. Three-column tableless layout using CSS with absolute positioning

Optimizing JavaScript Performance

Since the JavaScript referenced by a page needs to be parsed and executed by the browser, you should take care to make sure that it performs well. In addition to the techniques that you might apply to a compiled language, a few performance guidelines are specific to JavaScript.

Some IE-specific optimizations are possible that allow you to reference elements more efficiently. For example, with `<img id="tagId" />`, you can use just `tagId.src` instead of any of the following:

- `document.all.tagId.src`

- `document.getElementById("tagId").src`

- `document.all["tagId"].src` (which is the slowest)

However, note that the short version doesn't work with forms.

For all browsers, you should use temporary variables when accessing multiple values, especially in loops. For example, in IE don't do this:

```
for (i = 0; i < document.all.formx.length; i++)
    if (document.all.formx.taken[i].checked)
        dostuff();
```

Do this instead:

```
var tf = document.all.formx;
var tfl = tf.length;
for (i = 0; i < tfl; i++)
    if (tf.taken[i].checked)
        dostuff();
```

The `innerHTML` property is very powerful and a useful way to dynamically modify your page, particularly as part of leveraging Ajax or Silverlight. However, for IE only you can use the much faster `innerText` property instead when the content contains only text and no HTML.

For all browsers, in the event that a number of strings will eventually be written into the page with `document.write()`, it's more efficient to write them individually rather than concatenating them together first. For example, don't do this:

```
var str = "The value for " + myname + " is this: " + myvalue;
document.write(str);
```

Do this instead:

```
document.write("The value for ");
document.write(myname);
document.write(" is this: ");
document.write(myvalue);
```

Summary

In this chapter, I covered the following:

- The steps that the browser follows when requesting and processing a page and how you can use that information to optimize your HTML for faster load times.

- Why you should include a few requests in the first 500 bytes or so of your page.

- Using early and late loading to request images according to their priority to the user instead of their position on the screen.

- Using consistent case for your URLs and consistent names for your files to avoid having clients download the same files more than once, even when they're cacheable.

- Assigning your static files to multiple domains to help the browser download them in parallel.

- Placing `<script>` includes late in your HTML or preceding them with one or more images to help increase network parallelism.

- Minimizing the number of script files in your project by combining them and by avoiding the need for `document.write()`.

- Using absolute positioning or DOM manipulation to reorder scripts that you can't modify.

- Using the page `onload` handler to load large, low-priority images, or images that are below the fold or that might not be used (such as rollover images).

- Using CSS to replace text images.

- How to minify your HTML, CSS, and JavaScript, including using tools such as `jsmin` as part of your build process.

- Using lowercase URLs, tag names, property names, and so on, to help maximize the compressibility of your HTML.

- How to reduce the number and size of the images you need through careful requirements analysis.

- Using transparency as an alternative to rollover images.

- Optimizing the size of your images with careful cropping and the choice of the right image format, quality level, bit depth, and dimensions.

- Using image slicing to improve perceived performance when you're loading large images.

- Using client-side image maps instead of multiple images or slicing.

- Why you should specify the size of images in your `<img>` tags, using the native image size or larger.

- Including a web site icon file in your project and specifying a near-term cache expiration date for it.

- Applying general HTML, CSS, and JavaScript optimizations such as removing redundant tags and using self-closing tags.

- Using the **Optimize HTML** feature in Expression Web.

- Avoiding optimization techniques that violate the HTML standards.

- Eliminating CSS round-trips for the first page view.

- Using JavaScript to gate page requests by strategically disabling buttons and links.

- Using JavaScript to reduce HTML size by generating repetitive HTML or by adding frequently repeating text to tag properties.

- Minimizing the amount of data that clients have to upload when they are requesting objects on a page.

- Reducing the bandwidth and time consumed by cookies by using the `path` property, by not associating cookies with static files and by using short or encoded names and values.

- Replacing CSS `style` properties with classes, IDs, or other selectors in a separate (cacheable) CSS file.

- Merging duplicate CSS styles and common elements and to minimize the size of your CSS with property inheritance, shorthand, cascading, and other optimizations.

- Using image sprites and clustering to reduce round-trips.

- Using DHTML to make certain types of page changes entirely on the client.

- Using Ajax for partial-page updates.

- Using Silverlight to generate HTML controls and insert them into your page.

- Improving page rendering speed.

- Using precaching to help the next page that the user is likely to see load quickly.

- Using tableless layout to help optimize the order of content in your HTML so that users see what's important to them right away when the page starts to render.

- Improving the performance of your JavaScript.

CHAPTER 3

■ ■ ■

Caching

Caching is an important cornerstone of high-performance web sites. You can use it to accomplish the following:

- *Reduce round-trips*: Content cached at the client or in proxies can eliminate web server round-trips. Content cached at the web server can eliminate database round-trips.

- *Move content closer to clients*: The farther away from clients content is located, the longer it takes to retrieve.

- *Avoid time-consuming processes of regenerating reusable content*: For content that takes a lot of time or resources to generate, system performance and scalability are improved if you can generate content once and then reuse it many times.

- *Optimize state management*: Caching state information at the client is more scalable than storing it in a central location (within certain bounds, as discussed later).

In this chapter, I'll cover how and when to use caching in all tiers of your application:

- Browser cache

- `ViewState`

- Cookies

- Silverlight isolated storage

- Proxy cache

- Web server cache

- SQL Server caching

- Distributed caching

- Cache expiration times

Caching at All Tiers

As discussed in Chapter 1, the end-to-end system called a *web application* contains a number of layers, or *tiers*, where caching is possible. See Figure 3-1.

```
┌─────────────────────────────────────────────────────┐
│ Web Browser                                          │
│  ┌─────────┐ ┌───────────┐ ┌─────────┐ ┌───────────┐ │
│  │  Files  │ │ ViewState │ │ Cookies │ │Silverlight│ │
│  └─────────┘ └───────────┘ └─────────┘ └───────────┘ │
└─────────────────────────────────────────────────────┘
┌ ─ ─ ─ ─ ─ ─ ─ ─ ─ ─ ─ ─ ─ ─ ─ ─ ─ ─ ─ ─ ─ ─ ─ ─ ─ ┐
                    Local Proxy
└ ─ ─ ─ ─ ─ ─ ─ ─ ─ ─ ─ ─ ─ ─ ─ ─ ─ ─ ─ ─ ─ ─ ─ ─ ─ ┘
┌ ─ ─ ─ ─ ─ ─ ─ ─ ─ ─ ─ ─ ─ ─ ─ ─ ─ ─ ─ ─ ─ ─ ─ ─ ─ ┐
                     ISP Proxy
└ ─ ─ ─ ─ ─ ─ ─ ─ ─ ─ ─ ─ ─ ─ ─ ─ ─ ─ ─ ─ ─ ─ ─ ─ ─ ┘
┌─────────────────────────────────────────────────────┐
│ Web Server                                           │
│  ┌────────────────────────────────────────────────┐ │
│  │                    http.sys                      │ │
│  └────────────────────────────────────────────────┘ │
│  ┌────────────────────────────────────────────────┐ │
│  │                IIS Output Cache                  │ │
│  └────────────────────────────────────────────────┘ │
│  ┌────────────────────────────────────────────────┐ │
│  │             ASP.NET Output Cache                 │ │
│  └────────────────────────────────────────────────┘ │
│  ┌──────────────────────┐ ┌───────────────────────┐ │
│  │ ASP.NET Object Cache │ │ ASP.NET Request Cache │ │
│  └──────────────────────┘ └───────────────────────┘ │
│  ┌────────────────────────────────────────────────┐ │
│  │              Disk Controller Cache               │ │
│  └────────────────────────────────────────────────┘ │
│  ┌────────────────────────────────────────────────┐ │
│  │                Disk Drive Cache                  │ │
│  └────────────────────────────────────────────────┘ │
└─────────────────────────────────────────────────────┘
┌─────────────────────────────────────────────────────┐
│                     SQL Server                       │
└─────────────────────────────────────────────────────┘
┌─────────────────────────────────────────────────────┐
│                     Disk Array                       │
└─────────────────────────────────────────────────────┘
```

Figure 3-1. Caching options that are available to web applications

Boxes at the same horizontal level in the figure are mutually exclusive content stores, and their vertical location gives a rough sense of how far away they are from each other, in terms of relative access time. For example, you wouldn't normally store the same data in both the ASP.NET object cache and in the ASP.NET request cache, or in both cookies and `ViewState`, and the browser can retrieve content cached by `http.sys` faster than content from SQL Server.

Although you can (and should) cache certain resources in multiple tiers, some types of data should be stored only in a single location. For example, state information stored in a cookie might be stored only there, or a pre-calculated result might exist only in the ASP.NET object cache.

You should *consider* caching in all tiers, though, and take relative content uniqueness and access frequency into account when deciding whether to cache in a particular tier. For example, content that is unique per user is generally not a good candidate to cache at the web server tier, since it is relatively unlikely to be reused, particularly in an environment with a large number of load-balanced servers. However, it might be perfectly acceptable to have the user's browser cache it.

You can configure caching in four different ways:

- Using IIS Manager (a GUI front-end to the underlying XML configuration files)
- By directly editing an XML configuration file
- Declaratively, in an ASP.NET page or control
- Programmatically, in code-behind or in an `HttpModule`

I will describe each approach in the following sections.

Browser Cache

Files that the browser retrieves from the server should be stored in the browser's cache as long as possible to help minimize server round-trips. If a page and all the resources it requires are in the browser's cache, no server round-trips at all are required; the browser can render the page using only the cached content. Since that presents no load on the network or the server, it is obviously very good for scalability!

Caching Static Content

Every object stored in the browser cache includes an expiration time, beyond which the browser considers the content stale or invalid. You can manage those expiration times with the `Cache-Control: max-age` HTTP header. The `Expires` header performed the same function with HTTP 1.0, but `Cache-Control` overrides `Expires` when both are present. I prefer to use only `Cache-Control` when possible, thereby avoiding the confusion that might arise when you have two headers that specify the same thing.

If neither the `Expires` nor `Cache-Control: max-age` HTTP headers is set, then IE still stores the content in its cache, although it's marked stale.

Avoiding Conditional GETs

For stale content, IE does a conditional `GET` when it is referenced the second and subsequent times (only once per page), asking the server to confirm that the content hasn't changed since the last time it was retrieved. Here's what a conditional HTTP request looks like:

```
GET /check.png HTTP/1.1
Accept: */*
Accept-Language: en-us
UA-CPU: x86
Accept-Encoding: gzip, deflate
If-Modified-Since: Sat, 10 May 2008 10:52:45 GMT
If-None-Match: "80fc52fa8bb2c81:0"
User-Agent: Mozilla/4.0 (compatible; MSIE 7.0; Windows NT 6.0; SLCC1;
  .NET CLR 2.0.50727; Media Center PC 5.0; InfoPath.2; .NET CLR 3.5.21022;
  .NET CLR 1.1.4322; .NET CLR 3.5.30428; MS-RTC LM 8; .NET CLR 3.5.30729;
  .NET CLR 3.0.30618; OfficeLiveConnector.1.3; OfficeLivePatch.0.0)
Host: www.12titans.net
Connection: Keep-Alive
```

IE has included the `If-Modified-Since` and `If-None-Match` headers to ask the web server whether the content has changed since the last time it was requested. Here's the response:

```
HTTP/1.1 304 Not Modified
Cache-Control: max-age=1
Last-Modified: Sat, 10 May 2008 10:52:45 GMT
Accept-Ranges: bytes
ETag: "80fc52fa8bb2c81:0"
Server: Microsoft-IIS/7.0
Date: Mon, 16 Mar 2009 04:07:01 GMT
```

IIS responds with `304 Not Modified`, indicating that the content hasn't changed. It also includes headers with the current values of `Cache-Control`, `Last-Modified`, and `ETag`.

Even though the responses to conditional `GET`s are short, the round-trips alone can have a big effect on performance. Until the interval that you specify with `Cache-Control: max-age` passes, the content will remain active in the cache, and the browser won't make those extra server round-trips.

Setting Cache-Control: max-age

You can set `Cache-Control: max-age` for static content using IIS Manager. First, select **HTTP Response Headers**. Then click **Set Common Headers** on the upper right, and select **Expire Web content**, as in Figure 3-2.

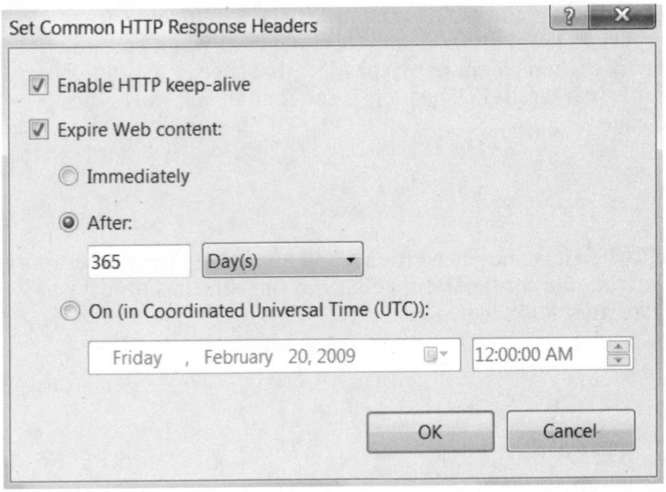

Figure 3-2. Set a far-future expiration time for static content using IIS Manager.

The HTTP 1.1 standard recommends one year in the future as the maximum expiration time. You should use that as the default for all static content on your site, as in Figure 3-2. Since `max-age` is specified in seconds, that will result in the following HTTP header:

```
Cache-Control: max-age=31536000
```

You can also apply this configuration setting in your `web.config` file, as follows:

```
<configuration>
  . . .
  <system.webServer>
    . . .
    <staticContent>
     <clientCache cacheControlMode="UseMaxAge" cacheControlMaxAge="365.00:00:00" />
    </staticContent>
  </system.webServer>
</configuration>
```

Once you've established a site-wide default, you can then set shorter expiration times for specific static files or folders if needed.

Disabling Browser Caching

You can disable browser caching for a particular static file or folder by selecting it first in the left-hand panel in IIS Manager, then bringing up the same dialog box shown in Figure 3-2, and finally selecting **Expire Web Content** and **Immediately**. This results in the following HTTP header:

```
Cache-Control: no-cache
```

You can also disable static file caching in `web.config`. For example, for a file called `image.jpg` in the top-level folder of your site, you'd have the following:

```
<configuration>
  . . .
  <location path="image.jpg">
    <system.webServer>
      <staticContent>
        <clientCache cacheControlMode="DisableCache" />
      </staticContent>
    </system.webServer>
  </location>
</configuration>
```

As implied by the name of the previous `<staticContent>` XML element, this approach works only for static content. You will need to set client cache expiration times for dynamic content declaratively in the `.aspx` file or set it programmatically.

Caching Dynamic Content

In general, dynamic content should have an expiration time of between 1 and 30 days, depending on the details of your application. An example of doing that declaratively is to place an OutputCache directive at the top of your .aspx page (see dyn-client.aspx):

```
<%@ Page . . . %>
<%@ OutputCache Duration="86400" Location="Client" VaryByParam="None" %>
```

That tells the runtime to generate HTTP headers that ask the browser to cache the page for 86,400 seconds (one day). You must include VaryByParam, or the parser will generate an error. A value of None means that multiple versions of the page do not need to be cached independently. The resulting HTTP headers are as follows:

```
Cache-Control: private, max-age=86400
Expires: Tue, 17 Mar 2009 01:34:17 GMT
```

Cache-Control: private prevents proxies from caching the response. ASP.NET also includes an Expires header, even though it's technically redundant.

■ **Note** In this example, the page will *not* be cached on the server.

You can also generate the same headers programmatically, either from code-behind or from an HttpModule. Here's an example (see dyn-client2.aspx):

```
protected void Page_Load(object sender, EventArgs e)
{
    this.Response.Cache.SetExpires(DateTime.Now.AddDays(1.0));
    TimeSpan ds = new TimeSpan(1, 0, 0, 0);
    this.Response.Cache.SetMaxAge(ds);
}
```

The call to SetExpires() is optional and can be safely omitted. Cache-Control: private is the default and does not need to be set explicitly.

If your content changes more often than once per day, even short client-side expiration times (1 to 10 minutes) can be useful to prevent extra round-trips when users click the **Back** button in the browser to go back to one of your pages.

Using Cache Profiles

When you're using OutputCache directives, it's also a good idea to use centralized cache profiles to help ensure consistency and to minimize the effort needed to make subsequent changes. The first step is to define a cache profile in your web.config file. Using the previous example, define a profile called Cache1Day:

```
<system.web>
  <caching>
    <outputCacheSettings>
      <outputCacheProfiles>
        <add name="Cache1Day" duration="86400"
             location="Client" varyByParam="none" />
      </outputCacheProfiles>
    </outputCacheSettings>
  </caching>
</system.web>
```

After you define the profile, just reference it from the OutputCache directive (see dyn-client3.aspx):

```
<%@ OutputCache CacheProfile="Cache1Day" %>
```

Disabling Caching

You should disable browser caching of dynamic content only in cases where data must always be the absolute latest, where it can change in response to the user's state (such as whether they are logged on), or where the page contains sensitive data that should not be stored on the browser. Unfortunately, you can't disable browser caching declaratively with the OutputCache directive. Instead, it requires a programmatic approach. Here's an example (see dyn-disable.aspx):

```
protected void Page_Load(object sender, EventArgs e)
{
    this.Response.Cache.SetCacheability(HttpCacheability.NoCache);
}
```

HttpCacheability.NoCache will disable caching on both the client and the server. The resulting HTTP headers are as follows:

```
Cache-Control: no-cache
Pragma: no-cache
Expires: -1
```

The runtime includes the Pragma and Expires headers even though they aren't needed in HTTP 1.1 and are therefore redundant in most cases. You can eliminate the Expires header as follows (see dyn-disable2.aspx):

```
this.Response.Cache.SetAllowResponseInBrowserHistory(true);
```

The Expires: -1 header is supposed to prevent the page from being placed on the browser's history list so that you can't use the browser's **Back** button to navigate to it again. However, in my testing with IE7, it doesn't work that way; the page is always present in the history list. Perhaps it has some effect in other browsers.

ViewState

ViewState is a collection of information generated by controls on an .aspx page that's used by the controls to restore their state during a postback. State in this context can include the values of control properties, results of data binding, or input from users. The specifics vary by control.

As I mentioned in Chapter 1, there are a few places where technologies that help improve performance interact strongly with security. ViewState is one example. Using it correctly is important for both performance and security, and the issues on both fronts are compounded by the fact that it is visible to end users and is therefore subject to manipulation and abuse.

ViewState does not re-create custom controls on the page or restore posted values to controls, and you should not use it for session data, since it's specific to a page, not a session. It cannot be used for server-only objects, such as database connections, and it is not valid after you do a server-side redirect with Server.Transfer().

Unlike vanilla HTML, controls do have their posted values restored during an ASP.NET postback, but the mechanism doesn't use ViewState. For example, let's say that you have a page with ViewState disabled that contains an <asp:DropDownList>. If the user selects a value from the list and then submits the form, the runtime will restore the value on the page that it generates for the postback. The same is not true for static HTML.

ViewState is useful from a caching perspective because it allows you to cache information that is associated only with a particular page as part of the page itself.

For example, let's say you have a page that displays a list of strings, along with a link that allows the user to alternate between sorting the list either ascending or descending. How do you keep track of that? One way would be with a query string. Although that's appropriate in some circumstances, it means that search engines would see multiple versions of the page, which might not be desirable. It also exposes a string in the URL that hackers could change and that you would therefore need to write additional code to validate.

As an alternative to using the query string, you can store the current sort order in ViewState. Here's an example (see view.aspx):

```
private const string SortStateKey = "SO";
private const string SortAscending = "a";
public bool IsSortAscending { get; set; }

protected void Page_Load(object sender, EventArgs e)
{
    if (IsPostBack)
    {
        string prevSort = (string)this.ViewState[SortStateKey];
        this.IsSortAscending = prevSort == SortAscending;
    }
    else
    {
        this.ViewState[SortStateKey] = SortAscending;
        this.IsSortAscending = true;
    }
}
```

If the current page request is not a postback, the code stores a value into the `ViewState` object to indicate that the default sort order is ascending. If the request is a postback, you retrieve the previously stored value. Elsewhere in the code, when the user clicks a link or a button to alternate between ascending and descending sort order, you would use this information to determine which sort order to use and then change the value to indicate that you should do the opposite next time.

`ControlState` is similar to `ViewState`, in that it also contains page-specific, control-specific state information. However, unlike with `ViewState`, you can't disable `ControlState`. It contains information that is required in order for a control to work at all. I will walk you through an example of using `ControlState` in Chapter 8.

As part of the page-rendering process, the runtime serializes `ViewState` and `ControlState`, encodes them in base-64, and stores them *together* as a single hidden `<input>` field on the page called `__VIEWSTATE`. To be serialized, the objects stored in `ViewState` must be marked with the `[Serializable]` attribute or have a custom `TypeConverter`.

The browser sends the hidden field back to the server when the `<form>` is submitted, as it does with all `<input>` fields. When the runtime receives the field, it is decoded, deserialized, and used to restore the state of the controls. `ViewState` can be read and written only after the `Page_Init()` event and before `Page_PreRender()`.

■ **Note** The presence of the `__VIEWSTATE` hidden field in an HTTP POST is how ASP.NET determines the value of `Page.IsPostBack`.

For example, consider the following ASP.NET markup:

```
<form id="form1" runat="server">
</form>
```

Here's the corresponding HTML that the runtime generates:

```
<form name="form1" method="post" action="viewstate1.aspx" id="form1">
<div>
<input type="hidden" name="__VIEWSTATE" id="__VIEWSTATE"
       value="/wEPDwULLTE2MTY2ODcyMjlkZExMOiM4ebB6mDGwogfzmhu/UroP" />
</div>
</form>
```

You can see the `<input>` tag containing the `__VIEWSTATE` field.

Protecting ViewState Data Integrity

Since `ViewState` contains a collection of serialized objects that will be reconstituted on the server, it presents the possibility of abuse, including hacking and denial-of-service attacks. To prevent tampering and help ensure data integrity, the runtime can generate a message authentication code (MAC). The runtime can also encrypt the field in the event you need to use it to store sensitive data.

The default setting for `ViewState` validation uses the SHA-1 algorithm to generate a MAC, with an automatically generated `validationKey`. Using the MD5 algorithm instead is a little faster and generates a few less bytes in your pages. The extra cryptographic strength of SHA-1 would reduce the chances (very slightly) that an attacker could find some other random string that would result in the same hash code, but that's not something that you care about in this case; protecting against injection of *arbitrary* text is more important, and MD5 does that just fine.

In an environment with multiple web servers, be sure to configure the `validationKey` to be the same on all servers. Otherwise, with the default automatically generated keys, `ViewState` generated on one server will not be valid on other servers, since the MACs would be different. Even in single-server environments, it's a good practice to set a specific `validationKey`. That helps avoid surprises down the road, including things such as inadvertently invalidating form-containing web pages that are cached by search engines in the event you move to a new server or reload the operating system. Here are the relevant settings in `web.config`:

```
<system.web>
  . . .
  <pages enableViewStateMac="true">
    . . .
  </pages>
  <machineKey
    validationKey="50B3847462938741422FF158A5B42D0E8DB8CB5CDA174257"
    validation="MD5" />
</system.web>
```

The `validationKey` is a random hex string, between 40 and 128 characters long.

You should generally not require site-wide encryption of `ViewState`. If you need to store sensitive information in `ViewState`, you can encrypt it separately. If you need to protect the *structure* of the objects, then you can write a custom serializer, or you can serialize into memory first and encrypt the result.

Other Uses of ViewState

To understand more thoroughly how `ViewState` works and how to avoid several potential pitfalls, I've found that it's helpful to cover a few security-oriented applications.

For example, you can use `ViewState` to prevent *one-click attacks*. The way they usually work is that an attacker creates HTML that includes a form and a link, which, when clicked, submits the form to the server being attacked. The form might do something like register a new user that the attacker will subsequently use to spam the target site. The power of the technique stems from the forms being submitted from IP addresses that aren't directly associated with the attacker. The HTML is often sent to third parties using e-mail, along with socially engineered link text, such as "click here to claim your prize."

One way to use `ViewState` to prevent one-click attacks is to set the `ViewStateUserKey` property on a `Page`. That value is stored in `ViewState` when the runtime initially renders the page. Then, during a postback, the runtime checks the stored field to make sure that it's equal to the current `ViewStateUserKey`. If it isn't, then the runtime throws an exception, and the page is aborted. You should choose `ViewStateUserKey` so that it is unique per user. Here's an example that sets the user's IP address as the key (see `view2.aspx`):

```
protected void Page_Init(object sender, EventArgs e)
{
    this.ViewStateUserKey = Request.UserHostAddress;
}
```

The result is that the __VIEWSTATE hidden field will be different for each different IP address, and users who submit the form from an IP address that's different from the one that the containing page was originally sent to will receive an error. That prevents attackers from copying the hidden field from one form and using it in a one-click attack.

■ **Note** ViewStateUserKey must be set in Page_Init(), which is before ViewState is restored.

If you're using sessions, a session ID is another candidate for ViewStateUserKey, although you should be aware that with the standard implementation, the runtime doesn't send a session cookie to the browser until you save something in the Session object. Session IDs won't be repeatable until the cookie is set.

Minimizing ViewState Size

Some controls, such as GridView, can easily generate many kilobytes of ViewState. Since the browser sends ViewState back to the server as part of an HTTP POST, it can adversely affect page load times if it gets too large. See Figure 3-3 for a graph of upload times for various data sizes and uplink speeds.

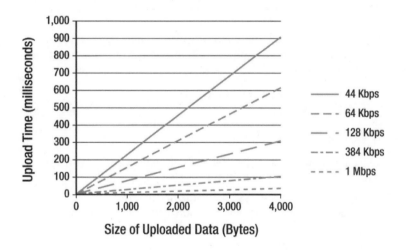

Figure 3-3. Upload times based on data size and upload speed

Keep in mind that it is sometimes faster to refetch data from the database for controls such as GridView than to have it sent back to the server as ViewState. From Figure 3-3 you can see that just 4KB of ViewState would take around 300ms to send over a DSL connection with a 128Kbps uplink. You can retrieve a lot of data from SQL Server in 300ms, particularly if it's still in SQL Server's RAM cache.

Because of the potentially large upload times, you should disable ViewState by default, on a per-page basis. You can do that by setting EnableViewState="false" in the Page directive (see view3.aspx):

```
<%@ Page Language="C#" EnableViewState="false" AutoEventWireup="true"
    CodeFile="view3.aspx.cs" Inherits="view3" %>
```

You can disable ViewState for your entire application in web.config:

```
<system.web>
    . . .
    <pages enableViewState="false">
    . . .
    </pages>
</system.web>
```

Unfortunately, you can't override that setting in web.config at the page level, so you can't selectively turn it back on when you need it. Therefore, disabling it on a per-page basis is more flexible.

■ **Tip** You should enable ViewState only in pages that post back to the server; pages that don't post back don't need ViewState.

Many ASP.NET controls rely on ViewState to implement various features. When you need it, you should enable it at the page level, and then disable it for the controls where you don't need it, using the EnableViewState property. Here's an example:

```
<asp:GridView ID="mygrid" runat="server" EnableViewState="false" />
```

Using a Custom Template in Visual Studio

You can create a custom template in Visual Studio that disables ViewState by default so that you don't have to remember to apply it for every new page. To do that, follow these steps:

1. Create a page with the settings and content the way you would like to have them, including the code-behind file. Then select File ➤ Export Template, which will start the Export Template Wizard, as in Figure 3-4.

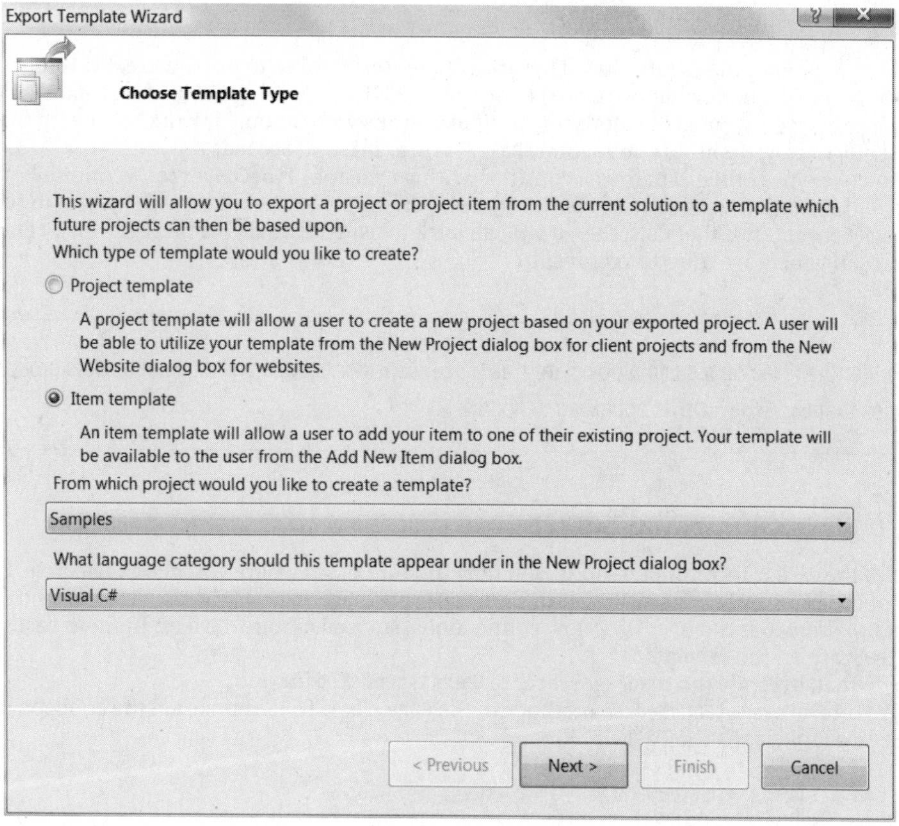

Figure 3-4. The Export Template Wizard in Visual Studio

2. Select **Item Template**, set the project from which you would like to create the template, and set the appropriate language category.

3. Click **Next**, and select the page that you created earlier. Visual Studio only shows the .aspx file; the code-behind will also be included.

4. Click **Next**, and select any **Item References** that should be associated with the template. For basic settings as I'm describing here, no additional references are needed.

5. Click **Next** again, and enter a name and description for the template.

6. Click **Finish**, and Visual Studio will create and import the template.

To use the template, select it when you add a new item to your project. Notice that Visual Studio will automatically set some values in the .aspx file, such as CodeFile and Inherits, along with corresponding values in the code-behind, when you create a new item from the template.

Minimizing Serialization Overhead

In addition to latency that's introduced because of the time it takes to upload ViewState, serialization overhead is another performance-related concern. ASP.NET uses an optimized serializer for ViewState called LosFormatter, where Los stands for "limited object serialization." It works best with the following types: String, Array, Hashtable, ArrayList, Pair, Triple, int, and Boolean.

If you use types other than those, consider writing a custom TypeConverter to minimize serialization overhead. If the object is not one of the "limited object" types, LosFormatter will first try to serialize it with a TypeConverter. If that fails, then it will fall back to using a BinaryFormatter, which can be very slow and can generate a much larger result.

■ **Tip** Rather than placing a custom object in ViewState, consider using a collection of objects grouped using the basic types that LosFormatter is optimized to handle.

Storing ViewState on the Server

In spite of the earlier recommendations, you may run into cases where you need ViewState, but it's so large that it significantly impairs the performance of your page. You might also need to support certain types of browsers that run over very slow connections, such as mobile devices. In those cases, you can store ViewState on the server side.

To do that, override the LoadPageStateFromPersistenceMedium and SavePageStateToPersistenceMedium methods in the Page class. To demonstrate the concept, consider the following example (see view4.aspx):

```
public const string ViewKeyName = "__viewkey";

protected override void SavePageStateToPersistenceMedium(object state)
{
    string key = Guid.NewGuid().ToString();
    this.ClientScript.RegisterHiddenField(ViewKeyName, key);
    this.Cache[key] = state;
}

protected override object LoadPageStateFromPersistenceMedium()
{
    string key = this.Request[ViewKeyName];
    if (key == null)
        throw new InvalidOperationException("Invalid ViewState Key");
    object state = this.Cache[key];
    if (state == null)
        throw new InvalidOperationException("ViewState too old");
    return state;
}
```

The first method creates a new GUID as a key and includes it in the page as a hidden field. Then you store the `ViewState` object in server-side `Cache` using that key. Note that this would work only on a site with a single IIS worker process, and if IIS had to restart, all `ViewState` would be lost. In a production environment, it should be stored in a database or some similar "persistence medium," as the name of the methods imply.

The second method retrieves the GUID key from the hidden field and then uses it to retrieve the `ViewState` from the `Cache`.

To support low-speed devices in a generalized way, you could make both methods conditional on browser type or `ViewState` size, and so on, and include them in a common base class.

Cookies

Cookies are name/value pairs of strings that are stored on the client. Cookies are set when the browser receives a `Set-Cookie` HTTP header in a response from the server. Browsers send the cookie back to the server later if the requested URL matches the `path` and `domain` restrictions associated with the cookie when it was first set and if the cookie hasn't expired. I covered some of the limitations and guidelines surrounding cookies in Chapter 2.

■ **Tip** Cookies should be used to cache state information and other data that is specific to a particular user and that is needed across multiple pages.

Typical uses of cookies include user preferences, shopping cart, advertising history, last-visit date, authentication, and so on. As with `ViewState` and query strings, you can't use cookies to store server-side state such as database connections.

You can set cookies either by setting HTTP headers from ASP.NET, by using JavaScript on the client, from Silverlight, or through configuration settings in IIS. They can be set in the response from a standard `.aspx` page, from an `.asmx` web service, or even with static content such as an image. You can also set them from some WCF services, although the approach is somewhat convoluted since WCF is designed to be protocol independent and cookies are a feature of HTTP.

Cookies are another area where security and performance concerns overlap to some extent. Since the information in cookies is visible to users, they are unfortunately subject to abuse. A fast architecture isn't useful if it's not secure, and in spite of their benefits from a caching perspective, incorrect use of cookies is a good way to expose your site to a variety of attacks. To help mitigate those concerns, I will cover a few issues related to cookies and security in this section.

Data that might be used to hack into your site or that is so large that it will cause performance problems should not be stored in cookies; it should be kept on the server side instead and referenced indirectly with a unique key. That is one feature of session state, which I will cover in detail in Chapter 5.

Setting Session Cookies

Here's an example that sets a cookie programmatically from an `.aspx` page (see `cookie1.aspx`):

```
protected void Page_Load(object sender, EventArgs e)
{
    HttpCookie cookie = new HttpCookie("name");
    cookie.Value = "value";
    this.Response.AppendCookie(cookie);
}
```

That will create a *session cookie*, since you didn't set an expiration time. A *session* in this context means that the cookie lasts only as long as the browser is running. If the user closes the browser or reboots their machine, all session cookies are dropped.

To create a session cookie from JavaScript, you can use this function:

```
function SetCookie(name, value) {
    document.cookie = name + '=' + escape(value);
}
```

To create a session cookie from Silverlight, use this:

```
public void SetCookie(string name, string value) {
    HtmlPage.Document.Cookies = name + "=" + value;
}
```

See Figure 2-6 for an example of the configuration-based approach to setting cookies.

Multiple Name/Value Pairs in a Single Cookie

In addition to the single name/value per cookie approach, ASP.NET also provides a mechanism to store multiple name/value pairs in a single cookie. This can be useful to help work around the browser's limitation of no more than 20 cookies per domain, as described in Chapter 2. It is also more efficient than setting many cookies that all have the same properties. Here's an example (see `cookie2.aspx`):

```
HttpCookie cookie = new HttpCookie("name");
cookie.Values["v1"] = "value1";
cookie.Values["v2"] = "value2";
```

That results in a single cookie that looks like this when the server sends it to the browser:

```
name=v1=value1&v2=value2
```

Cookie Properties

In addition to name/value pairs, the `Set-Cookie` HTTP header supports several properties that influence the way the browser handles cookies.

Expires

The expires property contains a date that tells the browser how long it should store the cookie. Setting the expires property makes a cookie become *persistent* so that the browser can save it across sessions. When the expiration date passes, the browser can delete the cookie and no longer send it to the server.

Here's an example that sets expires to one year in the future from an .aspx page (see cookie3.aspx):

```
protected void Page_Load(object sender, EventArgs e)
{
    HttpCookie cookie = new HttpCookie("name");
    cookie.Value = "value";
    cookie.Expires = DateTime.Now.AddYears(1);
    this.Response.AppendCookie(cookie);
}
```

From JavaScript, a semicolon precedes properties, as in the HTTP header. The following function accepts an expiration time as minutes in the future:

```
function SetCookie(name, value, minutes) {
    var exp = new Date((new Date()).getTime() + minutes*60000);
    document.cookie = name + '=' + escape(value) + '; expires=' + exp.toGMTString();
}
```

Silverlight is similar, since you're just setting the same JavaScript property:

```
public void SetCookie(string name, string value, double minutes) {
    DateTime expires = DateTime.UtcNow.AddMinutes(minutes);
    HtmlPage.Document.Cookies = name + "=" + value +
        "; expires =" + expires.ToString("R");
}
```

To delete a cookie, set an expires date in the past using the original cookie name, path, and domain.

Path

The path property is a case-sensitive string, with which the path name of a URL must start in order for the browser to send the cookie to the server. The path is not limited to being a folder name. The URL that sets path must begin with the specified path property in order for the property setting to be accepted.

For example, valid path settings for http://www.12titans.net/ch03/page1.aspx include /ch, /ch03, /ch03/, and /ch03/page1. If your intent is to specify a folder name as the path, then the path should end with a slash. If you tried to specify a path of /ch04/ from that page, the browser wouldn't accept it, since the URL doesn't start with that string.

■ **Caution** Browsers can store multiple cookies with the same name at different paths in the same domain. It is therefore possible for the server to receive more than one cookie with the same name. Disambiguation isn't always easy (or even possible), since cookie properties such as `path` are not sent back to the server along with the name/value pairs.

To minimize the bandwidth that your cookies use, and the latency they introduce, you should configure them so the browser uploads them only once per page. That means you should avoid sending cookies with static content, where the server will probably never even look at them. You can also limit how often the browser sends cookies to the server by partitioning your pages by folder name or file name prefix, based on which cookies they need.

The default `path` is /, which means the browser will send the cookie to the server for all URLs from that domain, including static content, since all URL path names start with a slash. To accomplish these goals, be sure to set a more restrictive `path` on *all* your cookies, even if it means you need to reorganize the hierarchy of the files in your web site in order to do so.

Here's an example that sets the `path` from an `.aspx` page (see `cookie4.aspx`):

```
protected void Page_Load(object sender, EventArgs e)
{
    HttpCookie cookie = new HttpCookie("name");
    cookie.Value = "value";
    cookie.Path = "/ch03/";
    this.Response.AppendCookie(cookie);
}
```

Here's an example from JavaScript:

```
function SetCookie(name, value, path) {
    document.cookie = name + '=' + escape(value) + '; path=' + path;
}
```

Here's an example from Silverlight:

```
public void SetCookie(string name, string value, string path) {
    HtmlPage.Document.Cookies =
        String.Format("{0}={1}; path={2}", name, value, path);
}
```

Domain

The `domain` property tells the browser which domains should be associated with the cookie. You would use this if you needed to set cookies that should be visible on multiple subdomains. The value of the `domain` property is compared to the domain of the URL being requested, using an `EndsWith` (tail) match. Note that the browser bases the comparison strictly on the strings, ignoring case; the IP addresses of the servers don't matter.

The domain property must match the domain of the page that sets it, and it must contain at least three dots, unless the domain ends with .com, .edu, .net, .org, .gov, .mil, or .int, in which case only two dots are required. The default is the domain of the URL that set the cookie.

To set a cookie on www.12titans.net that's also visible on pages.12titans.net, you would set the domain property to .12titans.net (note the leading dot).

Here's an example that sets domain programmatically (see cookie5.aspx):

```
protected void Page_Load(object sender, EventArgs e)
{
    HttpCookie cookie = new HttpCookie("name");
    cookie.Value = "value";
    cookie.Domain = ".12titans.net";
    this.Response.AppendCookie(cookie);
}
```

From JavaScript, it's similar to the path property:

```
function SetCookie(name, value, dom) {
    document.cookie = name + '=' + escape(value) + '; domain=' + dom;
}
```

From Silverlight, it looks like this:

```
public void SetCookie(string name, string value, string dom) {
    HtmlPage.Document.Cookies = name + "=" + value + "; domain=" + dom;
}
```

HttpOnly

The HttpOnly property tells the browser not to make the cookie visible to JavaScript. You should set it by default to help reduce your application's attack surface, including the risk of things such as script-based session hijacking. You should disable HttpOnly only when you have script that explicitly needs access to a particular cookie.

Here's an example that sets HttpOnly programmatically (see cookie6.aspx):

```
protected void Page_Load(object sender, EventArgs e)
{
    HttpCookie cookie = new HttpCookie("name");
    cookie.Value = "value";
    cookie.HttpOnly = true;
    this.Response.AppendCookie(cookie);
}
```

Since its purpose is to restrict script access, HttpOnly cannot be set from JavaScript or Silverlight.

Secure

If the data in a cookie contains sensitive information or if it might be subject to abuse by a third party, then you should generally send it over SSL-protected connections only. Those cookies should also be marked with the secure property, which prevents the browser from sending them to the server unless the connection uses SSL.

Here's an example that sets secure programmatically (see cookie7.aspx):

```
protected void Page_Load(object sender, EventArgs e)
{
    HttpCookie cookie = new HttpCookie("name");
    cookie.Value = "value";
    cookie.Secure = true;
    this.Response.AppendCookie(cookie);
}
```

This is how to do it from JavaScript:

```
function SetCookie(name, value) {
    document.cookie = name + '=' + escape(value) + '; secure';
}
```

This is how to do it from Silverlight:

```
public void SetCookie(string name, string value) {
    HtmlPage.Document.Cookies = name + "=" + value + "; secure";
}
```

Reading Cookies

When the browser sends cookies to the server or when you use script or Silverlight to read them on the client, the only thing they contain is the name/value pair. Any properties that were originally set on them are not visible.

Here's an example of reading cookie values programmatically (see cookie8.aspx):

```
protected void Page_Load(object sender, EventArgs e)
{
    HttpCookie cookie = this.Request.Cookies["name"];
    if (cookie != null)
    {
        string value = cookie.Value;
    }
}
```

JavaScript only provides a way to get *all* cookies and values. You need a little extra code to extract the particular one of interest:

```
function getcookie(name) {
    var allcookies = document.cookie;
    var start = allcookies.indexOf(name + '=');
    if (start == -1)
        return null;
    start += name.length + 1;
    var end = allcookies.indexOf(';', start);
    if (end == -1)
        end = allcookies.length;
    var cookieval = allcookies.substring(start, end);
    return unescape(cookieval);
}
```

In `document.cookie`, an equals sign separates name/value pairs, and one cookie is separated from another with a semicolon.

Similarly, here's how to read cookies from Silverlight:

```
private static string GetCookie(string name)
{
    string allcookies = HtmlPage.Document.Cookies;
    int start = allcookies.IndexOf(name + "=", StringComparison.OrdinalIgnoreCase);
    if (start == -1)
        return null;
    start += name.Length + 1;
    int end = allcookies.IndexOf(';', start);
    if (end == -1)
        end = allcookies.Length;
    string cookieval = allcookies.Substring(start, end - start);
    return cookieval;
}
```

Storing Binary Data in Cookies

Since cookies are intended to hold strings only, if you want to store binary data in a cookie, it will need to be encoded into a string. One way to do that is with *base-64* encoding. Base-64 takes a sequence of 8-bits-per-byte binary data and encodes it as a string that uses 6-bits-per-character; 6 bits is 64 values, which is why it's called base-64. The 64 values consist of the 52 characters A–Z and a–z, plus 0–9, /, and +, with = used for padding.

As an example of how to store binary data in a cookie, let's look at encrypted cookies.

If SSL isn't practical or desirable or if you need to protect certain cookies from your users as well as from others, you can encrypt them using symmetric encryption. Since the results of encryption are binary, you can encode them using base-64.

Here's a class to handle the encryption (see **App_Code\Secure.cs**):

```
using System.IO;
using System.Security.Cryptography;
using System.Text;

public class Secure
{
    private static RijndaelManaged Cryptor(string keySeed, string saltString)
    {
        byte[] salt = UTF8Encoding.UTF8.GetBytes(saltString);
        Rfc2898DeriveBytes derivedBytes =
            new Rfc2898DeriveBytes(keySeed, salt, 1000);
        RijndaelManaged cryptor = new RijndaelManaged();

        //
        // KeySize must be set before the Key
        //
        cryptor.KeySize = 128;
        cryptor.Key = derivedBytes.GetBytes(16);
        cryptor.IV = derivedBytes.GetBytes(16);
        return cryptor;
    }
```

This method returns a `RijndaelManaged` object that you can use to do encryption or decryption. It takes a `keySeed` as an argument that it uses to generate a strong password, along with a salt string. The salt helps ensure that when two strings are encrypted with the same `keySeed`, they don't generate the same ciphertext.

```
    public static string EncryptToBase64(string clearText,
                                         string keySeed, string salt)
    {
        using (MemoryStream ms = new MemoryStream())
        {
            using (ICryptoTransform encryptor =
                    Cryptor(keySeed, salt).CreateEncryptor())
            {
                using (CryptoStream encrypt =
                        new CryptoStream(ms, encryptor, CryptoStreamMode.Write))
                {
                    byte[] data = new UTF8Encoding(false).GetBytes(clearText);
                    encrypt.Write(data, 0, data.Length);
                    encrypt.Close();
                    return Convert.ToBase64String(ms.ToArray());
                }
            }
        }
    }
```

This method encrypts a string and encodes the result in base-64.

```
public static string DecryptFromBase64(string cipherText,
                                       string keySeed, string salt)
{
    byte[] data = Convert.FromBase64String(cipherText);
    using (MemoryStream ms = new MemoryStream())
    {
        using (ICryptoTransform decryptor =
                Cryptor(keySeed, salt).CreateDecryptor())
        {
            using (CryptoStream decrypt =
                    new CryptoStream(ms, decryptor, CryptoStreamMode.Write))
            {
                decrypt.Write(data, 0, data.Length);
                decrypt.FlushFinalBlock();
                return new UTF8Encoding(false).GetString(ms.ToArray());
            }
        }
    }
}
```

This method decodes the base-64 ciphertext and decrypts the result.

You can use that class to protect some secret text in a cookie. Let's use the requesting host's IP address as salt so that two users won't see the same ciphertext for the same secret (see encrypt.aspx):

```
protected void Page_Load(object sender, EventArgs e)
{
    HttpCookie cookie = new HttpCookie("name");
    cookie.Value = Secure.EncryptToBase64("my secret text",
                        "password", this.Request.UserHostAddress);
    this.Response.AppendCookie(cookie);
}
```

Looking at the page with Fiddler, you can see the encrypted cookie in the HTTP header:

```
Set-Cookie: name=EMRtCOJ3tZFHNfQdaJEZPA==; path=/
```

You can recover the secret from the encrypted cookie by providing the same password and salt that you used to encrypt it (see decrypt.aspx):

```
protected void Page_Load(object sender, EventArgs e)
{
    HttpCookie cookie = this.Request.Cookies["name"];
    if (cookie != null)
    {
        string secret = Secure.DecryptFromBase64(cookie.Value,
                            "password", this.Request.UserHostAddress);
    }
}
```

The results of compressing text using `GzipStream` can be similarly processed and encoded. However, `GzipStream` is not suitable for use with short strings, since it generates header information that can make the length of the output longer than the input.

Using a Compact Privacy Policy

Although most browsers readily accept cookies, Safari and IE6 and later make it possible for users to *selectively* accept them using "privacy" settings.

First-party cookies are set from pages that are in the same domain as the top-level page (the one in the address bar). Cookies set from all other domains are considered third-party. The default privacy setting in IE6 and later is Medium, which blocks third-party cookies that don't have a compact privacy policy.

The Medium privacy setting also blocks third-party cookies and restricts first-party cookies that include information that can be used to contact you without your explicit consent. The browser figures that out based on a compact privacy policy that the site provides.

You can see the privacy setting in IE7 or IE8 by selecting **Tools ➤ Internet Options**. Then click the **Privacy** tab. See Figure 3-5.

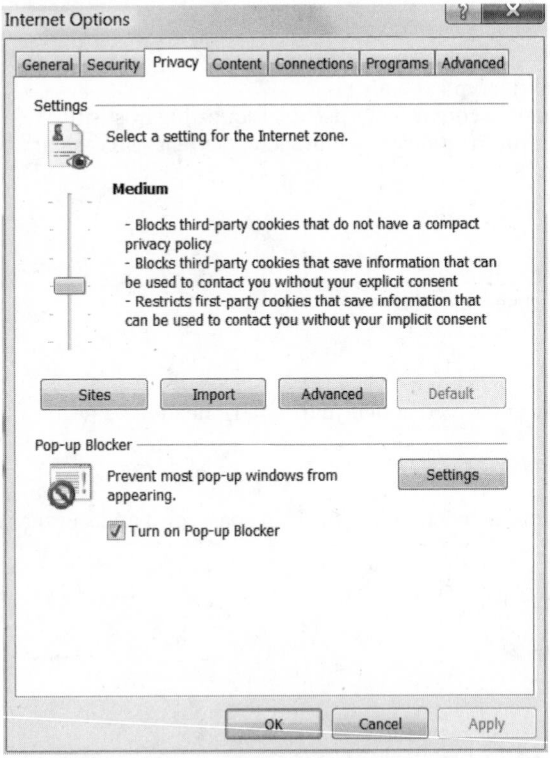

Figure 3-5. Default privacy options in IE7

The default settings aren't a problem for sites with all of their content in a single domain. However, as I've shown in Chapter 2, there are good reasons why your site might perform better if you split it across multiple domains. If you mix domains on a single page, IE can block cookies unless you have a compact privacy policy. The Medium setting can also be a problem if other sites reference your pages in frames or if you use frames (including <iframe>s) with some content from one domain and other content from a different domain.

If users select the High privacy setting, then IE blocks even first-party cookies unless your site has a compact privacy policy. If you're using cookie-based sessions or authorization cookies, those users may not be able to register or log in to your site. For those reasons, including a compact privacy policy at least whenever you set a cookie is a good idea.

Compact privacy policies are encoded in an HTTP header that is sent to the browser along with the rest of the response to a web request. The process of creating one normally involves filling out a lengthy questionnaire. Several sites online can help you create one that's appropriate for your site, although they often charge a fee. Free software is also available that can help you. As an example only, here's a simple one:

```
P3P: CP="NID DSP CAO COR"
```

With that HTTP header in place, IE would accept both first-party and third-party cookies from your site. See Table 3-1 for the meaning of the values.

Table 3-1. Meaning of the Values in the Example Compact Privacy Policy

Value	Meaning
P3P	The name of the HTTP header for privacy information. P3P stands for The Platform for Privacy Preferences.
CP=	Indicates that the quoted string that follows is a compact policy.
NID	The information collected is not personally identifiable.
DSP	The policy contains at least one dispute-resolution mechanism.
CAO	Access is available to contact and other information.
COR	Violations of this policy will be corrected.

You can set the header from IIS using the same procedure shown in Figure 2-6 or declaratively in web.config as shown after the figure.

Here's an example that sets the header programmatically (see p3p.aspx):

```
protected void Page_Load(object sender, EventArgs e)
{
    this.Response.AddHeader("P3P", "CP=\"NID DSP CAO COR\"");
}
```

Managing Cookies

To help simplify the management of cookies, including site-wide consistency, it's a good idea to centralize cookie handling into a common library. The functions of the library might include the following:

- Enforcing the browser's limits of 20 cookies per domain and no more than 4KB per cookie

- Enforcing project-specific policies for maximum cookie length and cookie naming

- Setting cookie expiration times based on the type of data they contain, rather than hard-coding time intervals into your pages

- Setting the HttpOnly cookie property by default

- Requiring the path property always to be set and not allowing it to be set to the root path

- Consistent serialization, encryption, compression, and encoding

- Automatic rollover from cookies to database storage for objects that are too long or for certain browser types, such as slow mobile devices

An HttpModule can help to enforce cookie policies. I describe HttpModules in detail in Chapter 7.

Silverlight Isolated Storage

Silverlight applications can cache data on the user's disk using *isolated storage*. The default amount of space that's available is 1MB per application (considerably more than cookies), although the app can ask the user for a larger quota if needed.

The assigned storage is unique for each application URL, so two applications that are loaded from different URLs will not share the same space. Isolated storage is a good place to keep user-specific information that is needed when rendering certain pages. You can also use it as an alternative to cookies to store prior history or preferences in cases where only the client needs that information.

You might want to store user preferences in isolated storage. For example, things like the preferred position and size of web parts on a page, preferred colors or fonts, and so on.

In addition to standard HTTP-based web requests, Silverlight applications can also use Windows Communications Foundation (WCF) to make web services calls. This can be a good way for applications to interact with the server.

Sample Application: "Welcome Back"

Let's write a sample application to demonstrate how to use isolated storage and WCF from Silverlight. Imagine that you want to have every page on your site say "Welcome back, UserName" after users log on. If the text was inserted by the server, that would mean every page would be unique per user and therefore could not be placed in the high-performance output cache.

An alternative is to use a Silverlight application to display the welcome string. The HTML, the script on the page, and the Silverlight application file would then be identical for every user, so they could all be stored in the output cache on the server. The app could get the welcome string from a WCF service and store it in isolated storage so that it will be accessible from one page to the next.

WCF Service

Let's start by adding the WCF service to your web site. Select **Silverlight-enabled WCF Service** from the **Add New Item** dialog box in Visual Studio. Call it **LoginService.svc**, and click **Add**. In addition to adding the **LoginService.svc** file, Visual Studio will update **web.config** with information about the service and create **LoginService.cs** in your **App_Code** folder.

Open **LoginService.cs**, and replace the contents with the following code:

```
using System.ServiceModel;
using System.ServiceModel.Activation;

[ServiceContract(Namespace = "")]
[AspNetCompatibilityRequirements(RequirementsMode =
    AspNetCompatibilityRequirementsMode.Allowed)]
public class LoginService
{
    [OperationContract]
    public string Login(string userName)
    {
        return "Welcome back, " + userName;
    }
}
```

The Login() method creates the welcome string using the supplied argument.

XAML Markup

Next, right-click your solution and select **Add ➤ New Project** to open the **Add New Project** dialog box. Select **Visual C#** and **Silverlight** on the left and then **Silverlight Application** on the right. Call the project Welcome, and click **OK**.

Open **MainPage.xaml**, and edit it as follows:

```
<UserControl x:Class="Welcome.MainPage"
    xmlns="http://schemas.microsoft.com/winfx/2006/xaml/presentation"
    xmlns:x="http://schemas.microsoft.com/winfx/2006/xaml"
    xmlns:d="http://schemas.microsoft.com/expression/blend/2008"
    xmlns:mc="http://schemas.openxmlformats.org/markup-compatibility/2006"
    mc:Ignorable="d" d:DesignWidth="300" d:DesignHeight="120"
    Width="300" Height="120">
    <StackPanel Orientation="Vertical">
        <Border CornerRadius="6" Background="#ffdedede" Margin="0,0,4,0">
            <TextBlock x:Name="info" Foreground="#ff14517b" Margin="7,2,0,1"
                FontSize="20">Please Login</TextBlock>
        </Border>
        <TextBox x:Name="UserName" Margin="0,5,3,0" FontSize="20" />
        <Button x:Name="LoginButton" Content="Login" Margin="0,5,3,0"
            Click="LoginButton_Click" FontSize="20" />
    </StackPanel>
</UserControl>
```

You now have three controls arranged in a vertical `<StackPanel>`. The top one is a `<Border>` control with rounded corners that contains a `<TextBlock>` with the initial message `Please Login`. The middle control is a `<TextBox>` to allow the user to enter their name. The bottom control is a `<Button>` with the label `Login`. It has a `Click` handler assigned that's called `LoginButton_Click`. All three objects have `x:Name` attributes so that they can be referenced from the code-behind.

See Figure 3-6 for the resulting UI.

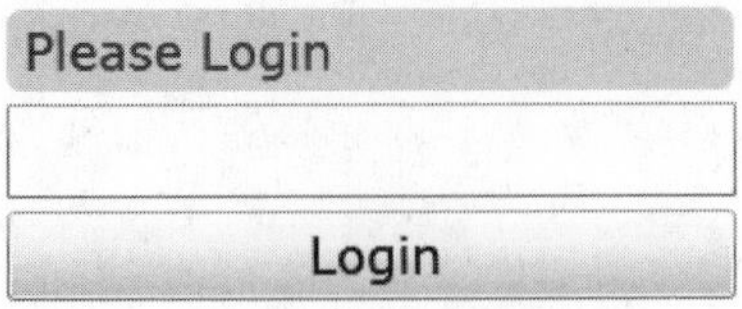

Figure 3-6. User interface for the sample Silverlight application

Using Isolated Storage and Calling a WCF Service

Next, add a reference to the WCF service in the Silverlight project. Right-click the Silverlight project, and select **Add Service Reference**. In the dialog box, click **Discover** to find `LoginService` in your web site. Set the **Namespace** to `LoginReference`, and click **OK**.

This approach will configure the Silverlight application to use the Cassini web server. If you're using the project from the code download for the book or when you're deploying a project like this, you will need to edit the `ServiceReferences.ClientConfig` file to set the URL of the service according to your environment.

Next, open `MainPage.xaml.cs`, and edit it as follows:

```
using System;
using System.IO.IsolatedStorage;
using System.Windows;
using System.Windows.Browser;
using System.Windows.Controls;
using Welcome.LoginReference;

namespace Welcome
{
    public partial class MainPage : UserControl
    {
        public const string WELCOME = "welcome";

        public MainPage()
        {
            this.Loaded += new RoutedEventHandler(Page_Loaded);
            InitializeComponent();
        }

        private void Page_Loaded(object sender, RoutedEventArgs e)
        {
            string welcome = null;
```

```
        IsolatedStorageSettings.SiteSettings.TryGetValue(WELCOME, out welcome);
        LoggedIn(welcome);
}

private void LoggedIn(string welcome)
{
    if (!String.IsNullOrEmpty(welcome))
    {
        this.info.Text = welcome;
        this.UserName.Visibility = Visibility.Collapsed;
        this.LoginButton.Content = "Logout";
    }
}
```

The constructor assigns the Page_Loaded() method as a handler for the application's Load event.

Page_Loaded() uses SiteSettings to get the value that may have been previously associated with the WELCOME string. The SiteSettings object implements what amounts to an on-disk hash table that's available to all applications from the same domain. SiteSettings objects are unique for each domain (based on the domain of the Silverlight application, not the domain of the containing page). The ApplicationSettings object performs a similar function, except the associated storage and settings are specific to a URL instead of a domain.

Page_Loaded() then calls LoggedIn(). If the stored string was present, LoggedIn() updates the <TextBlock> control with the string, hides the <TextBox> control, and changes the text on the <Button> to Logout.

```
private void LoginButton_Click(object sender, RoutedEventArgs e)
{
    if (this.UserName.Visibility == Visibility.Collapsed)
    {
        this.info.Text = "Please Login";
        this.UserName.Visibility = Visibility.Visible;
        this.LoginButton.Content = "Login";
        IsolatedStorageSettings.SiteSettings[WELCOME] = null;
    }
    else
    {
        string name = this.UserName.Text;
        if (!String.IsNullOrEmpty(name))
        {
            LoginServiceClient loginService = new LoginServiceClient();
            loginService.LoginCompleted +=
                new EventHandler<LoginCompletedEventArgs>
                    (loginService_LoginCompleted);
            loginService.LoginAsync(name);
        }
    }
}
```

As you specified in the XAML, LoginButton_Click() is called when a user clicks the <Button>. If the UserName <TextBox> isn't visible, then the user is already logged in, and by clicking the button they want to be logged out. In that case, update the info <TextBlock> to say Please Login, make UserName visible again, update the <Button> text to say Login, and clear the WELCOME setting from SiteSettings in isolated storage.

If the UserName is visible and if it contains text, create a proxy object to call the WCF service. Since all web service calls in Silverlight are asynchronous, the next step is to assign a handler to the LoginCompleted event, which the runtime will invoke when the service returns. Then call the service asynchronously using LoginAsync.

```
private void loginService_LoginCompleted(object sender,
    LoginCompletedEventArgs e)
{
    IsolatedStorageSettings.SiteSettings[WELCOME] = e.Result;
    LoggedIn(e.Result);
}
    }
}
```

When the service completes, the runtime calls loginService_LoginCompleted. It stores the result returned by the service into SiteSettings in isolated storage, using WELCOME as the key. Both SiteSettings and ApplicationSettings can store any serializable object, not just strings as in the example. LoggedIn() is called next to display the returned string, hide the text input box, and change the text on the button to Logout.

HTML and the User's Experience

Here's the HTML that Visual Studio autogenerates to host the Silverlight control into a web page:

```
<form id="form1" runat="server" style="height:100%">
<div id="silverlightControlHost">
    <object data="data:application/x-silverlight-2,"
        type="application/x-silverlight-2" width="100%" height="100%">
        <param name="source" value="ClientBin/Welcome.xap"/>
        <param name="onError" value="onSilverlightError" />
        <param name="background" value="white" />
        <param name="minRuntimeVersion" value="3.0.40624.0" />
        <param name="autoUpgrade" value="true" />
        <a href="http://go.microsoft.com/fwlink/?LinkID=149156&v=3.0.40624.0"
            style="text-decoration:none">
                <img src="http://go.microsoft.com/fwlink/?LinkId=108181"
                    alt="Get Microsoft Silverlight" style="border-style:none"/>
        </a>
    </object><iframe id="_sl_historyFrame"
        style="visibility:hidden;height:0px;width:0px;border:0px"></iframe></div>
</form>
```

The final application in this case was 7.1KB, which is about the size of a small image.

What you see after the app first loads is that when you enter your name and click the Login button, the welcome message is displayed and the button changes to say Logout.

If you refresh the page, or close the browser and open the page again, the welcome message is remembered and displayed, without calling the WCF service. If you click the Logout button, the welcome message goes away, and you're given another opportunity to log in.

Deploying and Updating Silverlight Applications

Silverlight applications are compiled into a `.xap` file, which is a renamed `.zip` file that contains the application DLLs and resources and a manifest file. From the server's perspective, a `.xap` is just a static file, so any web server or CDN can host it, not just IIS. You just need to configure the web server to return the correct MIME type, which is `application/x-silverlight-app`.

Since Silverlight applications are associated with client-side isolated storage based on their URL, `.xap` files that use isolated storage should be marked with a relatively near-term cache expiration time, such as a day or a week, to make them easier to update. With a far-future expiration time, in order to maintain high-performance server-side caching (no query strings), the URL would have to be changed when a new version is released, which would mean that the new version wouldn't have access to the old version's application-specific isolated storage.

Proxy Cache

Proxy caches, also known as *web proxies* or *web caches*, are a combined client and server that act as an intermediate between users and web servers. When a client browser issues an HTTP request through a proxy, the response can come directly from content cached in the proxy, or the proxy can obtain a response from the target server first and then forward it to the client, possibly caching it in the process.

Proxies can be located at the same premises as a user's computer, such as in a corporate environment, or at an ISP. In the former case, the proxies are usually visible, while in the latter they are usually invisible. A visible proxy is one that the browser knows about and to which it explicitly sends HTTP requests. An invisible proxy is one that the browser doesn't know about and that transparently intercepts all TCP connections to port 80 (HTTP), regardless of the destination IP address.

From a performance perspective, proxies can be helpful because they can cache content close to users. When content is present in the proxy, it results in higher-bandwidth delivery and less latency than delivering it from the source web server. If the content is not in the proxy, then latency increases, since the proxy will have to forward the HTTP request to the web server.

Other factors that often motivate the installation of a proxy include reducing bandwidth requirements and the ability to apply various types of filtering and logging.

You should engineer your web site so that proxies can cache your content as much as possible. The caching helps your site in ways that are similar to how it helps your users: improved performance (by offloading your site) and a reduction in bandwidth use.

Proxies determine which content to cache primarily by evaluating the HTTP response headers. The HTTP 1.1 standard provides some guidelines about caching, but most proxies also implement a number of heuristics in their decision process. You can help to remove ambiguity by setting HTTP headers that clearly indicate your intentions.

Proxies will not cache responses to SSL requests, or requests that use an HTTP `PUT`, `DELETE`, or `TRACE`. Proxies will not cache temporary redirect responses or responses to `POST` requests unless the response HTTP headers explicitly indicate that they should be.

Although there are still a small number of proxies that support only HTTP 1.0, in my experience they tend to be private proxies, rather than public ones. The other main source of HTTP 1.0 requests is likely to be from uncommon spiders or other low-volume corner cases. Because of potential security and site-performance issues, if I were building a large web site today, I would probably just block all HTTP 1.0 requests. The number of such requests would be very small, and blocking them would allow me to focus my limited resources in more productive, higher-impact areas than implementing and testing HTTP 1.0 compatibility.

Using the Cache-Control HTTP Header

The main HTTP header that controls caching in proxies is `Cache-Control`. When set to `private`, a proxy must not cache the response. When set to `public`, a proxy can cache the response, although it's not required to.

The ASP.NET runtime marks all dynamic content with `Cache-Control: private` by default so that proxies won't cache it. You should override that setting for dynamic content that is the same for all users by marking it with `Cache-Control: public`. The following example configures the `Cache-Control` header to tell both proxies and browsers that they can cache the page for 60 seconds (see `proxy1.aspx`):

```
protected void Page_Load(object sender, EventArgs e)
{
    TimeSpan age = TimeSpan.FromSeconds(60.0);
    this.Response.Cache.SetMaxAge(age);
    this.Response.Cache.SetCacheability(HttpCacheability.Public);
    this.Response.Cache.SetNoServerCaching();
}
```

Calling `SetCacheability(HttpCacheability.Public)` enables server-side output caching in addition to client and proxy caching. `SetServerNoCaching()` disables caching on the server without affecting client and proxy caching.

You can do the same thing declaratively, using the `OutputCache` directive (see `proxy2.aspx`):

```
<%@ Page . . . %>
<%@ OutputCache Duration="60" Location="Downstream" VaryByParam="None" %>
```

A `Location` setting of `Any` (the default) is similar, except it doesn't disable server caching. Usually, if a page can be stored in a proxy cache, it can also be stored in the server's cache.

■ **Note** Cassini, the development web server that's integrated with Visual Studio, always forces the `Cache-Control` header to be set to `private`.

Using Cookies with Proxies

Be careful when setting cookies on public pages. Even if the content of the page is the same for all users, the cookies may not be. Along with the content itself, proxies also cache the HTTP headers of the response, which can include `Set-Cookie`. Although some proxies won't cache responses that include cookies, others will, particularly if the response also includes `Cache-Control: public`. This means that if you mark a response with `Cache-Control: public` that includes a user-specific cookie, it can result in a security vulnerability since the proxy could deliver the cached cookie to a user other than the one you intended.

Because of this restriction, you should think twice about setting cookies on heavily referenced pages, such as your home page, since that could prevent those pages from being cacheable in proxies. In fact, ASP.NET will disable all output caching if you set a cookie, to avoid accidentally sending one user's cookies to another user. This is another reason to set cookies only when you actually need them. In particular, you should not immediately set a session cookie for every page. If you're using the built-in session mechanism, ASP.NET won't set a cookie as long as you don't store anything in the `Session` object.

The runtime will force `Cache-Control: private` for pages that require authentication to prevent the accidental caching of private content on public proxies.

Static Content

If you've assigned an expiration date to your static files as suggested in Chapter 2, the resulting headers generally allow proxies to cache them without taking any additional actions.

However, there are enough corner cases that it's a good idea to mark your static content explicitly with `Cache-Control: public`. For example, without that header, some proxies won't cache responses if the *request* includes cookies or if the URL includes a query string. You can configure IIS to generate the header for static content using the approach in Figure 2-6.

Proxies won't cache content that clients can't cache, so you can prevent caching on both proxies and clients by setting `Cache-Control: no-cache`, as described in the section on browser caching earlier in this chapter.

Managing Different Versions of the Same Content

You can direct proxies to store several different versions of the same content if the differences can be identified based on the HTTP request headers. For example, the `Accept-Language` header specifies the user's language preferences. To inform proxies that they should cache a different version of the content for different language preferences, you can call `SetVaryByCustom()`:

```
this.Response.Cache.SetVaryByCustom("Accept-Language");
```

That will set the `Vary` HTTP header to `Accept-Language`.

Using `Vary: *` is a special case, which says that proxies must consider responses different regardless of the request headers. Using `Vary: *` or `Vary: Cookie` are useful *defense-in-depth* techniques with responses that shouldn't be cached to help avoid accidentally storing user-specific content on proxies. Defense-in-depth is a strategy of protecting against attacks or vulnerabilities using multiple different techniques, in a layered way.

`Vary` headers are set automatically by the runtime in certain cases. For example, when compression is enabled, `Vary: Accept-Encoding` is set.

Web Server Cache

Web servers can cache content in a number of different ways to help improve performance. The server can cache an entire HTTP response in the kernel, in IIS, or in the ASP.NET output cache. It can also cache parts of response in the form of generated HTML fragments, as well as objects that the server uses to create the page, such as the results of database queries.

Windows Kernel Cache

Windows includes a kernel-mode HTTP driver called `http.sys`. Since HTTP is a networking protocol, the benefits of putting support for HTTP in the kernel are similar to those for putting TCP support there, including higher performance and increased flexibility.

Doing low-level protocol processing in the kernel makes it possible for multiple processes to bind to port 80, each receiving requests for a particular host—something that's not readily done with the regular TCP sockets-based mechanism. `http.sys` also handles request queuing and caching without the context switch overhead that would be involved with user-mode code.

The driver can return cached responses directly to clients, entirely bypassing user mode. That avoids several kernel/user context switches, which reduces latency and improves throughput.

Kernel HTTP caching is enabled by default for static files and is disabled by default for dynamic files.

Limitations

`http.sys` will cache responses only under certain limited conditions. The conditions that you're most likely to encounter that will prevent it from caching a response include the following:

- The request contains a query string.

- The requested file is accessed as a default document. For example, if `default.htm` is the default document in the top-level folder, then `http.sys` will not cache it if the incoming URL is `http://www.12titans.net/`. However, `http.sys` can cache the document when you access it using `http://www.12titans.net/default.htm`.

- Dynamic compression is enabled and is used for the response.

You're less likely to encounter the other conditions:

- The request is not anonymous.

- The request requires authentication (for example, the request contains an `Authorization` header).

- The web site is configured to use a footer.

- The static file is a Universal Naming Convention (UNC) file, and the `DoDirMonitoringForUnc` registry key is not enabled (UNC files are those that start with `\\hostname\` instead of a drive letter).

■ **Note** You can use the `DoDirMonitoringForUnc` registry property (a DWORD value) to switch the static file cache for UNC files back to a change notification cache. This is set at `HKLM\System\CurrentControlSet\Services\Inetinfo\Parameters`. The default value is 0, or not enabled. You can set it to 1 to enable caching of UNC static content based on change notification.

- The cache is disabled for the requested file or folder.

- The request has an entity body.

- Certificate mapping is enabled for the URL.

- Custom logging is enabled for the web site.

- The request HTTP version is not 1.1 or 1.0.

- The request contains a `Translate: f` header.

- An `Expect` header that does not contain exactly `"100 continue"` is present.

- The request contains either an `If-Range` header or a `Range` header.

- The total response size is larger than the configured per-response maximum size. The maximum is controlled by the `UriMaxUriBytes` registry key. The default value is 256KB.

- The response header size (which includes cookies) is larger than the configured per-response maximum header size. The default value is 1KB.

- The cache is full. The default size is proportional to the physical memory in the computer.

- The response is zero length.

Enabling Kernel Caching for Dynamic Content

You can enable `http.sys` caching of dynamic content declaratively, by using an `OutputCache` directive at the top of your `.aspx` file. Here's an example (see `kernel1.aspx`):

```
<%@ OutputCache Duration="86400" VaryByParam="None" %>
```

That will also enable ASP.NET output caching. The runtime will expire the cache entry for the page after 86,400 seconds (1 day). You can do the same thing programmatically as follows (see `kernel2.aspx`):

```
protected void Page_Load(object sender, EventArgs e)
{
    TimeSpan age = TimeSpan.FromDays(1.0);
    this.Response.Cache.SetMaxAge(age);
    this.Response.Cache.SetCacheability(HttpCacheability.Public);
}
```

Once `http.sys` caches a response, it is occupying kernel memory, which is a relatively scarce resource. To help optimize the use of that memory, if no clients request a cached item again within the next 120 seconds, `http.sys` will remove the cache entry. You can adjust the cache timeout period with the following registry entry:

```
HKLM\System\CurrentControlSet\Services\Http\Parameters\UriScavengerPeriod
```

You might want to use a longer timeout if the traffic on your site tends to arrive in bursts.

You can enable `http.sys` caching for all dynamic files with a particular file extension by using IIS Manager. After navigating to the folder or file in your web site that you want to cache, double-click

Output Caching in the **Features View**. Then click **Add** on the right-hand panel to bring up the **Add Cache Rule** dialog. Enter the **File name extension** of the type of file that you want to cache in `http.sys`, check the **Kernel-mode caching** checkbox, and click **OK**. See Figure 3-7.

■ **Note** With this approach, `Cache-Control: public` is *not* set, so the content would not be cacheable on proxies.

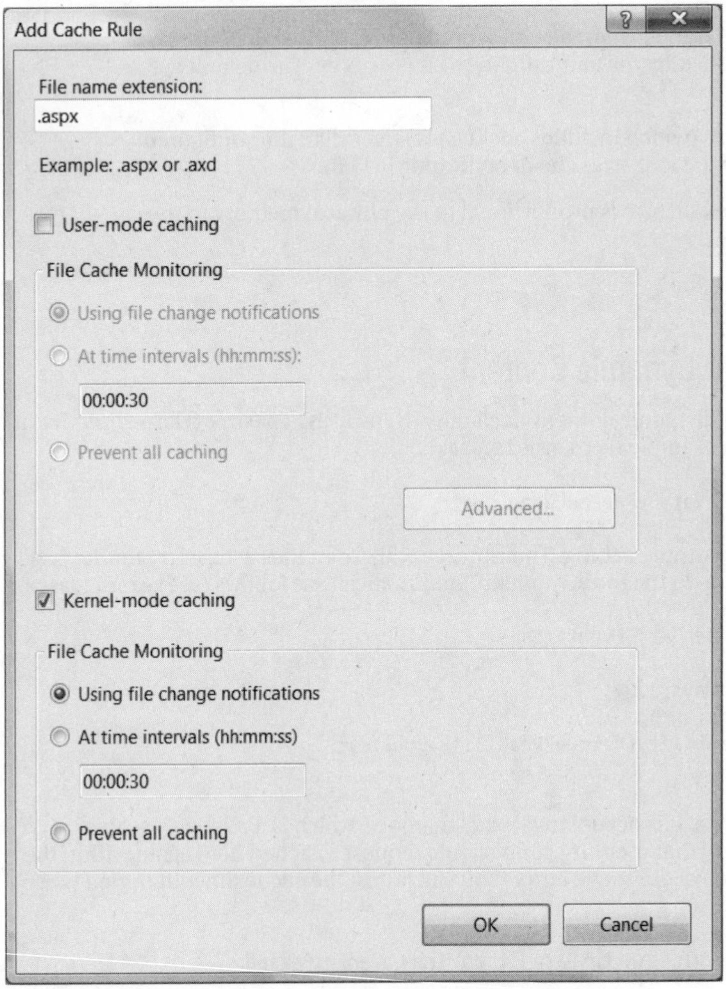

Figure 3-7. Enabling kernel-mode caching for dynamic files

Something else to be aware of when using the GUI is that it places the configuration setting in the IIS configuration file in `applicationHost.config`, which is located in `C:\Windows\System32\inetsrv\config`. That makes it a little more work to manage for `xcopy`-based deployments and source code management compared to settings in `web.config`.

You can also edit `applicationHost.config` directly, instead of using the GUI. Here's an example:

```
<configuration>
    . . .
    <location path="Samples/ch03">
      <system.webServer>
        <caching>
          <profiles>
            <add extension=".aspx" policy="DontCache"
                 kernelCachePolicy="CacheUntilChange" />
          </profiles>
        </caching>
      </system.webServer>
    </location>
</configuration>
```

Performance Comparison

To get a feeling for the performance difference when using `http.sys` compared to not using any output caching, let's run a quick test:

1. First, download and install the free IIS 6.0 Resource Kit Tools from Microsoft (the tools work with IIS 7 too): `http://www.microsoft.com/downloads/details.aspx?FamilyID=56FC92EE-A71A-4C73-B628-ADE629C89499&displaylang=en`.

2. Next, add a blank web form to your web site project in `pages/default.aspx`, and configure the site to be accessible from IIS, using `localhost`. Don't use the Cassini web server that's integrated with Visual Studio, and don't include the `OutputCache` directive for the first test.

3. From the Windows **Start** menu, open **IIS Resources** ➤ **WCAT Controller** ➤ **WCAT Controller**, to bring up a command window that's configured to use the Windows Capacity Analysis Tool. Use Notepad to create two configuration files in that folder. The first one is a script file you should call **s1.cfg**:

```
SET Server = "localhost"
SET Port = 80
SET Verb = "GET"
SET KeepAlive = true

NEW TRANSACTION
classId = 1
Weight = 100
NEW REQUEST HTTP
URL = "/pages/default.aspx"
```

This file tells the controller which pages you want to read and how you want to read them. In this case, you're reading `http://localhost/pages/default.aspx` using HTTP `GET`, with `KeepAlive` enabled (later, you might try disabling `KeepAlive` to get a feeling for how amazingly expensive it is to open a new connection for each request).

4. Next, create a test configuration file called `c1.cfg`:

    ```
    Warmuptime 5s
    Duration 30s
    CooldownTime 0s
    NumClientMachines 2
    NumClientThreads 10
    ```

    This specifies the `Warmuptime`, `Duration`, and `CooldownTime` for the test (in seconds), as well as how many client machines there will be and how many threads to use for each client.

5. Before running the test, bring up two windows for the **WCAT Client** (under IIS Resources in the Start menu). From one of those windows, run the following command to see the files that are currently present in the `http.sys` cache:

    ```
    netsh http show cachestate
    ```

    If you don't have any other web activity on your machine, it should report that there are no cache entries.

■ **Note** For the test results to be comparable, you need to make sure that CPU use during the test is close to 100 percent. On my test machine, I found that required two clients. You should verify that works for you as well, using Task Manager while the test is running.

---

6. Start the controller from its window:

    ```
    wcctl -a localhost -c c1.cfg -s s1.cfg
    ```

7. Then start both clients, one from each of the two other windows:

    ```
    wcclient localhost
    ```

8. After you start the second client, the test will begin. As soon as it completes, run the `netsh` command again. It should still show that the `http.sys` cache is empty.

9. Check the results from the controller to make sure there were no errors. For this test, you're most interested in how many requests per second you can get. Here are the results of the test on my machine at the 20-second point:

```
Total Requests           :          54135      (      2753/Sec)
```

10. Now edit the `.aspx` file to include the following `OutputCache` directive:

```
<%@ OutputCache Duration="86400" VaryByParam="None" %>
```

That will enable `http.sys` caching and ASP.NET output caching, as described earlier.

11. Repeat the test as shown earlier. The test configuration files don't need to be changed. This time, the result of the second `netsh` command should show that the `.aspx` file is in the cache:

```
URL: http://127.0.0.1:80/pages/default.aspx
    Status code: 200
    HTTP verb: GET
    Cache policy type: Time to live
    Cache entry Time to Live (secs): 86359
    Creation time: 2009.3.29:7.44.26:0
    Request queue name: Sample
    Headers length: 215
    Content length: 2247
    Hit count: 170778
    Force disconnect after serving: FALSE
```

The test results show a considerable improvement:

```
Total Requests          :        99746    (    5064/Sec)
```

In this case, you can process about 84 percent more requests per second with `http.sys` caching than without. Keep in mind too that this is in some ways a worst-case improvement, because the page is doing almost no real work: there are no database accesses or other off-box or out-of-process requests. The more work the page needs to do, the larger the percentage improvement will be.

IIS 7 Output Caching

The next caching layer below `http.sys` is in the user-mode IIS process. The biggest practical difference between IIS output caching and `http.sys` is that IIS can vary the cache output based on query strings or HTTP headers. If a query string is present in a URL, `http.sys` won't cache it.

You can demonstrate this by changing the `s1.cfg` file shown earlier to include a query string, while leaving the `OutputCache` directive in place. After running the test, you can see that `netsh` will show that the page is not in the `http.sys` cache.

Perhaps because output caching in IIS 7 is a relatively new feature, the ASP.NET API doesn't explicitly support it yet. Therefore, you won't normally need to explicitly enable or configure it for `.aspx` pages; the runtime manages the settings for you when you enable ASP.NET output caching.

However, if you are using `HttpHandlers` or non-ASP.NET dynamic content, such as PHP, then you will need to enable IIS 7 output caching explicitly. You can do that using the dialog box in Figure 3-7 and selecting the **User Mode Caching** box. After that, click the **Advanced** button to bring up the dialog box in Figure 3-8.

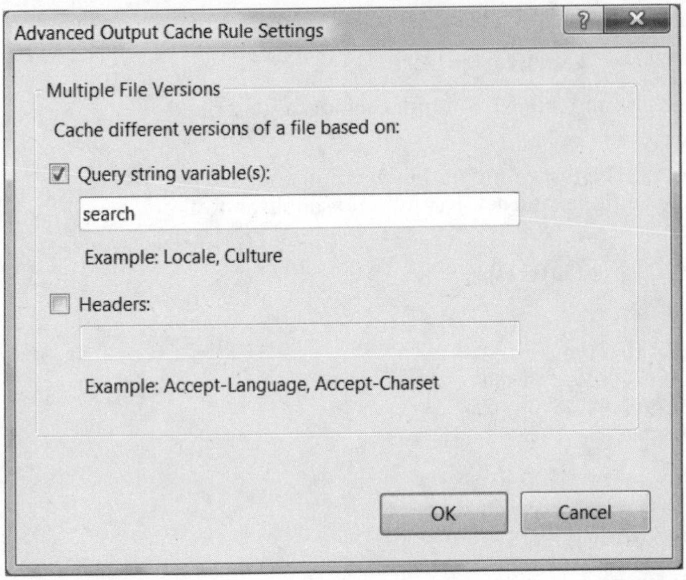

Figure 3-8. Advanced Output Cache Rule Settings dialog box for IIS 7 output caching

From there you can set the query string variables or HTTP headers that IIS should use to vary the cache output.

ASP.NET Output Caching

ASP.NET has an output cache that is separate from the one in IIS 7. You can enable it with the same `OutputCache` directive that you used earlier to enable `http.sys` caching. Unlike `http.sys` and IIS, the ASP.NET cache can vary its output based on parameters that are more complex than HTTP headers or query string values, such as a user's role or the content of a table in the database. In addition to entire pages, it can cache page fragments, and it also supports programmatic invalidation.

As with `http.sys` and IIS 7 caching, you should apply ASP.NET output caching only to pages and controls that have the same output for many users. Avoid caching output that is unique per user, since the chances of the same user requesting it again from the same server are not as good as they are for shared content. The more load-balanced web servers you have, the more unlikely it is that user-specific content generated on any one server will be reused.

Avoid caching output that is infrequently accessed, even if it's shared. You don't want to fill your cache with content that won't be reused. Good candidates for output caching include content that varies only based on which browser the user has, their selected language or role, certain query string values, a specific table in the database, and so on.

If pages have small user-specific variations, such as putting the user's name on the page, then you should store the relevant information in cookies or in Silverlight isolated storage and use script or Silverlight to place the content on the page, as described in Chapter 2 and in the Silverlight example earlier in this chapter. That way, all users will receive the same HTML, which you can place in the output cache. However, be sure not to set cookies from the cached page. ASP.NET will disable output caching in that case to avoid accidentally sending user-specific cookies to all users. Instead, you should set cookies from a page that the server doesn't cache.

You can use a similar approach for pages that vary from one request to the next only by information that's otherwise available directly from JavaScript or Silverlight. For example, you can display the current time on each page with script, rather than adding it on the server.

Caching Page Fragments with User Controls

For data-driven pages and other content that is best created on the server, you should build fixed content separately from dynamic content. You can do that in two ways: user controls (fragments) and substitution controls.

For example, here's a user control that displays just a string and the date (see `Controls\Date.ascx`):

```
<%@ Control Language="C#" AutoEventWireup="true"
    CodeFile="Date.ascx.cs" Inherits="Controls_Date" %>
<%@ OutputCache Duration="5" VaryByParam="None" %>
Control time: <%= DateTime.Now.ToString() %>
```

It has an `OutputCache` directive that will cause the text the control generates to be cached for five seconds.

To use the control, first place a `Register` directive near the top of your `.aspx` page (see `date1.aspx`):

```
<%@ Register Src="~/Controls/Date.ascx" TagPrefix="ct" TagName="Date" %>
```

Later in the page, call the control and display the date again:

```
<ct:Date runat="server" />
<br/>Page time: <%= DateTime.Now.ToString() %>
```

When you run the page, what you'll see is that the two times start out the same. If you refresh the page quickly a few times, the control time will stay the same for five seconds and then change, whereas the page time is updated after every refresh. That's because after the `Date` control runs, the runtime reuses its output for all requests that arrive over the following five seconds. After that, the runtime drops the cache entry and executes the control again the next time a request calls it.

You should use a fixed cache `Duration` for content that you need to update periodically but that you can't easily associate with an update event such as a SQL Server change notification. For example, let's say you have a page that shows several images, along with counts of how often users access the images. However, users don't need to see the absolute latest counts. Instead of retrieving all of the counts from the database each time users access the page, you could have a user control that retrieves them and then enable output caching on the control with a `Duration` of 300 seconds. The page would use the cached output of the control until it expires.

User controls are not instantiated as objects when the runtime retrieves them from the output cache, so before you place them in the output cache, you should make sure they don't need to participate programmatically with the rest of the page.

You will revisit user controls in more detail in Chapter 6.

Substitution Caching

You can think of substitution caching as the inverse of user controls. Instead of dynamically generating the outer page and retrieving inner parts of it from the cache, you cache the outer page and dynamically generate inner parts of it.

Let's use substitution caching to create output similar to the preceding example. You will cache the .aspx page and generate a new time value for each page view using the substitution control. Here's the .aspx page (see date2.aspx):

```
Cached time: <%= DateTime.Now.ToString() %>
<br />Page time:
<asp:Substitution ID="sub" runat="server" MethodName="SubTime" />
```

Next, add the method specified in the MethodName property of the substitution control to the code-behind. The runtime will call it to generate a string that it will insert in place of the substitution control:

```
public static string SubTime(HttpContext context)
{
    return DateTime.Now.ToString();
}
```

If you view the page at this point, the two date strings will always be the same.

Next, enable output caching on the page:

```
<%@ OutputCache Duration="5" VaryByParam="None" %>
```

Now when you view the page, the Page time will be different each time, since it's generated for every page view, but the Cached time will be updated only every five seconds.

■ **Note** Although the static method that generates the content for insertion into the substitution control can access the HttpContext object for the request, it cannot return an ASP.NET control. The returned string is inserted directly into the final output; it is not compiled and parsed into objects as with a user control.

Disabling Output Caching

Output caching is not appropriate for pages or fragments that require per-access logging or other back-end tracking, authorization, or accounting, since the code that's embedded in the page or that's located in code-behind will not be executed when the content is delivered from the cache.

You can programmatically disable output caching for a particular request as follows:

```
this.Response.Cache.SetNoServerCaching();
```

If you were to call that method from Page_Load() in the code-behind for the previous example, the two date strings on the page would always be the same, since the output would not be cached.

Removing Items from the Output Cache

Once you have placed a page in the ASP.NET output cache, you can remove it later. You might want to do this if something changes that was used to generate the page. Here's an example:

```
HttpResponse.RemoveOutputCacheItem("/pages/default.aspx");
```

■ **Caution** Using RemoveOutputCacheItem() by itself on one machine in a server farm will not remove the page from the cache on other machines or processes in the farm.

You can remove several related items from the cache at the same time by associating them with an item in the ASP.NET object cache.

For example, first let's add an object to the cache. You might do this from global.asax.cs or from an HttpModule.

```
HttpContext.Current.Cache.Insert("key", "value", null,
        DateTime.MaxValue, TimeSpan.Zero,
        CacheItemPriority.NotRemovable, null);
```

Next, associate output cache entries for the related pages with the same cache key:

```
protected void Page_Load(object sender, EventArgs e)
{
    this.Response.AddCacheItemDependency("key");
}
```

If you modify the value in the cache that's associated with the specified key, then all the pages with output caching enabled that have called AddCacheDependency with that key will have their cache entries expired. As with RemoveOutputCacheItem earlier in the chapter, this works only on a single server.

If the cache key doesn't exist at the time you call AddCacheDependency, then the page won't be cached at all.

■ **Note** You can't call AddCacheItemDependency from a user control. Instead, you can create a CacheDependency object and assign it to the control's Dependency property.

Database Dependencies

Pages or fragments that depend on the database can be associated with the corresponding tables or queries so that their cache entries automatically expire when those objects change. This also has the advantage of keeping the cache of all machines in a server farm in sync.

One way to do this is by setting the SqlDependency property in the OutputCache directive. Here's an example:

```
<%@ OutputCache VaryByParam="None" SqlDependency="CommandNotification" %>
```

What this does is to set a hidden flag that tells SqlCommand to include a SqlDependency request with all queries, which in turn tells SQL Server to send a notification when the results of those queries might have changed. SQL Server implements change notifications using Service Broker, which you will need to enable in order for this to work, as described in Chapter 8.

The net effect of enabling CommandNotification is that the runtime will place your page in the output cache unless one of the database queries it uses is not compatible with query notifications, such as using SELECT * or not specifying two-part table names. See Chapter 8 for details. Provided the underlying queries meet the requirements for SqlDependency, CommandNotification works even when you issue queries from other assemblies or from transactions or stored procedures.

Once in the output cache, if the database receives an INSERT, UPDATE, or DELETE command that might modify the results of those queries, even if the command originates from other machines, then it sends a notification back to all servers that posted dependencies. When the web servers receive the notification, they remove the page that issued the original query from the output cache.

If your page issues a number of queries or if you need to bypass queries that aren't compatible with SqlDependency, then you can instead use AddCacheDependency together with SqlCacheDependency. Here's an example (see depend1.aspx):

```
protected void Page_Load(object sender, EventArgs e)
{
    string cs = ConfigurationManager.ConnectionStrings["data"].ConnectionString;
    using (SqlConnection conn = new SqlConnection(cs))
    {
        string sql = "dbo.GetInfo";
        using (SqlCommand cmd = new SqlCommand(sql, conn))
        {
            cmd.CommandType = CommandType.StoredProcedure;
            conn.Open();
            SqlCacheDependency dep = new SqlCacheDependency(cmd);
            mygrid.DataSource = cmd.ExecuteReader();
            mygrid.DataBind();
            this.Response.AddCacheDependency(dep);
        }
    }
}
```

Execute the query and bind the results to a control as usual, but just before calling ExecuteReader, create a SqlCacheDependency object. Then pass a reference to that object to AddCacheDependency, which will cause the runtime to remove the page from the output cache when it receives a query change notification.

Here's the corresponding markup:

```
<%@ Page Language="C#" AutoEventWireup="true"
    CodeFile="depend1.aspx.cs" Inherits="depend1" %>
<%@ OutputCache Duration="86400" VaryByParam="None" %>
<!DOCTYPE html PUBLIC "-//W3C//DTD XHTML 1.0 Transitional//EN"
  "http://www.w3.org/TR/xhtml1/DTD/xhtml1-transitional.dtd">
```

```
<html xmlns="http://www.w3.org/1999/xhtml">
<head runat="server">
    <title></title>
</head>
<body>
    <form id="form1" runat="server">
    <div>
        Last updated: <%= DateTime.Now %><br />
        <asp:GridView runat="server" ID="mygrid" />
    </div>
    </form>
</body>
</html>
```

The first time you request the page, the runtime will execute the database query and place the rendered page in the output cache. If you refresh the page, you will see that the Last updated time doesn't change. If you use Server Explorer or SSMS to modify the table that's the target of the query, then behind the scenes the runtime will receive a notification and remove the page from the cache. The next time you refresh the page, you will see the current time and the updated data in the GridView.

Varying the Output Cache

For cases where the output of a page or control varies based on things like cookie values or a user's role, you can use the VaryByCustom property of the OutputCache directive. For example, let's say you have a page that generates different output based on the value of a cookie. First, set the OutputCache directive (see vary1.aspx):

```
<%@ OutputCache Duration="300" VaryByParam="None" VaryByCustom="info" %>
```

Then in your Global.cs file (the code-behind for global.asax), override the GetVaryByCustomString method:

```
public override string GetVaryByCustomString(HttpContext context, string arg)
{
    if (arg == "info")
    {
        HttpCookie cookie = context.Request.Cookies[arg];
        if (cookie != null)
            return cookie.Value;
    }
    return base.GetVaryByCustomString(context, arg);
}
```

All pages in your application that use this feature share the same method. When the method is called, the arg string will have the same value that you set in the VaryByCustom property on the page. The runtime will generate and store different versions of the page for each unique value that GetVaryByCustomString returns (think of the return value as the key for a hash table). In this case, you're returning the value of a cookie, so the runtime will cache a different version of the page for each value of the cookie. For more complex cases, you can return a string that's a composite of several different values.

115

If you specify the special value of `browser` to `VaryByCustom`, then the runtime caches different versions of the page based on the browser's type and major version number.

Cache Validation

If it would be better for your application to determine programmatically whether a cache entry is still valid, you can use a cache validation callback. The runtime will invoke the callback to determine whether it should return an entry that's already in the cache or whether it should flush the cache entry and re-create the page.

Let's say that your site has a requirement that members of the `admin` group should always receive an uncached version of a particular page. When `admin` users log on, the site sets a cookie called `admin`, which you can use in the validation callback (see `valid1.aspx`):

```
public static void ValidateCache(HttpContext context, Object data,
                                 ref HttpValidationStatus status)
{
    HttpCookie cookie = context.Request.Cookies["admin"];
    if (cookie != null)
        status = HttpValidationStatus.Invalid;
    else
        status = HttpValidationStatus.Valid;
}
```

The callback checks to see whether the cookie is present in the `Request`. If it is, then setting status to `HttpValidationStatus.Invalid` tells the runtime to invalidate the current cache entry and to re-create the page. If the cookie isn't there, then setting status to `HttpValidationStatus.Valid` tells the runtime to return the already cached page.

You should keep the validation method short, since the runtime will call it for every page view.

Next, associate the callback with the page by calling `AddValidationCallback`:

```
protected void Page_Load(object sender, EventArgs e)
{
    HttpCacheValidateHandler val = new HttpCacheValidateHandler(ValidateCache);
    this.Response.Cache.AddValidationCallback(val, null);
}
```

When you have pages that use any of the server-side validation or dynamic expiration methods, you generally should avoid caching them in proxies. When the runtime invalidates a page in the output cache on the server, it does not change any copies that might be cached in proxies. To enable server-side output caching while disabling proxy caching, you should set the `Location` property of the `OutputCache` directive to `Server`. Here's an example (see `server1.aspx`):

```
<%@ OutputCache Duration="300" VaryByParam="None" VaryByCustom="info"
    Location="Server" %>
```

That's equivalent to the following code (see `server2.aspx`):

```
TimeSpan expires = TimeSpan.FromSeconds(300.0);
this.Response.Cache.SetMaxAge(expires);
this.Response.Cache.SetVaryByCustom("info");
```

```
this.Response.Cache.SetCacheability(HttpCacheability.Server);
this.Response.Cache.SetValidUntilExpires(true);
```

The call to SetValidUntilExpires() prevents Cache-Control cache invalidation headers that are sent by the client from causing the server's cache to expire.

ASP.NET Object Caching

ASP.NET can cache objects that are frequently referenced or expensive to create. There are several different options, depending on the object's scope and expected lifetime.

Caching Objects with Global Scope and Indefinite Lifetime

You can use static variables to cache objects that should *always* be in memory and that different web pages can use at the same time. For best performance, use initializers instead of static constructors. Better yet, only set the variables when they are first referenced (lazy initialization).

You can use the HttpContext.Application object for similar purposes, although it's a bit slower, since it uses a hash table. As with most global variables that you can access from multiple threads, you should use some form of locking to ensure consistent state between two different operations. In this case, the Application object includes its own Lock() and UnLock() methods. Here's an example (see app1.aspx):

```
HttpApplicationState app = this.Context.Application;
string myValue = null;
app.Lock();
try
{
    myValue = (string)app["key"];
    if (myValue == null)
    {
        myValue = "value";
        app["key"] = myValue;
    }
}
finally
{
    app.UnLock();
}
```

Caching Objects Used Only by the Current Request

You should use HttpContext.Items for objects that are needed only during the current request. The runtime drops the collection when the current request is complete.

This is the preferred mechanism for passing data between an HttpModule and page-specific code. It can also be useful for sharing data with or between user controls, as an alternative to properties.

Since the `Items` collection is local to the current request, multiple threads don't usually access it at the same time, so it doesn't usually require locking. Here's an example:

```
this.Context.Items["key"] = "value";
```

Caching Objects Used by More Than One Page Request

You should use `HttpContext.Cache` for objects that are needed by more than one user and by more than one page request.

Examples include results of database queries, results of web service calls, the contents of frequently used local files, preparsed data structures, and so on.

Like with the `Application` object, multiple threads can access the `Cache` object at the same time, so you should establish a lock to ensure consistent state between related operations. Even though the `Cache` object is "thread safe," that applies to single operations only, not sequences. I don't recommend getting a lock directly on the `Cache` object, since other code not under your control might use the same object, resulting in deadlocks or performance issues. Here's an example that uses a static object to synchronize access:

```
public static Object lockObject = new Object();

. . .
lock (lockObject)
{
    if (this.Cache["key"] == null)
        this.Cache["key"] = "value";
}
```

Using the indexer to add an item to the cache, as in the example, is equivalent to calling `Cache.Insert("key", "value")`.

Without locking, it would be possible for the conditional to succeed in one thread, and then a context switch right after that could allow the conditional to succeed in another thread too. One thread would set the `Cache` entry, and then the other thread would set it again.

The runtime can remove objects from this cache at any time, depending on memory pressure and other factors. There is no guarantee that your data will still be there when you next look for it, even during the same web request.

■ **Note** When you reference a cached item more than once, you should store it in a temporary variable so you have a consistent reference.

When you add an object to the cache, you can specify how long the runtime should keep it there. However, the specification is only a hint; the runtime can still drop the object at any time. Here's an example (see `cache1.aspx`):

```
lock (lockObject)
{
    if (this.Cache["key"] == null)
        this.Cache.Add("key", "value", null, DateTime.Now.AddSeconds(60),
            Cache.NoSlidingExpiration, CacheItemPriority.High, null);
}
```

You are asking the runtime to retain the object in the cache for up to 60 seconds.

You can also specify a sliding expiration time, as a TimeSpan, which advises the runtime to retain the object until the specified interval from when you last accessed it.

■ **Tip** It's a good idea to double-check how long the runtime is retaining your objects in the cache compared to the hints that you specify using the debugger or custom performance counters. By default, the Cache class has an aggressive policy of dropping objects; you might find that the runtime is dropping your objects much sooner than you expect.

To encourage the runtime to retain objects longer, you can increase the CacheItemPriority from the default setting of Normal. The previous example uses a setting of High.

File-Based Dependencies

You can associate a CacheDependency with a cache entry that's associated with a file so that when the file changes, the cache entry is removed (see App_Code\XmlDepend.cs):

```
using System;
using System.Web;
using System.Web.Caching;
using System.Xml;

public class XmlDepend
{
    public static Object lockObject = new Object();

    public static XmlDocument MyDocument(string path)
    {
        string key = "mydoc:" + path;
        Cache cache = HttpContext.Current.Cache;
        lock (lockObject)
        {
            XmlDocument doc = (XmlDocument)cache[key];
            if (doc == null)
            {
                doc = new XmlDocument();
                doc.Load(path);
                CacheDependency cd = new CacheDependency(path);
```

```
                    cache.Insert(key, doc, cd);
                }
                return doc;
            }
        }
    }
```

Pass the method a path to an XML file, which it uses to construct a unique key for the Cache. Since all pages on the site share the same Cache, this helps avoid possible collisions. Next, establish a lock using a shared lock object. If the XmlDocument is still in the Cache, return it. Otherwise, load it from disk. Create a CacheDependency object, and include it along with the key when you insert the XmlDocument into the Cache.

The CacheDependency object registers with the operating system to listen for changes to the specified file. If the file changes, it receives a notification and removes the XmlDocument from the Cache.

Database Dependencies

You can use a similar mechanism with database queries (see App_Code\DataDepend.cs):

```
using System;
using System.Configuration;
using System.Data;
using System.Data.SqlClient;
using System.Web;
using System.Web.Caching;

public static class DataDepend
{
    public static Object lockObject = new Object();
    public const string DataKey = "key";

    public static DataSet MyData()
    {
        DataSet ds;
        Cache cache = HttpContext.Current.Cache;
        lock (lockObject)
        {
            ds = (DataSet)cache[DataKey];
            if (ds == null)
            {
                string cs = ConfigurationManager.ConnectionStrings["data"]
                                        .ConnectionString;
                using (SqlConnection conn = new SqlConnection(cs))
                {
                    string sql = "dbo.GetInfo";
                    using (SqlCommand cmd = new SqlCommand(sql, conn))
                    {
                        cmd.CommandType = CommandType.StoredProcedure;
                        using (SqlDataAdapter adapter = new SqlDataAdapter(cmd))
                        {
```

```
                    conn.Open();
                    SqlCacheDependency dep = new SqlCacheDependency(cmd);
                    adapter.Fill(ds);
                    cache.Insert(DataKey, ds, dep);
                }
              }
            }
          }
        }
        return ds;
    }
}
```

This code is like the earlier example with output caching. Before you issue the query, associate a `SqlCacheDependency` object with the `SqlCommand`. Then a `SqlDataAdapter` sends the query to SQL Server and reads the results into a `DataSet`. Insert the `DataSet` into the `Cache` and associate it with the `SqlCacheDependency` object.

Later, when SQL Server processes a command that might change the results of the query that generated the `DataSet`, it sends a notification event to the `SqlCacheDependency` object. The command that triggers the notification can originate from any host that's connected to the database; it's not limited to the one that originated the query. When the server receives the notification, it invalidates the cache entry; the next time your application needs the data, it will reissue the query and re-create the `DataSet`.

Using WeakReferences for Caching

You can also allow the .NET garbage collector (GC) to manage a cache for you. When you have objects that don't require an explicit expiration policy or when you'd like the policy to be "whatever fits in memory," you can store them in a static `WeakReference` or `Dictionary<Tkey, WeakReference>`. Here's an example (see `App_Code\Weak.cs`):

```
using System;
using System.Data;

public static class Weak
{
    public static WeakReference MyItem { get; set; }
    public static Object lockObject = new Object();

    public static DataSet WeakData()
    {
        DataSet ds = null;
        lock (lockObject)
        {
            if (MyItem != null)
                ds = MyItem.Target as DataSet;
            if (ds == null)
            {
                ds = new DataSet();
                MyItem = new WeakReference(ds);
            }
```

```
        }
        return ds;
    }
}
```

If `MyItem` is not `null`, and if the GC hasn't reclaimed the object held by the `WeakReference` yet, then cast it to the right type and return it. Otherwise, create the object and associate it with a `WeakReference`.

If the GC decides that it needs more memory, it will reclaim the `DataSet`. If there is no memory pressure, then the `DataSet` will still be available the next time it's needed.

You might consider using `WeakReferences` for "speculative" caching, where there's a chance that an object might be reused but you're not sure.

An advantage compared to using the `Cache` class is that the GC and memory pressure alone drive `WeakReferences`. It should also be more efficient, since the GC replaces the `Cache` object's policy management logic.

SQL Server Caching

In addition to caching the results of database queries in the ASP.NET part of your application, as described earlier, SQL Server itself can also act as a cache. This type of caching is largely transparent and automatic. Even so, there are a few things you can do to encourage and take advantage of it.

While processing your queries, SQL Server may need to read data pages into RAM from disk. It will keep those pages in RAM for as long as it can, depending on the memory requirements of other requests. It's similar to the ASP.NET `Cache` object in that way. If the server doesn't need the RAM for something else after the query is first issued, SQL Server can very quickly return results using the pages in memory, rather than fetching them again from disk first. The net effect is that with enough RAM, it can act as a large cache once it has processed a query the first time.

To take advantage of this, first make sure that your database server has plenty of memory. See Chapter 8 for more details on how SQL Server manages memory and how you can determine whether you need more.

Next, you can prefetch data pages so that they will be available for future queries. Let's say that after you've completed processing a page, you can anticipate the user's next action, along with an associated query. In that case, you can queue a request to a background thread on the web server to issue that query (or a related one) to cause SQL Server to read the pages you will need into memory. That way, when the user takes the action you anticipated, the data they require will already be in memory, and the query will complete more quickly. Even if the anticipated query is an `UPDATE`, `INSERT`, or `DELETE`, the query you use for precaching should always be a `SELECT` that references the same rows and indexes. The goal is not necessarily to perform the actual action, just to get the needed data into memory. Of course, if it's appropriate, you can also cache the results on the web server.

This technique works best for data that your application doesn't access too frequently. For example, if most of the pages on your site query a particular table, there's no reason to precache that table from the few web pages that don't use it; since so many other pages use the data frequently, it will be there anyway.

An example where it would make sense is an image gallery. After issuing a query to retrieve the data for the current page, you might know that there's a good chance the user will want to see the next page too. After completing the current page, you can queue a query for the next page's data in a background thread. Even if a different web server in your server farm processes the next page, the data will still be in memory on the database server, where SQL Server can return it quickly.

I will cover data precaching in more detail in Chapter 8.

Distributed Caching

To help offload database servers and ease scale out, it's possible to store some content in a dedicated in-memory-only caching tier instead of in the database. Since the content is not persisted to disk, short-lived content is generally most appropriate, such as session state. To achieve scale-out, you distribute the caching tier among a number of servers and include support for high-availability, failover, and so on.

The premise of distributed caching systems is that they are faster, easier to scale, and less expensive than database-oriented solutions. They can be the right solution for some environments. However, you should also watch for a number of pitfalls.

One argument in support of distributed caches is that they are faster because they don't have to persist the data. However, in order to support the failure of individual nodes, the data does have to be stored in at least two servers. Therefore, a properly designed distributed caching architecture will have to wait for an acknowledgment after the data is sent to another node, before returning to the user. You are effectively trading off disk bandwidth on a database server for network bandwidth. Different distributed cache architectures approach this problem in different ways (multicast, unicast, and so on), but the net effect is the same.

Write throughput on SQL Server is largely determined by the speed of writing sequentially to the database log. Just adding a few additional drives can significantly increase write throughput. Adding battery-backed write cache on a disk controller or a SAN can also help. I will cover this in more detail in Chapters 8 and 10.

Read overhead in a distributed cache can require more than one round-trip, depending on the details of the cache and application architecture. Some systems use multicast to query many servers at once, but that has the disadvantage of consuming network bandwidth to all the cache servers, which can decrease write throughput when the system is under load. Regardless of the technique to read the distributed cache, if the data you need isn't there, then you may still have to go to the database to get it, which will increase latency.

Some systems rely on a directory to determine where a given object resides, part of which you can cache on the web servers. However, the larger your system is, the less effective the directory cache tends to be. As the size of the directory increases and as you spread the cached entries out among a large number of servers, the hit rate will naturally decline.

On the scalability front, the argument in favor of distributed caches is that they are easy to scale in theory by just adding more cheap servers, whereas scaling up a database server is perceived as expensive, and scaling out is perceived as technically difficult.

However, the usual initial approach to scaling up your database should involve just adding more RAM to improve caching and adding more drives to make the log or data volumes faster, which is almost certainly no more expensive than adding distributed cache servers. Scaling out does require some code, but it doesn't have to be difficult or complex.

From a cost perspective, you should consider whether your application might be able to use the free SQL Server Express. It uses the same relational database engine as the full SQL Server Standard but is limited in terms of how much RAM it can use and how large the database can be (a few features are also limited by edition).

I'll cover partitioning and scaling techniques and ways to leverage SQL Server Express in Chapters 5 and 8.

The advantage of using SQL Server instead of a distributed cache is that it simplifies your architecture by eliminating an entire tier. Deployment, testing, software maintenance, debugging, and operations efforts are all reduced. Having fewer tiers also tends to increase your ability to be agile, responding quickly to new business opportunities gets easier, which is in keeping with the ultra-fast approach, as described in Chapter 1.

I'm not saying that there is never a role for distributing caching; in some applications it can be a great tool. However, I prefer to rely on time-tested logic to handle critical functions such as locking, memory management, updates, transactions, queries, and so on, when I can. Those algorithms can be complex and difficult to implement correctly and efficiently, and small mistakes might not be noticed or found right away. For me, having one less component in the architecture that might introduce bugs and latency is a good thing.

Cache Expiration Times

You can manage the expiration of cached content in a few ways. One way is to use relatively short expiration times. With that approach, the client checks back frequently with the server to see whether newer content is available. The extra round-trips that causes, though, are undesirable.

Another way is to arrange for a cache flush mechanism of some kind so that content is ejected from the cache when the underlying data changes. Most tiers don't support this type of mechanism; it's not possible to tell a client or a proxy proactively to flush their caches, for example. ASP.NET does have a comprehensive cache flush system, including integration with SQL Server, using `SqlDependency`, as discussed earlier.

Another approach is to set far-future expiration times. Then, when the content is changed, its name is also changed, instead of waiting for the remote caches to expire.

In most web sites, you will use all three methods: relatively short expiration times for content where the name shouldn't be changed, such as dynamic content, Silverlight applications that use isolated storage and `favicon.ico`; active invalidation for certain SQL Server queries; and far-future expiration dates for most static content.

Dynamic Content

For most sites, I like to set a relatively short default expiration time of between 1 and 30 days for dynamic content, depending on the nature of the application. Shorter or longer times are then set on an exception basis, including the possibility of disabling caching.

When you're thinking about disabling caching because a page changes frequently, consider using very short expiration times instead, particularly for heavily referenced content. For example, let's say you have a page that takes 50ms to execute and that your users view once per second per server. If you assign the page a 5-second lifetime in the output cache, where a cache hit takes 1ms or less to process, then for each 5-second interval that would result in a 78 percent reduction in the CPU time needed to render that page.

Static Content

For long-lived content such as static files, expiration times aren't as useful, since the content will not change in sync with the expiration times. In those cases, you should use a far-future expiration date and manage changes in the contents of the files by changing their names, perhaps by including a date string in the name of the files or their folders. You should then update references to the changed file in your project.

■ **Tip** You can isolate references to regularly updated static content in a user control, a master page, a CSS file, or an ASP.NET `.skin` file to minimize the number of places that have to be updated when the content changes. See Chapter 6.

As your content's frequency-of-change increases, it starts to make sense to get the location of the content (or even the content itself) from a database, instead of embedding it in your source files and trying to manage it with new deployments of your site. Of course, at some point, "static" content starts to become "dynamic" content, and the dynamic content rules apply instead.

A *very* common problem, even on large web sites, is allowing static content to expire too quickly. I suggest using one year as a default expiration time. You can then set it to a shorter time on an exception basis, if needed. Remember, every time a client requests content that could have been cached, it presents an extra load on the server and slows down the page and the site.

Including old static data with new releases allows things such as old pages that are cached by search engines, or old e-mails that reference external images, to still work correctly after updates are applied.

Summary

In this chapter, I covered following:

- Taking content uniqueness and access frequency into account when deciding whether to cache in a particular tier.

- Using IIS and ASP.NET to enable or disable browser caching.

- Using `ViewState` to cache information that's specific to a particular page.

- Understanding the importance of minimizing the size of `ViewState`. You should disable it by default on a per-page basis and enable it only when you need it.

- Creating a custom template in Visual Studio and using it to help simplify the process of establishing consistent per-page defaults.

- Storing `ViewState` on the server when needed.

- Using cookies to cache state information on the client.

- Setting cookies and their properties and reading the resulting name/value pairs from ASP.NET, JavaScript, and Silverlight.

- Setting the `path` property on cookies to limit how often the browser sends them to the server, since cookies consume bandwidth and add latency.

- Encoding binary data in cookies.

- Using a compact privacy policy to help make sure that your user's browser accepts your cookies.

- Using isolated storage to cache data in the user's filesystem.

- Using ASP.NET and IIS to make your content cacheable by proxies by setting the `Cache-Control: public` HTTP header.

- Enabling the high-performance kernel cache on your web servers to cache your dynamic content.

- Comparing caching a page with and without `http.sys` and finding that using it produced 84 percent more requests per second.

- Using IIS to cache dynamic content that varies based on query strings or HTTP headers.

- Configuring ASP.NET output caching for pages and page fragments using the `OutputCache` directive.

- Using substitution caching.

- Removing items from the output cache with `RemoveOutputCacheItem()` and `AddCacheItemDependency()`.

- Using page-level database dependencies with the `SqlDependency` parameter in the `OutputCache` directive.

- Varying the output cache based on custom objects such as cookies.

- Using a cache validation callback to decide whether the cached version of your content is still valid.

- Caching objects using static fields such as `HttpApplicationState`, `HttpContext.Items`, `HttpContext.Cache`, and `WeakReferences`.

- Using file and database dependencies with cached objects.

- Using locking around references to static fields and cached objects that might be accessible to more than one thread.

- Using SQL Server as an extended cache.

- Some potential pitfalls to watch for if you're considering distributed caching.

- Managing cache expiration times, with suggested defaults of 1 year for static content and between 1 and 30 days for dynamic content.

■ ■ ■

CHAPTER 4

IIS 7

Internet Information Services (IIS) is the web server that's included with (and integrated into) Windows. As the application that sits between your web site and the operating system, IIS has a big impact on the performance and scalability of your site.

In this chapter, I'll cover the following:

- Application pools and web gardens

- The IIS request-processing pipeline

- Windows System Resource Manager

- Common HTTP issues

- Compression

- HTTP keep-alives

- Optimizing your URLs

- Managing traffic

- Failed request tracing

- Miscellaneous IIS performance tuning

Application Pools and Web Gardens

When you configure a single web site to run under IIS with default settings, you can see the worker process running in Task Manager as **w3wp.exe**. However, IIS isn't limited to running as a single worker process. You can configure it to use multiple processes, with each one handling requests for one or more web sites or for the same web site (as a *web garden*). Each group of IIS processes handling requests for the same collection of web sites is called an *application pool* (or *AppPool*). A single AppPool can support a large number of web sites.

To specify settings for an AppPool, select **Application Pools** in the **Connections** pane in IIS Manager, then select an AppPool in the center panel, and finally click **Advanced Settings** in the right-hand pane. Available settings include **Managed Pipeline Mode** (**Classic** or **Integrated**), **Maximum Worker Processes**, **CPU Limit**, **Processor Affinity**, the Windows **Identity** used to run the process, parameters for health monitoring, **Rapid-Fail**, and **Recycling** parameters. See Figure 4-1.

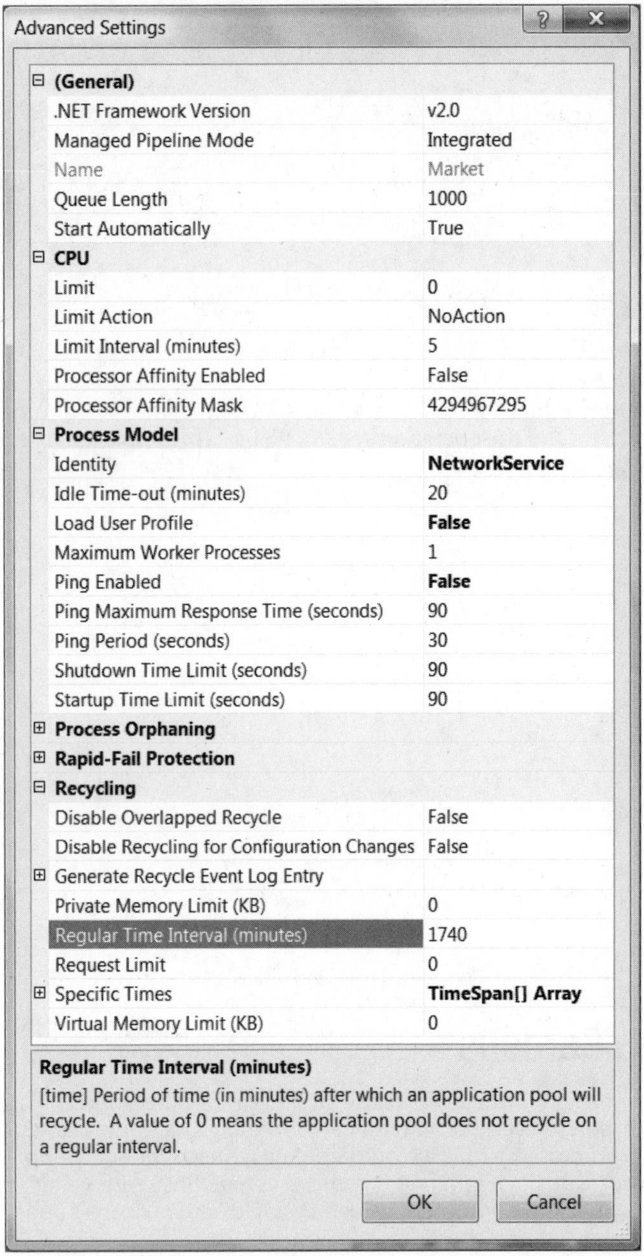

Advanced Settings	？ ✕
⊟ (General)	
.NET Framework Version	v2.0
Managed Pipeline Mode	Integrated
Name	Market
Queue Length	1000
Start Automatically	True
⊟ CPU	
Limit	0
Limit Action	NoAction
Limit Interval (minutes)	5
Processor Affinity Enabled	False
Processor Affinity Mask	4294967295
⊟ Process Model	
Identity	**NetworkService**
Idle Time-out (minutes)	20
Load User Profile	**False**
Maximum Worker Processes	1
Ping Enabled	**False**
Ping Maximum Response Time (seconds)	90
Ping Period (seconds)	30
Shutdown Time Limit (seconds)	90
Startup Time Limit (seconds)	90
⊞ Process Orphaning	
⊞ Rapid-Fail Protection	
⊟ Recycling	
Disable Overlapped Recycle	False
Disable Recycling for Configuration Changes	False
⊞ Generate Recycle Event Log Entry	
Private Memory Limit (KB)	0
Regular Time Interval (minutes)	1740
Request Limit	0
⊞ Specific Times	**TimeSpan[] Array**
Virtual Memory Limit (KB)	0

Regular Time Interval (minutes)

[time] Period of time (in minutes) after which an application pool will recycle. A value of 0 means the application pool does not recycle on a regular interval.

OK	Cancel

Figure 4-1. IIS application pool Advanced Settings

By default, AppPools are set to recycle every 1,740 minutes (29 hours). When they recycle, the IIS processes in the AppPool are shut down and restarted in an overlapped manner, so that no requests are lost. Recycling can help prevent outages due to memory leaks or other resource leaks or due to application bugs that might cause a thread in the AppPool to use all available CPU, disk, or network resources. However, it also presents an additional load on your server that can affect performance and throughput.

To avoid disrupting your users more than necessary, one approach is to configure recycling to happen at a specific time every day when you know the traffic on your site will be low. Although that usually works well for smaller sites, for larger ones you might prefer to configure recycling based on processing a certain number of requests. Combined with the right load balancing algorithm, such as one based on the number of connections per server (as opposed to round robin), that should prevent your servers from all recycling at the same time.

Another possibility is to disable recycling. However, based on experience, I've generally found that's not a good idea, except on sites that are using active monitoring, where you can detect and act on faults in other ways. Even on very large sites, it's surprisingly common that application bugs will occasionally cause problems that are resolved by restarting the AppPool.

Web sites running in an AppPool share the resources available to those processes. Thread pools, for example, are allocated on a per-process basis. This also means that if one web site does something that causes a process in the AppPool to crash or reset, then all of the web sites using that AppPool will also be affected.

Web gardens can help mitigate this risk by having more than one worker process handle requests for the same web sites. However, web gardens also cause all application-specific memory to be duplicated in each worker process, including user-mode output caches. I therefore don't recommend using them except in some cases where your site is running from a single web server, rather than in the usual load-balanced configuration used by larger sites. With enough RAM, web gardens can provide a basic level of redundancy; if one worker process crashes, another will still be available to handle requests.

Another scenario where web gardens can be useful is when you are running on a single server but you're planning to move up to a multiserver load-balanced environment later. In the interim, you can use a web garden to help work out any issues that you might have with a load-balanced architecture, such as cache and state management.

One of the main reasons to consider using additional AppPools is if you have web sites with uptime or reliability requirements that are significantly different from one another. By segregating the applications into separate AppPools, you can help prevent bugs or outages in one site from causing problems in the other.

For example, let's say that one part of your site is responsible for handling customer order processing and another part allows users to browse your product catalog. The former is business-critical, while the latter is not. Let's also say that the catalog part of the site includes content created by relatively junior staff, and it tends to have more bugs. To avoid having outages in the catalog part of the site also bring down the business-critical order-processing part, you could separate the two applications into different AppPools.

Since context switching between threads is faster than between processes, there is a performance cost in using more worker processes. I generally recommend no more than one to two per CPU core to help minimize context switch overhead. For example, a server with a single quad-core CPU should usually have no more than about four to eight worker processes.

Request-Processing Pipeline

IIS has two request-processing pipeline modes: *Integrated* and *Classic*. Integrated mode allows both native code and managed code to process events as requests move through the pipeline. In Classic mode, only native code (C++) can process IIS events. I recommend using Integrated mode (which is the default) whenever possible.

Each request that IIS receives goes through a sequence of states. In Integrated mode, managed `HttpModules` can register event handlers before, at, and after each state transition, as shown in Figure 4-2.

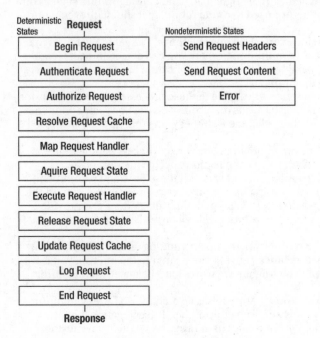

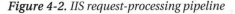

Figure 4-2. IIS request-processing pipeline

`HttpModules` are just organized collections of event handlers for IIS state transitions. IIS invokes the event handlers in all `HttpModules` that have registered for a particular event before moving to the next state.

Deterministic states progress from the top of Figure 4-2 to the bottom. There are also three nondeterministic states, which can happen at various times in the pipeline. The `Error` state, for example, can happen at any time or may not happen at all.

Examples of the functions implemented by standard `HttpModules` include forms authentication, authorization, and logging.

The *request handlers* called from the pipeline are responsible for retrieving the resource that's associated with a particular URL. Handlers are mapped to specific file extensions. For example, the ASP.NET handler is associated with `.aspx` files.

You can have ASP.NET process additional file extensions other than `.aspx` by adding them to the **Handler Mappings** section of IIS Manager. You might want to do this when you're migrating to ASP.NET from another technology so that you can maintain your existing search engine entries and links from other sites without redirects. For example, you could turn your static `.htm` pages into dynamic pages this way, including support for code-behind, ASP.NET directives, and so on. You can use the same technique to generate `.css` or `.js` files dynamically.

Similarly, if you wanted to support another dynamic page-generation technology such as PHP or Perl, you would do so by adding an appropriate handler and mapping it to the desired file extension.

Windows System Resource Manager

Windows System Resource Manager (WSRM) is a feature that comes standard with Windows Server 2008 that allows you to reserve a minimum amount of CPU or memory for different groups of processes.

Let's walk through an example. Start by creating two AppPools, one for an online catalog and another for purchase transactions. Call the first one `Catalog` and the second one `Trans`.

Under normal (unmanaged) conditions, let's say that you've measured CPU use by `Catalog` to be 50 percent, `Trans` is 10 percent, and the operating system uses an additional 10 percent for things such as network processing and kernel mode caching.

You can use WSRM to protect against bugs or load spikes in one application impairing the performance of the other. In this example, I will show how to use it to ensure that `Catalog` gets at least 65 percent of the CPU if it needs it, `Trans` gets 20 percent, and everything else gets 15 percent, including the operating system.

To do that, first add the WSRM feature from **Server Manager** and start the WSRM service. Then start the WSRM console by selecting **Start ➤ Administrative Tools ➤ Windows System Resource Manager**. When the **Connect to Computer** dialog box comes up, select **This Computer**, and click **Connect**.

To configure WSRM, the first step is to tell the software how to identify the processes that you want it to manage. Right-click **Process Matching Criteria** in the left panel, and select **New Process Matching Criteria**. In the dialog box that comes up, click **Add**. The next dialog box that opens is where you define the files or command lines that will be included in this rule. Select **IIS App-Pool** in the option box, and click **Select**. In the dialog box that comes up, select the `Catalog` **AppPool**, and click **OK**. The result should be as in Figure 4-3.

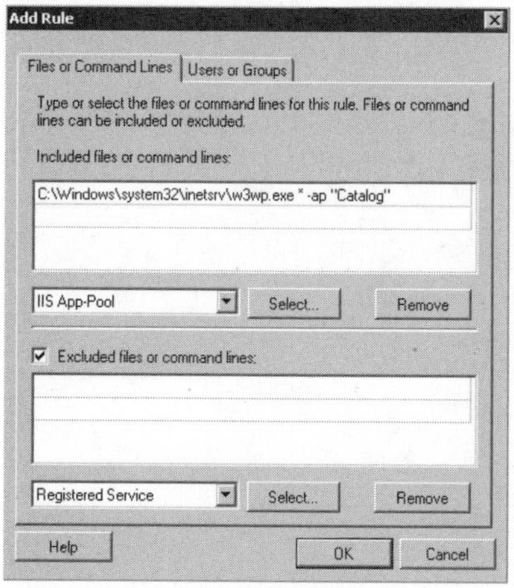

Figure 4-3. Add Rule dialog box in Windows System Resource Manager

Click **OK** to dismiss the dialog box. In the **New Process Matching Criteria** dialog box, give the criteria a name. Let's call it `CatalogAppPool` (spaces aren't allowed). See Figure 4-4.

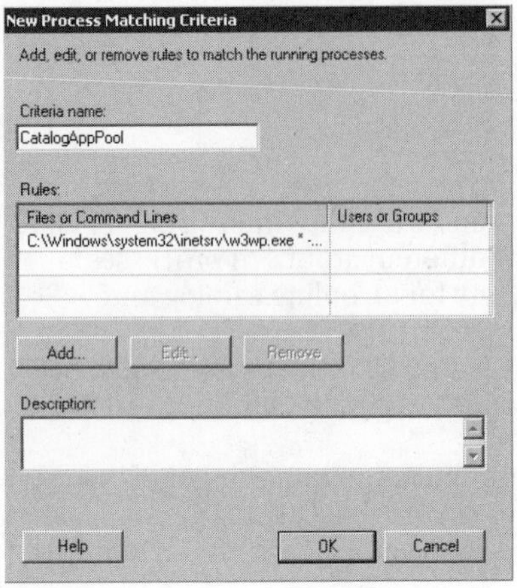

Figure 4-4. New Process Matching Criteria dialog box in Windows System Resource Manager

Click **OK** to dismiss the dialog box and complete the definition of the first process matching criteria. Repeat the process for the other AppPool. Call the second criteria `TransAppPool`.

Next, right-click **Resource Allocation Policies**, and select **New Resource Allocation Policy**. In the dialog box that comes up, click **Add**. In the next dialog box, in the **Process matching criteria** option box, select `CatalogAppPool`, and set the **Percentage of processor allocated for this resource** to **65**, as in Figure 4-5.

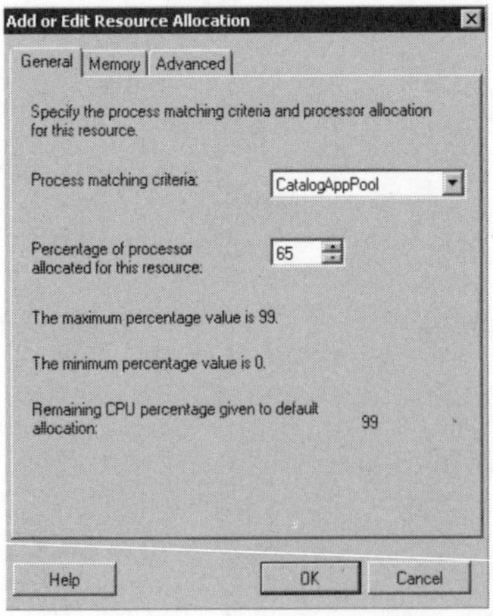

Figure 4-5. Add or Edit Resource Allocation dialog box in Windows System Resource Manager

That defines the minimum CPU time that will be available to this AppPool. Click **OK** to dismiss the dialog box. Repeat the process to add `TransAppPool` to the policy, giving it a 20 percent allocation. Give the policy a name, such as `CatalogTrans`. The dialog box should look like Figure 4-6.

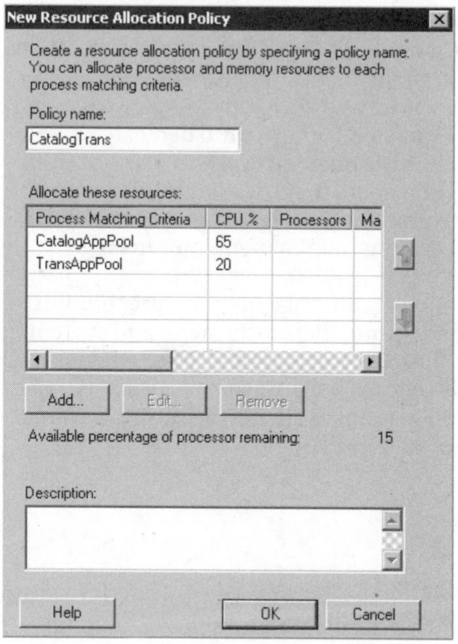

Figure 4-6. New Resource Allocation Policy dialog box in Windows System Resource Manager

Notice that **Available percentage of processor remaining** is 15 percent. That's the residual allocation that will be available for the OS and other processes. Click **OK** to dismiss the dialog box and create the policy.

To activate the policy, first right-click it in the left panel and select **Set as Managing Policy**. Then right-click **Windows System Resource Manager (Local)** at the top of the left panel and select **Start Windows System Resource Manager management**.

When enforcing CPU limitations, WSRM doesn't become active until aggregate total CPU use exceeds 70 percent. Applications can use more than their allocated share of the CPU until another managed application needs its share. At that point, WSRM lowers the priority of the application that's using more than its allocated share, which will decrease its CPU use.

For example, let's say that `Catalog` needs 80 percent of the CPU (vs. 65 percent allocated), `Trans` needs 5 percent (vs. 20 percent allocated), and the OS needs 10 percent (vs. 15 percent allocated), which is 95 percent altogether. WSRM will not adjust CPU usage or process priorities, because none of the managed process groups is limited within its specified minimums and because free CPU cycles are still available. However, if the load on `Trans` increases to where it *could* use 15 percent, then WSRM will lower the priority of `Catalog` so that it uses only 75 percent.

Another way of looking at this is that available CPU cycles aren't wasted. If one of the managed processes can use the CPU without limiting the cycles available to another managed process to something below its minimum allocation, then WSRM will allow that to happen. This allows more efficient sharing of hardware resources.

That behavior leads to a different way of using WSRM than described in the example. Instead of reserving minimum CPU use to a value somewhat above average use, you could make sure that a high-priority AppPool can always get as much of the CPU as it needs to cover loads during peak periods. Extending the earlier example, you might allocate 80 percent to `Trans`, 10 percent to `Catalog`, and 10 percent to residual. Average use as described earlier would be unimpaired. The difference is that if there were a load spike on `Trans`, it would be allowed to use 80 percent of the CPU, at the expense of the `Catalog` application.

In most environments, WSRM can reduce the need to segregate applications onto dedicated hardware so that they don't interfere with one another. Segregating business-critical applications from other apps, particularly when the other apps can change frequently or are much less stable, is a sound architectural principle. However, placing them on separate machines for that reason alone often introduces another set of problems related to things such as operations, deployment, monitoring, capacity planning, and so on.

WSRM has several other advanced features, including the ability to manage memory use, binding processes to certain processors, matching processes by the user or group that starts them, and switching to different policies at certain times. I suggest managing by CPU use instead of memory use whenever possible, since restricting memory use can have unexpected side effects, including results such as increased disk activity (paging). The other features tend to be most useful in environments with a large number of AppPools or ones that are running applications other than just IIS.

Common HTTP Issues

As sites grow and evolve, file and folder names change regularly. One side effect is inadvertent HTTP `404 Not Found` errors. Since errors can have a negative impact on both performance and site functionality, it's important to establish a process to identify `404 Not Found` errors when they appear. One way is to analyze your IIS log files regularly using a tool like Log Parser.

You can download Log Parser from this location:

```
http://www.microsoft.com/DownLoads/
    details.aspx?FamilyID=890cd06b-abf8-4c25-91b2-f8d975cf8c07&displaylang=en
```

Here's an example that uses Log Parser to find the `404 Not Found` errors in all the logs for my primary site and to display how many times the error has happened, along with the URL:

```
C:\>logparser "select count(*) as Times, cs-uri-stem as URL
    from <1>
    where sc-status = 404
    group by cs-uri-stem
    order by Times desc"

Times   URL
------  -----------------------------------
157807  /pages/defaultx.aspx
42      /static/myimage.jpg
```

The `<1>` in the query tells Log Parser to find the site with an ID of 1 (usually the default site) and to locate and process all of its log files. You can find the ID for your site either in the site's **Advanced**

Settings dialog box in IIS Manager or in the `applicationHost.config` file. Log Parser also supports several other ways of selecting a site.

Log Parser uses a SQL-like query language to parse, summarize, or transform a wide variety of source data, not just IIS logs. The documentation that's included in the download describes the syntax in detail. In addition to text output, it can also generate graphics and insert results into other data stores, such as SQL Server. It's a powerful and flexible tool, and I recommend it highly.

The process of searching logs like this becomes increasingly time-consuming and error prone on large sites, since the log files have to be collected from each server. For `.aspx` pages and other dynamic content, you can ease the process by logging HTTP errors (including `404 Not Found`s) to a central database. With the data in SQL Server, it is much easier to do reporting.

Handling HTTP errors related to images and other static content is best done by automated multiserver monitoring, rather than directly in your application. I'll cover that approach in more detail in Chapter 10.

■ **Caution** Be sure not to enable custom logging in IIS, since that disables kernel-mode caching (`http.sys`).

Keep in mind that `http.sys` generates its own log files, separate from IIS.

HTTP Redirects

IIS issues some HTTP redirects automatically. For example, IIS redirects requests to a folder that don't end in a slash to a URL that does end in a slash. For example, the following URL (without the slash):

```
http://www.12titans.net/samples
```

will be redirected to this:

```
http://www.12titans.net/samples/
```

Here's what the HTTP response looks like:

```
HTTP/1.1 302 Found
Cache-Control: private
Content-Type: text/html; charset=utf-8
Location: /samples/
X-Powered-By: ASP.NET
Server: Microsoft-IIS/7.0
X-AspNet-Version: 2.0.50727
Date: Tue, 17 Feb 2009 00:31:44 GMT

<html><head><title>Object moved</title></head>
<body><h2>Object moved to
<a href="%2fsamples%2f">here</a>.
</h2></body></html>
```

IIS will obtain the content for a folder-based URL from one of the configured default files. For example, with the previous URL, the content might come from this location:

```
http://www.12titans.net/samples/default.aspx
```

That means there are three equivalent URLs for default pages. Therefore, in order to avoid "hidden" redirects like these, it's important to use consistent URLs to reference default pages. The browser will also treat all three URLs as distinctly different from a caching perspective. After experiencing a redirect on the first URL in the previous example, if a user later clicked a link that referenced the third version, they would end up with two copies of the page in their browser cache.

Consistently using full, explicit URLs on your site is the best solution because it helps minimize the chances of duplicate caching on clients and proxies. In addition, `http.sys` won't cache "implied default" URLs like the first two shown earlier.

Notice that the redirect response in the previous example includes some HTML. The same is true for error responses such as a `404 Not Found`. Even when the requested object is an image, the server will still return HTML-formatted error text. The text is there for human readability, but people rarely see redirect responses, since the browser should immediately reissue the request. People sometimes see HTTP error pages, although usually they don't since browsers tend to display their own error pages instead.

For those reasons, it is advisable to use custom error pages and to keep the error text very short. Custom error pages that users are unlikely to see should be implemented with "plain" HTML and should not reference any images or external JavaScript or CSS files to avoid possible circular errors (such as if the image on a `404 Not Found` error page also can't be found).

Custom error pages that you use in association with the `Application_Error` event or with Web Events usually don't need to be as restrictive. Although simplicity is still a good idea, you might use `.aspx` pages in some cases. Just be sure that your error pages can't generate the same type of errors that you are using them for.

Since redirects require an additional server round-trip, you should avoid using them for your regular content. The most appropriate use of redirects is to manage situations where you would like to provide a way for old or archived pages to find content that you have recently moved or renamed. However, those redirects should be permanent, not temporary. Browsers can cache redirects if they're permanent, but not if they're temporary.

I'll cover some additional techniques in Chapter 5 for programmatically minimizing redirects for dynamic content, using ASP.NET.

HTTP Headers

As you saw earlier in the HTTP response for redirects, IIS and ASP.NET insert a few "informational" HTTP headers that are useful mostly for third-party statistical purposes. You can easily see them with a tool like the Fiddler proxy. They have no impact on either the browser or the web server, other than to add extra traffic to every request, so it's a good idea to remove them.

The issue with these headers is not that they are performance killers. Rather, their elimination is in keeping with the ultra-fast philosophy as explained earlier: every little bit helps, and lots of little bits *in the right places* add up quickly. HTTP headers, for example, can have an impact on *every* response generated by the server.

There is a minor side issue here relating to site security. There is a chance that a hacker might choose to target sites based on which operating system or web server the sites are using. Although there are many techniques a hacker might use to figure that out, there's no reason you need to make it easy for them by advertising your web server type and .NET version number in every HTTP response you generate.

Removing the headers doesn't do anything to make your site more secure, but it does reduce the risk that a hacker will use them to identify and target your site in the event that a specific IIS or .NET security vulnerability is identified. Like with performance and scalability, lots of small security improvements add up: every little bit helps.

■ **Tip** I recommend regularly looking at the HTTP responses generated by your site using a web proxy tool like Fiddler. That can help identify HTTP errors, unexpected HTTP headers, hidden redirects, and the like; it can be a very enlightening experience.

Removing the X-Powered-By Header

To remove the `X-Powered-By` header, first double-click **HTTP Response Headers** in IIS Manager. Then click the header, and select **Remove** on the right side, as in Figure 4-7.

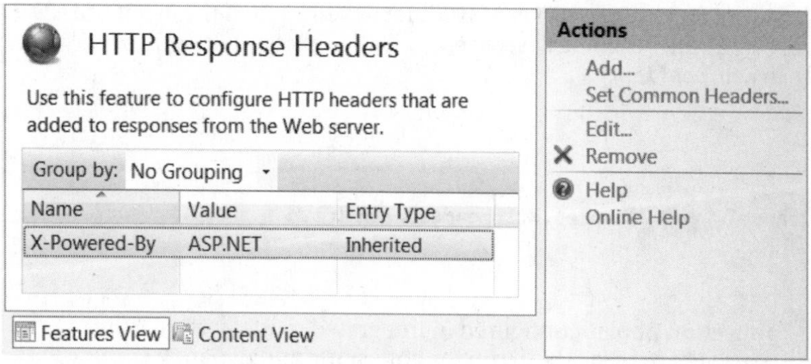

Figure 4-7. Removing informational HTTP headers using IIS Manager

Since the header type is `Inherited`, you can remove it either on a per-site basis (as shown in Figure 4-7) or for all web sites on your server by selecting the top-level machine node before opening the **HTTP Response Headers** panel.

Removing the Server Header

The next informational header in the example response shown earlier is `Server`. Unfortunately, you can't remove it using IIS Manager. Here's some example code for a custom `HttpModule` to remove it (see `App_Code\HttpHeaderCleanup.cs`):

```
using System;
using System.Web;

namespace Samples
```

```
{
    public class HttpHeaderCleanup : IHttpModule
    {
        public void Init(HttpApplication context)
        {
            context.PreSendRequestHeaders += OnPreSendRequestHeaders;
        }

        void OnPreSendRequestHeaders(object sender, EventArgs e)
        {
            HttpResponse response = HttpContext.Current.Response;
            response.Headers.Remove("Server");
        }

        public void Dispose()
        {
        }
    }
}
```

The code registers an event handler for the PreSendRequestHeaders event. When the event fires, the handler removes the Server header from the outgoing Response.

Next, register the HttpModule in web.config:

```
<system.webServer>
  <modules>
    . . .
    <add name="HttpHeaderCleanup" type="Samples.HttpHeaderCleanup" />
  </modules>
</system.webServer>
```

For this to work, be sure the application pool is configured in Integrated mode (which is the default). Setting it up this way will cause the HttpModule to run for both static and dynamic content.

Removing the ETag Header

IIS generates ETag headers for static content. For example, after cleaning up the headers as described earlier, the HTTP response for an image might look something like this:

```
HTTP/1.1 200 OK
Cache-Control: max-age=31536000,public
Content-Type: image/png
Last-Modified: Mon, 16 Jun 2008 10:17:50 GMT
Accept-Ranges: bytes
ETag: "f0f013b9acfc81:0"
Date: Tue, 17 Feb 2009 01:26:21 GMT
Content-Length: 4940
```

The idea behind the ETag header is that if the content expires, the browser can use an HTTP If-Modified-Since request to ask the server to send a new copy only if it has changed since it was first retrieved. For example:

```
If-Modified-Since: Mon, 16 Jun 2008 10:17:50 GMT
If-None-Match: "f0f013b9acfc81:0"
```

Although the concept sounds good in principle, with far-future expiration times, it's just as likely that your site will no longer be using the same content once it expires, so the If-Modified-Since call may never happen; the basic HTTP responses will vastly outnumber the potential If-Modified-Since calls. In addition, the round-trip to make such a call takes almost as long as retrieving small static objects, so you save very little unless the objects are large or costly to generate on the server side. Unless you have a specific application for them, you should therefore disable ETags, since that will shorten all of your static file response headers.

Unfortunately, as with the Server header, IIS doesn't provide a configuration setting to disable ETags. Luckily, though, you can handle them in the same way by adding the following code to the end of OnPreServerRequestHeaders():

```
response.Headers.Remove("ETag");
```

Removing the X-Aspnet-Version Header

You can remove the X-Aspnet-Version header from ASP.NET pages by setting the enableVersionHeader property to false in the <httpRuntime> tag in web.config:

```
<configuration>
  ...
 <system.web>
   <httpRuntime enableVersionHeader="false" />
   ...
 </system.web>
```

Using HTTP 1.1 Headers

Modern browsers now universally support HTTP 1.1, so in most environments there is no longer any need to explicitly support HTTP 1.0. The ASP.NET runtime will handle this automatically for you, but in case you are tempted to add your own headers for some reason, you should use the HTTP 1.1 version of headers that were intended to replace their HTTP 1.0 equivalents. In particular, Cache-Control: max-age should be used instead of Expires, and Cache-Control: no-cache should be used instead of a "back-dated" Expires header or Pragma: no-cache. There should never be a need to use either Expires or Pragma.

Compression

Compression of text files, including HTML, CSS, and JavaScript, can often reduce file sizes by 60 percent or more. This has several advantages:

- Server bandwidth is reduced.

- The content is received by the client more quickly (reduced latency).

- For content that the runtime doesn't have to recompress for every request, servers can deliver more requests per second when it is compressed.

There are also a couple of disadvantages:

- It takes server CPU resources to compress the file the first time. After that, compressed static files are cached by IIS.

- Special configuration is required to cache compressed dynamic files.

- Additional server disk space and RAM are required.

Note that Cassini, the development web server that's included with Visual Studio, does not support compression. However, during development on Vista or Windows Server, you can easily configure IIS to run your site instead of Cassini and set the startup URL in Visual Studio accordingly. When you're developing multiple web sites on the same machine, you can either use different port numbers on `localhost` for each one or create several aliases in your `hosts` file.

Enabling Compression

Before enabling compression, first install the dynamic compression role service for IIS if you haven't already (from Server Manager). Next, configure basic settings at the machine level by selecting your computer from IIS Manager and then double-clicking the **Compression** feature. See Figure 4-8.

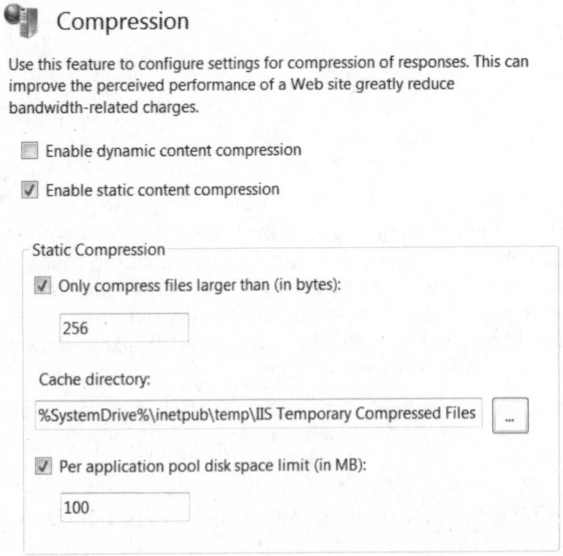

Figure 4-8. Compression configuration panel at the machine level in IIS Manager

From there, you can set a minimum size that files must be before the runtime will compress them, set the folder where the files should be cached once they are compressed, and set the maximum disk space to be allocated to the cache folder. Those settings are available only at the machine level, not at the web site level or below. You can also enable static or dynamic compression for all web sites on your machine. I suggest enabling static compression here, but not dynamic compression, as in Figure 4-8.

You can override server-wide enabling or disabling of compression at the web site, folder, or file level by selecting the target in IIS Manager and double-clicking the **Compression** feature. See Figure 4-9.

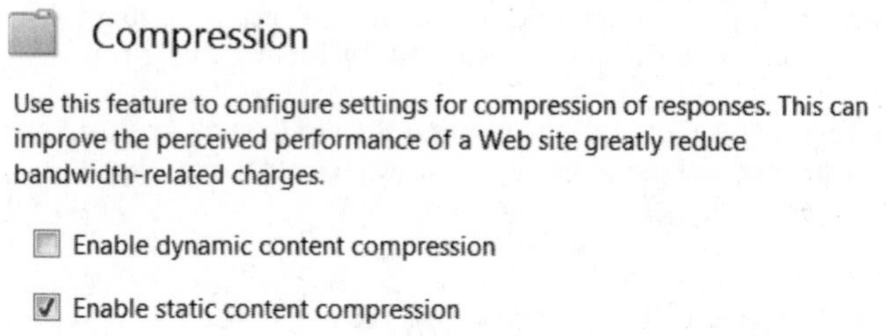

Compression

Use this feature to configure settings for compression of responses. This can improve the perceived performance of a Web site greatly reduce bandwidth-related charges.

☐ Enable dynamic content compression

☑ Enable static content compression

Figure 4-9. Compression configuration panel at the site, folder, or file level in IIS Manager

If you have entire folders where all of the dynamic files they contain can be compressed, you can enable that this way.

When enabling dynamic compression, the GUI modifies the main IIS configuration file at C:\Windows\System32\inetsrv\config\applicationHost.config by default, rather than web.config. You can do the same thing by adding a <urlCompression> section near the end of the file. For example:

```
<location path="Default Web Site/pages">
    <system.webServer>
        <urlCompression doDynamicCompression="true" />
    </system.webServer>
</location>
```

Enabling compression typically increases CPU use by roughly 3 to 5 percent for an active site. For most sites, the trade-off is generally worth it. However, if you have heavily accessed pages that are always unique per user and if your web servers are operating at high CPU loads, then you might consider not enabling compression for those files.

Setting Compression Options

Browsers tend to understand two different compression algorithms: gzip and deflate. IIS supports gzip in its default configuration but not **deflate**, even though the algorithm is available in the standard gzip.dll.

The gzip and deflate algorithms both support varying levels of compression. The higher the level, the more CPU time they spend trying to optimize and improve the degree of compression. Levels vary from zero to ten. The default is seven for both static and dynamic compression. A light level of compression for dynamic files minimizes the extra CPU load, while still providing most of the benefits.

Heavy compression for static files provides maximum benefits with minimal additional cost, since the compression is done only once and the file is then served many times.

Another configuration option controls whether the runtime disables compression if CPU use reaches a certain threshold. I don't suggest using that feature. On a heavily loaded site, where the load never drops below the default threshold of 50 percent for static content, your content might never be compressed. For dynamic content, even if your server is behaving normally, CPU use might periodically peak at 100 percent while delivering regular traffic. If IIS suddenly disabled dynamic compression when your server reached the default 90 percent point, network traffic might spike from sending uncompressed content, which could cause more problems than it solves; the number of requests per second that the server can deliver could easily decline. It's much better to allow the system to degrade gracefully when it reaches maximum CPU use. You can turn those features off by raising the "disable" thresholds to 100 percent.

You can make the changes suggested in this section, including enabling the `deflate` algorithm, by modifying the `<httpCompression>` section in `applicationHost.config` as follows (control over these settings is not available from the GUI; see `compress.config`):

```
<httpCompression
    directory="%SystemDrive%\inetpub\temp\IIS Temporary Compressed Files"
    staticCompressionDisableCpuUsage="100"
    dynamicCompressionDisableCpuUsage="100">
  <scheme name="gzip" dll="%Windir%\system32\inetsrv\gzip.dll"
      staticCompressionLevel="10" dynamicCompressionLevel="5" />
  <scheme name="deflate" dll="%Windir%\system32\inetsrv\gzip.dll"
      staticCompressionLevel="10" dynamicCompressionLevel="5" />
  <staticTypes>
    <add mimeType="text/*" enabled="true" />
    <add mimeType="message/*" enabled="true" />
    <add mimeType="application/x-javascript" enabled="true" />
    <add mimeType="*/*" enabled="false" />
  </staticTypes>
  <dynamicTypes>
    <add mimeType="text/*" enabled="true" />
    <add mimeType="message/*" enabled="true" />
    <add mimeType="application/x-javascript" enabled="true" />
    <add mimeType="*/*" enabled="false" />
  </dynamicTypes>
</httpCompression>
```

■ **Tip** If you are serving a particular MIME type that would benefit from compression, you should make sure that it's included in either `<staticTypes>` or `<dynamicTypes>`, or both, as appropriate.

Using web.config to Configure Compression

The default settings don't allow you to override `<urlCompression>` in `web.config`. As discussed, this tag is used to enable dynamic compression; it's set in `applicationHost.config` by default. To make it possible to use web.config instead, you could add the following XML after </configSections> in applicationHost.config, with the path attribute set to your web site:

```
<location path="Default Web Site" overrideMode="Allow">
    <system.webServer>
        <urlCompression />
    </system.webServer>
</location>
```

Alternatively, to enable this capability for all sites on your server, edit the <section> entry for urlCompression as follows (see compress.config):

```
<section name="urlCompression" overrideModeDefault="Allow" />
```

From a development, tracking, maintenance, and deployment perspective, it's preferable to keep site-specific configuration-related details in web.config when you can.

With the previous change, for folder-specific settings the GUI will create a small web.config file in each folder. I prefer to group settings together in the top-level web.config, which means making the entries by hand rather than using the GUI. For example:

```
<location path="pages">
  <system.webServer>
    <urlCompression doDynamicCompression="true" />
  </system.webServer>
</location>
```

Caching Compressed Content

By default, IIS only stores uncompressed content in the output cache. The runtime then compresses it right before sending it to the client. It's much more efficient to cache the compressed version instead. You can enable that feature with the dynamicCompressionBeforeCache property:

```
<system.webServer>
    <urlCompression dynamicCompressionBeforeCache="true" />
    . . .
</system.webServer>
```

With this feature enabled, if most of your pages can be output cached, then you might consider increasing dynamicCompressionLevel accordingly, since the runtime would not need to recompress every requested page.

Consider caching both compressed and uncompressed versions of your pages. You can do that using the VaryByContentEncoding property of the OutputCache directive. For example:

```
<%@ OutputCache Duration="86400" VaryByParam="None" VaryByContentEncoding="gzip;deflate" %>
```

You can also specify that property in a cache profile in web.config:

```
<add name="Cache1Day" duration="86400" varyByParam="none"
    varyByContentEncoding="gzip;deflate" />
```

However, be aware that `VaryByContentEncoding` will disable `http.sys` caching since the runtime needs to decide which cached version to use. You should therefore use it selectively.

Programmatically Enabling Compression

There are cases where it's not optimal to compress a page. For example, pages that can't be output cached and are less than about 1KB in size, and that therefore fit in a single TCP packet, are generally not good candidates for dynamic compression. Since the usual delay between successive response packets doesn't exist when there's only one packet, the reduction in data size may not be worth the increase in latency caused by the compression.

In addition, if your servers are frequently running close to 100 percent CPU utilization, you might want to consider selectively disabling dynamic compression, particularly for pages that can't be output cached.

You can programmatically enable dynamic compression by adding the following code to your `Page_Load()` method (see `compress.aspx`):

```
if (!String.IsNullOrEmpty(this.Request.ServerVariables["SERVER_SOFTWARE"]))
    this.Request.ServerVariables["IIS_EnableDynamicCompression"] = "1";
```

The check for `SERVER_SOFTWARE` is to make sure we're running on IIS, since Cassini doesn't allow us to set `ServerVariables`, nor does it support compression.

HTTP Keep-Alives

You should not disable HTTP keep-alives. If you do, IE will revert to the HTTP 1.0 behavior of one request per TCP connection. If the browser is forced to open a new connection for every object on the page, it can have a very negative impact on performance.

The default settings for IIS are to enable keep-alives, with a 120-second timeout; if the browser hasn't reused the connection after 120 seconds, IIS will close it. Depending on the nature of how your users interact with your site, since opening a new connection increases request latency, you might consider extending the timeout. If users tend to navigate to a page, read for a while, and then click to a new page, then a longer timeout might make sense. If they tend to click a few links quickly and leave your site quickly, then there's no need to change the default.

Although keeping the connection open does consume memory on the server, it's only roughly 1KB per connection, or 1MB per 1,000 connections. It's a small price to pay for a significant improvement in performance.

Optimizing Your URLs

Since URLs appear in HTTP request headers, as well as in your HTML, it's a good idea to avoid excessively long ones. Yahoo, for example, has a long history of using single-character paths in certain parts of its site.

As a rule of thumb, you should try to keep both file names and folder names less than about eight characters long (two to six is best), except where search engine optimization comes into play. Folder hierarchies should be flat, rather than deep. For example, the following:

```
http://s1.12titans.net/images/mypic.jpg
```

is much better than this:

```
http://coolstaticfiles.12titans.net/reallycoolimages/picsfromlastyear/mycoolpic.jpg
```

If you need to work with an existing hierarchy that uses long names or if your system needs longer names to ease some aspects of development or maintenance, then you can shorten the long URLs using virtual directories or URL rewriting.

Virtual Directories

You can use virtual directories with short names to refer to the actual folders. You may be able to bypass one or more levels of an on-disk folder hierarchy this way.

For example, if you wanted to map the long path shown earlier to a shorter one under the `images` folder, then right-click the folder in IIS Manager, and select **Add Virtual Directory**. See Figure 4-10.

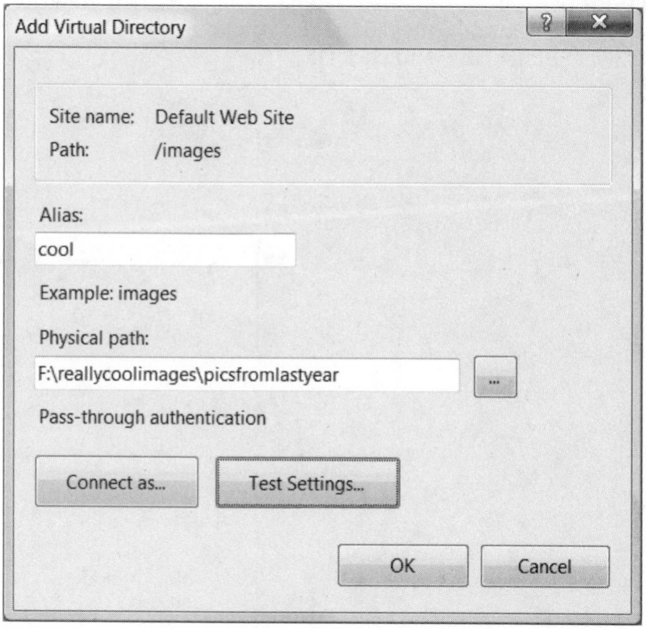

Figure 4-10. Adding a virtual directory to shorten your URLs

Type in the alias you'd like to use and the physical path that you want to map to that alias. In the example, IIS would map all files in the folder `F:\reallycoolimages\picsfromlastyear` to `http://s1.12titans.net/images/cool/`.

URL Rewriting

Although URL rewriting is often used to make URLs search engine friendly, you can also use it to make them shorter. You might want to do this in cases where you are unable to rename the existing files or folders for some reason or when you want to have a local file structure different from the public one. You can also use URL rewriting to hide query strings from `http.sys`, which can make a page cacheable that wouldn't be otherwise.

You can rewrite URLs in IIS using the URL Rewrite Module or in ASP.NET using an `HttpModule`. Because of the way that URL rewriting interacts with web forms, the `HttpModule` approach is generally better for `.aspx` pages. The IIS approach tends to be better for static content, although there are also cases where you may want to use the two approaches together. See Chapter 7 for details on the `HttpModule` approach.

To use the URL Rewrite Module with IIS, first download and install it:

`http://www.iis.net/extensions/URLRewrite`

As an example, let's use it to shorten a URL. Create a folder in your web site called `mylongfoldername`, put an image in it called `logo.png`, and configure the web site in IIS.

Next, click your web site in the **Connections** panel in IIS Manager. Then double-click **URL Rewrite** in the center panel to enter the configuration area. Click **Add Rules** in the right-hand panel to bring up the **Add rule(s)** dialog box as in Figure 4-11. Select **Blank rule**, and click **OK**.

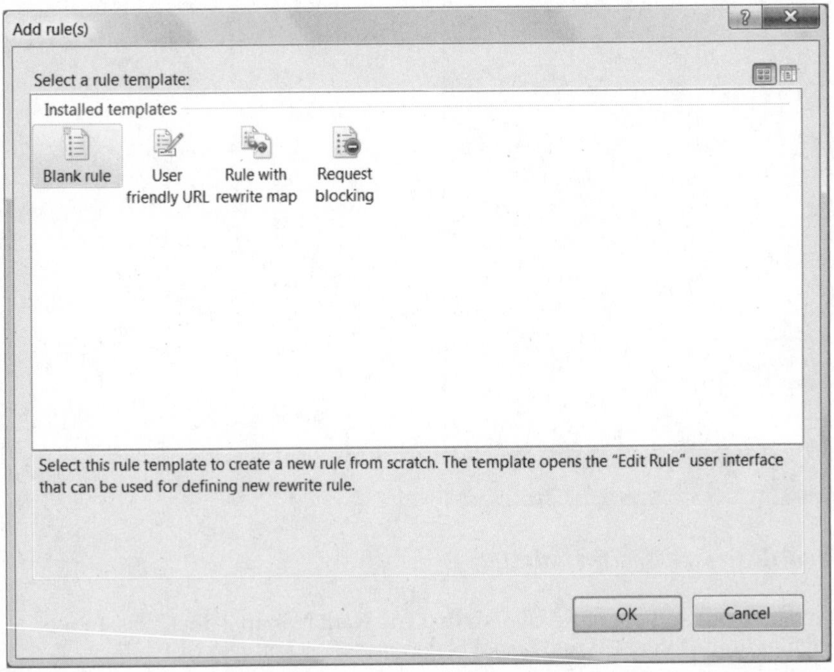

Figure 4-11. Selecting the blank URL rewriting rule template

Next, in the **Edit Rule** screen, enter a name in **Name** for the rule, and enter ^m/(.*) in **Pattern**. See Figure 4-12.

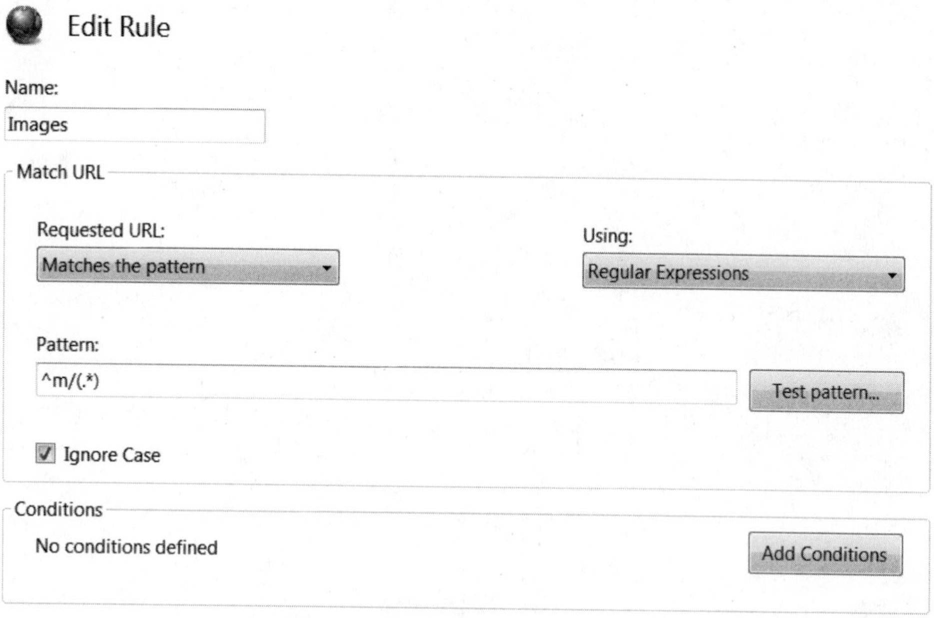

Edit Rule

Name:

```
Images
```

Match URL

Requested URL:

```
Matches the pattern          ▾
```

Using:

```
Regular Expressions          ▾
```

Pattern:

```
^m/(.*)
```

Test pattern...

☑ Ignore Case

Conditions

No conditions defined

Add Conditions

Figure 4-12. Entering a regular expression pattern for the incoming URL

The **Pattern** field contains a regular expression that matches the incoming URL. In this case, you're looking for a URL that starts with the letter *m*, then a slash, and anything else after that. You use the parentheses to establish a *capture group*, which you can reference later in the rewritten URL. Capture groups are numbered from left to right, from one to *N*. Capture group zero is a special case that represents the entire incoming URL.

To test the regular expression, click **Test pattern**. Enter an example of an incoming URL that the pattern is supposed to match as the **Input data to test**. Click the **Test** button to see the results of the test, including the capture groups. See Figure 4-13.

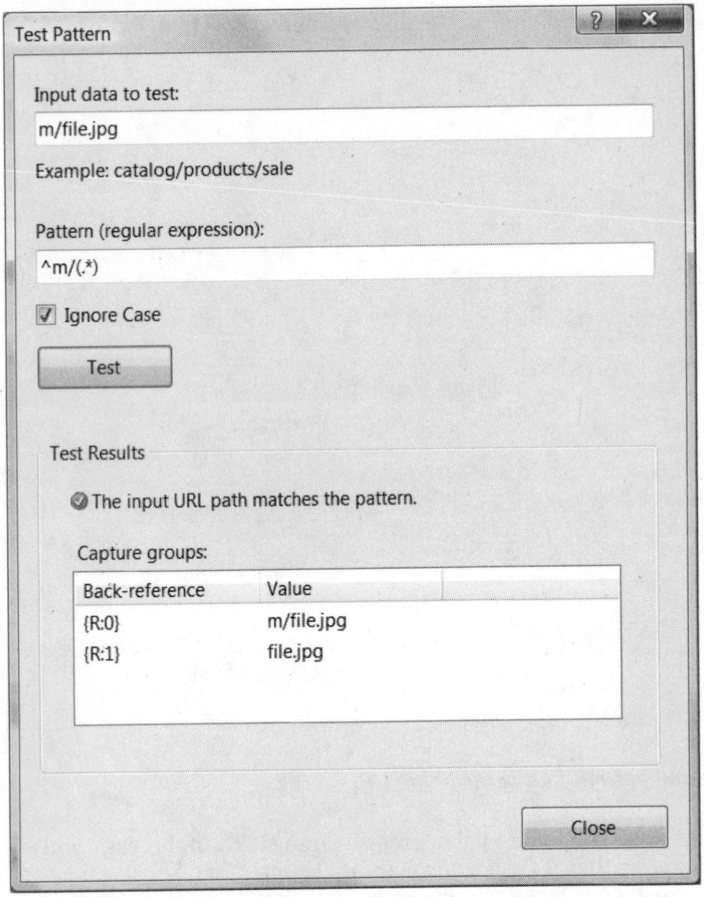

Figure 4-13. Testing the regular expression

Click **Close** to dismiss the **Test Pattern** dialog box, and enter `mylongfoldername/{R:1}` in **Rewrite URL**. Leave the other settings at their defaults. See Figure 4-14.

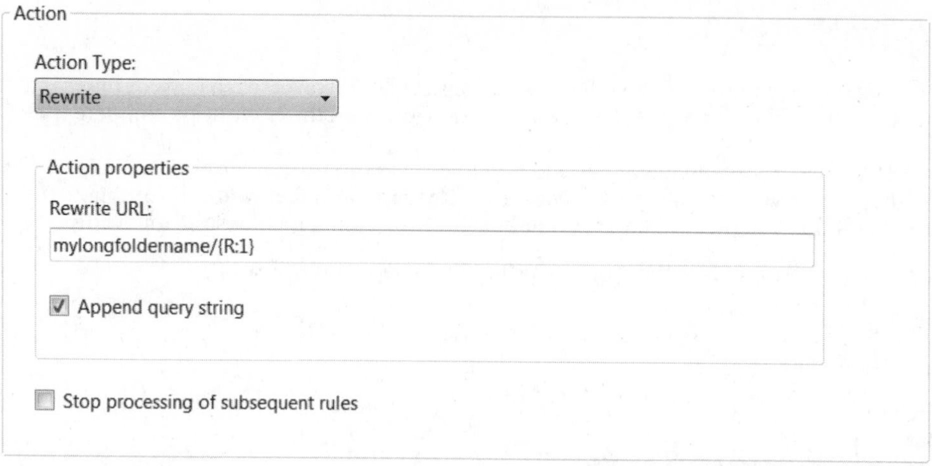

Figure 4-14. *Entering the rewrite URL using a capture group from the regular expression*

This is the name of the local resource, so you have the long folder name, followed by {R:1}, which is the first capture group from the regular expression.

Click **Apply** at the upper right of the screen, which will activate the rewrite rule and save it in the web site's web.config.

■ **Note** Since adding a new URL rewrite rule updates web.config, it will also cause your site to restart.

After applying the rule, IIS will map an incoming URL like http://localhost/m/logo.png to http://localhost/mylongfoldername/logo.png.

If you have a number of rules, you might find it easier to edit web.config directly, instead of using the GUI. For example:

```
<system.webServer>
  . . .
  <rewrite>
    <rules>
      <rule name="Images">
        <match url="^m/(.*)" />
        <action type="Rewrite" url="mylongfoldername/{R:1}" />
      </rule>
    </rules>
  </rewrite>
</system.webServer>
```

Managing Traffic

For most sites, having search engines visit regularly is very desirable. However, each page or file that a search engine requests presents a load on your servers and network, and those requests compete with your regular users.

For some sites, the load from search engines and other bots can be substantial. You can help manage the load they put on your site by using `robots.txt`, site maps, and bandwidth throttling.

The type of content that you may want to prevent bots from accessing includes the following:

- Images, CSS, and other files that you use primarily for layout purposes

- JavaScript files

- Registration pages

- Search results

- Certain file types, such as `.zip`, `.avi`, `.docx`, `.pptx`, and so on

- Pages that require authentication

- Lists of users who are currently online, and similar content that's only meaningful to someone connected to your site

In addition, it's a good idea to partition your images into folders, based on those that would be suitable for image search and those that wouldn't be, to make it easier to block access to the latter. For example, in an image gallery application, you might want to allow access to thumbnails but not to full-size images.

Using robots.txt

You can place a `robots.txt` file in the root of your site to help inform search engines and other bots about the areas of your site that you don't want them to access. For example, you may not want bots to access the content of your `images` folder:

```
User-agent: *
Disallow: /images/
```

You can also provide instructions for particular bots. For example, to exclude Google image search from your entire site, use this:

```
User-agent: Googlebot-Image
Disallow: /
```

The `robots.txt` standard is unfortunately very limited; it only supports the `User-agent` and `Disallow` fields, and the only wildcard allowed is when you specify it by itself in `User-agent`, as in the previous example.

Google has introduced support for a couple of extensions to the `robots.txt` standard. First, you can use limited patterns in pathnames. You can also specify an `Allow` clause. Since those extensions are specific to Google, you should probably only use them with one of the Google user agents or with `Googlebot`, which all of its bots recognize.

For example, you can block PNG files from all Google user agents as follows:

```
User-agent: Googlebot
Disallow: /*.png$
```

As with regular expressions, the asterisk means to match any sequence of characters, and the dollar sign means to match the end of the string. Those are the only two pattern matching characters that Google supports.

To disable all bots except for Google, use this:

```
User-agent: *
Disallow: /

User-agent: Googlebot
Allow: /
```

To exclude pages with sort as the first element of a query string that can be followed by any other text, use this:

```
User-agent: Googlebot
Disallow: /*?sort
```

One trick with robots.txt that you might consider is to set a cookie on clients that read it, using the technique for static files that I covered earlier (see Figure 2-6). Since most bots read robots.txt and most users don't, you can use the presence of the cookie as an indication that the client is probably a bot.

Although many bots accept cookies, not all of them do, and every once in a while a real user might access your robots.txt. That means you shouldn't consider the cookie to be a foolproof indication that a user is a bot; it's just a hint, although often it's a more reliable one than trying to decode user-agent strings, which are sometimes forged by bots.

Another trick to consider is generating robots.txt dynamically, rather than having it be static. That would allow you to log information about the associated requests (such as IP address and user agent string), to set custom performance counters, and to quickly adapt to new bots or new content.

Site Maps

Site maps are XML files that list all of the URLs on your site, along with when the content was last modified, an indication regarding how often it changes, and a relative priority. By providing a site map, you can help search engines optimize how often they revisit your site. If the content on a particular page never changes, you can let search engines know so they don't keep reading it repeatedly.

You can find the site map specification online at http://www.sitemaps.org/. Here's an example:

```
<?xml version="1.0" encoding="UTF-8"?>
<urlset xmlns="http://www.sitemaps.org/schemas/sitemap/0.9">
  <url>
    <loc>http://www.12titans.net/p/default.aspx</loc>
    <lastmod>2009-12-01</lastmod>
    <changefreq>daily</changefreq>
    <priority>0.8</priority>
  </url>
</urlset>
```

You list each URL in a separate `<url>` block. Only the `<loc>` tag is required; the others are optional.

Several tools are available online to help you generate site maps and submit them to search engines. If you choose to do it yourself, be sure to use correct XML syntax, including escaping entities such as ampersands.

You can advertise the availability of a site map in your `robots.txt` file:

```
Sitemap: http://www.12titans.net/sitemaps/sitemap.xml.gz
```

You can also submit the URL of the site map file directly to search engines. The details vary by search engine. For Google, you should do it using its Webmaster Tools.

Bandwidth Throttling

Although it's most often used when serving media content, you can also use bandwidth throttling as a traffic and load management technique. One aspect of the concept involves sending content more slowly to bots than to real users. That can allow more bandwidth and CPU cycles to be available to real users when your site is being heavily used so your user's content will load faster than it would otherwise.

You can also use bandwidth throttling to make sure that you give users a chance to change their minds about whether they really want a file they're downloading. For example, with streaming video, a user might watch the first few seconds and then decide they don't want to download the whole thing. If you send it to them in a high-speed mode, it might be too late to cancel when the time comes. Using bandwidth throttling, you can slow things down and give them time to cancel, while not interfering with the user's streaming experience. In addition to improving overall system performance, this can also help reduce your bandwidth costs, both by reducing the total amount of data transferred and by lowering your peak transfer rate.

To use bandwidth throttling, install the IIS extension:

```
http://www.iis.net/extensions/BitRateThrottling
```

To enable it from IIS Manager, first click the site or machine in the **Connections** pane that you want to enable it for. Double-click **Bit Rate Throttling** in the center panel, and click **Enable** in the **Actions** pane on the right side. That will enable throttling for most media content, such as `.avi` and `.mp3` files.

For media content, IIS will start by sending the files in high-speed burst mode. After a little while, the throttling module will reduce the rate to the encoded bit rate. For example, consider an `.avi` file that's encoded at 500Kbps. IIS will start by sending 20 seconds of the file at full speed and then limit bandwidth to 100 percent of the encoded 500Kbps rate after that.

For our purposes here, the real power of the Bit Rate Throttling extension comes into play using its programmability. You can set server variables to control the speed of a given response. You could do that from an `.aspx` page, an `HttpModule`, or even an `HttpHandler`.

You might consider applying bandwidth throttling programmatically according to conditions such as the following:

- Based on the `User-Agent` string (search engines and other bots, media players, and so on)

- Particular pages, folders, images, domains, and so on

- Time of day

- Day of the week or month

- Cookies (user or role, VIP users, banned users, and so on)

- Leeched content (images used directly on other sites; determined with the HTTP referrer)

- Request rate (use cookies or session state to track the history)

- HTTP 1.0 requests (identify using `Request.ServerVariables["SERVER_PROTOCOL"]`)

- Requests from proxies (identify using the `Via` HTTP header)

- IP addresses (countries or states, identified using a Geo-IP database; or certain IP ranges)

- Performance counters (CPU, network, disk)

As an example, let's create an `HttpModule` that limits the download speed of `.zip` files (see `App_Code\Throttle.cs`):

```
using System;
using System.Web;

namespace Samples
{
    public class Throttle : IHttpModule
    {
        public void Init(HttpApplication context)
        {
            context.PostRequestHandlerExecute += OnPostRequestHandlerExecute;
        }

        void OnPostRequestHandlerExecute(object source, EventArgs e)
        {
            HttpApplication application = (HttpApplication)source;
            HttpContext context = application.Context;
            HttpResponse response = context.Response;
            if (response.ContentType == "application/x-zip-compressed")
            {
                HttpRequest request = context.Request;
                if (!String.IsNullOrEmpty(request.ServerVariables["SERVER_SOFTWARE"]))
                {
                    request.ServerVariables["ResponseThrottler-InitialSendSize"] = "20";
                    request.ServerVariables["ResponseThrottler-Rate"] = "10";
                }
            }
        }

        public void Dispose()
        {
        }
    }
}
```

After the request handler runs, you check the MIME type of the response to see whether it's a `.zip` file. If it is and if you're running under IIS instead of Cassini, you set two server variables. `ResponseThrottler-InitialSendSize` indicates that you want the first 20KB of the file to be downloaded at full network speed, and `ResponseThrottler-Rate` says that you want the rest of the file to be download at 10Kbps (about 1.25KB/s).

Next, register the `HttpModule` in `web.config`:

```
<system.webServer>
  . . .
  <modules>
    . . .
    <add name="ThrottleModule" type="Samples.Throttle, App_Code"/>
  </modules>
</system.webServer>
```

This tells IIS to run it with static content too.

Next, put a `.zip` file in the web site and access it from a browser. After an initial burst, you will see the download rate settle in at around the target (the rate displayed by IE is an average, not the current rate). See Figure 4-15.

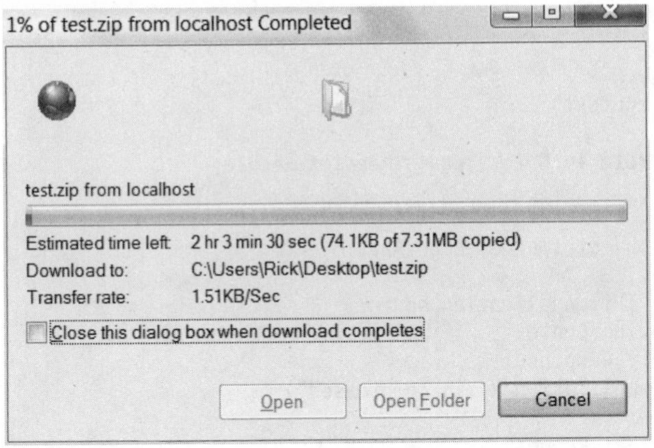

Figure 4-15. Bandwidth-limited download

Failed Request Tracing

Don't let the name of the IIS *Failed Request Tracing* (FRT) feature fool you. In addition to tracing requests that *fail*, you can also use it to trace successful requests. In particular, you can use it to trace requests that take too long or that aren't being processed in a way that you expect, such as with caching or compression.

For example, let's analyze a case where `http.sys` is not caching a particular image. First, you will need to install the feature. From Server Manager, select **Go To Roles**. In the **Web Server (IIS)** section, under **Role Services**, select **Add Role Services**. Under **Health and Diagnostics**, select **Tracing**, and click **Install**.

Next, open IIS Manager, open your web site in the **Connections** panel, and click the folder that contains the files of interest. Then double-click the **Failed Request Tracing Rules** icon in the IIS section of the **Features View**, and click **Add** in the right-hand panel. For this example, you're interested in all PNG files in the selected folder, so in the **Specify Content to Trace** dialog box, select **Custom** and enter *.png as the filename pattern, as in Figure 4-16.

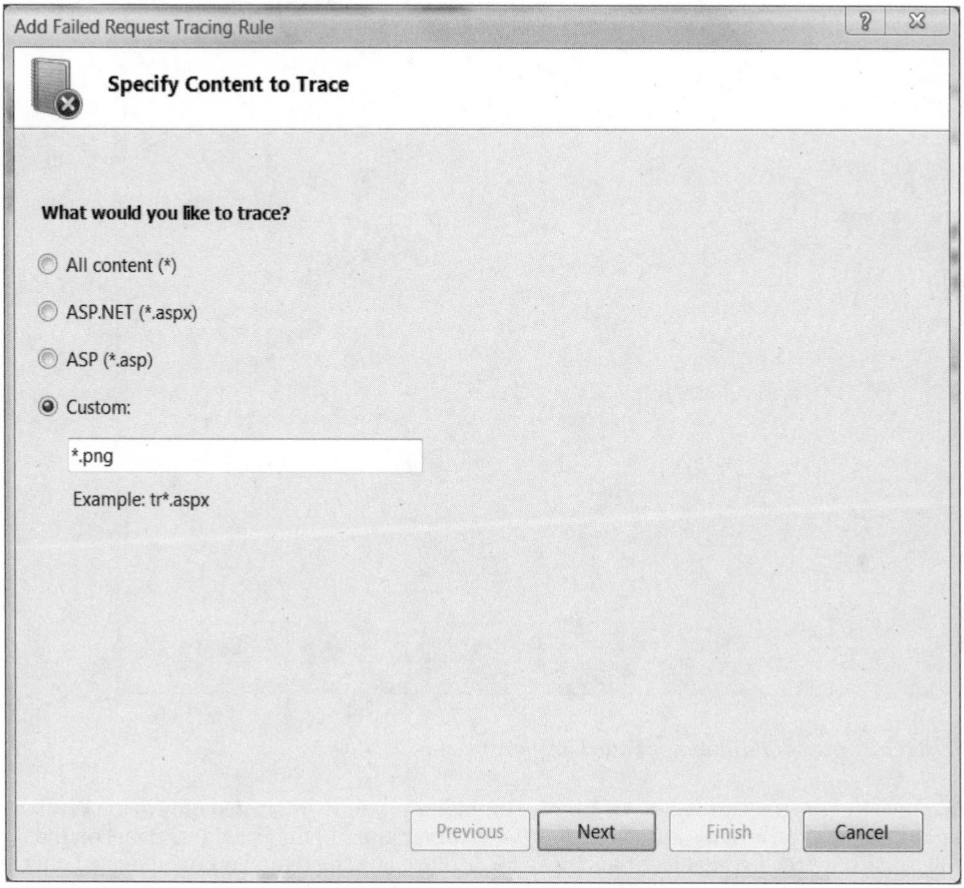

Figure 4-16. Specifying content to trace for Failed Request Tracing

Click the **Next** button, and specify the trace conditions. In this case, you're interested in successful responses rather than errors or pages that take too long to execute (which are, however, very useful in their own right). Select the **Status code(s)** box, and enter **200**, which is the HTTP response code that indicates success. See Figure 4-17.

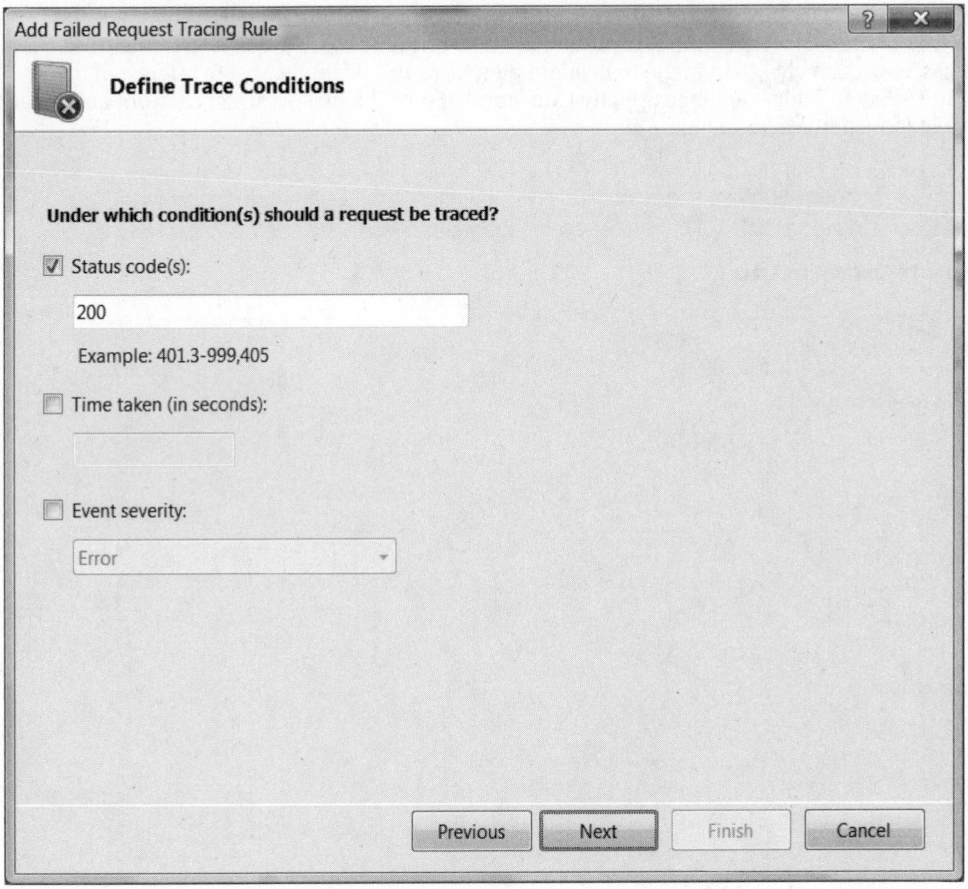

Figure 4-17. *Defining trace conditions for Failed Request Tracing*

Click **Next** to select the trace providers of interest. In this case, you're interested only in the **WWW Server** provider. Uncheck the others, and select the **WWW Server** entry in the **Providers** panel on the left, which will cause the **Areas** available for tracing to be displayed on the right. You're interested only in the **Cache** area, so uncheck the others as in Figure 4-18. Since the trace information is written to disk as an XML file, it's a good idea to select only the information you're interested in to limit the size of the file, particularly when using tracing on a server in production.

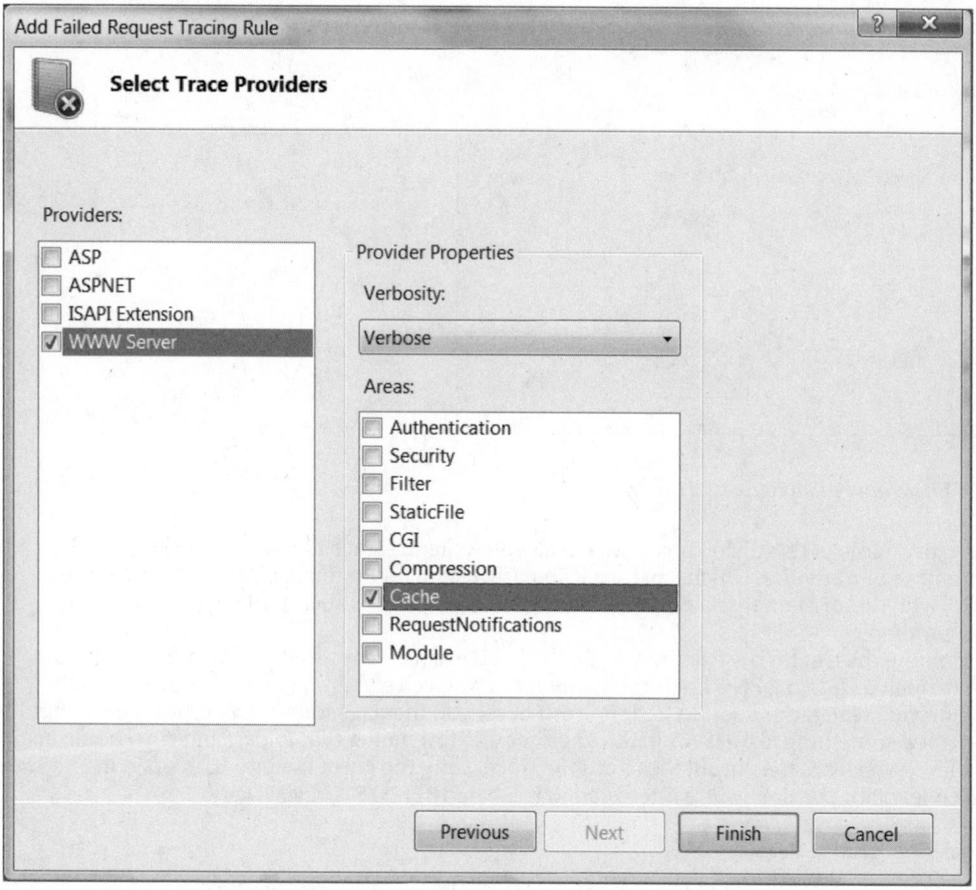

Figure 4-18. Selecting trace providers for Failed Request Tracing

Click **Finish** to complete creation of the rule.

Next, you need to enable FRT to activate the rule. Click the web site in the **Connections** panel. Then click **Failed Request Tracing** on the right-hand panel, under **Manage Web Site ➤ Configure**. In the dialog box that comes up, select **Enable**, as in Figure 4-19. Then click **OK** to activate FRT.

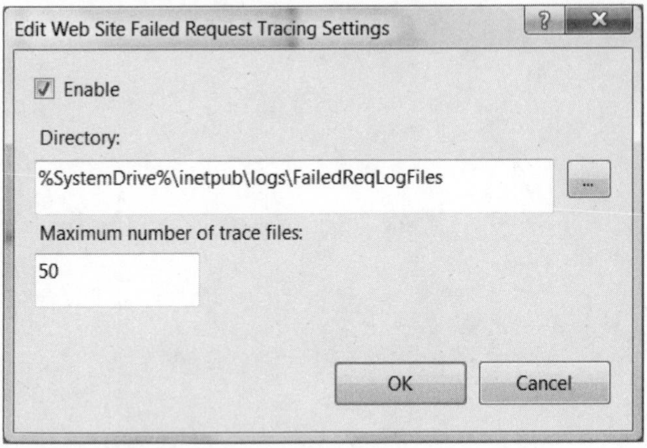

Figure 4-19. Enabling Failed Request Tracing

The directory name in this dialog box is where IIS will write the trace files. You can also specify a maximum number of trace files, which can be particularly useful for systems in production, to avoid filling the disk with them. In many cases, you will only need a small number of trace files in order to diagnose the problem.

Before running the test for the example, open the `FailedReqLogFiles` folder in Windows Explorer. Next, use IE to open a URL to a PNG file from the folder in the web site under test that you originally specified when you created the rule. Hit Ctrl+Refresh to refresh the page four or five times. There should be a folder named something like `W3SVC1` in the Explorer window. Open that folder, and you should see several XML files, which are the output files from the trace. Drag the latest file into IE to open it, and click the **Compact View** tab. The line you're interested in is labeled `HTTPSYS_CACHEABLE`:

```
HttpsysCacheable="true", Reason="OK",
CachePolicy="USER_INVALIDATES", TimeToLive="0"
```

This says that the file is cacheable by `http.sys`. If you hit Ctrl+Refresh enough times in a row, you'll notice that FRT stops creating new trace files after the file starts to be served from `http.sys`.

Now let's change the URL to include a query string, which will prevent `http.sys` from caching it. Just adding a question mark to the end of the URL will be enough. Hit Ctrl+Refresh a bunch of times in a row, as before. This time, notice that the files don't stop appearing in the folder as they did before. Open the latest XML file in IE, and click the **Compact View** tab as discussed earlier. The `HTTPSYS_CACHEABLE` line reads as follows:

```
HttpsysCacheable="false", Reason="STATIC_REQUEST_QUERYSTRING",
CachePolicy="NO_CACHE", TimeToLive="0"
```

This tells you that the file is not cacheable by `http.sys`, and the reason is that the request includes a query string.

You can use FRT to help diagnose unexpected behavior in caching, in compression, or during many of the other steps in the IIS pipeline. It's also useful to catch pages that are running slowly. For example, you might collect tracing on all of the requests that take longer than one second to execute to help identify bottlenecks. In production environments, I suggest enabling it on as few servers as you can and only for as long as you need it, since there is a performance cost when it's running.

Miscellaneous IIS Performance Tuning

Here are a few tips for tuning IIS:

- Order the list of file types for default documents by their approximate frequency of use, and delete any file types that you don't use. For example, if most of your default pages are `default.aspx` and you have a few `index.htm`, then place `default.aspx` at the top of the list, followed by `index.htm`, and remove all the other entries. If `default.aspx` is located at the end of the list, then IIS will look for all the other files every time users access the default page. You can make this change at both the site level and for individual folders.

- Remove modules that you aren't using. For example, public-facing web sites generally don't require `WindowsAuthentication`. Configured modules still handle pipeline events, even if you're not using them. This also helps from a security perspective by reducing the attack surface of the application.

- Don't allow the use of `web.config` files in subdirectories of your applications. You should have only a single `web.config` at the top level. With that restriction in place, you can modify `applicationHost.config` as follows so that IIS doesn't have to search for config files where they won't exist, including in odd places such as `file.htm/web.config`, where IIS is checking to see whether the file name might be a folder:

```
<system.applicationHost>
    <sites>
        . . .
        <virtualDirectoryDefaults allowSubDirConfig="false" />
    </sites>
</system.applicationHost>
```

Summary

In this chapter, I covered the following:

- When you should use multiple AppPools or a web garden

- Configuring recycling on your AppPools

- How `HttpModules` and request handlers fit into the IIS request-processing pipeline

- Using WSRM to help manage contention between AppPools

- Using Log Parser to find HTTP errors in your log files

- Using consistent URLs to help eliminate unnecessary HTTP redirects

- How to remove the `X-Powered-By`, `Server`, `ETag`, and `X-Aspnet-Version` HTTP headers

- Enabling static and dynamic compression, and optimizing the compression configuration settings

- Enabling caching for compressed content

- Programmatically enabling compression

- Why it's important not to disable HTTP keep-alives

- Using virtual directories to reduce the length of your URLs

- Using URL rewriting to optimize your URLs

- Using `robots.txt` and site maps to help limit the load on your site from search engines and other bots

- Using bandwidth throttling to help manage network traffic and total data transferred

- Using Failed Request Tracing to trace requests that take too long or that aren't being processed in a way that you expect, such as with caching or compression

- Miscellaneous tips for tuning IIS

■■■

CHAPTER 5

ASP.NET Threads and Sessions

For many ASP.NET-based web sites, an effective way to improve site performance and scalability is by thoroughly addressing issues related to threads and sessions.

In this chapter, I'll cover the following:

- The very negative impact of using synchronous pages when you make out-of-process or off-box calls

- Improving the scalability of your site by using asynchronous pages and background worker threads

- A brief overview of locking as it applies to asynchronous programming

- The scalability impact of the default session state provider, why it's best to avoid session state if you can, and what the alternatives are

- An approach to building a customized and highly scalable session state provider

Threads Affect Scalability

I've noticed that many large sites end up spending a lot of effort optimizing their systems in the wrong places. As an example, let's say that you identify a slow page. You find that it takes 100ms to retrieve the page on an unloaded system, even though it takes much longer when the system is under load. Table 5-1 shows a breakdown for where the page is spending its time, including the time to receive the request and send the response.

Table 5-1. Example Performance Measurement Results

Task	Time
Receive request at web tier	0.5KB @ 128Kbps = 5ms
Obtain needed data from database	77ms
Generate response HTML	2ms
Send response	5KB @ 384Kbps = 16ms

When faced with this data, the first place many people would look for improvements is the long-running task, which in this case is the database access. In some environments, the database is a black box, so it can't be tuned and is written off. When it can be tuned, the usual approach is to put a lot of emphasis on query optimization. Although that certainly can be helpful, it often doesn't solve the problem. In later chapters, I'll show some reasons why that's the case and what you can do about it. For this example, let's assume the queries are already fully tuned.

The next place to look would probably be the send and receive times. However, a typical initial response is that "you can't do anything about the client's data transmission rates, so forget about the request and response times." As I've shown in Chapter 2, that clearly is not the whole story.

That leaves the time to generate the HTML, which in this case is only 2 percent of the total request-processing time. Because that's the part of the application most readily under the control of developers, optimizing the time spent there is often where performance improvement efforts are spent. However, even if you improve that time by 50 percent, down to 1ms, the overall end-to-end improvement seen by end users may only be 1 percent.

I would like to suggest looking at this problem in a much different way. In a correctly designed architecture, *the CPU time spent to process a request at the web tier should not be a **primary** factor in overall site performance or scalability.* In the previous example, an extra 2ms one way or the other won't be noticeable by an end user. When a web site gets to the point where web servers are CPU limited, with proper design it should be possible to simply add another load-balanced server. That should distribute the load and either allow the site to scale or push the scalability issues into another tier, such as the database.

Let's say that in this example, you repeated the test under a target load of 1,200 simultaneous users on a single server and found that the same page takes 10 seconds to execute. To keep the response time under a goal of 1 second, you have to scale the load back by a factor of 10 and find that the system can handle only 120 users (120 requests per second) per server. At that load and with 2ms of CPU time per request, a single-CPU server is only 24 percent busy (`0.002 * 120`). However, as the number of users increases, the CPU use does not (instead, response time increases).

If you add another server, you can support only another 120 users. If your goal is thousands or tens of thousands of users, that's a lot of hardware. Reducing the CPU time spent by the web tier in generating the pages reduces the CPU load on each machine, but it doesn't improve throughput or reduce the number of machines you need. Your site isn't scalable.

What's happening in the example is that the site's throughput is limited by the IIS and ASP.NET thread pools. By default, they process only 12 requests at a time per CPU. Above that, requests are queued. Each request takes 100ms to process from end to end, so one thread can process 10 requests per second. With 12 requests at a time, that becomes 120 requests per second.

In the example, caching helps when you can use it to eliminate the database request. Threads come into play when you can't. When the CPU time used by your application increases, you can compensate for it by adding more servers or upgrading to faster CPUs, more CPU cores, and so on. For most small to medium-scale sites, buying or leasing moderate amounts of hardware is usually less expensive than developer labor spent focused on optimizing CPU time. For larger sites, when CPU use per server averages 70 to 80+ percent under peak load, then it makes sense to put effort into optimizing the CPU time used by the application. However, the goal in that case would normally be to minimize the number of servers needed, not to improve performance from the user's perspective. Of course, there are cases where CPU use is the dominant factor that you should address first, but once a site is in production, those cases tend to be the exception and not the rule. Developers and testers tend to catch those cases early. Unfortunately, threading issues often don't appear until a site goes into production and is under heavy load.

ASP.NET Page Life Cycle

As I discussed in Chapter 4, HTTP requests processed by IIS go through a series of states on the way to generating a response. Similarly, ASP.NET pages also go through a series of states. As with IIS, the runtime generates events at each state that you can register a handler for and take action on. See Figure 5-1 for a diagram of the standard synchronous page life cycle and associated events.

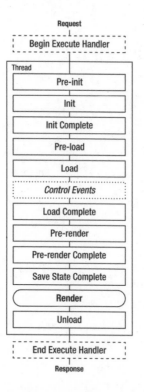

Figure 5-1. ASP.NET page processing life cycle and events

The HTTP request enters the page-processing pipeline at the top of the figure, when IIS starts to execute the Page Handler (see also Figure 4-2). As the processing progresses, the runtime moves from one state to another, calling all registered event handlers as it goes. In the synchronous case, a single thread from the ASP.NET thread pool does all the processing for the page.

■ **Note** The Render phase is not an event. All pages and controls have a Render() method that's responsible for generating the output that will be sent to the client.

Instead of the usual serial and synchronous approach, it's possible to configure a page to run asynchronously. For asynchronous pages, ASP.NET inserts a special "async point" into the page life cycle, after the PreRender event. One thread executes the part of the life cycle before the async point. The original thread or possibly other threads from the thread pool will then begin the async requests. Then one of those threads or a different one executes the rest of the life cycle after the async point. See Figure 5-2.

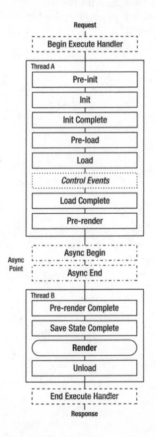

Figure 5-2. Asynchronous page processing life cycle and events

Application Thread Pool

Let's put together a test case to demonstrate how the application thread pool processes both sync and async pages.

Synchronous Page

Add a new web form in Visual Studio, and call it `sql-sync.aspx`. Keep the default markup, and use the following code-behind:

```
using System;
using System.Data.SqlClient;
using System.Web.UI;

public partial class sql_sync : Page
{
    public const string ConnString = "Data Source=.;Integrated Security=True";

    protected void Page_Load(object sender, EventArgs e)
    {
        using (SqlConnection conn = new SqlConnection(ConnString))
        {
            conn.Open();
            using (SqlCommand cmd =
                new SqlCommand("WAITFOR DELAY '00:00:01'", conn))
            {
                cmd.ExecuteNonQuery();
            }
        }
    }
}
```

The code connects to SQL Server on the local machine and issues a T-SQL command that waits for one second.

■ **Note** I'm using a connection string that's compatible with a local default instance of a "full" edition of SQL Server, such as Developer, Enterprise, Standard, or Workgroup. If you're using SQL Server Express, which works with most (but not all) of the examples in the book, the `Data Source` field should be `.\SQLEXPRESS`. In both cases, the dot is shorthand for `localhost` or your local machine name. I'm showing connection strings in-line for clarity. In a production application, you should usually store them in `web.config`.

You don't need to specify which database to connect to, since you aren't accessing any tables or other securables.

Asynchronous Page

Next, create another page called `sql-async.aspx`. Change the `Page` directive in the markup file to include `Async="true"`:

```
<%@ Page Language="C#" Async="true" AutoEventWireup="true"
    CodeFile="sql-async.aspx.cs" Inherits="sql_async" %>
```

That tells the runtime that this page will be asynchronous, so it will create the async point as in Figure 5-2.

Next, create the code-behind as follows:

```
using System;
using System.Data.SqlClient;
using System.Web;
using System.Web.UI;

public partial class sql_async : Page
{
    public const string ConnString =
        "Data Source=.;Integrated Security=True;Async=True";
```

Here you are including `Async=True` in the connection string to inform SQL Server that you will be issuing asynchronous queries. Using async queries requires a little extra overhead, so it's not the default.

```
    protected void Page_Load(object sender, EventArgs e)
    {
        PageAsyncTask pat =
            new PageAsyncTask(BeginAsync, EndAsync, null, null, true);
        this.RegisterAsyncTask(pat);
    }
```

In the `Page_Load()` method, you create a `PageAsyncTask` object that refers to the `BeginAsync()` method that the runtime should call to start the request and the `EndAsync()` method that it should call when the request completes. Then you call `RegisterAsyncTask()` to register the task. The runtime will then call `BeginAsync()` before the `PreRenderComplete` event, which is fired before the markup for the page is generated.

```
    private IAsyncResult BeginAsync(object sender, EventArgs e,
        AsyncCallback cb, object state)
    {
        SqlConnection conn = new SqlConnection(ConnString);
        conn.Open();
        SqlCommand cmd = new SqlCommand("WAITFOR DELAY '00:00:01'", conn);
        IAsyncResult ar = cmd.BeginExecuteNonQuery(cb, cmd);
        return ar;
    }
```

The BeginAsync() method opens a connection to SQL Server and starts the WAITFOR DELAY command by calling BeginExecuteNonQuery(). This is the same database command that was used in the synchronous page, but BeginExecuteNonQuery() doesn't wait for the response from the database like ExecuteNonQuery() does.

```
private void EndAsync(IAsyncResult ar)
{
    using (SqlCommand cmd = (SqlCommand)ar.AsyncState)
    {
        using (cmd.Connection)
        {
            int rows = cmd.EndExecuteNonQuery(ar);
        }
    }
}
```

The runtime will call EndAsync() when the async database call completes. EndAsync() calls EndExecuteNonQuery() to complete the command. You have two using statements that ensure that Dispose() is called on the SqlConnection and SqlCommand objects.

Load Test

Add the two new pages to a web site that's running under IIS. Ideally, the site should be on Windows Server 2008, since threading behaves differently with IIS on Vista. Test the pages with a browser to make sure they're working.

Let's use the same load test tool as in Chapter 3, WCAT. Create the configuration file as follows in the WCAT Controller folder, and call it c2.cfg:

```
Warmuptime 5s
Duration 30s
CooldownTime 0s
NumClientMachines 1
NumClientThreads 100
```

The test will warm up for 5 seconds and run for 30 seconds, using a single client process with 100 threads.

Let's test the synchronous case first. Create the test script in the same folder, and call it s2.cfg:

```
SET Server = "localhost"
SET Port = 80
SET Verb = "GET"
SET KeepAlive = true

NEW TRANSACTION
classId = 1
Weight = 100
NEW REQUEST HTTP
URL = "/sql-sync.aspx"
```

You can of course adjust the server name or port number if needed.

You are now ready to run the first test. Open one window with the WCAT Controller and another with the WCAT Client. In the controller window, start the controller as follows:

```
wccat -a localhost -c c2.cfg -s s2.cfg
```

In the client window, start the client:

```
wcclient localhost
```

The results of interest, as shown in the client window at the 20-second point on my dual-processor server, are as follows:

```
Total 200 OK              :          180      (       9/Sec)
Avg. Response Time (Last) :        10287 MS
```

Even though the only thing the page does is to sleep for one second, the server is only able to process nine requests per second, and the average response time is more than ten seconds.

Next, change the URL in s2.cfg to refer to the async page, and repeat the test. Here are the results:

```
Total 200 OK              :          480      (      24/Sec)
Avg. Response Time (Last) :        4189 MS
```

The number of requests per second has increased by almost a factor of 3, to 24 per second, and the response time has decreased to about 4.2 seconds.

Even with an async page, response time is still high. What's happening?

The default configuration limits the number of simultaneous requests to 12 per CPU. The size of the thread pool is managed separately. Creating new threads is a relatively expensive operation, so the runtime creates them only when it decides you really need them. In the sync test case, one thread can handle only one request at a time. Since there were 9 requests per second, you know that there were 9 threads. In the async case, when the async operation is started, a thread can go on to process other requests. That means that the same 9 threads can process many more requests. In this case, I'm limited by the default of 12 simultaneous requests per CPU, which is 24 total on my dual-processor server. Since each request takes 1 second to process, I end up with 24 requests per second of throughput.

Tuning the IIS Application Thread Pool

To improve this further, start by inserting the following XML into the Aspnet.config file in C:\Windows\Microsoft.NET\Framework\v2.0.50727:

```
<configuration>
    . . .
    <system.web>
        <applicationPool maxConcurrentRequestsPerCPU="12"
                         maxConcurrentThreadsPerCPU="0"
                         requestQueueLimit="5000" />
    </system.web>
</configuration>
```

After updating the file, you will need to restart IIS in order for the changes to take effect. The parameters specified are the same as the defaults. If you rerun the previous tests, you should see that they both produce the same results.

Using these configuration parameters, you can adjust the limits on the number of concurrent requests and/or the threads per CPU. A value of 0 means that the limits are not enforced. One parameter or the other can be set to 0, but not both. Both can also have nonzero values. Enforcing thread limits is slightly more expensive than enforcing request limits.

The logic behind these limits is that in some scenarios, serializing requests to some degree at the web tier is desirable in order to avoid overloading remote resources. For example, this is often the case when you make heavy use of web services. However, in this test case and in sites whose primary off-box calls are to SQL Server, it's usually better to let the database handle serializing the requests. Some requests can be completed quickly and easily, and in a large-scale environment, there might be multiple partitioned database servers. The web server just doesn't have enough information for a policy of limiting the number simultaneous requests to be an effective performance-enhancing mechanism.

Let's modify those two parameters to several different values and repeat the tests (be sure to restart IIS after each change). I've summarized the results in Table 5-2. *RPS* is requests per second, *Requests* is the value of `maxConcurrentRequestsPerCPU`, and *Threads* is the value of `maxConcurrentThreadsPerCPU` in the previous configuration XML.

Table 5-2. *Load Test Results for Synchronous and Asynchronous Pages*

Requests	Threads	Sync RPS	Sync Ave Time	Async RPS	Async Ave Time
12	0	9	10s	24	4.2s
24	0	9	10s	48	2.1s
0	12	9	10s	100	1s
0	1	2	16.5s	100	1s

The setting with 0 concurrent requests and 12 concurrent threads is the same as the default in IIS 6.

Notice that increasing the number of concurrent requests from 12 to 24 did not increase the number of requests per second for the sync case. That's because of the same reason that there are only 9 requests per second instead of 12, as described earlier: the number of active threads is conservatively managed, and even with a higher limit on the number of concurrent requests, there are still only 9 threads in the pool for the duration of this test. That change did increase the throughput of the async page, though. On my dual-CPU machine, the throughput matched the expected maximum of 24 RPS per CPU.

Disabling the concurrent request-based limit and switching to a thread limit instead shows no change for the sync page. Throughput is still limited by the number of active threads. However, notice that the async page is now running at full speed. With 100 clients, throughput is 100 requests per second, and the average time per page has dropped to 1 second, indicating no queuing.

Carrying this to an extreme, decreasing the number of threads to only 1 per CPU (2 total), reduces the sync throughput to 2 per second as expected. Much more interesting, though, is that async throughput stayed the same as with the higher number of threads. Just 2 threads can still process 100 requests per second.

I only ran the previous tests for 30 seconds. If you let them run longer, after about 3 minutes, in response to the large number of blocked requests, IIS will create additional threads for the sync scenario, and performance will increase accordingly. This will help if your load is continuous but not if it arrives in bursts.

When to Use Asynchronous Pages

The bottom line is this:

- Use asynchronous web pages whenever possible for database requests, web services, file I/O, and other network I/O.

- For database-oriented workloads, configure thread-based concurrency with a moderate number of threads per CPU.

- Consider using code rather than the runtime to enforce concurrency limits in scenarios where the load on the remote system is an issue, such as with some web services.

Keep in mind when writing async pages that it doesn't help to perform CPU-intensive operations asynchronously. The goal is to give up the thread *when it would otherwise be idle waiting for an operation to complete* so that it can do other things. If the thread is busy with CPU-intensive operations and does not go idle, then using an async task just introduces extra overhead that you should avoid.

Improving the Scalability of Existing Synchronous Pages

Since increasing concurrency of requests or threads didn't help the sync test case, if you have a large site with all-sync requests, you might be wondering whether there's anything you can do to improve throughput while you're working on converting to async. If your application functions correctly in a load-balanced arrangement and you have enough RAM on your web servers, then one option is to configure your AppPools to run multiple worker processes as a web garden.

In the previous sync test case, if you configure the AppPool to run two worker processes, throughput will double to 18 requests per second. One price you pay for multiple workers is increased memory use; another is increased context switch overhead. Data that can be shared or cached will need to be loaded multiple times in a web garden scenario, just as it would if you were running additional web servers.

Executing Multiple Async Tasks from a Single Page

While developing async pages, you will often run into cases where you need to execute multiple tasks on a single page, such as several database commands. Some of the tasks may not depend on one another and so can run in parallel. Others may generate output that is then consumed by subsequent steps. From a performance perspective, it's usually best to do data combining in the database tier when you can. However, there are also times where that's not desirable or even possible.

Executing Tasks in Parallel

The first solution to this issue works when you know in advance what all the steps will be and the details of which steps depend on which other steps. The fifth (last) argument to the `PageAsyncTask` constructor is the executeInParallel flag. You can register multiple PageAsyncTask objects with the page. When you do, the runtime will start them in the order they were registered. Tasks that have executeInParallel set to true will be run at the same time. When the flag is set to false, those tasks will run one at a time, in a serialized fashion.

For example, let's say that you have three tasks, the first two of which can run at the same time, but the third one uses the output of the first two, so it shouldn't run until they are complete (see async-parallel.aspx):

```
protected void Page_Load(object sender, EventArgs e)
{
    PageAsyncTask pat = new PageAsyncTask(BeginAsync1, EndAsync1, null, null, true);
    this.RegisterAsyncTask(pat);
    pat = new PageAsyncTask(BeginAsync2, EndAsync2, null, null, true);
    this.RegisterAsyncTask(pat);
    pat = new PageAsyncTask(BeginAsync3, EndAsync3, null, null, false);
    this.RegisterAsyncTask(pat);
}
```

The executeInParallel flag is set to true for the first two tasks, so they run simultaneously. It's set to false for the third task, so the runtime doesn't start it until the first two complete.

The fourth argument to the PageAsyncTask constructor is a state object. If you provide a reference to one, it will be passed to your BeginEventHandler. This option can be helpful if the BeginEventHandler is in a different class than your page, such as in your data access layer (DAL).

Executing Async Tasks After the PreRender Event

The other approach to this issue relies on the fact that the runtime won't advance to the next state in the page-processing pipeline until all async tasks are complete. That's true even if you register those tasks during the processing of other async tasks. However, in that case, you need to take one extra step after registering the task, which is to start it explicitly.

The following builds on the previous sql-async.aspx example (see async-seq.aspx):

```
private void EndAsync(IAsyncResult ar)
{
    using (SqlCommand cmd = (SqlCommand)ar.AsyncState)
    {
        using (cmd.Connection)
        {
            int rows = cmd.EndExecuteNonQuery(ar);
        }
    }
    PageAsyncTask pat = new PageAsyncTask(BeginAsync2, EndAsync2,
        null, null, true);
    this.RegisterAsyncTask(pat);
    this.ExecuteRegisteredAsyncTasks();
}
```

The call to ExecuteRegisteredAsyncTasks() will start any tasks that have not already been started. It's not required for tasks that you've registered before the end of **PreRender** event processing. This approach also allows the tasks to be conditional or to overlap in more complex ways than the executeInParallel flag allows.

You can also call ExecuteRegisteredAsyncTasks() earlier in the page life cycle, which will cause the runtime to execute all registered tasks at that time, rather than at the async point. Tasks are called only once, regardless of how many times you call ExecuteRegisteredAsyncTasks().

Handling Timeouts

As the third parameter in the **PageAsyncTask** constructor, you can pass a delegate that the runtime will call if the async request takes too long to execute:

```
PageAsyncTask pat = new PageAsyncTask(BeginAsync, EndAsync,
    TimeoutAsync, null, true);
```

You can set the length of the timeout in the **Page** directive in your markup file:

```
<%@ Page AsyncTimeout="30" . . . %>
```

The value of the **AsyncTimeout** property sets the length of the timeout in seconds. However, you can't set a separate timeout value for each task; you can set only a single value that applies to all of them.

You can set a default value for the async timeout in **web.config**:

```
<system.web>
    <pages asyncTimeout="30" . . . />
    . . .
</system.web>
```

You can also set the value programmatically:

```
protected void Page_Load(object sender, EventArgs e)
{
    this.AsyncTimeout = TimeSpan.FromSeconds(30);
    . . .
}
```

Here's an example that forces a timeout (see **async-timeout.aspx**):

```
using System;
using System.Data.SqlClient;
using System.Web.UI;

public partial class async_timeout : Page
{
    public const string ConnString =
        "Data Source=.;Integrated Security=True;Async=True";

    protected void Page_Load(object sender, EventArgs e)
    {
```

```
    this.AsyncTimeout = TimeSpan.FromSeconds(5);
    PageAsyncTask pat = new PageAsyncTask(BeginAsync, EndAsync,
        TimeoutAsync, null, true);
    RegisterAsyncTask(pat);
}
```

You set the timeout to five seconds and then create and register the task.

```
private IAsyncResult BeginAsync(object sender, EventArgs e,
    AsyncCallback cb, object state)
{
    SqlConnection conn = new SqlConnection(ConnString);
    conn.Open();
    SqlCommand cmd = new SqlCommand("WAITFOR DELAY '00:01:00'", conn);
    IAsyncResult ar = cmd.BeginExecuteNonQuery(cb, cmd);
    return ar;
}
```

The WAITFOR command waits for one minute, which is longer than the five-second timeout, so the page will display the error message when it runs.

```
private void EndAsync(IAsyncResult ar)
{
    using (SqlCommand cmd = (SqlCommand)ar.AsyncState)
    {
        using (cmd.Connection)
        {
            int rows = cmd.EndExecuteNonQuery(ar);
        }
    }
}

private void TimeoutAsync(IAsyncResult ar)
{
    errorLabel.Text = "Database timeout error.";
    SqlCommand cmd = (SqlCommand)ar.AsyncState;
    cmd.Connection.Dispose();
    cmd.Dispose();
}
}
```

The runtime doesn't call the end event handler if a timeout happens. Therefore, in the timeout event handler, you clean up the SqlCommand and SqlConnection objects that were created in the begin handler. Since you don't have any code that's using those objects here like you do in the end handler, you explicitly call their Dispose() methods instead of relying on using statements.

Asynchronous Web Services

Another type of long-running task that's a good candidate to run asynchronously is calls to web services. As an example, let's build a page that uses Microsoft's TerraServer system to get the latitude and longitude for a given city in the United States. First, right-click your web site in Visual Studio, select **Add Web Reference**, and enter the URL for the WSDL:

```
http://terraserver-usa.com/TerraService.asmx?WSDL
```

Click the **Go** button to display the WSDL. See Figure 5-3.

Add Web Reference

Navigate to a web service URL and click Add Reference to add all the available services.

◉ Back ◉ | ▤ ▣ ⌂

URL: http://terraserver-usa.com/TerraService.asmx?WSDL   ▾   ◲ Go

"TerraService" Description

Documentation
TerraServer Web Service

Methods
- **ConvertLonLatPtToNearestPlace** (*point* As LonLatPt) As string
- **ConvertLonLatPtToUtmPt** (*point* As LonLatPt) As UtmPt
- **ConvertPlaceToLonLatPt** (*place* As Place) As LonLatPt
- **ConvertUtmPtToLonLatPt** (*utm* As UtmPt) As LonLatPt
- **CountPlacesInRect** (*upperleft* As LonLatPt , *lowerright* As LonLatPt , *ptype* As PlaceType) As int
- **GetAreaFromPt** (*center* As LonLatPt , *theme* As Theme , *scale* As Scale , *displayPixWidth* As int , *displayPixHeight* As int) As AreaBoundingBox
- **GetAreaFromRect** (*upperLeft* As LonLatPt , *lowerRight* As LonLatPt , *theme* As Theme , *scale* As Scale) As AreaBoundingBox
- **GetAreaFromTileId** (*id* As TileId , *displayPixWidth* As int , *displayPixHeight* As int) As AreaBoundingBox
- **GetLatLonMetrics** (*point* As LonLatPt) As ArrayOfThemeBoundingBox
- **GetPlaceFacts** (*place* As Place) As PlaceFacts
- **GetPlaceList** (*placeName* As string , *MaxItems* As int , *imagePresence* As boolean) As ArrayOfPlaceFacts

Figure 5-3. *Adding a web reference for TerraService*

Keep the default **Web reference name**, and click **Add Reference** to finish adding it.
Next, add a web form called `terra1.aspx`.
Set `Async="True"` in the Page directive, and add two `<asp:Label>` tags to hold the eventual results:

```
<%@ Page Async="true" Language="C#" AutoEventWireup="true"
    CodeFile="terra1.aspx.cs" Inherits="terra1" %>
<!DOCTYPE html PUBLIC "-//W3C//DTD XHTML 1.0 Transitional//EN"
  "http://www.w3.org/TR/xhtml1/DTD/xhtml1-transitional.dtd">
<html xmlns="http://www.w3.org/1999/xhtml">
<head runat="server">
    <title></title>
```

```
</head>
<body>
    <form id="form1" runat="server">
    <div>
        <asp:Label runat="server" ID="LA" />
        <br />
        <asp:Label runat="server" ID="LO" />
    </div>
    </form>
</body>
</html>
```

In the code-behind, add a using statement for the new web reference (see terra1.aspx.cs):

```
using System;
using System.Web;
using System.Web.UI;
using com.terraserver_usa;

public partial class terra1 : Page
{
    protected void Page_Load(object sender, EventArgs e)
    {
        this.AsyncTimeout = TimeSpan.FromSeconds(30);
        PageAsyncTask pat = new PageAsyncTask(BeginAsync, EndAsync, TimeoutAsync,
            null, true);
        RegisterAsyncTask(pat);
    }
```

In Page_Load(), set the timeout programmatically to 30 seconds and then create and register a PageAsyncTask object.

```
private IAsyncResult BeginAsync(object sender, EventArgs e,
    AsyncCallback cb, object state)
{
    TerraService terra = new TerraService();
    Place place = new Place();
    place.City = "Seattle";
    place.State = "WA";
    place.Country = "US";
    IAsyncResult ar = terra.BeginGetPlaceFacts(place, cb, terra);
    return ar;
}
```

In BeginAsync(), create an instance of the TerraService web service proxy that Visual Studio created for you, build a test argument with the Place class, and call BeginGetPlaceFacts() to start the web service call. In addition to the conventional synchronous calls, Visual Studio also creates Begin and End methods when it creates the proxy class to facilitate asynchronous use.

It's important to pass the `AsyncCallback` object to the `BeginGetPlaceFacts()` method. You also pass a reference to the `TerraService` object as the state object so that you can recover it easily when the runtime calls the `End` handler. Another option would have been to store it as an instance variable.

```
private void EndAsync(IAsyncResult ar)
{
    TerraService terra = (TerraService)ar.AsyncState;
    PlaceFacts facts = terra.EndGetPlaceFacts(ar);
    this.LA.Text = String.Format("Latitude: {0:0.##}", facts.Center.Lat);
    this.LO.Text = String.Format("Longitude: {0:0.##}", facts.Center.Lon);
}
```

If the call completes before it times out, the runtime calls the `End` handler. First, get the reference to the `TerraServer` object from the provided `IAsyncResult`. Next, call `EndGetPlaceFacts()` to end the web service call and retrieve the results object. Then format the results and store them in the labels that you put in the markup earlier.

```
private void TimeoutAsync(IAsyncResult ar)
{
    this.LA.Text = "Web service call timed out.";
}
}
```

In the event of a timeout, put an error message in one of the labels.

Asynchronous File I/O

For an asynchronous file I/O example, start by creating a new web form called `file1.aspx`. Make the same changes to the markup as you did for the web service example earlier.

Here's the code-behind:

```
using System;
using System.IO;
using System.Web;
using System.Web.UI;

public partial class file1 : Page
{
    private byte[] Data { get; set; }

    protected void Page_Load(object sender, EventArgs e)
    {
        PageAsyncTask pat = new PageAsyncTask(BeginAsync, EndAsync,
            null, null, true);
        RegisterAsyncTask(pat);
    }
}
```

As before, you create and register the async task. You're not using a timeout handler here since local file access shouldn't need it.

```
private IAsyncResult BeginAsync(object sender, EventArgs e,
    AsyncCallback cb, object state)
{
    FileStream fs = new FileStream(this.Server.MapPath("csg.png"),
        FileMode.Open, FileAccess.Read, FileShare.Read, 4096,
        FileOptions.Asynchronous | FileOptions.SequentialScan);
    this.Data = new byte[64 * 1024];
    IAsyncResult ar = fs.BeginRead(this.Data, 0, this.Data.Length, cb, fs);
    return ar;
}
```

To use a `FileStream` for asynchronous file I/O, be sure to either set the `useAsync` parameter to `true` or include the `FileOptions.Asynchronous` bit in the `FileOptions` flag. For best performance, you should use a buffer size of 1KB or more; I've used 4KB in the example. You may see a slight performance improvement with buffers up to about 64KB in size. If you know the access pattern for your file (random vs. sequential), it's a good idea to include the corresponding flag when you create the `FileStream`, as a hint that the OS can use to optimize the underlying cache. I've specified `FileOptions.SequentialScan` to indicate that I will probably read the file sequentially.

■ **Tip** When you're reading just a few bytes, async file I/O can be considerably more expensive than synchronous I/O. The threshold varies somewhat, but I suggest a 1KB file size as a reasonable minimum: for files less than 1KB in size, you should prefer synchronous I/O.

```
private void EndAsync(IAsyncResult ar)
{
    using (FileStream fs = (FileStream)ar.AsyncState)
    {
        int size = fs.EndRead(ar);
        this.LA.Text = "Size: " + size;
    }
}
}
```

When the I/O is done, you call `EndRead()` to get the number of bytes that were read and then write that value in one of the labels on the page.

The process for async writes is similar. However, in many cases even when you request an async write, the operating system will handle it synchronously. The usual reason is that the OS forces all requests that extend files to happen synchronously. If you create or truncate a file and then write it sequentially, all writes will be extending the file and will therefore be handled synchronously. If the file already exists, you can get around that by opening it for writing and, rather than truncating it, use `FileStream.SetLength()` to set the length of the file as early as you can. That way, if the old file is as long as or longer than the new one, all writes will be asynchronous. Even if the file doesn't already exist, calling `FileStream.SetLength()` as early as you can is still a good idea, since it can allow the operating system to do certain optimizations, such as allocating the file contiguously on disk.

In addition, reads and writes to compressed filesystems (not individual compressed files) and to files that are encrypted with NTFS encryption are forced by the OS to be synchronous.

■ **Tip** During development, it's a good practice to double-check that the OS is really executing your calls asynchronously. You can do that by checking the `IAsyncResult.CompletedSynchronously` flag after you issue the `Begin` request.

Asynchronous Web Requests

Following what by now I hope will be a familiar pattern, let's walk through an example of how to execute a web request asynchronously. First, create a new web form, and call it **webreq1.aspx**. Make the same changes to the markup file that you did for the previous examples: set the **Async** flag in the **Page** directive, and add the `<asp:Label>` controls.

Here's the code-behind:

```
using System;
using System.Net;
using System.Text;
using System.Web;
using System.Web.UI;

public partial class webreq1 : Page
{
    protected void Page_Load(object sender, EventArgs e)
    {
        this.AsyncTimeout = TimeSpan.FromSeconds(30);
        PageAsyncTask pat = new PageAsyncTask(BeginAsync, EndAsync,
            TimeoutAsync, null, true);
        RegisterAsyncTask(pat);
    }
```

`Page_Load()` is identical to the web services example; set the timeout to 30 seconds, and then create and register the `PageAsyncTask`.

```
    private IAsyncResult BeginAsync(object sender, EventArgs e,
        AsyncCallback cb, object state)
    {
        WebRequest request = WebRequest.Create("http://www.apress.com/");
        IAsyncResult ar = request.BeginGetResponse(cb, request);
        return ar;
    }
```

In `BeginAsync()`, create a `WebRequest`, and call `BeginGetResponse()` to start the request asynchronously, passing it the provided `AsyncCallback` object and the **request** reference as state information.

```
private void EndAsync(IAsyncResult ar)
{
    WebRequest request = (WebRequest)ar.AsyncState;
    WebResponse response = request.EndGetResponse(ar);
    StringBuilder sb = new StringBuilder();
    foreach (string header in response.Headers.Keys)
    {
        sb.Append(header);
        sb.Append(": ");
        sb.Append(response.Headers[header]);
        sb.Append("<br/>");
    }
    this.LO.Text = sb.ToString();
}
```

In EndAsync(), recover the WebRequest object from AsyncState and use it to call EndGetResponse() to end the request and collect the results of the call. Then collect the response header keys and values into a StringBuilder, along with a <br/> between lines, and display the resulting string in one of the labels on the page. The WebRequest and WebResponse objects don't implement IDisposable, so you don't need to call Dispose() as you did in the other examples.

```
private void TimeoutAsync(IAsyncResult ar)
{
    this.LO.Text = "Web request timed out.";
}
}
```

If the web request takes longer than 30 seconds to complete, it will timeout, and you will output an error message.

Background Worker Threads

Another approach to offloading the ASP.NET worker threads is to defer activities that might take a long time. One way to do that is with a background worker thread. Rather than performing the task in-line with the current page request, you can place the task in a local queue, which is then processed by a background worker thread.

Background worker threads are particularly useful for tasks where you don't require confirmation that they've executed on the current page before returning to the user and where a small probability that the task won't be executed is acceptable, such as if the web server were to crash after the request was queued but before it was executed. For example, logging often falls in this category. Service Broker is useful for longer tasks that you can't afford to skip or miss, such as sending an e-mail or recomputing bulk data of some kind. I will cover Service Broker in Chapter 8.

ASP.NET does provide ThreadPool.QueueUserWorkItem() for executing work items in the background. However, I don't recommend using it in web applications for two reasons. First, it uses threads from the same thread pool that your pages use and is therefore competing for that relatively scarce resource. Second, multiple threads can execute work items. One of the things that I like to use a background thread for is to serialize certain requests. Since the standard ThreadPool is a shared object whose configuration shouldn't be adjusted to extremes, task serialization isn't possible with QueueUserWorkItem() without using locks, which would cause multiple threads to be blocked.

Similarly, the .NET Framework provides a way to asynchronously execute delegates, using `BeginInvoke()`. However, as earlier, the threads used in this case also come from the ASP.NET thread pool, so you should avoid using that approach too.

There is a fundamental difference between native asynchronous I/O and processing I/O requests synchronously in background threads (so they *appear* asynchronous). With native async, a single thread can process many I/O requests at the same time. Doing the same thing with background threads requires one thread for each request. Although threads are lighter weight than processes, they are still relatively expensive to create. Native async, as you've been using in the examples, is therefore much more efficient in addition to not putting an extra load on the worker thread pool, which is a limited resource.

C# Using and Lock Statements

The `using` statement in C# has the following syntax:

```
using (IDisposable disposable = (IDisposable)statement)
{
    . . .
}
```

That code is shorthand for the following:

```
IDisposable disposable = (IDisposable)statement;
try
{
    . . .
}
finally
{
    if (disposable != null)
        disposable.Dispose();
}
```

The idea is to make sure that `IDisposable` objects have their `Dispose()` methods called, even in the event of an exception, an early return, or other changes in the flow of control.

The `lock` statement has the following syntax:

```
lock (obj)
{
    . . .
}
```

That's shorthand for the following:

```
Monitor.Enter(obj);
try
{
    . . .
}
```

```
finally
{
    Monitor.Exit(obj);
}
```

The lock is released if an exception is thrown. However, it's important to note that when processing exceptions thrown from inside the lock, it might be possible for the objects to be left in an inconsistent state. For that reason, using an additional `try/catch` block inside a `lock` is sometimes necessary.

Background Thread for Logging

Here's a detailed example of using a background thread, which demonstrates a number of key principles for async programming, such as locks (monitors), semaphores, queues, and signaling between threads. The goal of the code is to allow multiple foreground threads (incoming web requests) to queue requests to write logging information to the database in a background worker thread.

The code supports submitting logging requests to the worker thread in batches, rather than one at a time, for reasons that will become clear later in the book.

See `App_Code\RequestInfo.cs`:

```
namespace Samples
{
    public class RequestInfo
    {
        public string Page { get; private set; }

        public RequestInfo()
        {
            this.Page = HttpContext.Current.Request.Url.ToString();
        }
    }
}
```

The `RequestInfo` object encapsulates the information that you will want to write to the database later. In this case, it's just the URL of the current page.

See `App_Code\WorkItem.cs`:

```
namespace Samples
{
    public enum ActionType
    {
        None = 0,
        Add = 1
    }
```

The `ActionType` enum defines the various actions that the background worker thread will perform. I use `None` as a placeholder for an unassigned value; it is not valid for a queued work item.

```
public class WorkItem
{
    private static Queue<WorkItem> queue = new Queue<WorkItem>();
    private static Semaphore maxQueueSemaphore =
        new Semaphore(MaxQueueLength, MaxQueueLength);
    private static Object workItemLockObject = new Object();
    private static WorkItem currentWorkItem;
    private static Thread worker;
    public delegate void Worker();
```

The WorkItem class manages a collection of requests for work to be done, along with a static Queue of WorkItems.

You use a Semaphore to limit how many WorkItem objects can be queued. When a thread tries to queue a WorkItem, if the queue is full, the thread will block until the number of items in the queue drops below MaxQueueLength. You use workItemLockObject to serialize access to currentWorkItem to allow multiple threads to enqueue requests before the WorkItem is submitted to the background worker thread.

```
public ActionType Action { get; set; }
public ICollection<RequestInfo> RequestInfoList { get; private set; }

public static int MaxQueueLength
{
    get { return 100; }
}

public int Count
{
    get { return this.RequestInfoList.Count; }
}

public static int QueueCount
{
    get { return queue.Count; }
}

public WorkItem(ActionType action)
{
    this.Action = action;
    this.RequestInfoList = new List<RequestInfo>();
}
```

The constructor stores the specified ActionType and creates a List to hold RequestInfo objects. Using a List maintains the order of the requests.

```
private void Add(RequestInfo info)
{
    this.RequestInfoList.Add(info);
}
```

The `Add()` method adds a `RequestInfo` object to the end of `RequestInfoList`.

```
private void Enqueue()
{
    if (maxQueueSemaphore.WaitOne(1000))
    {
        lock (queue)
        {
            queue.Enqueue(this);
            Monitor.Pulse(queue);
        }
    }
    else
    {
        EventLog.WriteEntry("Application",
            "Timed-out enqueueing a WorkItem.  Queue size = " + QueueCount +
            ", Action = " + this.Action, EventLogEntryType.Error, 101);
    }
}
```

The `Enqueue()` method adds the current `WorkItem` to the end of the `Queue` and signals the worker thread. You write an error to the Windows event log if the access to the `Semaphore` times out.

This method waits up to 1,000ms to enter the semaphore. If successful, the semaphore's count is decremented. If the count reaches zero, then future calls to `WaitOne()` will block until the count is incremented by calling `Release()` from `Dequeue()`.

After entering the semaphore, obtain a lock on the queue object since `Queue.Enqueue()` is not thread safe. Next, save the current `WorkItem` in the queue. Then call `Monitor.Pulse()` to signal the worker thread that new work is available in the queue.

```
public static void QueuePageView(RequestInfo info, int batchSize)
{
    lock (workItemLockObject)
    {
        if (currentWorkItem == null)
        {
            currentWorkItem = new WorkItem(ActionType.Add);
        }
        currentWorkItem.Add(info);
        if (currentWorkItem.Count >= batchSize)
        {
            currentWorkItem.Enqueue();
            currentWorkItem = null;
        }
    }
}
```

The `QueuePageView()` method starts by getting a lock on `workItemLockObject` to serialize access to `currentWorkItem`. If `currentWorkItem` is null, then create a new `WorkItem` with a type of `ActionType.Add`. After adding the given `RequestInfo` object to the `List` held by the `WorkItem`, if the number of objects in that `List` is equal to the specified `batchSize`, then the `WorkItem` is enqueued to the worker thread.

```
public static WorkItem Dequeue()
{
    lock (queue)
    {
        for (;;)
        {
            if (queue.Count > 0)
            {
                WorkItem workItem = queue.Dequeue();
                maxQueueSemaphore.Release();
                return workItem;
            }
            Monitor.Wait(queue);
        }
    }
}
```

The worker thread uses the `Dequeue()` method to obtain the next `WorkItem` from the `Queue`. First, lock `queue` to serialize access. If the queue has anything in it, then `Dequeue()` the next item, `Release()` the semaphore, and return the `WorkItem`. Releasing the semaphore will increment its count. If another thread was blocked with the count at zero, it will be signaled and unblocked.

If the queue is empty, then the code uses `Monitor.Wait()` to release the lock and block the thread until the `Enqueue()` method is called from another thread, which puts a `WorkItem` in the queue and calls `Monitor.Pulse()`. After returning from the `Wait`, the code enters the loop again at the top.

```
public static void Init(Worker work)
{
    lock (workItemLockObject)
    {
        if (worker == null)
            worker = new Thread(new ThreadStart(work));
        if (!worker.IsAlive)
            worker.Start();
    }
}
```

The `Init()` method obtains a lock on the `workItemLockObject` to serialize the thread startup code, ensuring that only one worker thread is created. Create the worker thread with the entry point set to the provided `Worker` delegate and then start the thread.

```
public static void Work()
{
    try
    {
        for (;;)
        {
            WorkItem workItem = WorkItem.Dequeue();
            switch (workItem.Action)
            {
                case ActionType.Add:
```

The code that's executed by the worker thread starts with a loop that calls Dequeue() to retrieve the next WorkItem. Dequeue() will block if the queue is empty. After retrieving a work item, the switch statement determines what to do with it, based on the ActionType. In this case, there is only one valid ActionType, which is Add.

```
string sql = "[Traffic].[AddPageView]";
using (SqlConnection conn = new SqlConnection(ConnString))
{
    foreach (RequestInfo info in workItem.RequestInfoList)
    {
        using (SqlCommand cmd = new SqlCommand(sql))
        {
            cmd.CommandType = CommandType.StoredProcedure;
            SqlParameterCollection p = cmd.Parameters;
            p.Add("pageurl", SqlDbType.VarChar, 256).Value
                = (object)info.Page ?? DBNull.Value;
            try
            {
                conn.Open();
                cmd.ExecuteNonQuery();
            }
            catch (SqlException e)
            {
                EventLog.WriteEntry("Application",
                    "Error in WritePageView: " +
                    e.Message + "\n",
                    EventLogEntryType.Error, 104);
            }
        }
    }
}
break;
        }
    }
}
catch (ThreadAbortException)
{
    return;
}
catch (Exception e)
{
    EventLog.WriteEntry("Application",
        "Error in MarketModule worker thread: " + e.Message,
        EventLogEntryType.Error, 105);
    throw;
}
}
}
```

The remainder of the method uses ADO.NET to call a stored procedure synchronously to store the URL of the page. The stored procedure has a single argument, and you call it once for each `RequestInfo` object that was stored with the `WorkItem`. I will cover several techniques for optimizing this code later in the book.

The `ThreadAbortException` is caught and handled as a special case, since it indicates that the thread should exit. The code also catches and logs generic `Exceptions`. Even though it's not a good practice in most places, `Exceptions` that are thrown from a detached thread like this would be difficult to trace otherwise.

Using the worker thread is easy. First, start the thread:

```
WorkItem.Init(Work);
```

You can do that from the `Init()` method of an `HttpModule`, or perhaps from `Application_Start()` in `Global.asax.cs`.

After that, just create a `RequestInfo` object and pass it to `QueuePageView()` along with the batch size:

```
WorkItem.QueuePageView(new RequestInfo(), 10);
```

Task Serialization

You can also use background threads as a way of executing certain types of tasks one at a time, as an alternative to locking for objects that experience heavy contention. The advantage over locking is that the ASP.NET worker thread doesn't have to block; you could write the request to a queue in a `BeginAsyncHandler` method, and the thread would continue rather than block. Later, when the task completes, the background thread could signal an associated custom `IAsyncResult`, which would cause the `EndAsyncHandler` method to execute.

However, because of the significant additional overhead, this makes sense only when threads are frequently blocking for relatively long periods.

If your code accesses different areas of disk at the same time, the disk heads will have to seek from one area to another. Those seeks can cause throughput to drop by a factor of 20 to 50 or more, even if the files are contiguous. That's an example of where you might consider using task serialization with a background thread. By accessing the disk from only one thread, you can limit seeks by not interleaving requests for data from one part of the disk with requests for data from another part.

Locking Guidelines and Using ReaderWriterLock

Whenever you have multiple threads, you should use locks to prevent race conditions and related problems. Locking can be a complex topic, and there's a lot of great material that's been written about it, so I won't go into too much detail here. However, for developers who are new to asynchronous programming, I've found that it's often helpful to establish a couple of basic guidelines:

- Use a lock to protect access to all writable data that multiple threads can access at the same time. Access to static data, in particular, should usually be covered with a lock.

- Avoid using a lock within another lock. If absolutely required, ensure that the order of the locks is always consistent to avoid deadlocks.

- Lock the minimum amount of code necessary (keep locks short).

- When deciding what code to lock, keep in mind that interrupts can happen between any two nonatomic operations and that the value of shared variables can change during those interrupts.

The standard C# lock statement serializes access to the code that it surrounds. In other words, the runtime allows only one thread at a time to execute the code; all other threads are blocked. For cases where you mostly read and only infrequently write the static data, there is a useful optimization you can make. The .NET Framework provides a class called ReaderWriterLock that allows many readers, but only one writer, to access the locked code at the same time. The standard lock doesn't differentiate between readers and writers, so all accesses of any type are serialized.

For example, here are two shared variables, whose values need to be read or written at the same time in order for them to be consistent:

```
public static double Balance;
public static double LastAmount;
```

Here's the declaration of the lock:

```
public static ReaderWriterLock rwLock = new ReaderWriterLock();
```

Here's the code to read the shared data:

```
rwLock.AcquireReaderLock(1000);
double previousBalance = Balance + LastAmount;
rwLock.ReleaseReaderLock();
```

The argument to AcquireReaderLock() is the maximum amount of time to wait for the lock before timing out, in milliseconds. If there was any chance of the locked code throwing an exception or otherwise altering the flow of control, you should wrap it in a try/finally block to ensure that ReleaseReaderLock() is always called.

Here's the code to write the shared data:

```
rwLock.AcquireWriterLock(1000);
LastAmount = currentAmount;
Balance -= LastAmount;
rwLock.ReleaseWriterLock();
```

Nested locks work correctly. If you acquire a ReaderWriterLock again after you've already acquired it once, the runtime will increment an internal counter. Releasing the lock will decrement the counter until it reaches zero, when the lock will actually be released.

Session State

Web applications often have a requirement for managing information that is carried over from one HTTP request to another. For example, this information could include a logged-on user's name, their role, their shopping cart contents, and so on.

In a load-balanced environment, each HTTP request from a given client might be routed to a different web server, so storing that state information on the web tier won't work. The HTTP protocol itself is stateless; each connection carries no history with it about anything that has happened before.

Session state is "historical" or *state* information that is useful only for the duration of a session. A *session* is the period that a client is "active," which might be the time that they are logged on or perhaps the time that the browser is open.

The management of session state, or more often its mismanagement, is one of the issues that rapidly growing sites often encounter. Because it's easy to use and yet presents a significant load to your back-end data store, it can become a significant barrier to scalability. From a scalability perspective, *the best solution to avoiding session state problems is not to use it*; most sites can get along fine with just cookies. Having said that, there definitely are times when it's useful and desirable.

ASP.NET includes a comprehensive set of mechanisms for managing session state. While the built-in system can work great for small to medium sites, it's not sufficiently scalable as-is for large sites, although the system does have several hooks that will allow you to improve its scalability substantially.

Here's an example of how to set session state from a web page:

```
this.Session["info"] = "this is my info";
```

You can then read the information in a subsequent request on the same page or a different one:

```
string myinfo = (string)this.Session["info"];
if (myinfo != null)
{
    // myinfo will be set to "this is my info"
}
```

The `Session` object is a specialized dictionary that associates a key with a value. The semantics are similar to those of the `ViewState` object, as described in Chapter 3.

Session IDs

Session state works in part by associating some client-specific data with a record that's stored somewhere on the server side. The usual approach is to set a *session ID* cookie. The session ID is a key that's used to store the client's serialized session state.

An alternative approach is to use *cookieless* session IDs, where the session ID is placed in the URL. In many applications, providing ready access to session IDs, such as is possible when they are encoded in a URL, is a potential security risk. As I mentioned in Chapter 1, modern public-facing web sites will encounter very few real clients (as opposed to spiders) that don't support cookies. For those reasons, I recommend using only the cookie-based approach.

The default implementation of session ID cookies by ASP.NET doesn't assign an explicit expiration time to them. That causes the browser to consider them *temporary*, so it can delete the cookies only when the browser's window is closed. Temporary cookies never timeout on their own; they are active as long as the window is open. When you provide an expiration time, the browser writes the cookies to disk, and they become (semi) *permanent*. The browser deletes them after they expire.

Both types of cookies have a role in implementing session state or alternatives, depending on the requirements for your site. You might want users to stay logged in for a while, even if they close the browser. You might also want the user's session to timeout if they walk away from their computer for a while without closing the browser. In most cases, I prefer cookies to be permanent, with specific expiration times. If your application requires the session to end when a user closes the browser, then you might consider a custom provider with both a temporary cookie and a permanent one. Together, you will have all the information you need to take the correct action on the server. From a code complexity perspective, I prefer that approach to using temporary cookies with timeout information encoded into them.

InProc Mode

The default configuration is to store session state information in the memory of the IIS worker process using `InProc` mode, which is enabled by default. The advantage of this approach is that it's very fast, since session objects are just stored in (hidden) slots in the in-memory `Cache` object. The stored objects aren't serialized and don't have to be marked as serializable.

Since one worker process doesn't have access to the memory in another, the default configuration won't work for a load-balanced site, including web gardens. Another issue is that if the web server crashes or reboots or if the IIS worker process recycles, all current state information will be lost. For those reasons, I don't recommend using `InProc` mode, even for small sites.

One approach that some web sites take to address the problems with `InProc` mode is to configure their load balancer to use sticky connections to the web servers. That way, the load balancer will assign all connections from a particular client to a particular web server, often based on something like a hash code of the client's IP address. Although that solution partly addresses the scalability issue, the data is still stored in RAM only and will therefore still be lost in the event of a server failure or a worker process recycle.

In addition, using sticky connections introduces a host of additional problems. Since the load balancer is no longer free to assign incoming connections in an optimized way (such as to the server with the least number of active connections), some servers can experience significant and unpredictable load spikes, resulting in an inconsistent user experience. Those load spikes might result not just in purchasing more hardware than you would otherwise need, but they can also interfere with your ability to do accurate capacity planning and load trend forecasting.

Using StateServer

Another option for storing session state is to use `StateServer`, which is included as a standard component of ASP.NET. `StateServer` has the advantage of running outside of IIS, and potentially on a machine of its own, so your site will function correctly without sticky connections when it's load balanced or a web garden.

However, as with the `InProc` mode, `StateServer` stores state information only in memory, so if you stop the process or if the machine reboots, all session data is lost. With `StateServer`, you are effectively introducing a single point of failure. For those reasons, I don't recommend using `StateServer`.

Using SQL Server

Storing session state in a database addresses the reliability issues for both `InProc` and `StateServer`. If the database crashes or reboots, session state is preserved.

To enable use of the built-in SQL Server session provider, execute the following command from `C:\Windows\Microsoft.NET\Framework\v2.0.50727`:

```
aspnet_regsql -E -S localhost -ssadd -sstype p
```

The `-E` flag says to use a trusted connection (Windows authentication). The `-S` flag specifies which database server instance to use; for SQL Server Express, you should specify `.\SQLEXPRESS`, as you would with a connection string. -ssadd says to add support for SQL Server session state. -sstype p says to store both session state and the associated stored procedures in the newly created ASPState database.

If you have trouble getting aspnet_regsql to work correctly in your environment, the /? flag will display a list of options.

If you're curious, you can look in the InstallPersistSqlState.sql file in that same folder for an idea of what the previous command will do. However, you shouldn't execute that script directly; use aspnet_regsql as shown earlier.

After you run aspnet_regsql, if you take a look at SQL Server using SSMS, you'll notice a new database called ASPState, which has two tables and a bunch of stored procedures. You might need to configure the database to allow access from the identity that your web site's AppPool uses, depending on the details of your security setup.

A SQL Agent job is also created, which runs once a minute to delete old sessions. You should enable SQL Agent so that the job can run.

Next, enable SQL Server session state storage by making the following change to web.config:

```
<system.web>
  <sessionState mode="SQLServer"
    sqlConnectionString="Data Source=.;Integrated Security=True"
    timeout="20"
    cookieName="SS" />
  . . .
</system.web>
```

The timeout property specifies how long a session can be idle before it expires, in minutes.

The sqlConnectionString property specifies the server to use. The database name of ASPState is implied; the runtime won't allow you to specify it explicitly unless you also set the allowCustomSqlDatabase property to true. As an alternative to including a full connection string, you can also use the name of one from the connectionStrings section of your web.config.

Using the cookieName property, I've specified a short two-character name for the name of the session ID cookie instead of the default, which is ASP.NET_SessionId.

If you're interested in exploring how sessions work in more details, after running a small test page, along the lines of the earlier Session example, you can query the tables in the ASPState database to see that they are in fact being used. You can also take a look at the HTTP headers using Fiddler to see how the session ID cookie is handled and view the session-related database queries with SQL Profiler.

Selectively Enabling Session State and Using ReadOnly Mode

In spite of its positive aspects, database storage of session state does have some drawbacks. The biggest is that the standard implementation doesn't address scalability.

Having many web servers that talk to a single session database can easily introduce a bottleneck. One database round-trip is required at the beginning of a web request to read the session state and update the session's expiration time, and a second round-trip is required at the end of the request to update the database with the modified state. The runtime also needs to deserialize and reserialize the state information, which introduces even more overhead.

Writes to the database are particularly expensive from a scalability perspective. One thing you can do to help minimize scalability issues is to heavily optimize the database or file group where the session state is stored for write performance, as described in later chapters.

Something that can have even more impact is to limit which pages use session state and to indicate whether it's only read and not written. You can disable session state for a particular page by setting the EnableSessionState property to false in the Page directive:

```
<%@ Page EnableSessionState="false" . . . @>
```

If you try to access the `Session` object from a page that has session state disabled, the runtime will throw an exception.

With session state disabled, even if you don't access the `Session` object, the session code still accesses the database in order to update the session timeout. This helps keep the session alive, but it also presents additional load on the database.

You can use the same property to indicate that the session data used by the page is read-only:

```
<%@ Page EnableSessionState="ReadOnly" . . . @>
```

Setting read-only mode helps performance by eliminating the write to the database at the end of the request. It also causes the session management code to take out a read lock on the database record, rather than an exclusive lock. The read lock allows other read-only pages from the same client to access the session data at the same time. That can help improve parallelism and is particularly important when a single client can issue many requests for dynamic content at the same time, such as with some Ajax-oriented applications or with sites that use frames.

You can set the default for the `EnableSessionState` property in `web.config`:

```
<configuration>
    <system.web>
        <pages enableSessionState="false">
            . . .
        </pages>
        . . .
    </system.web>
</configuration>
```

In most environments, I suggest setting the default to `false` and then explicitly enabling session state on the pages that need it. That way, you avoid accidentally enabling it on pages that don't need it.

It's also a good idea to split functions that need session data only in read-only form onto separate pages from those that need read/write access to minimize further the write load on the database.

Scaling Session State Support

As I mentioned earlier, the standard support for session state using SQL Server unfortunately isn't scalable for large sites. However, if it's an important part of your architecture, the framework does provide a couple of hooks that make it possible to modify several key aspects of the implementation, which you can use to make it scalable.

Although the cost of serializing session state data can be significant, it normally has an impact mostly on the performance side, rather than on scalability. Since it's a CPU-intensive activity, if your site is scalable, you should be able to add more servers to offset the serialization cost, if you need to do so. The time it takes to write the session data to the database is where scalability becomes an issue.

It is possible to use distributed caching technology, such as Microsoft's Velocity, as a session state store. See the "Distributed Caching" section in Chapter 3 for a discussion of that option.

Scaling Up

With enough RAM, SQL Server can act like a large cache, and read queries tend to execute very quickly, often with no access to disk. However, all INSERT, UPDATE, and DELETE operations must wait for the database to write the changes to disk. I'll cover database performance in more detail in later chapters. For now, the main point is that database scalability is often driven more by writes than reads.

To increase database write performance, the first step is to maximize the performance of your database hardware. Database write performance is largely driven by the speed with which SQL Server can write to the database log. Here are a few high-impact things you can do:

- Place the session database log file on a dedicated set of disks.

- Use RAID-10 and avoid RAID-5 for the log disks.

- Add spindles to increase log write performance.

I'll discuss those optimizations in more detail in later chapters.

Scaling Out

Once you reach the limit of an individual server, the next step is to scale out. Your goal should be to distribute session state storage onto several different servers in such a way that you can figure out which server has the state for a particular request without requiring yet another round-trip. See Figure 5-4.

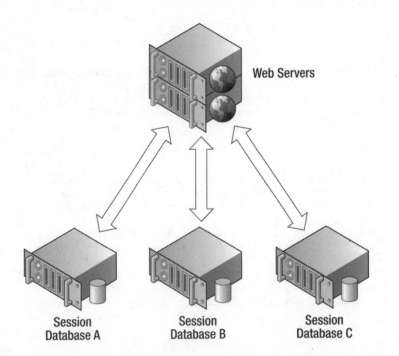

Figure 5-4. *Scaled-out databases for session state storage*

Custom Session ID Manager

The default session ID is a randomly generated 24-character string. A simple approach you might use is to convert part of that string to integer, take its modulo, and use that to determine which database server to use. If you had three servers, you would take the ID modulo three.

What complicates the issue for large sites is the possibility that you might want to change the number of session state servers at some point. The design shouldn't force any existing sessions to be lost when you make such a change. Unfortunately, algorithms such as a simple modulo function that are based entirely on a set of random inputs aren't ideal in that sense, since without accessing the database you don't have any history to tell you what the server assignment used to be before a new server was added.

A better approach is to encode the identity of the session server directly into the session ID, using a custom session ID generator. Here's an example (see App_Code\ScalableSessionIDManager.cs):

```
using System;
using System.Web;
using System.Web.SessionState;

namespace Samples
{
    public class ScalableSessionIDManager : SessionIDManager
    {
```

Here you are going to extend the default SessionIDManager class. You only need to override two methods to implement custom session IDs. If you also wanted to modify the way the session cookies are handled, you would implement the ISessionIDManager interface instead.

```
public static string[] Machines = { "A", "B", "C" };
private static Object randomLock = new Object();
private static Random random = new Random();

public override string CreateSessionID(HttpContext context)
{
    int index;
    lock (randomLock)
    {
        index = random.Next(Machines.Length);
    }
    string id = Machines[index] + "." + base.CreateSessionID(context);
    return id;
}
```

Pick a random number between zero and the length of the Machines array. This index determines which database server you'll use to store the session state.

If the hardware you're using for each of your session servers is not identical, you should apply weighting to the random assignments to allow for the difference in performance from one server to another.

Since creating the Random class involves some overhead, use a single instance of it to generate the random numbers. Since its instance methods are not thread safe, get a lock first before calling Random.Next(). In keeping with best practices for locking, create a separate object for that purpose.

Although you could lock on the Random object itself or on the Type of the ScalableSessionIDManager, subtle bugs can arise if other code were to lock those same objects in an uncoordinated way.

Finally, you create the session ID by concatenating the machine ID with a separator character and the ID provided by the base class. This approach will allow you to add new session servers later if needed, without disturbing the existing ones, since the session server assignment is encoded in the session ID.

```
public static string[] GetMachine(string id)
{
    if (String.IsNullOrEmpty(id))
        return null;
    string[] values = id.Split('.');
    if (values.Length != 2)
        return null;
    for (int i = 0; i < Machines.Length; i++)
    {
        if (Machines[i] == values[0])
            return values;
    }
    return null;
}

public override bool Validate(string id)
{
    string[] values = GetMachine(id);
    return (values != null) && base.Validate(values[1]);
}
```

The static GetMachine() method parses your new session IDs and makes sure that they contain a valid session server ID. The overridden Validate() method first calls GetMachine() to parse the session ID and then passes the part of it that originally came from the base class to the Validate() method in the base class.

Partition Resolver

To map your new session IDs into appropriate database connection strings, you use a *partition resolver*. See App_Code\ScalablePartitions.cs:

```
using System.Web;

namespace Samples
{
    public class ScalablePartitions : IPartitionResolver
    {
```

Implement the `IPartitionResolver` interface, which contains only two methods: `Initialize()` and `ResolvePartition()`.

```
private string[] sessionServers = {
    "Data Source=ServerA;Initial Catalog=session;Integrated Security=True",
    "Data Source=ServerB;Initial Catalog=session;Integrated Security=True",
    "Data Source=ServerC;Initial Catalog=session;Integrated Security=True"
};
```

Specify the connection strings for the different servers. During testing, you might configure this either with different database instances or with different databases on the same machine.

```
public void Initialize()
{
}

public string ResolvePartition(object key)
{
    string id = (string)key;
    string[] values = ScalableSessionIDManager.GetMachine(id);
    string cs = null;
    if (values != null)
    {
        for (int i = 0; i < ScalableSessionIDManager.Machines.Length; i++)
        {
            if (values[0] == ScalableSessionIDManager.Machines[i])
            {
                cs = sessionServers[i];
                break;
            }
        }
    }
    return cs;
}
```

`Initialize()` is called once per instance of the class. This implementation doesn't require any instance-specific initialization, so that method is empty.

`ResolvePartition()` receives the session ID as its argument. Pass the ID to the static `GetMachine()` shown earlier, which will parse the ID and return a two-element array if it's properly formatted. The first element in the array is the key that determines which session server to use. After finding that key in `ScalableSessionIDManager.Machines`, use its index to determine which connection string to return.

Configuring the Custom Session ID Manager and Partition Resolver

To tell the runtime to use the new code, make the following change to web.config:

```
<system.web>
  <sessionState sessionIDManagerType="Samples.ScalableSessionIDManager"
    partitionResolverType="Samples.ScalablePartitions"
    mode="SQLServer" timeout="20" cookieName="SS"
    allowCustomSqlDatabase="true" />
  . . .
</system.web>
```

The sessionIDManagerType property specifies the class name for the custom session ID manager. The partitionResolverType property specifies the class name for the partition resolver. Setting mode to SQLServer causes the SQL Server session provider to be used. The cookieName property gives a nice short name for the session state cookie.

Setting allowCustomSqlDatabase to true allows you to include the name of a database in the connection strings returned by the partition resolver. That's particularly useful during development, when you might want to use several different databases on the same server. The default setting of false prevents that, which in effect always forces use of the default ASPState database.

The database connection string that you may have previously included in the <sessionState> section is no longer needed, since the partition resolver will now provide them.

Testing the New Code

To test the code, create a new web form, and call it session1.aspx. Enable session state in the Page directive:

```
<%@ Page EnableSessionState="True" Language="C#" AutoEventWireup="true"
    CodeFile="session1.aspx.cs" Inherits="session1" %>
```

Next, replace the code-behind with the following:

```
using System;
using System.Web.UI;

public partial class session1 : Page
{
    protected void Page_Load(object sender, EventArgs e)
    {
        this.Session["test"] = "my data";
    }
}
```

Unless you store something in the Session object, the runtime won't set the session cookie.

Bring the new page up in a browser, and start the Fiddler web debugger. Replace localhost with ipv4.fiddler in the requested URL, and reissue the request to allow Fiddler to intercept the HTTP request and response. The response should include a Set-Cookie header, something like the following:

```
Set-Cookie: SS=C.ssmg3x3t1myudf3osq3whdf4; path=/; HttpOnly
```

Notice the use of the cookie name that you configured, along with the session server key at the beginning of the session ID.

ASP.NET also displays the session ID on the page when you enable tracing:

```
<%@ Page Trace="True" . . . %>
```

You can verify the use of the correct database by issuing an appropriate query from SSMS. For example:

```
select * from ASPStateTempSessions where
    SessionID = 'C.ssmg3x3t1myudf3osq3whdf4e62629bf'
```

Fine-Tuning

You should address several additional issues in your support for performance-optimized session state. Notice that the standard session provider doesn't set an expiration date on the session ID cookie, which results in a browser session cookie. That means if the user closes the browser's window, the cookie may be dropped. If the user never closes the browser, the cookie will never be dropped. Notice too that the path is set to /, so the cookie will be included with all requests for the given domain. That introduces undesirable overhead, as I discussed in Chapters 2 and 3. Unfortunately, the default implementation doesn't provide a way to override the path.

The default session IDs aren't self-validating. The server needs to issue queries to the database to make sure that the session hasn't expired and to update its expiration date. Also, as I mentioned earlier, even when sessions have been disabled on a page, once a user activates a session, a database round-trip is still made in order to update the session's expiration time. In keeping with the core principles as outlined in Chapter 1, it would be nice to eliminate those round-trips.

One approach would be to encode the session expiration time in the session cookie (or perhaps a second cookie), along with a hash code that you could use to validate the session ID and the expiration time together. You could implement that as a custom ISessionIDManager.

Full-Custom Session State

To get full control over the way session state is managed, you will need to replace the default session HttpModule. Such a solution would involve implementing handlers for the AcquireRequestState and ReleaseRequestState events to first retrieve the session data from the database and then to store it back at the end of the request. You will need to handle a number of corner cases, and there are some good opportunities for performance optimization. Here is a partial list of the actions your custom session HttpModule might perform:

- Recognize pages or other HttpHandlers that have indicated they don't need access to session state or that only need read-only access

- Implement your preferred semantics for updating the session expiration time

- Call your ISessionIDManager code to create session IDs and to set and retrieve the session ID cookie

- Call your IPartitionResolver code to determine which database connection string to use

- Serialize and deserialize the Session object

- Implement asynchronous database queries and async HttpModule events

- Implement your desired locking semantics (optimistic writes vs. locks, and so on)

- Handle creating new sessions, deleting old or abandoned sessions, and updating existing sessions

- Ensure that your code will work in a load-balanced configuration (no local state)

- Store and retrieve the Session object to and from HttpContext, and raise SessionStart and SessionEnd events (perhaps using the SessionStateUtility class)

There are also details on the database side, such as whether to use the default schema and stored procedures or ones that you've optimized for your application.

You might also consider transparently storing all or part of the Session object in cookies, rather than in the database. That might eliminate the database round-trips in some cases.

Session Serialization

The standard session state provider uses a serialization mechanism that efficiently handles basic .NET types, such as integers, bytes, chars, doubles, and so on, as well as DateTime and TimeSpan. Other types are serialized with BinaryFormatter, which, unfortunately, can be slow. You can reduce the time it takes to serialize your session state by using the basic types as much as possible, rather than creating new serializable container classes.

If you do use serializable classes, you should consider implementing the ISerializable interface and including code that efficiently serializes and deserializes your objects. Alternatively, you can mark your classes with the [Serializable] attribute and then mark instance variables that shouldn't be serialized with the [NonSerialized] attribute.

Something to be particularly cautious about when you're using custom objects is to avoid accidentally including more objects than you really need. BinaryFormatter will serialize an entire object tree. If the object you want to include in session state references an object that references a bunch of other objects, they will all be serialized.

■ **Tip** It's a good idea to take a look at the records that you're writing to the session table to make sure that their sizes seem reasonable.

With a custom session HttpModule, you might also want to check the size of the serialized session and increment a performance counter or write a warning message to the log if it exceeds a certain threshold.

Alternatives to Session State

For cases where you only need the data on the client, Silverlight can provide a good alternative to session state. Once in Silverlight, you can use the data locally on the client, without requiring the browser to send it back to the server. If the server does need it, you can send it under program control, rather than with every request as would happen with cookies. Instead of using the Session-based API, your web application would simply pass state information to your Silverlight app as part of the way it communicates for other tasks, such as with web services. The Silverlight app can then use the isolated storage API to persist the state to the user's local disk, as described in Chapter 3.

Cookies are another alternative. As with the Silverlight approach, the easy solution here involves using cookies directly and avoiding the Session-based API.

However, if your site already makes heavy use of the Session object, it is also possible to write a custom session provider that would save some state information to cookies. You could save data that is too big for cookies or that might not be safe to send to clients even in encrypted form in a database. For sites that need session state with the highest possible performance, that's the solution I recommend.

Cookies have the disadvantage of being limited to relatively short strings and of potentially being included with many HTTP requests where the server doesn't need the data. They are also somewhat exposed in the sense that they can be easily sniffed on the network unless you take precautions. In general, you should therefore encrypt potentially sensitive data (such as personal information) before storing it in a cookie. In Chapter 2, I've provided an example for encrypting and encoding data for use in a cookie.

When using cookies as an alternative to session state, you should set their expiration times in a sliding window so that as long as a user stays active, the session stays alive. For example, with a 20-minute sliding expiration time, when the user accesses the site with 10 minutes or less to go before the cookies expire, then the server should send the session-related cookies to the client again with a new 20-minute expiration time. If users wait more than 20 minutes between requests, then the session times out and the cookies expire.

The other guidelines that I described for cookies in Chapter 2 also apply here, including things such as managing cookie size and using the httpOnly, path, and domain properties.

Summary

In this chapter, I covered the following:

- How synchronous I/O can present a significant barrier to system scalability

- How you should use asynchronous I/O on web pages whenever possible for database accesses, filesystem I/O, and network I/O such as web requests and web services

- How proper configuration of the maximum number of simultaneous requests and ASP.NET worker threads can have a significant impact on performance and scalability

- Using background worker threads to offload the processing of long-running tasks

- Why you should avoid using session state if you can, and why cookies or Silverlight isolated storage are preferable

- In the event your application requires session state, how you can improve its scalability by strategically limiting the way it's used, and by using custom session IDs, a partition resolver, and a custom session management HttpModule

CHAPTER 6

■ ■ ■

Using ASP.NET to Implement and Manage Optimization Techniques

You can use a number of standard ASP.NET mechanisms to implement many of the optimization techniques described in Chapters 2 and 3. Implementations that use shared or centralized code can help reduce the time and effort required to create new high-performance content or to modify existing content. Speed in those dimensions is an important part of the ultra-fast approach.

In this chapter, I will cover the following:

- How to use master pages, user controls, and themes and skins to help centralize and manage your optimized code and markup

- How to quickly and reliably customize your content on the server based on the browser type, rather than using fragile JavaScript on the client

- How to customize the output of standard user controls to generate optimized output that implements some of the strategies from Chapter 2

- How to generate JavaScript and CSS dynamically

- How to automatically retrieve your static files from multiple domains

- How to resize and recompress images from your application

Master Pages

Master pages can help improve consistency and reliability by allowing you to share a single copy of frequently referenced code and markup among multiple pages. Reusing a common implementation can also help simplify the process of performance optimizing your pages.

Improving the speed with which you can effectively respond to changing requirements from customers or from your business and being able to find and fix bugs quickly are also aspects of the ultra-fast approach that are supported by master pages. With master pages, you can make changes to a single file that will be reflected immediately through your entire site.

As an example, let's say you've decided to use `DOCTYPE Strict` for your site. Since that's not the default in the standard web form template used by Visual Studio and since you might want to change it in the future, you decide to create a top-level master page that contains your desired `DOCTYPE` setting.

That way, other developers on the team can use the master page, and you don't have to worry about them remembering to use the right DOCTYPE or a custom template. In addition, since the standard web form template includes a server <form> tag, you decide to remove that from the top-level master so that content-only pages won't include the extra HTML for the <form> tag itself and the ViewState information that comes along with it.   Here's the markup for the master page (see Master\Master.master):

```
<%@ Master Language="C#" AutoEventWireup="true" CodeFile="Master.master.cs"
    Inherits="Master" %>
<!DOCTYPE html PUBLIC "-//W3C//DTD XHTML 1.0 Strict//EN"
    "http://www.w3.org/TR/xhtml1/DTD/xhtml1-strict.dtd">
<html xmlns="http://www.w3.org/1999/xhtml">
<head runat="server">
    <title></title>
</head>
<body>
    <asp:ContentPlaceHolder id="BD" runat="server">
    </asp:ContentPlaceHolder>
</body>
</html>
```

The first line is the Master directive, which indicates to ASP.NET that this is a master page.

■ **Note** You can't include an OutputCache directive in a master page.

In addition to the DOCTYPE tag and the removal of the <form> tag, notice that there is an <asp:ContentPlaceHolder> tag, which defines where content will be placed that is provided by pages that are derived from the master page. You can have as many of them as you need. Also, notice that the ID that you've used for that tag is very short: only two characters long. That ID string will often appear directly in the generated HTML, so it's a good idea to keep it short.

Next, let's create a page that uses that master page. When you create the new web form, select the **Select master page** box. Then choose the one that you just created. Visual Studio will automatically insert an <asp:Content> control for each <asp:ContentPlaceHolder> in the master page. Add an <asp:HyperLink> tag in the <asp:Content> section as the content for the page.

Here's the final markup (see page1.aspx):

```
<%@ Page Title="Test" Language="C#" MasterPageFile="~/Master/Master.master"
    AutoEventWireup="true" CodeFile="page1.aspx.cs" Inherits="page1" %>
<asp:Content ID="Content1" ContentPlaceHolderID="BD" Runat="Server">
<asp:HyperLink runat="server" ID="home" NavigateUrl="~/default.aspx">
Home
</asp:HyperLink>
</asp:Content>
```

In the Page directive, Visual Studio has specified a MasterPageFile that refers to the new master page. You have also included a title for the page, which the runtime will place in the <head> section of the generated HTML, replacing the empty <title> tag in the master page.

View this page in a browser, and then view the source of the page. Notice that the hidden field for `ViewState` is not present, since you don't have a server-side `<form>`. Here is the `<a>` tag that's generated by `<asp:HyperLink>`:

```
<a id="ctl00_BD_home" href="default.aspx">
```

Notice that the IDs of both the `<asp:ContentPlaceHolder>` and the `<asp:HyperLink>` are included in the generated ID of the `<a>` tag. You can keep that string short by using short IDs in your markup. Even better, when you don't need to reference that object from the code-behind or from JavaScript, you can simply omit the ID tag, and it won't be generated in the HTML.

You can also disable the feature in Visual Studio that automatically adds an ID to controls when you copy and paste them. Go to **Tools** ➤ **Options**, select **Text Editor** ➤ **HTML** ➤ **Miscellaneous** in the left panel, deselect **Auto ID elements on paste in Source view** on the right side (as in Figure 6-1), and click OK.

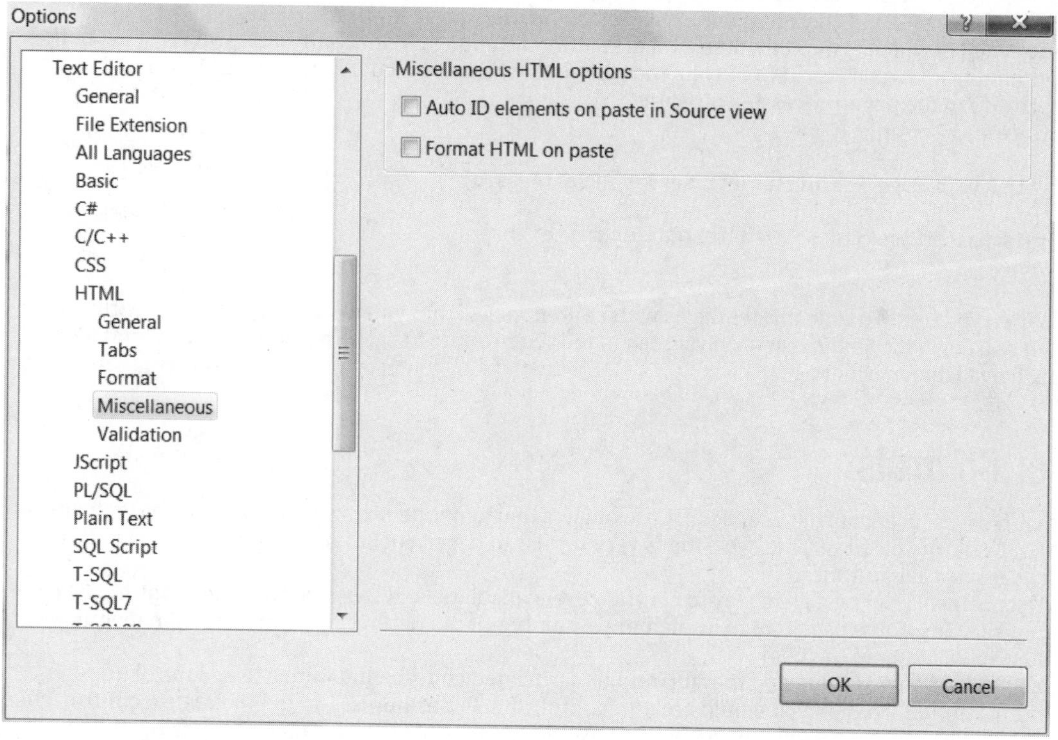

Figure 6-1. Disable "Auto ID elements on paste in Source view" in Visual Studio

ASP.NET supports nested master pages. You create them by deriving a master page from another master page, which is easily done by simply using the same `MasterPageFile` property in the `Master` directive as you use with `Pages`.

For example, here's a nested master page that includes a server `<form>` tag (see `Master\Form.master`):

```
<%@ Master Language="C#" MasterPageFile="~/Master/Master.master"
    AutoEventWireup="true" CodeFile="Form.master.cs" Inherits="Master_Form" %>
<asp:Content ID="Content1" ContentPlaceHolderID="BD" Runat="Server">
 <form id="mainform" runat="server">
   <asp:ContentPlaceHolder ID="IC" runat="server">
   </asp:ContentPlaceHolder>
 </form>
</asp:Content>
```

Notice that you replaced the `ContentPlaceHolder` `BD` in the original master page with the `<form>` tag and a new `ContentPlaceHolder` `IC`, which will be the one that pages derived from this master page will replace with content (although you had the option of reusing `BD` in this scope).

Instead of assigning a page to a particular master page using the `MasterPageFile` property in the `Page` directive, it's also possible to make the assignment dynamically at runtime. You might want to do that as part of a personalization scheme, where you provide a way for users to select different page layouts, each of which is implemented by a different master page. For this to work, you must make the assignment from `Page_PreInit()` in your code-behind, which is called before `Page_Init()` and `Page_Load()` in the page-processing pipeline.

Here's an example:

```
protected void Page_PreInit(object sender, EventArgs e)
{
    this.MasterPageFile = "~/Master/Master.master";
}
```

When you use dynamic master pages with content pages that you would like to be compatible with output caching, you should use `VaryByCustom` to tell the runtime to cache different versions of the page for each available master page.

User Controls

Like with pages, user controls in ASP.NET are objects that generate text, which is usually, but not always, HTML. User controls have a life cycle that's very similar to pages, including the same set of events, and you can cache their output.

User controls can be a great way to centralize, encapsulate, and reuse performance-optimized code for your site. You could use them to implement a number of the performance optimization techniques that I covered earlier in the book.

You should consider moving markup and its associated code-behind into a user control under conditions similar to when you would create a subroutine. For example, you might create a control when it's likely to be reusable in other places, when it would help to split it off for maintenance or development purposes, or when it helps improve code clarity, provides an optimized implementation, implements best practices or standardized business rules, and so on.

■ **Tip** You can access most regular HTML tags from the code-behind by adding `runat="server"` and an `ID`; you don't have to convert them to custom or `<asp>`-type user controls to do so.

As with the example in the previous section on master pages, when you're using ASP.NET controls, be aware that they often output all or part of the strings you choose as object IDs in the HTML. Therefore, unlike conventional software wisdom that correctly advocates descriptive and potentially long names, you should try to use short IDs whenever you can. In addition, although IDs are generally recommended, they are not required unless you need to reference the object from code-behind, from another declarative statement, or from JavaScript. It's therefore reasonable to simply leave them off unless they are explicitly used somewhere.

Example

I briefly discussed user controls in Chapter 3, in the section on page fragment output caching. Here's another example that implements a couple of the recommendations from Chapter 2:

- URLs used in `<img>` tags should use consistent case throughout your application so that the browser downloads an image only once when there are multiple references to it. Ideally, the URLs should be in lowercase to maximize compressibility.

- You should always include a `height` and `width` with `<img>` tags to speed up the browser's rendering of the page to the screen.

Here's the markup for the control (see `Controls\image.ascx`):

```
<%@ Control Language="C#" AutoEventWireup="true" CodeFile="image.ascx.cs"
    Inherits="Controls_image" %>
<%@ OutputCache Duration="86400" VaryByControl="src" Shared="true" %>
<img src="<%= src %>" height="<%= height %>" width="<%= width %>"
    alt="<%= alt %>" />
```

Since the control might have to do some work to determine the size of the image, you enable output caching to cache the results. Setting `VaryByControl` to `src` tells the runtime to cache a different version of the control for each different value of the `src` property. Setting `Shared` to `true` allows multiple pages to share a single instance of the cached control.

The way control caching works is that the runtime constructs a key that it uses to store and retrieve information about the control in the cache, along with its rendered contents. The key includes the fully qualified ID of the control, so if you have three instances of the control on one page, they will all be cached separately. Similarly, if you have multiple instances that you reference in nested controls, they will also be cached separately, since their fully qualified path IDs will be different, even if the local or immediate IDs are the same. If `Shared` is set to `false` (the default), then the runtime also includes the page class name in the cache key, so you will have different versions of the control cached for each page, even when their fully qualified path names are the same.

From a practical perspective, this means that you should be sure to use the same ID from one page to another for controls that should use cached output. If you use different IDs, it might appear to work, but you will in fact have multiple copies of the control in the cache, even when `Shared` is `true`.

Conversely, if you set Shared to true and use the same IDs from one page to another, don't let it surprise you when the page uses a version that may have been created and cached on a different page.

If your control varies based on more than one input property, you can include them in VaryByControl by separating them with semicolons. In that case, the runtime will include all listed property values in the cache key, so you will have different versions for each combination.

You can also specify a list of fully qualified control IDs in VaryByControl using a dollar sign as the path separator, such as MyControl$OtherControl$MyTextBox. In that case, the runtime includes the hash code of the control (from GetHashCode()) as a component of the cache key. Unfortunately, the fully qualified path name approach can be somewhat fragile, particularly when you're using master pages.

The properties on the <img> tag are set from properties of the same name in the control to make it easy to modify existing HTML to use it.

Here's the code-behind for the control (see Controls\image.ascx.cs):

```
[PartialCaching(86400, null, "src", null, true)]
public partial class Controls_image : UserControl
{
    private string _src;

    protected void Page_Load(object sender, EventArgs e)
    {
        if (this.height <= 0 || this.width <= 0)
        {
            string path = Server.MapPath(this.src);
            using (Stream stream = new FileStream(path, FileMode.Open))
            {
                using (System.Drawing.Image image =
                        System.Drawing.Image.FromStream(stream))
                {
                    width = image.Width;
                    height = image.Height;
                }
            }
        }
    }

    public string src
    {
        get
        {
            return this._src;
        }
        set
        {
            this._src = ResolveUrl(value).ToLowerInvariant();
        }
    }
    public int height { get; set; }
    public int width { get; set; }
    public string alt { get; set; }
}
```

The `PartialCaching` attribute is an optional alternative to the `OutputCache` directive that specifies the same information (so you need only one or the other, not both as in the example). Although it's useful in some projects, most of the time I prefer the `OutputCache` directive, since using the same pattern as pages is usually easier to understand and maintain.

The code defines public properties for `src`, `height`, `width`, and `alt`. For `src`, it uses `ResolveUrl()` to determine an absolute path to the image and converts the result to lowercase. That allows developers to use references starting with a tilde to indicate a path relative to the home directory.

If the size properties aren't set, the `Page_Load()` method reads the image from disk and determines its size. Note that production code should probably use asynchronous I/O.

Registering and Using the Control

To use the control, first you register it on the page with the following directive after `<%@ Page . . . %>`:

```
<%@ Register Src="~/Controls/image.ascx" TagPrefix="ctl" TagName="image" %>
```

Then you invoke the control at the desired location on the page:

```
<ctl:image runat="server" src="~/CSG.png" alt="Test Image" />
```

When you run the page and view the HTML source, here's the text generated by the control:

```
<img src="/samples/csg.png" height="343" width="56" alt="Test Image" />
```

Notice that the URL for the image has been determined and is in lowercase and that the `height` and `width` properties are filled in, even though you didn't provide them originally.

Placing Controls in a DLL

It's also possible to place controls in a DLL. Once there, although you can continue to use a version of the `Register` directive if you prefer, I find it's easier and less error prone to do the registration in `web.config`. Let's say that your controls are in an assembly called `Sample`, in a namespace called `MyControls`. You could register the controls in `web.config` as follows:

```
<configuration>
    <pages . . .>
        <add tagPrefix="ctl" assembly="Sample" namespace="MyControls" />
        . . .
    </pages>
    . . .
</configuration>
```

With that configuration change in place, you can reference controls in that assembly directly from your pages, without the need for a `Register` directive. Visual Studio will also provide IntelliSense for available control names.

Themes

As with master pages and user controls, themes are helpful from an ultra-fast perspective because they allow you to factor out common code and put it in a central, easily managed location. Using a single central copy makes it easier and faster for you to change, debug, or performance tune. Avoiding code duplication also helps save time during development and debugging.

Static Files

Themes provide a way to group static files such as images, CSS, and JavaScript and to dynamically switch between those groups. When you apply a theme to a page, references to the CSS and script files it contains are automatically included in the `<head>` section of the generated HTML.

You might use themes as one aspect of implementing roles. You might assign regular users to one theme and administrators to another, with each having different CSS and JavaScript files. You can also use themes as part of a version migration (and fallback) strategy.

Unfortunately, themes in their current form suffer from some significant drawbacks, so they aren't suitable for all projects. For example, you can't specify the order in which CSS files will appear on a page (they are always included in lexicographic order) or which CSS files will be included (it's always all of them). One of the biggest issues for me is that the runtime does not allow you to use any dynamic page generation technologies for theme files, so you can't use an `.aspx` file to generate script or CSS in a theme.

Skins

Skins are collections of default property values for user controls. They are associated with a particular theme and are contained in one or more `.skin` files. Each set of default property values can be either unnamed or associated with a particular `SkinId`. For custom user controls, you can place an attribute on public properties to tell ASP.NET which ones should not be settable from skins.

■ **Note** You can't specify certain control properties, such as `EnableViewState`, in a skin.

You might think of skins as a very restricted variant of user controls, where you can only specify property values, with no code or nesting.

Setting Themes Dynamically

There are two different kinds of themes: `StyleSheetTheme` and regular `Theme`. Properties from a `StyleSheetTheme` are applied to controls first. Then properties at the `Page` level are applied. Finally, properties from a regular `Theme` are applied. In other words, in your `Page` you can override properties that are set in a `StyleSheetTheme`, and properties set in a regular `Theme` override the properties you set on the `Page`.

To set a regular Theme dynamically from a page, you must do so in the PreInit event. Here's an example:

```
protected void Page_PreInit(object sender, EventArgs e)
{
    this.Theme = "mkt";
}
```

You can't set the StyleSheetTheme property directly from a Page. You must instead override the property:

```
public override string StyleSheetTheme { get { return "mkt"; } }
```

You can also set site-wide defaults in web.config for both types of themes:

```
<system.web>
    . . .
    <pages styleSheetTheme="mkt">
        . . .
    </pages>
</system.web>
```

If you need to set a site-wide default programmatically instead of declaratively in web.config, you can do so from the PreRequestHandlerExecute event in an HttpModule. In that case, you can set either theme property directly.

Here's an example:

```
public void Init(HttpApplication context)
{
    context.PostRequestHandlerExecute += this.Sample_PostRequestHandlerExecute;
}

private void Sample_PreRequestHandlerExecute(Object source, EventArgs e)
{
    HttpApplication application = (HttpApplication)source;
    HttpContext context = application.Context;
    Page page = context.Handler as Page;
    if (page != null)
    {
        page.StyleSheetTheme = "mkt";
    }
}
```

Normally, you would set a default theme programmatically or in web.config and then override the default declaratively or programmatically when required.

Themable Properties

When you're writing custom user controls, by default all public properties are themable. If there's a public property that you don't want to be settable from a skin, you should mark it with the [Themeable(false)] attribute.

For example, let's say that you don't want the alt property in the earlier user control example to be settable from a skin:

```
[Themeable(false)]
public string alt { get; set; }
```

You can disable theming for a control either by setting its EnableTheming property to false in the PreInit event handler or by overriding the EnableTheming property in a custom control.

Example

Images that you reference with a relative path from a skin or a CSS file in a theme will be contained in the theme.

Let's say you have an image that you normally reference with an <asp:Image> tag that you want to be able to change from one theme to another. Right-click your web site in Solution Explorer, and select **Add ASP.NET Folder** and then **Theme**. That will create a folder called **App_Themes** at the top level of your site, along with an empty folder inside it. Rename the empty folder to mkt, which will be the name of the theme. Then create another folder called images in the mkt folder, which is where you will place the image files. Now you're ready to create the .skin file. Call it mkt.skin, and place it in the mkt folder. The first part of the name of the .skin file is just for organizing or grouping; the runtime will collect all files in the theme that end in .skin and use them together. After including a few images and a CSS file, the resulting folder structure will look like Figure 6-2.

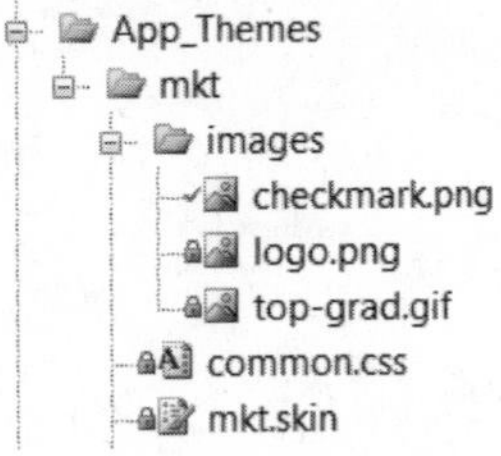

```
App_Themes
    mkt
        images
            checkmark.png
            logo.png
            top-grad.gif
        common.css
        mkt.skin
```

Figure 6-2. Folder structure for an ASP.NET theme

In the .skin file, add an <asp:Image> tag that references your image with a relative path, along with a SkinId that you will use later:

```
<asp:Image runat="server" SkinId="logo" ImageUrl="images/logo.png" />
```

As mentioned, the key here is that relative paths from a .skin file are resolved with respect to the skin, rather than with respect to the page. CSS files work the same way.

■ **Tip** To specify custom controls in a `.skin` file, either include a `Register` directive at the top of the `.skin` file, as with an `.aspx` page, or register the control or its DLL in `web.config`.

To use this image, first you need to specify the theme either at runtime, declaratively in the page itself, or in `web.config`. In this case, let's put it in the page:

```
<%@ Page Theme="mkt" Language="C#" AutoEventWireup="true"
    CodeFile="default.aspx.cs" Inherits="_default" %>
```

Finally, to reference the image, simply specify its `SkinId` in an `<asp:Image>` tag:

```
<asp:Image runat="server" SkinId="logo" />
```

The runtime will get the `ImageUrl` property from the `.skin` file. If the name of the image file changes, you can update it in the `.skin` file, and all references to it will automatically be changed. You might use this approach to help manage name changes for static files when you version them, as I discussed in Chapter 2. Instead of changing many `.aspx` pages that reference your static files, you can change just one or a few `.skin` files and then easily test the changes or fall back to the old version if you need to do so.

This approach is also useful to help consistently associate particular properties with an image, such as a CSS class or `height` and `width`.

In addition to images, you can apply skins to most controls. For some of the same reasons that it's a good idea to move style-related information such as colors and fonts into CSS files, it's also a good idea to move similar types of information into skins when it's applied to controls in the form of properties.

Precaching Themed Images

An issue may come up when you're implementing image precaching from JavaScript, as I discussed in Chapter 2, when you're also using themes. A fixed path name won't work correctly, since the path name changes when the theme changes. Paths can also be different in Cassini than in IIS. The solution is to use `ResolveUrl()` and the current theme name to generate the required path:

```
<body onload="OnPageLoad">
. . .
<script type="text/javascript">
function OnPageLoad(evt) {
    var cim = new Image();
    cim.src = '<%= ResolveUrl("~/app_themes/" + this.StyleSheetTheme +
            "/images/logo.png") %>';
}
</script>
</body>
```

You could extend this technique to force lowercase URLs and to support multiple static domains for your images, along the lines shown later in this chapter.

Browser-Specific Code

Making browser-specific changes to web pages, whether on the server or on the client in the form of JavaScript, can sometimes become one of the more time-consuming and error-prone aspects of web site development. ASP.NET provides some cool features that will help minimize the time and effort you spend in this area.

As another aspect of the ultra-fast approach, your development time will be shorter and your site will tend to be faster if you can do these types of customizations on the server, rather than on the client. You will have fewer bugs when you write your code in a type-safe .NET language instead of in script, and when you do have bugs, you will be able to find and fix them more quickly.

Every HTTP request carries a `User-Agent` string that you can use to determine which browser made the request. You can of course parse the `User-Agent` string yourself. However, ASP.NET can also do it for you. The information that the runtime uses to determine the current browser is contained in a collection of `.browser` files, located in `C:\Windows\Microsoft.NET\Framework\v2.0.50727\CONFIG\Browsers`. Those XML-formatted files contain regular expressions to match against the `User-Agent` string, along with a number of *capabilities*, as string/value pairs. As an example, here are the first few lines from the `ie.browser` file:

```
<browsers>
    <browser id="IE" parentID="Mozilla">
        <identification>
            <userAgent match="^Mozilla[^(]*\([C|c]ompatible;\s*MSIE
                              (?'version'(?'major'\d+)(?'minor'\.\d+)
                              (?'letters'\w*))(?'extra'[^)]*)" />
            <userAgent nonMatch="Opera|Go\.Web|Windows CE|EudoraWeb" />
        </identification>
        <capture>
        </capture>
        <capabilities>
            <capability name="browser"           value="IE" />
            <capability name="extra"             value="${extra}" />
            <capability name="isColor"           value="true" />
            <capability name="letters"           value="${letters}" />
            <capability name="majorversion"      value="${major}" />
            <capability name="minorversion"      value="${minor}" />
            <capability name="screenBitDepth"    value="8" />
            <capability name="type"              value="IE${major}" />
            <capability name="version"           value="${version}" />
        </capabilities>
    </browser>
```

Each browser has a unique `id` and is associated with a `parentID` to form a hierarchical tree of relationships. For example, IE and Firefox share a common ancestor in this tree called `Mozilla`.

To determine the current browser, the runtime will start at the root of the tree, which is the `Default` browser. Next, all nodes with `parentID` set to `Default` (child nodes) will be examined to see whether their `<userAgent match>` regular expressions match against the current `User-Agent` string. If there is a match, then the runtime evaluates the `<userAgent nonMatch>` regular expression to see whether it should ignore the match on that basis. If zero or more than one child node matches, then the process is complete, and the last matched node is the result. If exactly one child node matches, then the process is recursively repeated for its child nodes. Each time there's a match, including at the original `Default` node, the runtime picks up all the capability values of the matching node, overriding any previous values.

You can add new system-wide `.browser` files by placing them in subdirectories in the `CONFIG\Browsers` folder. After doing so, you must run the following command, which is located in `C:\Windows\Microsoft.NET\Framework\v2.0.50727`:

```
aspnet_regbrowsers -i
```

That will make the `.browser` files visible to the runtime. As with a change to `machine.config`, that will cause IIS and your application to restart, so you should do it with care on a production server.

■ **Caution** Don't change the standard `.browser` files. Windows Update can overwrite them, which might cause your changes to be lost.

Alternatively, you can place new site-specific `.browser` files in the `App_Browsers` folder of your web site, which also makes them easier to manage from a deployment and source code control perspective.

If you need in-depth support for mobile devices, I suggest installing the Mobile Device Browser File (MDBF)) from CodePlex, which is available at `http://mdbf.codeplex.com/`. As of May 2009, the MDBF supports more than 400 different devices.

Using Request.Browser

Once the runtime has determined which browser description matches the current `User-Agent` string best, it exposes the associated ID and capabilities through the `Request.Browser` object. To demonstrate, create a new web form called `browser1.aspx`, and edit the markup as follows:

```
User-Agent: <%= Request.UserAgent %><br /><br />
ID: <%= Request.Browser.Id %><br />
Browser: <%= Request.Browser.Browser %><br />
Type: <%= Request.Browser.Capabilities["type"] %>
```

If you open `browser1.aspx` in IE7, here's what it displays:

```
User-Agent: Mozilla/4.0 (compatible; MSIE 7.0; Windows NT 6.0; SLCC1;
  .NET CLR 2.0.50727; Media Center PC 5.0; InfoPath.2; .NET CLR 3.5.21022;
  .NET CLR 1.1.4322; .NET CLR 3.5.30428; MS-RTC LM 8; .NET CLR 3.5.30729;
  .NET CLR 3.0.30618; OfficeLiveConnector.1.3; OfficeLivePatch.0.0)

ID: ie6to9
Browser: IE
Type: IE7
```

Opening the same file in Firefox produces this:

```
User-Agent: Mozilla/5.0 (Windows; U; Windows NT 6.0; en-US; rv:1.9.0.10)
  Gecko/2009042316 Firefox/3.0.10 (.NET CLR 3.5.30729)

ID: mozillafirefox
Browser: Firefox
Type: Firefox3.0.10
```

Be careful not to add new `.browser` files that might cause multiple matches among sibling nodes and not to add nodes with the same names as existing nodes. If you do, you might break the browser identification system in unexpected ways. Instead, when adding a `.browser` file for a new device, a good approach is to determine first where the matching process terminates in the current hierarchy. Then use that node as the parent for the new `.browser` file.

For example, if you wanted to change some of the reported capabilities for Firefox, you would set the `parentID` to `mozillafirefox`.

Browser-Specific Property Prefixes

One way to customize your pages based on the browser is to prefix the ID from one of the matching browser definitions to property names in your markup. The runtime will use the most specific definition of an ID that it can. For example, create another web form called `browser2.aspx`, and include the following markup:

```
<asp:Label runat="server" Text="No prefix" mozilla:Text="This is Mozilla" />
```

If you display that page in IE or Firefox, it will show "This is Mozilla." In a non-Mozilla browser like Opera, it will show "No prefix."

To display different text in IE, make the following change:

```
<asp:Label runat="server" Text="No prefix" mozilla:Text="This is Mozilla"
          ie:Text="This is IE" />
```

Even though the `mozilla` ID matches IE, the `ie` prefix is more specific (further down the browser hierarchy), so that's the one the runtime will use for IE browsers. Firefox, Chrome, and other Mozilla browsers will still see "This is Mozilla."

Browser prefixes work on all properties of server objects, including template objects and events. They even work on `Page` directive properties. For example, here's how you might specify a different CSS file for IE than for other browsers:

```
<head runat="server">
    <title></title>
    <link runat="server" rel="stylesheet" type="text/css"
          ie:href="ie.css" href="others.css" />
</head>
```

In the `Page` directive, here's an example of how to specify a different master page for IE than for other browsers:

```
<%@ Page MasterPageFile="~/others.master" ie:MasterPageFile="~/ie.master" . . . %>
```

A common use of browser prefixes is to select an alternate CSS class. Here's an example:

```
<asp:Label runat="server" Text="My text"
    CssClass="othclass" ie:CssClass="ieclass" />
```

The server-side approach is easier to understand and maintain, as well as faster and shorter than conventional client-side conditional comments:

```
<!–[if IE]>
. . .
<![endif]-->
```

If you have sections of HTML or ASP.NET controls on a page that are browser-specific, the `<asp:MultiView>` control provides a convenient way to show one section or another based on browser type.

Here's an example:

```
<asp:MultiView runat="server" ie:ActiveViewIndex="0" ActiveViewIndex="1">
  <asp:View runat="server">
    This is <a href="#">for IE</a>
  </asp:View>
  <asp:View runat="server">
    And this is <a href="#">for others</a>
  </asp:View>
</asp:MultiView>
```

The `ActiveViewIndex` property specifies which of the `<asp:View>` tags to use, with a zero-based index. In this case, you're using the first one for IE and the second one for other browsers. The `<asp:View>` tags can contain either plain HTML or controls.

Caching Browser-Specific Pages

Pages with browser-specific code on them require extra care in order to be correctly output cached. You should specify an appropriate value for `VaryByCustom` in the `OutputCache` directive, along with a corresponding `GetVaryByCustomString` method. The goal is to ensure that different versions of the page are rendered for the different browsers.

The brute-force approach is to set `VaryByCustom` to `browser`. That will cause the runtime to cache different versions of the page based on the browser's type and major version number. This approach doesn't require a custom `GetVaryByCustomString` method. However, if your only variations are for IE, Mozilla, and all others, the brute-force solution will result in caching many more versions of the page than you actually need. Instead, an optimized `GetVaryByCustomString` method would be better.

Here's an example:

```
public override string GetVaryByCustomString(HttpContext context, string custom)
{
    switch (custom.ToLower())
    {
        case "iemozilla":
            switch (context.Request.Browser.Browser.ToLower())
            {
                case "ie":
                case "blazer 3.0":
                    return "ie";
                case "mozilla":
                case "firebird":
                case "firefox":
                case "applemac-safari":
                    return "mozilla";
                default:
                    return "default";
            }
        default:
            return base.GetVaryByCustomString(context, custom);
    }
}
```

The runtime will cache different versions of the page for each different string that this method returns; the exact value of the strings doesn't matter. In this case, we have up to three versions of each `iemozilla` page: `ie`, `mozilla`, and `default` (plus the base method, which handles the case where `custom` is `browser`).

You can't base the cache variations on exactly the same values that you used as prefixes for control properties, because of the hierarchical nature of the prefix-to-ID matching process. Therefore, use the `Browser` property here instead of `Id`, since the latter contains the ID of the leaf node only and can present considerable variation among similar browsers, whereas the former is used to group browsers with similar capabilities.

Then to configure output caching, use this:

```
<%@ OutputCache Duration="60" VaryByParam="None" VaryByCustom="ieMozilla" %>
```

The `ieMozilla` string assigned to `VaryByCustom` is passed to the `GetVaryByCustomString` method.

Control Adapters

Part of the life cycle of a user control includes the `Render` phase, during which the control generates its output. It's possible to use a *control adapter* to alter the output that a control generates. Since one of the main reasons most developers would be interested in generating different output for a control is to customize it for a particular browser, it should come as no surprise that the mechanism is integrated with the browser identification system.

Control adapters are useful for several things related to performance. For example, you might want to change a control to use a tableless layout or to shorten the markup. You can also use control adapters to modify some of the control's properties before it's rendered. You can use that feature to implement some of the HTML optimization techniques from Chapter 2.

In the earlier example of a user control, one of the things that you did was to convert the image URL to lowercase. Let's build a control adapter to do that automatically for *all* `<asp:Image>` controls (see `App_Code\ImageControlAdapter.cs`):

```
using System;
using System.Web.UI.WebControls;
using System.Web.UI.WebControls.Adapters;

namespace Samples
{
    public class ImageControlAdapter : WebControlAdapter
    {
        public ImageControlAdapter()
        {
        }
```

Since the `Image` control derives from `WebControl`, derive the control adapter from `WebControlAdapter`.

```
protected override void BeginRender(System.Web.UI.HtmlTextWriter writer)
{
    Image image = Control as Image;
    if ((image != null) && !String.IsNullOrEmpty(image.ImageUrl))
    {
        if (!image.ImageUrl.StartsWith("http"))
        {
            image.ImageUrl = this.Page.ResolveUrl(image.ImageUrl).ToLower();
        }
    }
    base.BeginRender(writer);
}
```

You need to override only one method in this case. The adapter will call `BeginRender` at the start of the rendering process. If the associated control is `Image`, and if its `ImageUrl` property is present and doesn't refer to an external site (where URL case might matter), then replace it with a lowercase version that includes the full path. After that, just call `base.BeginRender()`, which will render the control as usual.

Next, to configure the runtime to call the control adapter, create a file called `adapter.browser` in your `App_Browser` folder:

```
<browsers>
  <browser refID="Default">
    <controlAdapters>
      <adapter controlType="System.Web.UI.WebControls.Image"
               adapterType="Samples.ImageControlAdapter" />
    </controlAdapters>
  </browser>
</browsers>
```

You specify the ID of the browsers that you want this control adapter to be used for in the `refID` property. Since you want it to be used for all browsers in this case, specify the `Default` ID, which is the root of the hierarchy. Specify the full type name of the `Image` control in the `controlType` property and the type of the new control adapter in the `adapterType` property.

To test the adapter, create a new web form and add an `<asp:Image>` control with an uppercase `ImageUrl` property. When you view the page in a browser and examine the source, you should see the URL in lowercase.

I suggest looking into the *CSS Friendly Control Adapters* project available from `http://www.codeplex.com/cssfriendly`. Those adapters produce table-free, CSS-friendly markup for some of the more commonly used controls. Unfortunately, the code hasn't been updated in a while and is known to have several bugs, but even so, it provides a comprehensive example of how to use control adapters to generate more optimal HTML.

■ **Note** .NET 4.0 introduces the `RenderTable` property for the `<asp:FormView>` control. When set to `false`, it will prevent the content of the control from being surrounded by a `<table>`.

Browser Providers

.NET 4.0 introduces a feature called `HttpCapabilitiesProviders`, which allows you to determine the browser type and related capabilities programmatically, completely bypassing the default semistatic mechanisms described earlier.

One advantage of this technique from a performance perspective is that it allows you to look at more than just the `User-Agent` string. You might use this approach to identify search engines and other bots, for example, by looking at cookies or access patterns.

As an example, after making sure that your project is configured to use .NET 4.0, create a file called `BrowserProvider.cs` in your `App_Code` folder:

```
using System;
using System.Collections;
using System.Web;
using System.Web.Caching;
using System.Web.Configuration;

namespace Samples
{
    public class BrowserProvider : HttpCapabilitiesProvider
    {
        public BrowserProvider()
        {
        }
```

The class inherits from `HttpCapabilitiesProvider`. You need to override only one method:

```
public override HttpBrowserCapabilities GetBrowserCapabilities(HttpRequest request)
{
    string key = "bw-" + request.UserAgent;
    Cache cache = HttpContext.Current.Cache;
    HttpBrowserCapabilities caps = cache[key] as HttpBrowserCapabilities;
    if (caps == null)
    {
        //
        // Determine browser type here...
        //
        caps = new HttpBrowserCapabilities();
        caps.AddBrowser("test");
        Hashtable capDict = new Hashtable(StringComparer.OrdinalIgnoreCase);
        capDict["browser"] = "Default";
        capDict["cookies"] = "true";
        capDict["ecmascriptversion"] = "0.0";
        capDict["tables"] = "true";
        capDict["w3cdomversion"] = "0.0";
        caps.Capabilities = capDict;
        cache.Insert(key, caps, null, Cache.NoAbsoluteExpiration,
            TimeSpan.FromMinutes(60.0));
    }
    return caps;
}
```

First, construct a key to use with the cache to see whether you have previously determined the `HttpBrowserCapabilities` object for the current `User-Agent`. The results are cached because this method can be called multiple times during a single request and because the lookup process might be time-consuming. To generate the cache key, prepend a fixed string to the `User-Agent` string to avoid potential collisions with other pages or applications.

If the cache lookup fails, then parse `request.UserAgent` (not shown in the example), construct the result, and insert it into the cache. The `Id` property is an accessor that retrieves the last item in the list of matched browsers, which you build using the `AddBrowser()` method. This would normally be the list of matches in the hierarchy when using the default approach. The properties added in the example are the minimum set needed to display a very simple web page.

To enable the provider, make the following change to `Global.asax.cs`:

```
using System.Web.Configuration;

void Application_Start(object sender, EventArgs e)
{
    HttpCapabilitiesBase.BrowserCapabilitiesProvider =
        new Samples.BrowserProvider();
}
```

To test the provider, create a page that displays `Request.Browser.Id` and `Request.Browser.Browser`. Notice that the results are different after enabling the provider.

Cloaking

With the ability to generate different content for different User-Agents, one thing that you might be tempted to do is to create different pages for search engines than you do for regular browsers. This practice is known as *cloaking*, and it is strongly discouraged by search engines. The reason is to prevent misleading their users when they present information on one topic as the result of a search, while you deliver completely unrelated information when users click through to your site.

However, I believe that there is a very narrow range of conditions where presenting different content to a search engine is actually the right thing to do, because it *helps* end users correctly identify what's on your page.

One example is where a Silverlight application, which none of the major search engines currently index, dominates the page content. When the User-Agent is a bot, you might want to include some descriptive text and appropriate links on the page instead of the Silverlight control.

Dynamically Generating JavaScript and CSS

JavaScript undoubtedly plays a critical role in all modern web sites. Unfortunately, though, the ugly reality is that JavaScript is not a type-safe language, and it's interpreted rather than compiled. As a result, it tends to be a rich source of bugs, even on some of the world's largest and busiest sites.

I've worked with development teams that seem to spend more time chasing bugs in JavaScript than they do in server-side code, even though the script is a small fraction of the size. Fortunately, the script debugging feature in Visual Studio 2008 and later is a huge help in that regard, even though it doesn't address the underlying problem.

As an aside, I usually leave the JavaScript debug feature enabled in IE because of the development work I do. That causes IE to display a warning dialog box whenever it runs into a script exception (in the default configuration, all script errors are silently ignored). I would say that roughly 10 to 20 percent of the sites I visit have JavaScript bugs that are severe enough to throw an exception and pop up that warning dialog box. Imagine how many more bugs there must be that aren't quite that bad.

You can minimize these types of problems in two ways. The first, as described earlier, is to replace script with Silverlight on the client when possible. The second is to minimize the size and complexity of your script by generating it dynamically on the server. On many sites, considerable script ends up being devoted to detecting and handling various browser differences. Since the server knows which browser the client is using, you can handle most of those kinds of conditionals on the server instead, using the techniques described earlier.

There is a similar story for CSS. I've seen extremely inventive yet terribly convoluted and hard to maintain code that handles browser differences in CSS. You can make your life much easier by simply generating the correct CSS on the server.

Another reason to generate both JavaScript and CSS dynamically is so that you can combine multiple files into a single file of each type to help minimize client-to-server round trips. Using multiple files often makes good sense from a development perspective, particularly when multiple teams are involved. However, there is usually no reason for them to be downloaded to clients separately. I've seen sites with a dozen or more JavaScript files on a page. Particularly with the way browsers can serialize requests to download script, that's a scenario that you should try to avoid.

When thinking about how to make dynamic JavaScript and CSS work, consider for a moment what .aspx pages (and user controls) really are: a fancy way to generate *text* in response to an HTTP request. In the usual case, that text happens to be HTML, but it doesn't have to be.

Example

For example, create a new web form called **script1.aspx**, and replace the markup with the following:

```
<%@ Page EnableTheming="false" StylesheetTheme="" EnableViewState="false"
    AutoEventWireup="true" Language="C#" CodeFile="script1.aspx.cs"
    Inherits="script1" %>
alert('<%= "User Agent = " + Request.UserAgent %>');
```

If you're planning to use themes on your site, it's important to set **EnableTheming** to **false** and **StyleSheetTheme** to an empty string. Otherwise, the runtime will generate an error saying that you need to include a **<head runat="true">** tag. Unfortunately, setting those values in an **HttpModule** won't work.

Notice that the argument to **alert()** includes text that will be dynamically generated when the file is requested.

In the code-behind, use the following **Page_Load()** method:

```
protected void Page_Load(object sender, EventArgs e)
{
    this.Response.ContentType = "text/javascript";
}
```

This sets the MIME type of the response, which tells the browser what type of data it contains. If you want to generate CSS instead, the MIME type would be **text/css**.

Next, create a web form called **script-test1.aspx**, and insert the following at the top of the **<body>**:

```
<script type="text/javascript" src="script1.aspx">
</script>
```

Now view **script-test1.aspx** in a browser, and you should see an alert displayed from **script1.aspx**. Notice that the alert text contains the **User-Agent** string of the browser you're using.

You could combine this approach with several of the techniques described earlier in this chapter to generate JavaScript or CSS. You could have user controls that generate script, use browser prefixes to generate browser-specific script, or use the **<asp:MultiView>** control to select blocks of script for each of several different browsers.

Here's an example (see **script2.aspx**):

```
<%@ Page EnableTheming="false" StylesheetTheme="" EnableViewState="false"
    Language="C#" CodeFile="script2.aspx.cs" Inherits="script2" %>
<%@ OutputCache Duration="86400" VaryByParam="None" VaryByCustom="ieMozilla" %>
 var Event = {
<asp:MultiView runat="server" ActiveViewIndex="0" ie:ActiveViewIndex="1">
<asp:View runat="server">
    Add: function(obj, evt, func, capture) {
        obj.addEventListener(evt, func, capture);
    },
    Remove: function(obj, evt, func, capture) {
        obj.removeEventListener(evt, func, capture);
    }
</asp:View>
```

```
<asp:View runat="server">
    Add: function(obj, evt, func, capture) {
        obj.attachEvent('on' + evt, func);
    },
    Remove: function(obj, evt, func, capture) {
        obj.detachEvent('on' + evt, func);
    }
</asp:View>
</asp:MultiView>
}
```

I've specified an `OutputCache` directive with the same `VaryByCustom` method from earlier examples. Using the same code-behind as in the previous example to set the MIME type of the response, this code will generate one version of the `Event` functions for IE and one for other browsers.

You can of course also apply these techniques to script or CSS that's in the same file as your generated HTML. However, it's generally better to factor that text out into separate include files when you can. That way, the browser can cache it on the client. The trade-off is a slightly higher PLT1 (if an include is required where it wasn't before) vs. an improved PLT2. You can improve maintenance and code reuse by keeping as much script and CSS as possible in include files.

Although it's possible to configure ASP.NET to process `.js` or `.css` files as though they were `.aspx` files; unfortunately, as of .NET 3.5, there are issues that prevent that from working right if you're using themes. In particular, as I mentioned earlier, the runtime doesn't allow dynamic files in the `App_Themes` folder, presumably to prevent accidental recursion; perhaps it will be fixed in a future release.

Accessing ASP.NET Controls from JavaScript

In the event that you would like to use script to interact with ASP.NET controls, I've found that it's helpful to associate a constant name in script with the possibly variable ID strings produced by the runtime. Although the IDs generated by the runtime in the final HTML are sometimes predictable, often they are not. The use of master pages, for example, will result in IDs that are different from the ones you specify for your controls. To demonstrate, let's say you have an `<asp:Label>` control on a page that uses a master page and you want to modify the content of the control on the client using script (see `script3.aspx`):

```
<%@ Page MasterPageFile="~/master/Main.master" Language="C#" AutoEventWireup="true"
    CodeFile="script3.aspx.cs" Inherits="script3" %>
<asp:Content runat="server" ID="NW" ContentPlaceHolderID="LG">
<asp:Label runat="server" ID="myInfo" Text="Initial text" />
<script type="text/javascript">
    function RegObj(clientId, anId) {
        eval('window.' + clientId + ' = document.getElementById(anId)');
    }
    RegObj('mytext', '<%= myInfo.ClientID %>');
    mytext.innerHTML = 'Reset text';
</script>
</asp:Content>
```

The runtime generates the following HTML for the `<asp:Label>` control:

```
<span id="ctl00_LG_myInfo">Initial text</span>
```

Rather than having to call the JavaScript getElementById() function everywhere the control is referenced, the RegObj() function associates an ID that you obtain on the server with an easily referenced variable name. The *generated* JavaScript looks like this:

```
<script type="text/javascript">
    function RegObj(clientId, anId) {
        eval('window.' + clientId + ' = document.getElementById(anId)');
    }
    RegObj('mytext', 'ctl00_LG_myInfo');
    mytext.innerHTML = 'Reset text';
</script>
```

After calling RegObj(), you can refer to the generated <span> tag with just mytext.

Multiple Domains for Static Files

One of the suggestions I made in Chapter 2 was to distribute your image files among multiple subdomains, which can allow the browser to do more downloading in parallel. To maximize cacheability on the client and in proxies, you shouldn't make that assignment randomly; you should do it in a deterministic way so that the same image is always mapped to the same subdomain.

One approach you could take for images is to extend the <ctl:image> user control that I discussed earlier in the "User Controls" section. Since you are already manipulating the URL of the image there, it would be straightforward to add support for multiple subdomains.

Here's an example (see Controls\imagesub.ascx.cs):

```
private string _src;
private static string[] subdomains = {
    "http://s1.12titans.net",
    "http://s2.12titans.net",
    "http://s3.12titans.net"
};

public string src
{
    get
    {
        HttpContext ctx = HttpContext.Current;
        if (ctx.Request.Url.Host != "localhost")
        {
            if (!String.IsNullOrEmpty(this._src) && !this._src.StartsWith("http"))
            {
                int n = Math.Abs(this._src.GetHashCode()) % subdomains.Length;
                return subdomains[n] + this._src;
            }
        }
        return this._src;
    }
```

```
        set
        {
            this._src = ResolveUrl(value).ToLowerInvariant();
        }
    }
    public int height { get; set; }
    public int width { get; set; }
    public string alt { get; set; }
```

The example code does not change the URL when it's running on your local machine or when the image comes from another site.

You could apply this same technique in a control adapter for the `<asp:Image>` control, in addition to making the URL lowercase as in the earlier example.

In a production version of this code, you might want to minimize the effects of adding new domains or removing old ones. This would also be a good place to automatically apply similar mappings for a content distribution network (CDN).

Image Resizing

As I mentioned in Chapter 2, images often represent a significant fraction of both the data required by the browser to render a page fully and a site's bandwidth use. For those reasons, it's important to make sure that you don't send large images to the client when smaller ones will work just as well. If your images are too big or have a much higher quality than your users need, you might of course choose to resize or recompress them statically: figure out all the right sizes and compression factors, run them through a tool of some kind, and you're done. However, if you have tens of thousands of images, or perhaps tens of millions like some sites do, that can be more than a little tedious.

An alternative is to resize and recompress your images dynamically and cache the results as you go. You might create a user control to do that, for example, or for a large library of images, you might do it in a background thread. Since the number and size of the images could be large and since IIS has an efficient method for caching static files, you should store the resized images as files, rather than in memory.

Here's an example of a routine that can resize most image types. For JPEG images, you can specify a level of compression between 0 and 100, with 0 being maximum compression and minimum size and with 100 being minimum compression and maximum size. You specify the size of the resized image as the length of the longest dimension. You might use this to create thumbnails, for example, that all fit in a 100 × 100 pixel area.

See `App_Code\ImageResizer.cs`:

```
using System;
using System.Drawing;
using System.Drawing.Imaging;
using System.Drawing.Drawing2D;
using System.IO;

namespace Samples
{
    public class ImageResizer
    {
```

```
    private static ImageCodecInfo jpgEncoder;

    public static void ResizeImage(string inFile, string outFile,
        double maxDimension, long level)
    {
        using (Stream stream = new FileStream(inFile, FileMode.Open))
        {
            using (Image inImage = Image.FromStream(stream))
            {
```

You access the image file with a **Stream**, which you use to build an **Image** object. If you intend to call this code while processing a page, instead of from a background thread, then you should use asynchronous file I/O.

```
                double width;
                double height;

                if (inImage.Height < inImage.Width)
                {
                    width = maxDimension;
                    height = (maxDimension / (double)inImage.Width) * inImage.Height;
                }
                else
                {
                    height = maxDimension;
                    width = (maxDimension / (double)inImage.Height) * inImage.Width;
                }
                using (Bitmap bitmap = new Bitmap((int)width, (int)height))
                {
                    using (Graphics graphics = Graphics.FromImage(bitmap))
                    {
```

After calculating the dimensions of the new image based on the given parameters and the dimensions of the original image, create an empty **Bitmap** object that will contain the resized image and a **Graphics** object that you can use to draw into the **Bitmap**.

```
                        graphics.SmoothingMode = SmoothingMode.HighQuality;
                        graphics.InterpolationMode =
                            InterpolationMode.HighQualityBicubic;
                        graphics.DrawImage(inImage, 0, 0, bitmap.Width, bitmap.Height);
```

Copy the original image into the **Bitmap** using the **Graphics** object, resizing it as you go according to the parameters specified for **SmoothingMode** and **InterpolationMode**.

```
                        if (inImage.RawFormat.Guid == ImageFormat.Jpeg.Guid)
                        {
                            if (jpgEncoder == null)
                            {
                                ImageCodecInfo[] ici =
                                    ImageCodecInfo.GetImageDecoders();
```

```
            foreach (ImageCodecInfo info in ici)
            {
                if (info.FormatID == ImageFormat.Jpeg.Guid)
                {
                    jpgEncoder = info;
                    break;
                }
            }
        }
```

If the original image is in the JPEG format and you haven't previously found the corresponding ImageCodecInfo object, then look it up now.

```
        if (jpgEncoder != null)
        {
            EncoderParameters ep = new EncoderParameters(1);
            ep.Param[0] = new EncoderParameter(Encoder.Quality,
                level);
            bitmap.Save(outFile, jpgEncoder, ep);
        }
        else
            bitmap.Save(outFile, inImage.RawFormat);
    }
    else
    {
        //
        // Fill with white for transparent GIFs
        //
        graphics.FillRectangle(Brushes.White, 0, 0, bitmap.Width,
            bitmap.Height);
        bitmap.Save(outFile, inImage.RawFormat);
    }
```

If the original image was a JPEG, then set the compression level of the output image based on the specified input parameter, and encode the image. Otherwise, encode the output image in the same format as the original image.

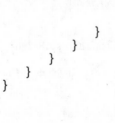

```
                }
              }
            }
          }
        }
      }
    }
```

Summary

In this chapter, I covered the following:

- Using master pages, user controls, and themes and skins to encapsulate high-performance implementations to improve code reuse and to reduce the time it takes you to make changes to your site

- Generating browser-specific markup efficiently using ASP.NET's built-in browser recognition system and extending that system

- Applying output caching to user controls and browser-specific pages

- Using control adapters to modify the output of user controls to produce optimized HTML and to implement some of the optimization techniques from Chapter 2

- Using `HttpCapabilitiesProvider` in .NET 4.0 to determine browser type and related capabilities programmatically

- Generating JavaScript and CSS dynamically using the same mechanisms you use to generate HTML

- Accessing HTML generated by ASP.NET controls from JavaScript

- Generating consistent domains for static files, as suggested in Chapter 2

- Dynamically resizing images, with optimized compression for JPEGs

CHAPTER 7

∎∎∎

Managing ASP.NET Application Policies

During the design and coding of your web site, you will often come up with actions that you would like to take for every page on your site, or perhaps for every control of a certain type. I call those actions *application policies*. You might apply them before or after a page generates its content or as part of page or control processing.

Application policies can have a big impact on performance in areas such as session management, caching, URL rewriting, output filtering, and control rendering. They also form an important part of the ultra-fast approach, since they allow you to easily centralize, manage, and monitor certain aspects of your application. That helps improve agility while minimizing code duplication and simplifying many system-wide debugging and analysis tasks.

In this chapter, I will cover the following:

- Using `HttpModules`, which allow you to apply policies at any point in the IIS request life cycle

- Using `HttpHandlers`, which allow you to bypass the policies and associated overhead imposed by the `Page` handler

- Implementing a page base class, which will allow you to override `Page` policies and to add others of your own

- Implementing URL rewriting programmatically to help shorten your URLs

- Using page adapters, tag mapping, and control adapters to implement application policies

- Using HTTP redirects and their alternatives

- Improving your user's experience by flushing the response buffer early

- Reducing the size of your page with HTML whitespace filtering

Custom HttpModules

ASP.NET requests have a life cycle that starts with an incoming HTTP request. IIS and the runtime then step through a number of states, ultimately producing the HTTP response. At each state transition, IIS and the runtime invoke all registered event handlers. Depending on the event, those event handlers might be located in your Global.asax file or in a standard or custom HttpModule.

When your site is running in IIS Integrated mode, as I suggest in Chapter 4, the pipeline events are as shown in Figure 4-2. The events happen for both static and dynamic content, and you can write event handlers in either managed or unmanaged code. For example, you could write an HttpModule in C# that handles events for your static images or even for files processed by a nonmanaged handler, such as PHP.

One of the differences between Global.asax and HttpModules is that events in Global.asax are executed only for requests that are processed by the ASP.NET handler, even when IIS is running in Integrated mode.

From an architectural perspective, I tend to discourage use of Global.asax as much as possible, since integrating a new HttpModule from another project into your site is much easier than merging multiple Global.asax files together. However, a couple of events are available only in Global.asax, and not in HttpModules, such as Application_Start and Application_Stop.

■ **Note** Cassini, the development web server that's used by Visual Studio, sends all requests through all HttpModules, even when the site is configured in Classic mode.

As with web pages, you can write HttpModules to operate asynchronously. Since they run for every request, it's particularly important for scalability to use async operations if your HttpModule does any I/O, including database requests.

The following are possible applications of HttpModules:

- Enforcing site-wide cookie policies

- Centralized monitoring and logging

- Programmatically setting or removing HTTP headers

- Wiring up post-processing of response output, such as removing extra whitespace

- Session management

- Authorization and authentication

Requirements for the Example HttpModule

I covered a simple example of an HttpModule in Chapter 4. However, since HttpModules can play a very important role in establishing site-wide consistency and because of their potential impact on performance, let's walk through a much more detailed example that includes some of the techniques that I've discussed.

Here's a list of the requirements for the example:

- Allow the default theme to be modified at runtime.

- Set a long-lasting cookie on each client that contains a unique ID, and record the value of that ID in the database.

- If the Page or the HttpModule itself sets a cookie, make sure that the P3P privacy header is also set (see Chapter 3).

- Differentiate between clients that retain cookies and those that don't (as a high-level indicator of whether they might be spider and not a real user).

- For all .aspx requests, log the client's unique ID and details about the page request in the database, using a background worker thread.

Init() Method

Create MainModule.cs in your App_Code folder:

```
using System;
using System.Collections.Generic;
using System.Data;
using System.Data.SqlClient;
using System.Diagnostics;
using System.Text;
using System.Threading;
using System.Web;
using System.Web.UI;

namespace Samples
{
    public class MainModule : IHttpModule
    {
        public const string CookiePath = "/Samples/pages/";
        public const string MachCookie = "MC";
        public const string MachId = "mi";
        public const string MachFirst = "mf";
        public const int PageViewBatchSize = 10;
        public const string ConnString =
            "Data Source=.;Initial Catalog=Sample;Integrated Security=True;Async=True";
```

The only methods in the IHttpModule interface are Init() and Dispose(). The bulk of the class will be event handlers that you will wire up in Init().

CookiePath is set to work with Cassini; under IIS, it wouldn't include the project name.

```
public void Init(HttpApplication context)
{
    WorkItem.Init(Work);
    context.AddOnAuthenticateRequestAsync(this.Sample_BeginAuthenticateRequest,
        this.Sample_EndAuthenticateRequest);
    context.PreRequestHandlerExecute += this.Sample_PreRequestHandlerExecute;
    context.EndRequest += this.Sample_EndRequest;
}

public void Dispose()
{
}
```

The Init() method starts by initializing a background worker thread, which you will use for logging as I discussed earlier in the section on thread management. I'm using the same background worker class that I walked you through in Chapter 5. Work is the name of the method that the worker thread will call to process WorkItem objects.

Since the code will need to access the database, use the async version of the AuthenticateRequest event, which happens early in the request life cycle. As with async pages, you do this by having one method to start the request and another that's called when the request completes.

Next, register an event handler for the PreRequestHandlerExecute event. As its name implies, this event is fired right before the request handler is executed. You may recall from Chapter 4 that the request handler is the code that's responsible for generating the primary output of the request. Request handlers are implementations of the IHttpHandler interface; the Page class is one example of a handler. There are also handlers for static files, ASMX web services, WCF, and so on. Your site might also include custom handlers. IIS determines which handler to invoke based on the extension of the URL that it's processing.

Finally, register an event handler for the EndRequest event, which happens near the end of the request life cycle.

PreRequestHandlerExecute Event Handler

Here's the PreRequestHandlerExecute event handler:

```
private void Sample_PreRequestHandlerExecute(Object source, EventArgs e)
{
    HttpApplication application = (HttpApplication)source;
    HttpContext context = application.Context;
    Page page = context.Handler as Page;
    if (page != null)
    {
        page.StyleSheetTheme = "mkt";
    }
}
```

The code checks to see whether the request handler assigned to the current request is a Page object, which is the case for all .aspx pages. If it is, then the StyleSheetTheme property is set to the name of the default theme. Since this happens before the handler is invoked, the Page itself can still override the setting in its Page_PreInit() method.

BeginAuthenticateRequest Event Handler

Here's the BeginAuthenticateRequest event handler:

```
private IAsyncResult Sample_BeginAuthenticateRequest(Object source, EventArgs e,
    AsyncCallback cb, Object state)
{
    IAsyncResult ar = null;
    HttpApplication application = (HttpApplication)source;
    HttpContext context = application.Context;
    string path = context.Request.Url.AbsolutePath;

    if (path.StartsWith(CookiePath, StringComparison.OrdinalIgnoreCase) &&
        (path.EndsWith(".aspx", StringComparison.OrdinalIgnoreCase) ||
         path.EndsWith("/", StringComparison.Ordinal)))
    {
```

Since this HttpModule will run in IIS Integrated mode and since you might use Cassini for testing, you need to check to make sure that this is a request for a page, rather than a CSS file or some other object. You do that by looking at the AbsolutePath of the URL, which doesn't include the query string, in case there is one.

In your site architecture, you have collected all the pages that you want to track with the ID cookie into one folder, which is specified by the CookiePath configuration parameter. In addition to checking what the path ends with, also make sure that it starts with CookiePath. Ignore case where appropriate, since URLs in IIS are case insensitive.

```
        RequestInfo info;
        HttpCookie machCookie = context.Request.Cookies[MachCookie];
        if ((machCookie == null) || !machCookie.HasKeys ||
            (machCookie.Values[MachId] == null))
        {
            info = new RequestInfo(Guid.NewGuid(), true, false);
        }
```

Encode the cookie with two subkeys, one for the ID itself and one as a flag that's set when you first create the ID and that's removed later if the client ever sends the cookie back to the server. The previous code checks to see whether the cookie is not already present or whether it is and it's not formatted correctly.

If the request meets those conditions, then create a new RequestInfo object, along with a new GUID, which you'll use as the ID. Use a GUID as an ID so that multiple load-balanced servers can create them independently, without involving the database. GUIDs are also semi-random, which makes it difficult for one client to impersonate another by guessing their ID.

The RequestInfo object here is an extension of the one I discussed earlier, in Chapter 5. The second parameter to the RequestInfo constructor indicates whether the ID value is new, and the third parameter indicates whether you've received the ID back from a client.

```
else
{
    string guidStr = machCookie.Values[MachId];
    try
    {
        Guid machGuid = new Guid(guidStr);
        bool firstResp = false;
        if (machCookie.Values[MachFirst] != null)
            firstResp = true;
        info = new RequestInfo(machGuid, false, firstResp);
    }
    catch (FormatException)
    {
        info = new RequestInfo(Guid.NewGuid(), true, false);
    }
}
```

If the cookie is present, then extract the ID string and convert it to a `Guid` object. If the GUID conversion was successful, then look to see whether the `MachFirst` flag was set in the cookie. If it was, then this is the first time you've seen this ID value come back from the client, and you set `firstResp` to `true`. Either way, create a new `RequestInfo` object that encapsulates the results.

Receiving a cookie back from a client tells you that the client has cookies enabled. That's a useful thing to know, because some spiders, including spam bots, some search engines, and so on, don't use cookies, whereas nearly all real users do. Of course, the `User-Agent` string is supposed to provide that sort of information, but some spider authors forge it, so relying on multiple detection mechanisms is usually prudent.

If the old cookie was malformed for some reason, then just create a new `RequestInfo` object as though the cookie wasn't there. In a production environment, this might be a good place to do some logging or increment a performance counter, since if this code path executes, the most likely causes are a bug on the server somewhere or users who are attempting to hack the system in some way.

```
context.Items[RequestInfo.REQ_INFO] = info;
```

All the code paths shown previously result in a `RequestInfo` object being created and stored in the `info` variable. Now, place a reference to that object in the `Items` collection in the `HttpContext` object. The reason for this is to make it available to other classes that are involved with this request. As I discussed in Chapter 3, the `Items` collection is scoped to a request.

```
if (info.FirstResponse)
{
    SqlConnection conn = new SqlConnection(ConnString);
    SqlCommand cmd = new SqlCommand("[Traffic].[AddMachine]", conn);
    cmd.CommandType = CommandType.StoredProcedure;
    cmd.Parameters.Add("id", SqlDbType.UniqueIdentifier).Value =
        info.MachineId;
    conn.Open();
    ar = cmd.BeginExecuteNonQuery(cb, cmd);
}
```

If this is the first time that a client has returned an ID that you previously sent to them, then record the ID in the database. Using GUIDs as IDs allows you to avoid a database round-trip when you first create the ID.

The first argument to `BeginExecuteNonQuery()` is the `AsyncCallback` that the runtime passed in as an argument to the event handler. The second argument will be stored in the `AsyncState` field of the `IAsyncResult`, where you can retrieve it later when the request completes.

```
    }
    return ar ?? CompletedResult.Create(state, cb);
}
```

The return value from the event handler is the `IAsyncResult` from the call to `BeginExecuteNonQuery`, if it was executed.

Unfortunately, you can't just return `null` from a `Begin` handler to indicate that you didn't start an async request of some kind. Therefore, if you didn't need to send a request to the database for this request, the return value is a new instance of `CompletedResult`, which is a custom implementation of `IAsyncResult` that always returns `true` for `CompletedSynchronously` and `IsCompleted`. The static `Create()` method also invokes the `AsyncCallback`.

EndAuthenticateRequest Event Handler

Here is the `EndAuthenticateRequest` event handler:

```
private void Sample_EndAuthenticateRequest(IAsyncResult ar)
{
    if (!(ar is CompletedResult))
    {
        SqlCommand cmd = ar.AsyncState as SqlCommand;
        if (cmd != null)
        {
            try
            {
                cmd.EndExecuteNonQuery(ar);
            }
            catch (SqlException e)
            {
                EventLog.WriteEntry("Application",
                    "SqlException in Sample_EndAuthenticateRequest: " + e.Message,
                    EventLogEntryType.Error, 201);
            }
            finally
            {
                cmd.Connection.Dispose();
                cmd.Dispose();
            }
        }
    }
}
```

This code is called when the database request has completed or immediately after BeginAuthenticateRequest returns a CompletedResult. If you executed a database request, then you can obtain the SqlCommand object that you previously stored in AsyncState. Using that, you call EndExecuteNonQuery, which completes the request.

As with all IDiposable objects, it's important for long-term performance to call Dispose() when you're done with them. A using statement is a syntactically cleaner way of doing so, but that won't work when you create the objects in one method and use them in another, so you can use the try/finally pattern here instead.

EndRequest Event Handler

Here's the EndRequest event handler:

```
private void Sample_EndRequest(Object source, EventArgs e)
{
    HttpApplication application = (HttpApplication)source;
    HttpContext context = application.Context;
    HttpResponse response = context.Response;
    RequestInfo info = (RequestInfo)context.Items[RequestInfo.REQ_INFO];
```

This code looks in the HttpContext.Items collection to see whether a RequestInfo object was previously stored there. Recall from the earlier discussion that you created a RequestInfo object and stored it in the Items collection only when the current request is for an .aspx page.

```
    if (info != null)
    {
        WorkItem.QueuePageView(info, PageViewBatchSize);
```

If the RequestInfo object was present, then queue a request to a background thread to log a record to the database that includes the page URL and the client's ID. All the data that you want to log is contained in the RequestInfo object. As described earlier, the PageViewBatchSize argument specifies how many RequestInfo objects need to be queued in a single WorkItem before the logging task will be triggered.

```
        if (info.FirstResponse || info.First)
        {
            HttpCookie machCookie = new HttpCookie(MachCookie);
            machCookie.Path = CookiePath;
            machCookie.HttpOnly = true;
            machCookie.Values[MachId] = info.MachineId.ToString();
            if (info.FirstResponse)
                machCookie.Expires = DateTime.Now.AddYears(50);
            else
                machCookie.Values[MachFirst] = "1";
            response.AppendCookie(machCookie);
        }
    }
}
```

If this is the first time that a new ID is being set or if it's the first time a client has sent an ID back to the server, then create the cookie and append it to the response. Set the `path` and `httpOnly` properties on the cookie, as per the best practices I covered earlier. Encode the ID GUID as a string, and insert it as a subkey into the cookie.

If this is the first time a client has sent the cookie back to the server, then set the expiration date to 50 years in the future. Otherwise, don't set an expiration date, so the cookie becomes a browser session cookie that will expire when the user closes their browser. In that case, also set the `MachFirst` flag as another subkey in the cookie, which will indicate to you in the client's next request that this is the first time the server has seen the ID coming back from the client.

```
if (!String.IsNullOrEmpty(context.Request.ServerVariables["SERVER_SOFTWARE"]))
{
    if ((response.Cookies.Count > 0) && (response.Headers["P3P"] == null))
    {
        response.AddHeader("P3P", "CP = \"NID DSP CAO COR\"");
    }
}
}
```

As I discussed earlier, the `P3P` HTTP header is required in some cases for the browser to accept your cookies. To avoid adding those extra bytes to all responses, the code here checks to see whether there are any cookies set in the response. If so and if the `P3P` header hasn't already been set somewhere else, then add it to the response.

The code also checks to see whether the `SERVER_SOFTWARE` server variable is set, which is one way to check whether you're running under Cassini. You need to do that here, since you can't view or manipulate the response headers unless you're running under IIS.

Database Table and Stored Procedure

Here are the definitions for the database table and the stored procedure that the example uses:

```
CREATE TABLE [Traffic].[Machines] (
    MachineId       UNIQUEIDENTIFIER,
    CreationDate    DATETIME
)

CREATE PROCEDURE [Traffic].[AddMachine]
    @id             UNIQUEIDENTIFIER
AS
BEGIN
    SET NOCOUNT ON
    DECLARE @trandate DATETIME
    SET @trandate = GETUTCDATE()
    INSERT INTO [Traffic].[Machines]
        ([MachineId], [CreationDate])
        VALUES
        (@id, @trandate)
END
```

The table is a heap, with no indexes, so inserts will be very fast.

Registering the HttpModule in web.config

To use the `HttpModule`, you will need to register it in `web.config`. For IIS Integrated mode, as recommended in Chapter 4, add it to the `<system.webServer>` section, as follows:

```
<system.webServer>
  <modules>
    <add name="MainModule" preCondition="managedHandler"
         type="Samples.MainModule" />
    . . .
  </modules>
  . . .
</system.webServer>
```

Setting `preCondition` to `managedHandler` tells IIS to call this `HttpModule` only if the request handler runs managed code, like the one for `.aspx` pages. If you want it to be executed for static content as well, you would omit the `preCondition` attribute.

To allow testing with Cassini, you should also configure the `<httpModules>` section:

```
<system.web>
    <httpModules>
        . . .
        <add name="MainModule" type="Samples.MainModule" />
    </httpModules>
    . . .
</system.web>
```

After it's registered, create a blank page in the **pages** folder of the **Sample** site, and view the page using Fiddler (by replacing `localhost` with `ipv4.fiddler` in the URL). The first time the page loads, it will set a cookie that includes the `MachFirst` flag. Here's an example:

```
Set-Cookie: MC=mi=f5489d25-2eb7-410b-87bf-f56b7e9a68a4&mf=1; path=/Samples/pages/; HttpOnly
```

The next time you request any page in that folder, the `HttpModule` will clear the `MachFirst` flag and set the cookie again with a far-future expiration date:

```
Set-Cookie: MC=mi=f5489d25-2eb7-410b-87bf-f56b7e9a68a4;
    expires=Fri, 12-Sep-2059 12:01:25 GMT; path=/Samples/pages/; HttpOnly
```

The code will also call the `AddMachine` stored procedure to `INSERT` a row into the `Machines` table, indicating that the ID is valid.

Custom HttpHandlers

As you saw in Chapter 4, as IIS is stepping through the HTTP request-processing life cycle, one of the things it does is to execute a request `HttpHandler`. The runtime uses an `HttpHandler` to process `.aspx` pages. In fact, the `Page` class, from which all `aspx` pages are derived, *is* an `HttpHandler`.

You can also create your own HttpHandlers. I find them to be most useful in cases where the markup file would have been empty, such as for dynamic image generation or delivering data directly from a file or a database.

From a performance perspective, HttpHandlers have the potential of being much lighter weight than an .aspx page. However, the downside is that you might also need to do more coding yourself to handle things such as output caching and returning appropriate HTTP error codes when needed.

As with Pages and HttpModules, for requests that include I/O or database accesses, you should use the asynchronous version, called IHttpAsyncHandler.

There are two ways to call HttpHandlers. One is to register them in web.config to be associated with a particular file extension. The other way is as an .ashx file, also known as a *generic* handler.

Beginning the Request

As an example, let's say you have some plain HTML pages stored in a database. The table has an integer key and a column that contains the HTML. Let's create a basic async HttpHandler that will determine the file ID from a query string parameter and call a stored procedure to retrieve the HTML.

To begin, right-click your web site, select **Add New Item**, and then select **Generic Handler**. Keep the default name of Handler.ashx. Modify the standard template code as follows:

```
<%@ WebHandler Language="C#" Class="Handler" %>

using System;
using System.Data;
using System.Web;
using System.Data.SqlClient;

public class Handler : IHttpAsyncHandler {
    public const string ConnString =
        "Data Source=.;Initial Catalog=Sample;Integrated Security=True;Async=True";
    HttpContext Context { get; set; }

    public void ProcessRequest(HttpContext context)
    {
    }
```

Derive the class from IHttpAsyncHandler, which itself inherits from IHttpHandler. You therefore need to implement the ProcessRequest() method, even though you won't use it.

```
    public IAsyncResult BeginProcessRequest(HttpContext context,
        AsyncCallback cb, object extraData)
    {
        this.Context = context;
        int fileid = 0;
        string id = context.Request.QueryString["id"];
        if (!String.IsNullOrEmpty(id))
            fileid = Convert.ToInt32(id);
        SqlConnection conn = new SqlConnection(ConnString);
        conn.Open();
        SqlCommand cmd = new SqlCommand("GetHtml", conn);
        cmd.CommandType = CommandType.StoredProcedure;
```

```
        cmd.Parameters.Add("fileId", SqlDbType.Int).Value = fileid;
        IAsyncResult ar = cmd.BeginExecuteReader(cb, cmd);
        return ar;
}
```

The BeginProcessRequest() method parses the id value in the query string, passes it as an integer parameter to the GetHtml stored procedure, starts the database query, and returns the associated IAsyncResult object. Keep in mind that you shouldn't use async .NET delegates here for the same reason you shouldn't use them in async pages: they will consume a worker thread, thereby defeating one of our scalability goals.

Ending the Request

Here's the EndProcessRequest() method:

```
public void EndProcessRequest(IAsyncResult ar)
{
    using (SqlCommand cmd = (SqlCommand)ar.AsyncState)
    {
        using (cmd.Connection)
        {
            SqlDataReader reader = cmd.EndExecuteReader(ar);
            while (reader.Read())
            {
                Context.Response.Write(reader["Html"]);
            }
        }
    }
    Context.Response.ContentType = "text/html";
}

public bool IsReusable
{
    get
    {
        return false;
    }
}
}
```

The code collects the result of the query and calls the Dispose() method of the SqlCommand and SqlConnection objects, by way of the using statements.

Write the result of the query to the output stream and then set the MIME type of the response to text/html.

The IsReusable property, which is required by IHttpHandler, is set to false to indicate that a single instance of this class cannot be used to service multiple requests.

The result of invoking this handler in a browser will be to asynchronously read the specified record from the database and send the result to the browser as HTML.

Page Base Class

During the process of developing your web site, it's likely that you will encounter one or more methods that you would like to have associated with all or most of your pages. A class derived from the Page class is a good way to do that.

Although there's nothing magic about abstract or derived classes, you might want to do a few other things at the same time, which have an impact on performance, project consistency, and overall ease of use.

The standard Page uses reflection to look for methods to call for each life-cycle event. Unfortunately, reflection is somewhat slow, so you can improve performance by disabling that feature and then overriding the built-in event handlers. To disable the default mechanism, set the AutoEventWireup flag to false in the Page directive:

```
<%@ Page Language="C#" AutoEventWireup="false"
    CodeFile="code.aspx.cs" Inherits="code" %>
```

In addition to the performance aspect, I like this approach because it allows me to use IntelliSense to find event handlers. Once selected, Visual Studio will then automatically create the method, including its arguments and a call to the base method.

I suspect that one reason this approach isn't the default is because it means that developers have to remember to call the base methods. If you don't, then your application might break in subtle or unexpected ways. I normally call the base method before my code, unless I explicitly need to override something that the base method would otherwise do.

In addition to providing some custom functionality, you might also use a custom page base class to implement certain application policies that an HttpModule can't effectively enforce, such as when protected methods are involved or when you need to intervene at some point in the page life cycle. For example, if the browser is a mobile device, you might want to persist ViewState in a database.

Here's an example of a custom base class, including two custom (but empty) methods for handling ViewState (see Chapter 3 for an example implementation):

```csharp
using System;
using System.Collections.Generic;
using System.Linq;
using System.Web;
using System.Web.UI;

public class MyBaseClass : Page
{
    public MyBaseClass()
    {
    }

    protected override object LoadPageStateFromPersistenceMedium()
    {
        return base.LoadPageStateFromPersistenceMedium();
    }
```

```
    protected override void SavePageStateToPersistenceMedium(object state)
    {
        base.SavePageStateToPersistenceMedium(state);
    }
}
```

Here's the code-behind for an empty page that uses the base class:

```
using System;
using System.Collections.Generic;
using System.Linq;
using System.Web;
using System.Web.UI;
using System.Web.UI.WebControls;

public partial class template1 : MyBaseClass
{
    protected override void OnLoad(EventArgs e)
    {
        base.OnLoad(e);
        //
        // Your code here
        //
    }
}
```

Once you have created a page base class and have selected customized page settings, you may also want to encapsulate them in a Visual Studio template to simplify the process of creating new pages that use them. I covered how to create a template in Chapter 3.

Page Adapters

One problem with trying to implement site-wide policies with page base classes is that developers might forget to use them. ASP.NET has a feature called *page adapters* that will allow you to globally override many functions of the default Page class, including ViewState management, how hyperlinks and postback events are rendered, the DHTML that should be used to reference forms, and arbitrary transformation of text on the page.

Example: PageStatePersister

For example, let's create a page adapter that implements a simple server-side ViewState caching mechanism. See AppCode\MyPageAdapter.cs.

The first class you need will inherit from PageStatePersister. You will override two methods, Save() and Load().

```
using System;
using System.Web.UI;
using System.Web.UI.Adapters;
```

```
namespace Samples
{
    public class MobilePersister : PageStatePersister
    {

        public const string ViewKeyName = "__viewkey";
        private const string _viewCache = "view";
        private const string _controlCache = "ctl";

        public MobilePersister(Page page)
            : base(page)
        {
        }

        public override void Save()
        {
            if ((this.ViewState != null) || (this.ControlState != null))
            {
                string key = Guid.NewGuid().ToString();
                this.Page.RegisterHiddenField(ViewKeyName, key);
                if (this.ViewState != null)
                    this.Page.Cache[key + _viewCache] = this.ViewState;
                if (this.ControlState != null)
                    this.Page.Cache[key + _controlCache] = this.ControlState;
            }
        }
```

The Save() method checks to see whether there is any ViewState or ControlState that should be persisted. If there is, it creates a new GUID and stores it in a hidden field on the page. ViewState and ControlState are stored in the shared cache using the GUID plus a short string as the key.

```
        public override void Load()
        {
            string key = this.Page.Request[ViewKeyName];
            if (key != null)
            {
                this.ViewState = this.Page.Cache[key + _viewCache];
                this.ControlState = this.Page.Cache[key + _controlCache];
            }
        }
    }
}
```

The Load() method retrieves the GUID from the hidden field and uses it plus the same short strings as in the Save() method to retrieve the ViewState and ControlState from the shared cache.

PageAdapter Class

Here's the MyPageAdapter class:

```
public class MyPageAdapter : PageAdapter
{
    public MyPageAdapter()
    {
    }

    public override PageStatePersister GetStatePersister()
    {
        if (this.Page.Request.Browser.IsMobileDevice)
        {
            return new MobilePersister(this.Page);
        }
        else
            return base.GetStatePersister();
    }
}
```

The code inherits from PageAdapter. The overridden GetStatePersister() method checks to see whether the current browser is a mobile device. If it is, then it returns an instance of the new MobilePersister class. Otherwise, it returns the default PageStatePersister.

Registering the PageAdapter

To use the page adapter, register it in a .browser file in the App_Browsers folder, in the same way that you did earlier for control adapters:

```
<browsers>
  <browser refID="Default">
    <controlAdapters>
      <adapter controlType="System.Web.UI.Page"
               adapterType="Samples.MyPageAdapter" />
    </controlAdapters>
  </browser>
</browsers>
```

The final result is that the page adapter will be called for all Pages on the site, providing a consistent implementation of ViewState and ControlState persistence for mobile devices.

URL Rewriting

URL rewriting is the process of transforming an externally visible URL into an internal one. Although search engine optimization is normally the primary motivation for URL rewriting, it's also useful from a performance perspective for two reasons. First, it allows you to create shorter URLs. As I discussed in

Chapter 2, shorter is better. Second, it can allow you to fool http.sys into caching a page that uses query strings, and so would otherwise not be cacheable there.

As I discussed in Chapter 4, it's possible to use an IIS plug-in to do URL rewriting using regular expressions. It's also possible to do URL rewriting programmatically in ASP.NET. A full-custom approach would make sense when you need more fine-grained control.

Rewriting URLs from an HttpModule

You can programmatically rewrite URLs either from an HttpModule or from Global.asax. Using an HttpModule will allow you to have access to all URLs processed by IIS, including those for static files.

Here's an example (see AppCode\RewriteModule.cs):

```
using System;
using System.Web;

namespace Samples
{
    public class RewriteModule : IHttpModule
    {
        public RewriteModule()
        {
        }

        public void Init(HttpApplication context)
        {
            context.BeginRequest += this.Sample_BeginRequest;
        }

        private void Sample_BeginRequest(Object source, EventArgs e)
        {
            HttpApplication application = (HttpApplication)source;
            HttpContext context = application.Context;
            string path = context.Request.RawUrl;
            if (path.Contains("/p/"))
            {
                string newUrl = path.Replace("/p/", "/mycoolproductpages/");
                context.RewritePath(newUrl, false);
            }
        }

        public void Dispose()
        {
        }
    }
}
```

The code starts by registering a handler for the BeginRequest event. The event handler checks to see whether the incoming URL contains a certain string. If it does, then you replace that string with your local (and much longer) path. The call to RewritePath() tells the runtime to process newUrl as though it was the page requested by the user. Setting the second argument of RewritePath() to false tells the runtime that the page should not be rebased to the new URL. That allows relative URLs on the destination page to work correctly.

The `http.sys` cache only sees the original URL, not the rewritten one. That means if you encode page parameters in the URL and then translate them into a query string during the rewrite process, then `http.sys` can cache the page if it's marked with an appropriate `OutputCache` directive.

Modifying Forms to Use Rewritten URLs

One issue that often comes up with rewritten URLs is that by default the URL for postbacks will use the original path, rather than the new one. Using the URL mapping from the earlier example, if you place a button on the destination page and hover over it, the original long name shows up in the browser's status area. If you view the source on the page, here's the problem HTML:

```
<form name="form1" method="post" action="../mycoolproductpages/Default.aspx"
    id="form1">
```

The best solution to this problem is to use a page adapter, similar to the one I went over earlier in this chapter:

```
using System;
using System.Web.UI;
using System.Web.UI.Adapters;
using System.Web;

namespace Samples
{
    public class RewritePageAdapter : PageAdapter
    {
        public RewritePageAdapter()
        {
        }

        protected override void OnInit(EventArgs e)
        {
            HttpContext context = HttpContext.Current;
            context.RewritePath(this.Page.Request.RawUrl);
            base.OnInit(e);
        }
    }
}
```

The adapter overrides the `OnInit` event handler and uses the `RewritePath()` method to set the URL of the current page back to the one that was originally requested. The runtime will use the adapter for all pages and will then render the `action` attribute of the `<form>` tag correctly:

```
<form name="form1" method="post" action="Default.aspx" id="form1">
```

Tag Transforms

You may occasionally encounter cases where you would like to replace the class for one control with another class everywhere it's used in your application. That can be much easier than writing a control adapter in certain cases.

As an example, let's use a tag transform to solve the postback problem. See App_Code\FormRewrite.cs:

```
using System.Web.UI;
using System.Web.UI.HtmlControls;

namespace Samples
{
    public class FormRewrite : HtmlForm
    {
        public FormRewrite()
        {
        }

        protected override void RenderAttributes(HtmlTextWriter writer)
        {
            this.Action = this.Page.Request.RawUrl;
            base.RenderAttributes(writer);
        }
    }
}
```

Inherit from the standard HtmlForm class, then override its RenderAttributes() method to set the action attribute to the original URL, and finally pass control to the base method.

Next, register the class in web.config:

```
<pages>
  . . .
  <tagMapping>
    <add tagType="System.Web.UI.HtmlControls.HtmlForm"
         mappedTagType="Samples.FormRewrite" />
  </tagMapping>
</pages>
```

That will cause the compiler to replace the HtmlForm class with the FormRewrite class everywhere it appears in your application.

Control Adapters Revisited

You can apply control adapters to standard Controls, as well as to WebControls as I discussed in the previous chapter.

As an example, let's use that approach to solve the same postback problem mentioned earlier. Here's the code for PostbackAdapter.cs:

```
using System.IO;
using System.Web;
using System.Web.UI;
using System.Web.UI.Adapters;

namespace Samples
{
    public class ActionHtmlWriter : HtmlTextWriter
    {
        public ActionHtmlWriter(TextWriter writer)
            : base(writer)
        {
        }

        public override void WriteAttribute(string name, string value, bool fEncode)
        {
            if (name == "action")
            {
                HttpContext context = HttpContext.Current;
                value = context.Request.RawUrl;
            }
            base.WriteAttribute(name, value, fEncode);
        }
    }
```

The first class inherits from `HtmlTextWriter` and overrides the `WriteAttribute()` method. If the name of the attribute being written is `action`, then its value is replaced with the new URL for the current page.

```
    public class PostbackAdapter : ControlAdapter
    {
        public PostbackAdapter()
        {
        }

        protected override void Render(HtmlTextWriter writer)
        {
            ActionHtmlWriter actionWriter = new ActionHtmlWriter(writer);
            base.Render(actionWriter);
        }
    }
}
```

The control adapter itself inherits from `ControlAdapter`, since the `<form>` control is indirectly derived from `Control`, rather than `WebControl` as in the earlier example. The class overrides the `Render()` method, which creates an instance of the new `ActionHtmlWriter` class and passes it to `base.Render()`.

As before, register the control adapter in a `.browser` file in the `App_Browsers` folder:

```
<browsers>
  <browser refID="Default">
    <controlAdapters>
```

```
    <adapter controlType="System.Web.UI.HtmlControls.HtmlForm"
            adapterType="Samples.PostbackAdapter" />
  </controlAdapters>
 </browser>
</browsers>
```

With those changes in place, the HTML produced by the test page now has a path to the new URL in the `action` attribute, rather than the post-rewriting relative path you had before:

```
<form name="form1" method="post" action="/Samples/p/Default.aspx" id="form1">
```

Redirects

Standard HTTP redirects cause the browser to request the specified URL in place of the original one, which results in an additional client-to-server round-trip. In keeping with our core principles, it's better to avoid that if you can.

Conventional Redirects

You can do a conventional `302 Found` redirect as follows:

```
this.Response.Redirect("~/pages/error.aspx", true);
```

Setting the second argument to `true` causes the runtime to terminate the current response by calling `Response.End()`, which in turn will throw a `ThreadAbortException`. To avoid the overhead and hassle of handling the exception, you can set the flag to `false`. However, in that case, both the ASP.NET and the IIS pipelines will continue to execute. You can tell IIS to skip the remaining events by calling `CompleteRequest()`:

```
HttpContext.Current.ApplicationInstance.CompleteRequest();
```

ASP.NET events will still execute in that case. Skipping them as well requires a little additional code. For example, you might set a flag when you call `CompleteRequest()` and then, in overridden event handlers, check to see whether that flag is set before calling the base handler. This might be another good task for a common base class.

This type of redirect is useful when you want to tell the browser to fetch a certain page conditionally, such as in the event of an error, as in the earlier example. The browser and proxies can't cache `302 Found` redirects, and search engines may not follow them.

Permanent Redirects

There are also cases when redirects should be permanent, such as when a page has moved. It's generally more efficient to issue permanent redirects from IIS, since the rest of the request pipeline can be short-circuited that way. You can also issue them programmatically, although with .NET 3.5 and earlier, there isn't an API call for permanent redirects, so you need to configure the HTTP response header yourself, as follows:

```
this.Response.StatusCode = 301;
this.Response.AddHeader("Location", "newpage.aspx");
this.Response.End();
```

■ **Note** .NET 4.0 introduces the `Response.RedirectPermanent()` method to do the same thing.

Browsers and proxies can cache permanent redirects, and search engines follow them.

It's a good idea to take a look at the text that accompanies your HTTP redirects to make sure you are returning as little as possible. Even though the browser doesn't display the body of the redirect, users can easily see it in a web debugger like Fiddler. In addition to the performance impact, if you did the redirect for security reasons and forgot to end the request afterward, you might accidentally still be rendering the page that you didn't want the user to see.

You can also configure conventional redirects from IIS, which is handy for static files or for cases where programmatic logic isn't required.

Using Server.Transfer()

One mechanism for avoiding the round-trip associated with redirects is the `Server.Transfer()` method. As with URL rewriting, the server doesn't tell the client to get a new page, so the URL in the browser's address bar doesn't change. You should use URL rewriting when the new path is known before the `HttpHandler` is called, such as from an `HttpModule`. Once the `HttpHandler` has been called, `RewritePath()` will no longer transfer control to a new page, and you should use `Server.Transfer()` instead.

Instead of putting the burden of making a new request back on the browser, `Server.Transfer()` reissues `HttpHandler.ProcessRequest()` without informing the client; no additional round-trips are required. As with calling `Response.Redirect()` when the `endResponse` flag is set to true, `Server.Transfer()` always ends the current request by calling `Response.End()`, which in turn throws a `ThreadAbortException`. Here's an example:

```
this.Server.Transfer("~/pages/error.aspx", false);
```

The purpose of setting the second parameter to `true` is supposed to be to allow you to see the query string and form parameters of the *current* page when the *new* page starts to execute. However, because of `ViewState` integrity verification (`enableViewStateMac`, which should be enabled, as described in Chapter 3), it will cause an exception if the current page contains any `ViewState`. You should therefore set the second parameter to `true` only if the current page does not use server-side forms or `ViewState` but does use query strings whose value you need in the destination page.

Of course, you can't use this mechanism to transfer control to another server, or even another AppPool. It works only for `.aspx` pages in the current AppPool.

The server does not reauthenticate users when you call `Server.Transfer()`. If you require authentication, you should apply it programmatically.

Early Response Flush

Unlike with ASP or PHP, the way ASP.NET creates a page involves recursively stepping through the life cycle of the page itself and all of its controls. The runtime doesn't render the page's output until almost the very end. That approach facilitates things like control-specific event handlers, and it allows controls that are located in one place on the page to make changes to output anywhere on the page.

When a page is ready to be rendered, the ASP.NET `HttpHandler` calls the `Render()` method of the page and all of its controls. By default, the output from `Render()` is buffered in memory. When the rendering phase is complete, the final size of the page is included in the HTTP headers, and the headers and the buffered content are sent to the client.

The standard approach works fine for pages that don't contain any long-running tasks. Although you should try hard not to have long-running tasks on a page, there are times when you can't avoid them. In keeping with the core principle of focusing on performance as perceived by users, for pages with long-running tasks it would be nice if you could send part of the response before sending the whole thing.

Before describing this technique, let me say that I prefer Ajax and partial-page updates most of the time. However, there are cases where you can't use Ajax. For example, search engines can't index content that you insert onto a page from an Ajax call.

ASP.NET provides a method called `Response.Flush()` that will flush the response buffer. However, by default nothing gets written into the response buffer until the rendering phase, so calling it before then doesn't do much. You might also be tempted to call `Flush()` in-line from your markup file, as you can from ASP (or equivalently from PHP). Unfortunately, the code in your markup file is called during the rendering phase, and by that time, whatever slow task you had on the page will have already completed.

Markup

The solution isn't pretty, but it works. As an example, create a web form called `flush1.aspx`:

```
<%@ Page StylesheetTheme="mkt" Title="Testing" Language="C#" AutoEventWireup="false"
    CodeFile="flush1.aspx.cs" Inherits="flush1" %>
<head runat="server">
    <title></title>
    <script type="text/javascript" src="test.js"></script>
</head>
<body>
    <form id="form1" runat="server">
    <div>
    <asp:Label runat="server" ID="test" Text="testing" />
    </div>
    </form>
</body>
</html>
```

Notice that I'm referencing a `StyleSheetTheme`, that `AutoEventWireup` is set to `false`, and that the `<!DOCTYPE>` and `<html>` tags are missing from the beginning of the file.

Code-Behind

Next, modify the code-behind file as follows:

```
using System;
using System.Web.UI;
```

```
public partial class flush1 : Page
{
    protected override void OnPreRender(EventArgs e)
    {
        base.OnPreRender(e);
        this.Response.Write("<!DOCTYPE html PUBLIC " +
            "\"-//W3C//DTD XHTML 1.0 Transitional//EN\" " +
            "\"http://www.w3.org/TR/xhtml1/DTD/xhtml1-transitional.dtd\">\n");
        this.Response.Write("<html xmlns=\"http://www.w3.org/1999/xhtml\">\n");
        HtmlTextWriter writer = this.CreateHtmlTextWriter(this.Response.Output);
        this.Header.RenderControl(writer);
        writer.Flush();
        this.Response.Flush();
        this.Controls.Remove(this.Header);
    }
}
```

Here's the tricky part. What you've done is to override the `OnPreRender()` event handler under the assumption that the slow tasks will happen either at the async point, which follows `PreRender`, or perhaps in the `PreRenderComplete` event.

After calling the base event handler, write the `<!DOCTYPE>` and `<html>` tags that you left out of the markup file into the response buffer.

Next, get an `HtmlTextWriter` object using `Page.CreateHtmlTextWriter()` and use it to render the page header control to the response buffer. The header will include the `<head>` tag and its contents, including CSS and JavaScript specified by the theme and the `<script>` tag you included in the markup.

Ideally, the initial content that you send to the browser should not only request a few of the files you'll need for the page but should also display something to indicate that the request is being processed. You might display a progress bar or graphic, for example.

Next, flush the `writer` and the response buffer, which writes its contents and the current HTTP headers to the network and waits for an acknowledgment.

Finally, remove the header from the control tree so that it won't be rendered a second time during the official render phase.

Waiting to do this until the `PreRender` event also allows any events to execute that are attached to the `Header` control or its children. Once you remove it from the control tree, events that are attached to it will no longer fire.

■ **Caution** After calling `Response.Flush()`, it is an error to set any additional HTTP headers (including from an `HttpModule`), since they are sent to the client when `Flush()` is called.

Packet Trace

To get a better feeling for what's happening, let's look at a packet trace. So that you can see what happens when the page executes a long-running task, let's sleep for two seconds after the call to `Response.Flush()`.

I ran the trace with Wireshark; the results are in Figure 7-1.

No..	Time	Source	Destination	Info
10	3.344351	192.168.1.108	192.168.1.105	31184 > 81 [SYN] Seq=0 Wi
11	3.344823	192.168.1.105	192.168.1.108	81 > 31184 [SYN, ACK] Seq
12	3.344885	192.168.1.108	192.168.1.105	31184 > 81 [ACK] Seq=1 Ac
13	3.345028	192.168.1.108	192.168.1.105	GET /flush1.aspx HTTP/1.1
14	3.540766	192.168.1.105	192.168.1.108	81 > 31184 [ACK] Seq=1 Ac
15	3.697567	192.168.1.105	192.168.1.108	[TCP segment of a reassem
16	3.701565	192.168.1.108	192.168.1.105	31185 > 81 [SYN] Seq=0 Wi
17	3.701838	192.168.1.105	192.168.1.108	81 > 31185 [SYN, ACK] Seq
18	3.701870	192.168.1.108	192.168.1.105	31185 > 81 [ACK] Seq=1 Ac
19	3.701970	192.168.1.108	192.168.1.105	GET /App_Themes/mkt/mkt.c
20	3.702704	192.168.1.105	192.168.1.108	HTTP/1.1 200 OK (text/cs
21	3.762294	192.168.1.108	192.168.1.105	GET /test.js HTTP/1.1
22	3.762902	192.168.1.105	192.168.1.108	HTTP/1.1 404 Not Found (
23	3.890860	192.168.1.108	192.168.1.105	31184 > 81 [ACK] Seq=705
24	3.960914	192.168.1.108	192.168.1.105	31185 > 81 [ACK] Seq=962
29	5.805397	192.168.1.105	192.168.1.108	HTTP/1.1 200 OK (text/ht
30	6.000983	192.168.1.108	192.168.1.105	31184 > 81 [ACK] Seq=705

Figure 7-1. Packet trace of an early response flush

- Packets 10, 11, and 12 are the browser opening a connection to the server. With three packets and one-and-a-half round-trips, you can see why opening a new connection is expensive. Notice that the destination port is 81 instead of the default of 80 for HTTP, since that's how I configured the test web site.

- At packet 13, the highlighted line in the figure, the browser sends the HTTP GET to the server.

- At packet 14, the server acknowledges the GET packet.

- At packet 15, the server sends the partial response after the Flush(). Wireshark considers this a partial response and can't correctly decode it yet.

- Packets 16, 17, and 18 are the browser opening a second connection to the server.

- At packet 19, the browser issues a GET request for a CSS file that's part of the theme. This means that the browser has parsed the partial response and is issuing a new HTTP request while it's waiting to receive the rest of the page.

- Packet 20 is the server's response to the GET for the CSS file (200 OK).

- Packet 21 is the browser issuing a GET request for the <script> that you included in the <head> section. Notice that it happens after the CSS request, for reasons explained in detail in Chapter 2.

- Packet 22 is the server's response to the GET for the script file (404 Not Found).

- Packet 23 is an ACK for the partial response in packet 15. Notice that two complete client-server request-response cycles happened in between the flushed data being sent and the corresponding ACK (although my machines are connected with a gigabit network, not over the Internet).

- Packet 29 is the server sending the rest of the response to the client. Notice that it arrives about two seconds after the ACK to the flushed packet, which indicates that the call to `Response.Flush()` waits for an acknowledgment before returning. After receiving this packet, Wireshark has enough information to decode the entire response, including packet 15. The packet number for this packet doesn't come right after the preceding one, since several other packets arrived for unrelated connections during the two-second gap, and I have configured Wireshark to filter them out.

- Finally, packet 30 is the client acknowledging the second part of the response in packet 29.

Chunked Encoding

To avoid closing the connection after using `Response.Flush()`, the runtime uses HTTP chunked encoding to send the response. In a normal response, the runtime knows the size of the entire response, since it's buffered before being sent. The server encodes the length in the HTTP `Content-Length` header, so the browser knows how much data to read before looking for the next HTTP response. With chunked encoding, the length is instead given right before the content. Here's the full server response:

```
HTTP/1.1 200 OK
Cache-Control: private
Transfer-Encoding: chunked
Content-Type: text/html; charset=utf-8
Date: Fri, 19 Jun 2009 09:18:07 GMT

153
<!DOCTYPE html PUBLIC "-//W3C//DTD XHTML 1.0 Transitional//EN"
"http://www.w3.org/TR/xhtml1/DTD/xhtml1-transitional.dtd">
<html xmlns="http://www.w3.org/1999/xhtml">
<head>
<link href="App_Themes/mkt/mkt.css" type="text/css" rel="stylesheet" />
<title>
Testing
</title>
<script type="text/javascript" src="test.js"></script>
</head>
136
<body>
    <form name="form1" method="post" action="flush1.aspx" id="form1">
<div>
<input type="hidden" name="__VIEWSTATE" id="__VIEWSTATE"
value="/wEPDwULLTEONDMxNDMoMTlkZEiWGdUcbeRgyeHWlKKfRp3d6Vq9" />
</div>
<div>
    <span id="test">testing</span>
</div>
</form>
</body>
</html>
0
```

Notice `Transfer-Encoding: chunked` in the header, and **153**, **136** and **0**, which indicate the number of characters in the following chunk. The packet boundary was right before the **136**.

Summary

When considering whether to use this approach, keep in mind that `Response.Flush()` doesn't return until after the associated `ACK` is received. On the Internet, where `ACK` times are often 100ms or more, you should be sure that your "long-running" task takes at least several multiples of that much time in order for this to be worthwhile. It's also important to understand that the worker thread will be blocked during that time, which can have a negative impact on scalability.

In addition to the hassle of using `Response.Write()` to put text into the response buffer, it's unfortunate that this technique produces some XHTML validation warnings in Visual Studio and that it breaks the visual designer. Also, the runtime doesn't allow code blocks in the markup file if you call `Controls.Remove()`. However, even with those shortcomings and restrictions, this approach can still be very useful on certain pages.

Whitespace Filtering

You can reduce the size of dynamically generated HTML that the server sends to the client by processing it first to remove extra whitespace. This is in the same spirit as the JavaScript minification that I discussed in Chapter 2, now applied to dynamic HTML. You might be surprised to see how much extra whitespace some HTML pages contain.

The first step is to write a filter that does the appropriate processing on the output stream of the `Page`. You should implement the filter using the `Stream` interface. The main method of interest is `Write()`, whose input is a byte array and an offset and a count. The fact that the runtime doesn't write all the output for the page at one time means you need to track some state information from one call to the next.

The resulting code is a bit too much to walk through as a detailed example, but here's an outline of what's required:

```
using System;
using System.IO;
using System.Text;

namespace Sample
{
    public class MinifyStream : Stream
    {
        private StreamWriter Writer { get; set; }
        private Decoder Utf8Decoder { get; set; }

        public MinifyStream(Stream stream)
        {
            this.Writer = new StreamWriter(stream, Encoding.UTF8);
            this.Utf8Decoder = Encoding.UTF8.GetDecoder();
        }
```

The class inherits from Stream, and the constructor wraps the provided Stream in a new StreamWriter, with UTF-8 encoding.

```
public override void Write(byte[] buffer, int offset, int count)
{
    . . .
}
```

The Write() method should process the input byte array as UTF-8 characters. The algorithm should filter out extra whitespace and write the filtered output to this.Writer, taking into account that the buffer boundary may not be on a line boundary.

You should override the Read(), SetLength(), and Seek() methods to throw NotImplementedException, since this is a write-only, forward-only Stream. Similarly, you should override the Position and Length properties to throw InvalidOperationException.

```
public override void Flush()
{
    this.Writer.Flush();
}

public override bool CanWrite
{
    get { return true; }
}

public override bool CanSeek
{
    get { return false; }
}

public override bool CanRead
{
    get { return false; }
}

public override void Close()
{
    this.Writer.Flush();
    this.Writer.Close();
    base.Close();
}
```

I've shown the remaining properties and methods here with straightforward overrides.

With the filter class in hand, the next step is to wire it up. In an HttpModule such as the one I walked you through earlier in this chapter, create and wire up a new event handler for the PostRequestHandlerExecute event, meaning that it will run right after the page handler finishes:

```
private void Sample_PostRequestHandlerExecute(Object source, EventArgs e)
{
    HttpApplication application = (HttpApplication)source;
    HttpResponse response = application.Context.Response;
```

```
    if(response.ContentType == "text/html")
        response.Filter = new MinifyStream(response.Filter);
}
```

You want to apply this filter to HTML output only; code that is optimized to remove whitespace from HTML won't work with anything else. You check that by looking at `Response.ContentType`, which contains the MIME type of the output.

The final step to making this whole thing work is to assign a new instance of the filter to `Response.Filter`. That will tell the runtime to call the filter code to output the page. You pass a reference to the old filter as an argument to the constructor so that your class will know where to send the output once it's done removing the extra whitespace.

▪ **Note** If you enable `dynamicCompressionBeforeCache`, as suggested in Chapter 4, the runtime applies compression before the response filters. In that case, the previous technique won't work as is; you will either need to modify it to not apply the filter if the content is compressed or disable `dynamicCompressionBeforeCache`.

Other Ways to Avoid Unnecessary Work

One of the standard performance-improvement tenants is to avoid doing more work than you need. In addition to the mechanisms I've described earlier, such as caching, you can also do a few more things along those lines.

Check Page.IsPostBack

Many controls cache their state in `ViewState`, and the runtime will restore that state during a postback. As I discussed in Chapter 3, you can also use `ViewState` to cache the results of page-specific long-running tasks, such as database queries. To avoid repeating those tasks during a postback, be sure to check the `Page.IsPostBack` flag:

```
protected override void OnLoad(EventArgs e)
{
    base.OnLoad(e);
    if (!this.IsPostBack)
    {
        //
        // Do expensive operations here that can be cached in ViewState,
        // cookies, etc.
        //
    }
}
```

Identify a Page Refresh

If your page performs any actions that should be done only once per page request per user, you may want to differentiate a normal page request from a page refresh. This is a good candidate method for a base class.

Fortunately, IE and Firefox both insert an extra HTTP request header for a refresh, although it's a different one for each browser. Here's some sample code:

```
protected virtual bool IsRefresh
{
    get
    {
        return this.Request.Headers["Pragma"] == "no-cache" ||
            this.Request.Headers["Cache-Control"] == "max-age=0";
    }
}
```

You might use this before updating a count of the number of times users have accessed the page, for example.

Cookies are another possible solution to this issue. The best approach depends on whether you want to apply restrictions to multiple accesses of any kind within some period (cookies) or just page refreshes (HTTP headers).

Avoid Redirects After a Postback

A coding pattern that I often see in ASP.NET sites is to have a web form that redirects to another page after it handles a postback in some way. You should try to avoid those redirects, either using `Server.Transfer()` as described earlier or perhaps by posting back to a different page. You can do that by specifying the `PostBackUrl` property on an `<asp:Button>` control:

```
<asp:Button runat="server" PostBackUrl="~/pages/otherpage.aspx" Text="Submit" />
```

You can simplify the process of accessing information from the previous page by declaring it with a directive in the destination page:

```
<%@ PreviousPageType VirtualPath="~/pages/firstpage.aspx" %>
```

With that directive in place, you can refer to the first page with the `PreviousPage` property:

```
this.PreviousPage.MyProperty = "value";
```

Check Response.IsClientConnected

There are times when a user requests a page and then cancels the request before the server has a chance to respond. They might click away to another page, hit the back button on the browser, hit the stop or refresh keys, or even close the tab or the browser entirely. In those cases, the browser or the client OS will close the network connection. You can tell when that happens by checking the `Response.IsClientConnected` flag.

The runtime checks `Response.IsClientConnected` before it sends a response. However, clients can abort requests at any time, including immediately after they send the request. It is therefore a good idea to check the flag before you perform any I/O, database requests, or long-running tasks. Here's an example:

```
protected override void OnLoad(EventArgs e)
{
    base.OnLoad(e);
    if (this.Response.IsClientConnected)
    {
        this.Server.Transfer("otherpage.aspx");
    }
}
```

Disable Debug Mode

Enabling debug mode in ASP.NET does the following:

- Disables page timeouts. This is to allow easy debugging from Visual Studio but is not appropriate for a live site.

- Disables most compiler optimizations so that symbols are guaranteed to align with source code statements (important for single stepping).

- Disables some batch optimizations, which causes compilation to take longer.

- Significantly increases the memory footprint of the running application.

- Disables caching of `WebResources.axd` by the client. This can have a big effect on pages that use Ajax and certain standard ASP.NET controls, since the browser will download the associated script files again for every page.

- Disables compression of `WebResources.axd`. When you disable debug mode, the output of `WebResources.axd` will be compressed.

- Generates source code files in the ASP.NET temporary files folder (which requires extra time and disk space). Although they might be useful while you're debugging, once again you shouldn't need them on a production server.

- Generates symbol (`.pdb`) files, which are useful not just with a debugger; they are also used to produce stack traces in the event of an error on the server. If you would like to have more detailed stack traces, you can compile your site first with `debug` set to `true` in a web deployment project (as described in Chapter 2), then recompile with `debug` set to `false` just prior to deployment. You can then include the `.pdb` files with the deployment, and they will be used to generate more detailed stack traces.

You can disable debug mode by setting the `debug` property to `false` on the `<compilation>` element in `web.config`:

```
<system.web>
    <compilation debug="false" . . .>
        . . .
    </compilation>
</system.web>
```

If you have a number of different sites on your production servers, you can force all of them to have `debug` set to `false` by adding the `<deployment>` element to `machine.config`:

```
<system.web>
    <deployment retail="true" />
</system.web>
```

That will also disable tracing output and the ability to show detailed stack traces remotely for all sites.

Batch Compilation

When your site is compiled, whether it's on-demand or precompiled, the `batch` property of the `<compilation>` element determines how assemblies are produced. When `batch` is set to `true`, an entire folder is compiled and grouped into a small number of assemblies (files such as `Global.asax` and controls are put in separate assemblies). When `batch` is set to `false`, the compiler puts each page into a separate assembly. Having a large number of assemblies like that can increase memory fragmentation and page load times.

If you normally update your live site with individual new pages instead of updating the full site at once, you may find that it sometimes get confused and out of sync if `batch` is `true`. Changing it to `false` usually alleviates those live update problems.

Summary

In this chapter, I covered the following:

- Using custom `HttpModules` with async I/O to implement site-wide application policies. Examples include tracking cookies, centralized logging and monitoring, HTTP header management, authentication, authorization, and so on.

- Using custom `HttpHandlers` with async I/O to improve performance for content that doesn't require ASP.NET-style markup or controls, such as dynamic images or content delivered directly from a file or a database.

- Using a page base class and a page adapter to override the behavior of a `Page` and to implement site-wide performance optimizations such as managing `ViewState` for mobile devices.

- Using tag mapping and control adapters to customize or optimize the way that controls work.

- Programmatically rewriting URLs to help improve performance by making them shorter and by allowing them to be cacheable by `http.sys`.

- Using a control adapter with URL rewriting to ensure that `<form>` controls use the new and pretty URLs instead of the old and ugly ones.

- Issuing `302 Found` and `301 Permanent` HTTP redirects and why you should avoid them if you can by using URL rewriting or `Server.Transfer()` instead.

- Flushing the response buffer early to improve the perceived performance of pages when you can't avoid long-running tasks.

- Helping prevent the server from doing more work than it has to by using `Page.IsPostBack` and `Response.IsClientConnected`, by checking for page refreshes, and by disabling debug mode.

CHAPTER 8

■ ■ ■

SQL Server Relational Database

In this chapter, I'll cover a few areas that can have a large impact on the performance of your data tier, even if you have already optimized your queries fully.

For example, our principle of minimizing round-trips also applies to round-trips between the web tier and the database. You can do that using change notifications, multiple result sets, and command batching.

The topics that I'll cover include the following:

- How SQL Server manages memory

- Stored procedures

- Command batching

- Transactions

- Table-valued parameters

- Multiple result sets

- Data precaching

- Data access layer

- Query and schema optimization

- Data paging

- Object relational models

- XML columns

- Data partitioning

- Full-text search

- Service Broker

- Data change notifications

- Resource Governor

- Scaling up vs. scaling out

- High availability

- Miscellaneous performance tips

How SQL Server Manages Memory

Similar to ASP.NET, it's possible to have a fast query (or page) but a slow database (or site). One of the keys to resolving this and to architecting your database for speed is to understand how SQL Server manages memory.

Memory Organization

On 32-bit systems, SQL Server divides RAM into an area that can hold only data pages and a shared area that holds everything else, such as indexes, compiled queries, results of joins and sorts, client connection state, and so on. 32 bits is enough to address up to 4GB at a time. The default configuration is that 2GB of address space is reserved for the operating system, leaving 2GB for the application. When running under one of the 32-bit versions of Windows Server, SQL Server can use Address Windowing Extensions (AWE) to map views of up to 64GB dynamically into its address space. (AWE isn't available for the desktop versions of Windows.) However, it can use memory addressed with AWE only for the *data* area, not for the shared area. This means that even if you have 64GB of RAM, with a 32-bit system you might have only 1GB available for shared information.

You can increase the memory available to SQL Server on machines with 16GB or less by adding the /3GB flag in the operating system's boot.ini file. That reduces the address space allocated to the operating system from 2GB to 1GB, leaving 3GB for user applications such as SQL Server. However, since limiting the RAM available to the OS can have an adverse effect on system performance, you should definitely test your system under load before using that switch in production.

On 64-bit systems, the division between data pages and shared information goes away. SQL Server can use all memory for any type of object. In addition, the memory usage limit increases to 2TB. For those reasons, combined with the fact that nearly all CPUs used in servers for quite a few years now are capable of supporting 64-bit operating systems (so there shouldn't be any additional hardware or software cost), I highly recommend using 64-bit systems whenever possible.

Reads and Writes

SQL Server uses three different kinds of files to store your data. The primary data store, or MDF file, holds tables, indexes, and their contents. You can also have zero or more secondary data stores, or NDF files, which hold the same type of content in separate *filegroups*. The LDF file holds the database log, which is a list of changes to the data file.

The MDF and NDF files are organized as 64KB *extents*, which consist of eight physically contiguous 8KB *pages*. Rows are stored on a page serially, with a header at the beginning of the page and a list of row offsets at the end that indicate where each row starts in the page. Rows can't span multiple pages. Large columns are moved to special "overflow" pages.

When SQL Server first reads data from disk, such as with a SELECT query, it reads pages from the data files into a pool of 8KB buffers, which it also uses as a cache. When the pool is full, the least-recently used buffers are dropped first to make room for new data.

Since SQL Server can use all available memory as a large cache, making sure your server has plenty of RAM is an important step when it comes to maximizing performance. It would be ideal if you have enough room to fit the entire database in RAM. See the "Scaling Up vs. Scaling Out" section in this chapter for some tips on how to determine whether your server needs more memory. Based on my experience, it's common in high-performance sites to see database servers with 32GB of RAM or more.

When you modify data, such as with an INSERT, UPDATE, or DELETE, SQL Server makes the requested changes to the data pages in memory, marks the associated data buffers as modified, writes the changes to the database log file (LDF), and then returns to the caller *after the log write completes.* A dedicated "lazy writer" thread periodically scans the buffer pool looking for modified buffers, which it writes to the data file (MDF). Modified buffers are also written to the MDF file if they need to be dropped to make room for new data or during periodic *checkpoints.*

Writes to the *log* file are always sequential. When properly configured on a disk volume by itself, the disk heads shouldn't have to move very much when writing to the log file, and write throughput can be very high.

Writes to the *data* file will generally be at random locations in the MDF file, so the disk heads will move around a lot; throughput is normally a small fraction of what's possible with an equivalently configured log drive. In fact, I've seen a factor of 50-to-1 performance difference or more between random and sequential writes on similar drives. See Chapter 10 for details.

To avoid seeks and thereby maximize write throughput, it's especially important to have the database log file on a set of dedicated spindles, separate from the data file.

Performance Impact

Understanding the way that SQL manages memory leads to several important conclusions:

- The first time you access data will be much slower than subsequent accesses, since it has to be read from disk into the buffer cache. This can be very important during system startup and during a database cluster failover, since those servers will start with an empty cache. It also leads to the beneficial concepts of database warm-up and precaching of database content.

- Aggregation queries (sum, count, and so on) and other queries that scan large tables or indexes can require a large number of buffers and have a very adverse effect on performance if they cause SQL Server to drop other data from the cache.

- With careful design, it's possible to use SQL Server as an in-memory cache.

- Write performance is determined largely by how fast SQL Server can sequentially write to the log file, while read performance is mostly determined by a combination of the amount of RAM available and how fast it can do random reads from the data file.

- When writes to the database log start happening simultaneously with the lazy writer thread writing modified pages to the data file, or simultaneously with data reads hitting the disk, the resulting disk seeks can cause the speed of access to the log file to decrease dramatically if the log and data files are on the same disk volume. For that reason, it's important to keep the log and data files on separate disk spindles.

Stored Procedures

Using stored procedures as your primary interface to the database has a number of advantages:

- Stored procedures allow easy grouping and execution of multiple T-SQL statements, which can help reduce the number of round-trips that the web server requires to perform its tasks.

- They allow you to make changes on the data tier without requiring changes on the web tier. This helps facilitate easy and fast application evolution and iterative improvement and tuning of your schema, indexes, queries, and so on.

- They more easily support a comprehensive security framework than dynamic SQL. You can configure access to your underlying tables and other objects so that your web tier can access them only through a specific set of procedures.

Another way to think of it is that stored procedures are a best practice for the same reason that accessors are a best practice in object-oriented code: they provide a layer of abstraction that allows you to modify easily all references to a certain object or set of objects.

When you submit a command to SQL Server, it needs to be compiled into a query plan before it can be executed. Those plans can be cached. The caching mechanism uses the command string as the key for the plan cache; commands that are exactly the same as one another, including whitespace and embedded arguments, are mapped to the same cached plan.

In dynamic ad hoc T-SQL, where parameters are embedded in the command, SQL Server performs an optimization that automatically identifies up to one parameter. That allows some commands to be considered the same so they can use the same query plan. However, if the command varies by more than one parameter, the extra differences are still part of the string that's used as the key to the plan cache, so the command will be recompiled for each variation. Using stored procedures and parameterized queries can help minimize the time SQL Server spends performing compilations, while also minimizing plan cache pollution (filling the cache with many plans that are rarely reused).

When you're writing stored procedures, one of your goals should be to minimize the number of database round-trips. It's much better to call one stored procedure that invokes ten queries than ten separate procedures that invoke one query each. I generally don't like to get *too* much business logic in them, but using things like conditionals is normally fine. Also, keep in mind that, as with subroutines or even user controls, it's perfectly acceptable for one stored procedure to call another one.

I suggest using dynamic T-SQL only when you can't create the queries you need with static T-SQL. For those times when it's unavoidable, be sure to use parameterized queries for best performance and security. Forming queries by simply concatenating strings has a *very* good chance of introducing SQL injection attack vulnerabilities into your application.

Here's an example of creating a table and a stored procedure to access it. I'm also using a SCHEMA, which is a security-related best practice:

```
CREATE SCHEMA [Traffic] AUTHORIZATION [dbo]

CREATE TABLE [Traffic].[PageViews] (
    [PvId]    BIGINT              IDENTITY NOT NULL,
    [PvDate]  DATETIME            NOT NULL,
    [UserId]  UNIQUEIDENTIFIER    NULL,
    [PvUrl]   VARCHAR(256)        NOT NULL
)
```

```
ALTER TABLE [Traffic].[PageViews]
    ADD CONSTRAINT [PageViewIdPK]
    PRIMARY KEY CLUSTERED ([PvId] ASC)

CREATE PROCEDURE [Traffic].[AddPageView]
    @pvid    BIGINT OUT,
    @userid  UNIQUEIDENTIFIER,
    @pvurl   VARCHAR (256)
AS
BEGIN
    SET NOCOUNT ON
    DECLARE @trandate DATETIME
    SET @trandate = GETUTCDATE()
    INSERT INTO [Traffic].[PageViews]
        (PvDate, UserId, PvUrl)
        VALUES
        (@trandate, @userid, @pvurl)
    SET @pvid = SCOPE_IDENTITY()
END
```

The stored procedure gets the current date, inserts a row into the [Traffic].[PageViews] table, and returns the resulting primary key as an output variable.

You will be using these objects in examples later in the chapter.

Command Batching

Another way to reduce the number of database round-trips is to batch several commands together and send them all to the server at the same time.

Using SqlDataAdapter

A typical application of command batching is to INSERT many rows. As an example, let's create a test harness that you can use to evaluate the effect of using different batch sizes. Create a new web form called sql-batch1.aspx, and edit the markup to include the following:

```
<form id="form1" runat="server">
<div>
Record count: <asp:TextBox runat="server" ID="cnt" /><br />
Batch size: <asp:TextBox runat="server" ID="sz" /><br />
<asp:Button runat="server" Text="Submit" /><br />
<asp:Literal runat="server" ID="info" />
</div>
</form>
```

You will use the two text boxes to set the record count and the batch size and an <asp:Literal> to display the results.

The conventional way to do command batching for INSERTs, UPDATEs, and DELETEs with ADO.NET is to use the SqlDataAdapter class. Edit the code-behind as follows:

```
using System;
using System.Collections;
using System.Data;
using System.Data.SqlClient;
using System.Diagnostics;
using System.Text;
using System.Web.UI;

public partial class sql_batch1 : Page
{
    public const string ConnString =
        "Data Source=server;Initial Catalog=Sample;Integrated Security=True";

    protected void Page_Load(object sender, EventArgs e)
    {
        if (this.IsPostBack)
        {
            int numRecords = Convert.ToInt32(this.cnt.Text);
            int batchSize = Convert.ToInt32(this.sz.Text);
            int numBatches = numRecords / batchSize;
            long pvid = -1;
            using (SqlConnection conn = new SqlConnection(ConnString))
            {
                conn.Open();
                conn.StatisticsEnabled = true;
                for (int j = 0; j < numBatches; j++)
                {
                    DataTable table = new DataTable();
                    table.Columns.Add("pvid", typeof(long));
                    table.Columns.Add("userid", typeof(Guid));
                    table.Columns.Add("pvurl", typeof(string));
```

After parsing the input parameters and creating a `SqlConnection`, in a loop that's executed once for each batch, create a new `DataTable` with three columns that correspond to the database table.

```
                    using (SqlCommand cmd =
                        new SqlCommand("[Traffic].[AddPageView]", conn))
                    {
                        cmd.CommandType = CommandType.StoredProcedure;
                        SqlParameterCollection p = cmd.Parameters;
                        p.Add("@pvid", SqlDbType.BigInt, 0, "pvid").Direction =
                            ParameterDirection.Output;
                        p.Add("@userid", SqlDbType.UniqueIdentifier, 0, "userid");
                        p.Add("@pvurl", SqlDbType.VarChar, 256, "pvurl");
```

Next, create a `SqlCommand` object that references the stored procedure, and define its parameters, including their data types and the names of the columns that correspond to each one. Notice that the first parameter has its `Direction` property set to `ParameterDirection.Output` to indicate that it's an output parameter.

```
using (SqlDataAdapter adapter = new SqlDataAdapter())
{
    cmd.UpdatedRowSource = UpdateRowSource.OutputParameters;
    adapter.InsertCommand = cmd;
    adapter.UpdateBatchSize = batchSize;
    Guid userId = Guid.NewGuid();
    for (int i = 0; i < batchSize; i++)
    {
        table.Rows.Add(0, userId,
            "http://www.12titans.net/test.aspx");
    }
    try
    {
        adapter.Update(table);
        pvid = (long)table.Rows[batchSize - 1]["pvid"];
    }
    catch (SqlException ex)
    {
        EventLog.WriteEntry("Application",
            "Error in WritePageView: " + ex.Message + "\n",
            EventLogEntryType.Error, 101);
        break;
    }
}
}
}
```

Next, set `UpdatedRowSource` to `UpdateRowSource.OutputParameters` to indicate that the runtime should map the **pvid** output parameter of the stored procedure back into the `DataTable`. Set `UpdateBatchSize` to the size of the batch, and add rows to the `DataTable` with the data. Then call `adapter.Update()` to synchronously send the batch to the server, and get the **pvid** response from the last row. In the event of an exception, write an entry in the operating system `Application` log.

```
StringBuilder result = new StringBuilder();
result.Append("Last pvid = ");
result.Append(pvid.ToString());
result.Append("<br/>");
IDictionary dict = conn.RetrieveStatistics();
foreach (string key in dict.Keys)
{
    result.Append(key);
    result.Append(" = ");
    result.Append(dict[key]);
    result.Append("<br/>");
}
this.info.Text = result.ToString();
}
}
}
}
```

Then you display the `pvid` of the last record along with the connection statistics, using the `<asp:Literal>` control. Each time you submit the page, it will add the requested number of rows to the `PageViews` table.

Results

The client machine I used for the examples in this chapter has a quad-core 2.4GHz Core 2 CPU with 4GB of RAM running 32-bit Vista Ultimate. It's connected over a 1Gbps network to a server with dual Opteron 250 CPUs at 2.4GHz and 4GB of RAM, running 32-bit Windows Server 2008 and SQL Server 2008. The disks on both machines are 7,200rpm SATA drives with 16MB of cache, configured as JBOD.

Here are the results after adding 20,000 rows on my test server, with a batch size of 50:

```
Last pvid = 20000
NetworkServerTime = 5997
BytesReceived = 982406
UnpreparedExecs = 400
SumResultSets = 0
SelectCount = 0
PreparedExecs = 0
ConnectionTime = 6257
ExecutionTime = 6217
Prepares = 0
BuffersSent = 1200
SelectRows = 0
ServerRoundtrips = 400
CursorOpens = 0
Transactions = 0
BytesSent = 7657600
BuffersReceived = 400
IduRows = 0
IduCount = 0
```

The test took 400 round-trips and about 6.2 seconds to execute. In Table 8-1, I've shown the results of running the test for various batch sizes, while maintaining the number of rows at 20,000.

Table 8-1. Insert Performance for Various Batch Sizes

Batch Size	Round-Trips	Execution Time (ms)
1	20,000	12,711
2	10,000	9,874
5	4,000	7,800
10	2,000	6,192
50	400	6,217

You can see that throughput roughly doubles as you increase the batch size from 1 to 10 and that larger batch sizes don't show any additional improvement, or they might even be a little slower. At that point, you are limited by disk speed rather than round-trips.

Limitations

Although this technique works reasonably well for INSERTs, it's not as good for UPDATEs and DELETEs, unless you already happen to have populated a DataTable for other reasons. Even then, SqlDataAdapter will send one T-SQL command for each modified row. In most real-life applications, a single statement with a WHERE clause that specifies multiple rows will be much more efficient.

This highlights a limitation of this approach, which is that it's not general purpose. If you want to do something other than reflect changes to a single DataTable or DataSet, you can't use the command batching that SqlDataAdapter provides.

Another issue with SqlDataAdapter.Update() is that it doesn't have a native async interface. Recall from earlier chapters that the general-purpose async mechanisms in .NET use threads from the ASP.NET thread pool, and therefore have an adverse impact on scalability. Since large batches tend to take a long time to run, not being able to call them asynchronously from a native async interface can cause or significantly compound scalability problems, as described earlier.

Building Parameterized Command Strings

The alternative approach is to build a parameterized command string yourself, separating commands from one another with semicolons. As crude as it might sound, it's very effective, and it addresses the problems with the standard approach in that it will allow you to send arbitrary commands in a single batch.

As an example, copy the code and markup from sql-batch1.aspx into a new web form called sql-batch2.aspx, and edit the code-behind as follows:

```
if (this.IsPostBack)
{
    int numRecords = Convert.ToInt32(this.cnt.Text);
    int batchSize = Convert.ToInt32(this.sz.Text);
    int numBatches = numRecords / batchSize;
    StringBuilder sb = new StringBuilder();
    string sql =
        "EXEC [Traffic].[AddPageView] @pvid{0} out, @userid{0}, @pvurl{0};";
    for (int i = 0; i < batchSize; i++)
    {
        sb.AppendFormat(sql, i);
    }
    string query = sb.ToString();
```

You construct the batch command by using EXEC to call your stored procedure, appending a number to the end of each parameter to make them unique, and using a semicolon to separate each command.

```
using (SqlConnection conn = new SqlConnection(ConnString))
{
    conn.Open();
    conn.StatisticsEnabled = true;
    SqlParameterCollection p = null;
    for (int j = 0; j < numBatches; j++)
    {
        using (SqlCommand cmd = new SqlCommand(query, conn))
        {
            p = cmd.Parameters;
            Guid userId = Guid.NewGuid();
            for (int i = 0; i < batchSize; i++)
            {
                p.Add("pvid" + i, SqlDbType.BigInt).Direction =
                    ParameterDirection.Output;
                p.Add("userid" + i, SqlDbType.UniqueIdentifier).Value = userId;
                p.Add("pvurl" + i, SqlDbType.VarChar, 256).Value =
                    "http://www.12titans.net/test.aspx";
            }
```

To finish building the batch command, assign a value to each numbered parameter. As in the previous example, **pvid** is an output parameter, **userid** is set to a new GUID, and **pvurl** is a string.

```
            try
            {
                cmd.ExecuteNonQuery();
            }
            catch (SqlException ex)
            {
                EventLog.WriteEntry("Application",
                    "Error in WritePageView: " + ex.Message + "\n",
                    EventLogEntryType.Error, 101);
            }
        }
    }
    StringBuilder result = new StringBuilder();
    result.Append("Last pvid = ");
    result.Append(p["pvid" + (batchSize - 1)].Value);
    result.Append("<br/>");
    IDictionary dict = conn.RetrieveStatistics();
    foreach (string key in dict.Keys)
    {
        result.Append(key);
        result.Append(" = ");
        result.Append(dict[key]);
        result.Append("<br/>");
    }
    this.info.Text = result.ToString();
}
}
```

Next, synchronously execute all the batches you need to reach the total number of records requested and collect and display the resulting statistics.

The performance of this approach is about the same as with `SqlDataAdapter`. Its advantage is the ability to include arbitrary commands and that you can execute the commands asynchronously, using `BeginExecuteNonQuery()`. You can also use it to improve performance with transactions, as I describe in the next section.

Transactions

As I mentioned earlier, each time SQL Server makes any changes to your data, it writes a record to the database log. Each of those writes requires a round-trip to the disk subsystem, which you should try to minimize. Each write also includes some overhead. Therefore, you can improve performance by writing multiple changes at once. The way to do that is by executing multiple writes within one transaction. If you don't explicitly specify a transaction, SQL Server transacts each change separately.

There is often a point of diminishing returns with regard to transaction size. Although larger transactions can help improve disk throughput, they can also block other threads if the commands acquire any database locks. For that reason, it's a good idea to adopt a middle ground when it comes to transaction length—not too short and not too long to give other threads a chance to run in between the transactions.

Using TransactionScope

You can apply transactions in a couple of ways. The one I prefer uses the `TransactionScope` object. That object isn't available in one of the libraries that ASP.NET references by default, so the first thing you need to do is add a reference. Right-click your web site, and select **Add Reference**. Make sure the **.NET** tab is selected, then scroll down and select `System.Transactions`, and finally click **OK**, as in Figure 8-1.

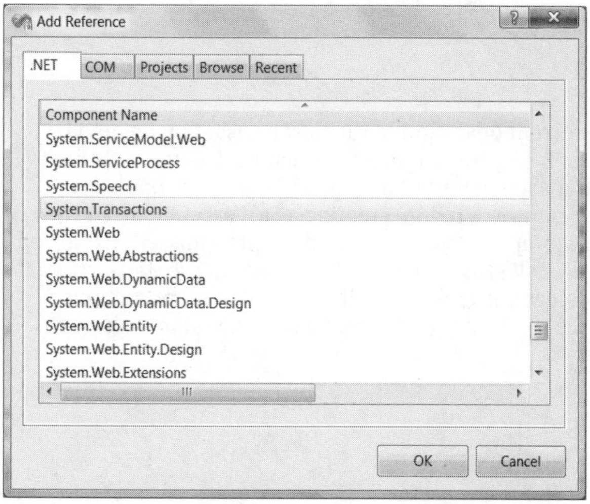

Figure 8-1. Adding a reference to System.Transactions

Copy the code and markup from `sql-batch2.aspx` into a new web form called `sql-batch3.aspx`, add `using System.Transactions` at the top, and edit the inner loop as follows:

```
for (int j = 0; j < numBatches; j++)
{
    using (TransactionScope scope = new TransactionScope())
    {
        using (SqlCommand cmd = new SqlCommand(query, conn))
        {
            conn.EnlistTransaction(Transaction.Current);
            p = cmd.Parameters;
            Guid userId = Guid.NewGuid();
            for (int i = 0; i < batchSize; i++)
            {
                p.Add("pvid" + i, SqlDbType.BigInt).Direction =
                    ParameterDirection.Output;
                p.Add("userid" + i, SqlDbType.UniqueIdentifier).Value = userId;
                p.Add("pvurl" + i, SqlDbType.VarChar, 256).Value =
                    "http://www.12titans.net/test.aspx";
            }
            try
            {
                cmd.ExecuteNonQuery();
                scope.Complete();
            }
            catch (SqlException ex)
            {
                EventLog.WriteEntry("Application",
                    "Error in WritePageView: " + ex.Message + "\n",
                    EventLogEntryType.Error, 101);
            }
        }
    }
}
```

Call `conn.EnlistTransaction()` to enlist the current operation in the new transaction created by `TransactionScope`. If you're writing code that doesn't require multiple transactions like the code here does, the `SqlConnection` object will enlist in the transaction automatically when you first open the connection (you would create a new `TransactionScope` first, before creating a `SqlConnection`). However, in this case you're opening the connection only once and then using it for multiple transactions, so you need to enlist explicitly. After the query is executed, call `scope.Complete()` to commit the transaction. If the query throws an exception, then `TransactionScope` will automatically roll back the transaction.

Table 8-2 shows the results of the performance tests, after truncating the table first to make sure you're starting from the same point.

Table 8-2. Insert Performance Using Basic Transactions

Batch Size	Round-Trips	Execution Time (ms)
1	60,000	24,072
2	30,000	12,835
5	12,000	7,404
10	6,000	4,382
50	1,200	2,849

Notice that the number of round-trips has tripled in each case. That's because ADO.NET sends the BEGIN TRANSACTION and COMMIT TRANSACTION commands in separate round-trips. That in turn causes the performance for the first two cases to be worse than the nontransaction case, since network overhead dominates. However, as the batch size increases, network overhead becomes less significant, and the improved speed with which SQL Server can write to the log disk becomes apparent. With a batch size of 50, inserting 20,000 records takes only 45 percent as long as it did when you didn't use explicit transactions.

Using Explicit BEGIN and COMMIT TRANSACTION Statements

Partly for fun and partly because the theme of this book is, after all, *ultra-fast* ASP.NET, you can eliminate the extra round-trips by including the transaction commands in the text of the command string. To illustrate, make a copy of sql-batch2.aspx (the version without transaction support), call it sql-batch4.aspx, and edit the part of the code-behind that builds the command string as follows:

```
StringBuilder sb = new StringBuilder();
string sql = "EXEC [Traffic].[AddPageView] @pvid{0} out, @userid{0}, @pvurl{0};";
sb.Append("BEGIN TRY; BEGIN TRANSACTION;");
for (int i = 0; i < batchSize; i++)
{
    sb.AppendFormat(sql, i);
}
sb.Append(
    "COMMIT TRANSACTION;END TRY\nBEGIN CATCH\nROLLBACK TRANSACTION\nEND CATCH");
string query = sb.ToString();
```

The T-SQL syntax allows you to use semicolons to separate all the commands except BEGIN CATCH and END CATCH. For those, you should use newlines instead.

Table 8-3 shows the test results. Notice the difference from the previous example is greatest for the smaller batch sizes and diminishes for the larger batch sizes. Even so, the largest batch size is about 19 percent faster, although the code definitely isn't as clean as when you used TransactionScope.

Table 8-3. Insert Performance Using Transactions with Minimal Round-Trips

Batch Size	Round-Trips	Execution Time (ms)
1	20,000	12,720
2	10,000	7,909
5	4,000	4,449
10	2,000	2,889
50	400	2,311

Table-Valued Parameters

T-SQL doesn't support arrays. In the past, developers have often resorted to things like comma-separated strings or XML as workarounds. SQL Server 2008 introduced *table-valued parameters*. The idea is that since tables are somewhat analogous to an array, you can now pass them as arguments to stored procedures. This not only provides a cleaner way to do a type of command batching, but it also performs well, assuming that the stored procedure itself uses set-based commands and avoids cursors.

To extend the previous examples, first use SQL Server Management Studio (SSMS) to add a new TABLE TYPE and a new stored procedure:

```
CREATE TYPE PageViewType AS TABLE (
    [UserId]  UNIQUEIDENTIFIER  NULL,
    [PvUrl]   VARCHAR(256)      NOT NULL
)

CREATE PROCEDURE [Traffic].[AddPageViewTVP]
    @pvid   BIGINT OUT,
    @rows   PageViewType READONLY
AS
BEGIN
    SET NOCOUNT ON
    DECLARE @trandate DATETIME
    SET @trandate = GETUTCDATE()
    INSERT INTO [Traffic].[PageViews]
        SELECT @trandate, UserId, PvUrl
            FROM @rows
    SET @pvid = SCOPE_IDENTITY()
END
```

You use the TABLE TYPE as the type of one of the arguments to the stored procedure. T-SQL requires that you mark the parameter READONLY. The body of the stored procedure uses a single insert statement to insert all the rows of the input table into the destination table. It also returns the last identity value that was generated.

To use this procedure, copy the code and markup from `sql-batch1.aspx` to `sql-batch5.aspx`, and edit the main loop as follows:

```
for (int j = 0; j < numBatches; j++)
{
    DataTable table = new DataTable();
    table.Columns.Add("userid", typeof(Guid));
    table.Columns.Add("pvurl", typeof(string));
    using (SqlCommand cmd = new SqlCommand("[Traffic].[AddPageViewTVP]", conn))
    {
        cmd.CommandType = CommandType.StoredProcedure;
        Guid userId = Guid.NewGuid();
        for (int i = 0; i < batchSize; i++)
        {
            table.Rows.Add(userId, "http://www.12titans.net/test.aspx");
        }
        SqlParameterCollection p = cmd.Parameters;
        p.Add("pvid", SqlDbType.BigInt).Direction = ParameterDirection.Output;
        SqlParameter rt = p.AddWithValue("rows", table);
        rt.SqlDbType = SqlDbType.Structured;
        rt.TypeName = "PageViewType";
        try
        {
            cmd.ExecuteNonQuery();
            pvid = (long)p["pvid"].Value;
        }
        catch (SqlException ex)
        {
            EventLog.WriteEntry("Application",
                "Error in WritePageView: " + ex.Message + "\n",
                EventLogEntryType.Error, 101);
            break;
        }
    }
}
```

Here's what the code does:

- Creates a `DataTable` with the two columns that you want to use for the database inserts.

- Adds `batchSize` rows to the `DataTable` for each batch, with your values for the two columns

- Configures the `SqlParameters` for the command, including setting `pvid` as an output value and adding the `DataTable` as the value of the rows table-valued parameter. ADO.NET automatically transforms the `DataTable` into a table-valued parameter.

- Synchronously executes the command and retrieves the value of the output parameter.

- Catches database exceptions and writes a corresponding message to the Windows error log.

In addition to providing a form of command batching, this version also has the advantage of executing each batch in a separate transaction, since the single insert statement uses one transaction to do its work.

It's worthwhile to look at the command that goes across the wire, using SQL Profiler. Here's a single batch, with a batch size of 2:

```
DECLARE @p1 BIGINT
SET @p1=0
DECLARE @p2 dbo.PageViewType
INSERT INTO @p2 VALUES
    ('AD08202A-5CE9-475B-AD7D-581B1AE6F5D1',N'http://www.12titans.net/test.aspx')
INSERT INTO @p2 VALUES
    ('AD08202A-5CE9-475B-AD7D-581B1AE6F5D1',N'http://www.12titans.net/test.aspx')
EXEC [Traffic].[AddPageViewTVP] @pvid=@p1 OUTPUT,@rows=@p2
SELECT @p1
```

Notice that the DataTable rows are inserted into an in-memory table variable, which is then passed to the stored procedure.

Table 8-4 shows the performance of this approach.

Table 8-4. Insert Performance Using a Table-Valued Parameter

Batch Size	Round-Trips	Execution Time (ms)
1	20,000	55,224
2	10,000	28,316
5	4,000	11,507
10	2,000	6,136
50	400	1,631
100	200	1,034
200	100	665
500	40	490

The performance isn't as good as the previous example (`sql-batch4.aspx`) until the batch size reaches 50. However, unlike with the previous examples, in this case write performance continues to improve even if you increase the batch size to 500. The best performance here has more than *25 times* the throughput of the original one-row-at-a-time example. A single row takes only about 25 microseconds to insert, which results in a rate of more than 40,000 rows per second.

Multiple Result Sets

If you need to process a number of queries at a time, each of which produces a separate result set, you can have SQL Server process them in a single round-trip. When executed, the command will return *multiple result sets*. This means that you should avoid issuing back-to-back queries separately; you should combine them into a single round-trip whenever possible.

You might do this by having a stored procedure that issues more than one SELECT statement that returns rows, or perhaps by executing more than one stored procedure in a batch, using the command batching techniques described earlier.

As an example, first create a new stored procedure:

```
CREATE PROCEDURE [Traffic].[GetFirstLastPageViews]
    @count          INT
AS
BEGIN
    SET NOCOUNT ON
    SELECT TOP (@count) PvId, PvDate, UserId, PvUrl
        FROM [Traffic].[PageViews]
        ORDER BY Pvid ASC
    SELECT TOP (@count) PvId, PvDate, UserId, PvUrl
        FROM [Traffic].[PageViews]
        ORDER BY Pvid DESC
END
```

The procedure returns the first and last rows in the PageViews table, in two result sets, using a parameterized count.

Using SqlDataReader.NextResult()

Create a web form called `sql-result1.aspx`, and edit the `<form>` part of the markup as follows:

```
<form id="form1" runat="server">
<div>
Count: <asp:TextBox runat="server" ID="cnt" /><br />
<asp:Button runat="server" Text="Submit" /><br />
<asp:GridView runat="server" ID="first" />
<br />
<asp:GridView runat="server" ID="last" />
</div>
</form>
```

The form has one text box for a count parameter, a submit button, and two data GridView controls.

Next, edit the code-behind as follows:

```csharp
using System;
using System.Collections;
using System.Data;
using System.Data.SqlClient;
using System.Diagnostics;
using System.Text;
using System.Web.UI;

public partial class sql_result1 : Page
{
    public const string ConnString =
        "Data Source=server;Initial Catalog=Sample;Integrated Security=True";

    protected void Page_Load(object sender, EventArgs e)
    {
        if (this.IsPostBack)
        {
            int numRecords = Convert.ToInt32(this.cnt.Text);
            using (SqlConnection conn = new SqlConnection(ConnString))
            {
                conn.Open();
                using (SqlCommand cmd =
                    new SqlCommand("[Traffic].[GetFirstLastPageViews]", conn))
                {
                    cmd.CommandType = CommandType.StoredProcedure;
                    SqlParameterCollection p = cmd.Parameters;
                    p.Add("count", SqlDbType.Int).Value = numRecords;
                    try
                    {
                        SqlDataReader reader = cmd.ExecuteReader();
                        this.first.DataSource = reader;
                        this.first.DataBind();
                        reader.NextResult();
                        this.last.DataSource = reader;
                        this.last.DataBind();
                    }
                    catch (SqlException ex)
                    {
                        EventLog.WriteEntry("Application",
                            "Error in GetFirstLastPageView: " + ex.Message + "\n",
                            EventLogEntryType.Error, 102);
                        throw;
                    }
                }
            }
        }
    }
}
```

The code executes the stored procedure and then binds each result set to a `GridView` control. Calling `reader.NextResult()` after binding the first result set causes the reader to advance to the next set of rows. This approach allows you to use a single round-trip to retrieve the two sets of rows generated by the stored procedure.

Using SqlDataAdapter and a DataSet

You can also use `SqlDataAdapter` to load more than one result set into multiple `DataTables` in a `DataSet`.

For example, make a copy of `sql-result1.aspx` called `sql-result2.aspx`, and edit the code-behind as follows:

```
using (SqlCommand cmd = new SqlCommand("[Traffic].[GetFirstLastPageViews]", conn))
{
    cmd.CommandType = CommandType.StoredProcedure;
    SqlParameterCollection p = cmd.Parameters;
    p.Add("count", SqlDbType.Int).Value = numRecords;
    using (SqlDataAdapter adapter = new SqlDataAdapter(cmd))
    {
        try
        {
            DataSet results = new DataSet();
            adapter.Fill(results);
            this.first.DataSource = results.Tables[0];
            this.first.DataBind();
            this.last.DataSource = results.Tables[1];
            this.last.DataBind();
        }
        catch (SqlException ex)
        {
            EventLog.WriteEntry("Application",
                "Error in GetFirstLastPageView: " + ex.Message + "\n",
                EventLogEntryType.Error, 102);
            throw;
        }
    }
}
```

The call to `adapter.Fill()` will check to see whether more than one result set is available. For each result set, it will create and load one `DataTable` in the destination `DataSet`. However, this approach doesn't work with asynchronous database calls, so it's only suitable for background threads or perhaps infrequently used pages where synchronous calls are acceptable.

Data Precaching

As I mentioned earlier, after SQL Server reads data from disk into memory, the data stays in memory for a while; exactly how long depends on how much RAM is available and the nature of subsequent commands. This aspect of the database points the way to a powerful and yet rarely used performance optimization technique: precaching at the data tier.

Approach

In the cases where you can reasonably predict the next action of your users and where that action involves database access with predictable parameters, you can issue a query to the database that will read the relevant data into RAM before it's actually needed. The goal is to precache the data *at the data tier*, so that when you issue the "real" query, you avoid the initial disk access. This can also work when the future command will be an UPDATE or a DELETE, since those commands need to read the associated rows before they can be changed.

There are a couple of tricks to making database precaching effective with a multiserver load-balanced web tier:

- You should issue the precache command either from a background thread or from an asynchronous Ajax call. You should not issue it in-line with the original page, even if the page is asynchronous.

- You should limit (throttle) the number precaching queries per web server to avoid unduly loading the server based solely on anticipated future work.

- Avoid issuing duplicate precaching queries.

- Don't bother precaching objects that will probably already be in database memory, such as frequently used data.

- You should discard precaching queries if they are too old, since there's no need to execute them after the target page has run.

- Execute precaching commands with a lower priority, using Resource Governor, so that they don't slow down "real" commands.

Precaching Forms-Based Data

As an example, let's take a forms-based login page. After viewing that page, it's likely that the next step for a user will be to log in, using their username and password. To validate the login, your application will need to read the row in the Users table that contains that user's information. Since the index of the row you need is the user's name and since you don't know what that is until after they've started to fill in the form, Ajax provides the best solution here for precaching.

When the user exits the username box in the web form, you can issue an async Ajax command to the server that contains the user's name. For precaching, you don't care about the password, since the name alone will be enough to find the right row.

On the web server, the other side of the Ajax call would queue a request to a background thread to issue a SELECT to read the row of interest. The server will process that request while the user is typing their password. Although you might be tempted to return a flag from the Ajax call to indicate that the username is valid, that's usually not recommended, for security reasons. In addition, the Ajax call can return more quickly if it just queues the request and doesn't wait for a result.

When the user clicks the Login button on the web form, the code on the server will validate the username and password by reissuing a similar query. At that point, the data will already be in memory on the database server, so the query will complete quickly.

Precaching Page-at-a-Time Data

Another example would be paging through data, such as in a catalog. In that case, there may be a good chance that the user will advance to the next page after they finish viewing the current one. To make sure that the data for the next page is in memory on the database server, you could do something like this:

- Queue a work item to a background thread that describes the parameters to read the next page of data from the catalog and a timestamp to indicate when you placed the query in the queue.

- When the background thread starts to process the work item, it should discard the request if it's more than a certain age (perhaps one to three seconds), since the user may have already advanced to the next page by then.

- Check the work item against a list of queries that the background thread has recently processed. If the query is on that list, then discard the request. This may be of limited utility in a load-balanced environment, but it can still help in the event of attacks or heavy burst-oriented traffic.

- Have the background thread use a connection to the server that's managed by Resource Governor (see later in this chapter), so that the precaching queries from all web servers together don't overwhelm database resources. That can also help from a security perspective by minimizing the impact of a denial-of-service attack.

- Cache the results of the query at the web tier, if appropriate.

- After issuing the query, the background thread might sleep for a short time before retrieving another work item from the queue, which will throttle the number of read-ahead requests that the web server can process.

The performance difference between using data that's already in memory and having to read it from disk first can be very significant—as much as a factor of ten or even much more, depending on the size of the data, the details of the query, and the speed of your disk subsystem.

Data Access Layer

An often-cited best practice for data-oriented applications is to provide a layer of abstraction on top of your data access routines. That's usually done by encapsulating them in a *data access layer* (DAL), which can be a class or perhaps one or more assemblies, depending on the complexity of your application.

The motivations for grouping the data access code in one place include easing maintenance, database independence (simplifying future migration to other data platforms), encouraging consistent patterns, and simplifying management of command batches, connections, transactions, and multiple result sets.

With synchronous database commands, the DAL methods would typically execute the command and return the result. If you use asynchronous commands everywhere you can, as I suggested in earlier chapters, you will need to modify your DAL accordingly. In the same style as the ADO.NET libraries, you should break up your code into one method that begins a query and another that ends it and collects the results.

Here's an example:

```
public class DAL : ADAL
{
    public override IAsyncResult AddBrowserBegin(RequestInfo info,
        AsyncCallback callback)
    {
        SqlConnection conn =
            new SqlConnection(ConfigData.TrafficConnectionStringAsync);
        SqlCommand cmd = new SqlCommand("[Traffic].[AddBrowser]", conn);
        cmd.CommandType = CommandType.StoredProcedure;
        cmd.Parameters.Add("id", SqlDbType.UniqueIdentifier).Value = info.BrowserId;
        cmd.Parameters.Add("agent", SqlDbType.VarChar, 256).Value = info.Agent;
        conn.Open();
        return cmd.BeginExecuteNonQuery(callback, cmd);
    }

    public override void AddBrowserEnd(IAsyncResult ar)
    {
        using (SqlCommand cmd = ar.AsyncState as SqlCommand)
        {
            if (cmd != null)
            {
                try
                {
                    cmd.EndExecuteNonQuery(ar);
                }
                catch (SqlException e)
                {
                    EventLog.WriteEntry("Application",
                        "Error in AddBrowser: " + e.Message,
                        EventLogEntryType.Error, 103);
                    throw;
                }
                finally
                {
                    cmd.Connection.Dispose();
                }
            }
        }
    }
}
```

The AddBrowserBegin() method creates a SqlConnection from an async connection string, along with an associated SqlCommand. After filling in the parameters, it opens the connection, begins the command, and returns the resulting IAsyncResult.

The AddBrowserEnd() method ends the command and calls Dispose() on the SqlConnection and SqlCommand objects (implicitly via a using statement for SqlCommand and explicitly for SqlConnection).

I'm also implementing the ADAL abstract class, which contains signatures for all the DAL methods, along with several static support methods. That will make it easier in the future to drop in a new class that performs the same functions, but with a different data store. You could also use this technique as part of your deployment and update strategy. One implementation of the abstract class could use an old API, while another version uses a new one. Dynamically selecting an implementation can help speed up the process of rolling a new schema to multiple database servers. You might also use it to switch between the "old way" and the "new way" at runtime, rather than requiring a full rollback in the event of problems.

You will probably also want to include connection and transaction management in your DAL. ADO.NET uses connection pools to reuse connections as much as it can. Connections are pooled based entirely on a byte-for-byte comparison of the connection strings; different connection strings will not share the same pooled connection. However, even with identical connection strings, if you execute a command within the scope of one `SqlConnection` object and then execute another command within the scope of the different `SqlConnection`, that will be considered a distributed transaction. To avoid the associated performance impact and complexity, it's better to execute both commands within the same `SqlConnection`. In fact, it would be better still to batch the commands together, as described earlier. Command batching and caching are also good things to include in your DAL.

Query and Schema Optimization

There's a definite art to query and schema optimization. It's a large subject worthy of a book of its own, so I'd like to cover just a few potentially high-impact areas.

Clustered and Nonclustered Indexes

Proper design of indexes, and in particular the choice between clustered and nonclustered indexes and their associated keys, is critical for optimal performance of your database.

As I mentioned earlier, SQL Server manages disk space in terms of 8KB pages and 64KB extents. When a *clustered* index is present, table rows within a page and the pages within an extent are ordered based on that index. Since a clustered index determines the physical ordering of rows within a table, each table can have only one clustered index.

A table can also have secondary, or *nonclustered*, indexes. Each nonclustered index is used to determine the physical order of the rows of the index. By default the rows in a nonclustered index only contain the indexed column itself and the clustered index column, if there is one and if it's unique. When you create a nonclustered index, you can also require other columns to be included. You can think of a nonclustered index as a separate table that only has a subset of the columns from the original table.

A table without any indexes is known as a *heap* and is unordered.

Neither a clustered nor a nonclustered index has to be unique or non-null, though both can be. Of course, both types of indexes can also include multiple columns, and you can specify an ascending or descending sort order. If a clustered index is not unique, then all nonclustered indexes include a 4-byte pointer back to the original row, instead of the clustered index.

Including the clustered index column in the nonclustered index allows SQL Server to quickly find the rest of the columns associated with a particular row, through a process known as a *key lookup*. SQL Server can also use the columns in the nonclustered index to satisfy the query; if all the columns you need to satisfy your query are present in the nonclustered index, then the key lookup can be skipped. We say that such a query is *covered*. You can help create covered queries and eliminate key lookups by adding the needed columns to a nonclustered index, assuming the additional overhead is warranted.

Index Performance Issues

Since SQL Server physically orders rows by the indexes, consider what happens when you insert a new row. For an ascending index, if the value of the index for the new row is greater than that for any previous row, then it is inserted at the end of the table. In that case, the table grows smoothly, and the physical ordering is easily maintained. However, if the new index places the new row in the middle of an existing page that's already full of other rows, then that page will be split by creating a new one and moving half of the existing rows into it. The result is fragmentation of the table; its physical order on disk is no longer the same as its logical order. The process of splitting the page also means that it is no longer completely full of data. Both of those changes will significantly decrease the speed with which you will be able to read the full table.

The fastest way for SQL Server to deliver a group of rows from disk is when they are physically next to each other. A query that requires key lookups for each row or that even has to directly seek to each different row will be much slower than one that can deliver a number of contiguous rows. You can take advantage of this in your index and query design by preferring indexes for columns that are commonly used in range-based WHERE clauses, such as BETWEEN.

When there are indexes on a table, every time you modify the table, the indexes may also need to be modified. Therefore, there's a trade-off between the cost of maintaining indexes and their use in allowing queries to execute faster. If you have a table where you are mostly doing heavy INSERTs and only very rarely do a SELECT, then it may not be worth the performance cost of maintaining an extra index (or any index at all).

If you issue a query with a column in the WHERE clause that doesn't have an index on it, the result is usually either a *table scan* or an *index scan*. SQL Server reads every row of the table or index. In addition to the direct performance cost of reading every row, there can also be an indirect cost. If your server doesn't have enough free memory to hold the table being scanned, then buffers in the cache will be dropped to make room, which might negatively affect the performance of other queries. Aggregation queries, such as COUNT and SUM, by their nature often involve table scans, and for that reason, you should avoid them as much as you can on large tables. See the next chapter for alternatives.

Index Guidelines

With these concepts in mind, you can formulate the following guidelines:

- Prefer narrow index keys that always increase in value, such as an integer IDENTITY. Keeping them narrow means that more rows will fit on a page, and having them increase means that new rows will be added at the end of the table, avoiding fragmentation.

- Avoid near-random index keys such as strings or UNIQUEIDENTIFIERs. Their randomness will cause a large number of page splits, resulting in fragmentation and associated poor performance. Having said that, even with their problems, there are times when the additional overhead implicit with UNIQUEIDENTIFIERs may be acceptable, such as if you can avoid a database round-trip by creating keys at the web tier.

- Although exact index definitions may evolve over time, begin by making sure that the columns you use in your WHERE and JOIN clauses have indexes assigned to them.

- Consider assigning the clustered index to a column that you often use to select a range of rows or that usually needs to be sorted. It should be unique for best performance.

- In cases where you have mostly INSERTs and almost no SELECTs (such as for logs), you might choose to use a heap and have no indexes. In that case, SQL Server will insert new rows at the end of the table, which prevents fragmentation. That allows INSERTs to execute very quickly.

- Avoid table or index scans. Some query constructs can force a scan even when an index is available, such as a LIKE clause with a wildcard at the beginning.

Although you can use NEWSEQUENTIALID() to generate sequential GUIDs, that approach has some significant limitations:

- It can be used only on the server, as the DEFAULT value for a column. One of the most useful aspects of GUIDs as keys is being able to create them from a load-balanced web tier without requiring a database round-trip, which doesn't work with this approach.

- The generated GUIDs are only guaranteed to be increasing for "a while." In particular, things like a server reboot can cause newly generated GUIDs to have values less than older ones. That means new rows aren't guaranteed to always go at the end of tables; page splits can still happen.

- Another reason for using GUIDs as keys is to have user-visible, non-guessable values. When the values are sequential, they become guessable.

Example with No Indexes

Let's start with a table by itself with no indexes:

```
CREATE TABLE ind (
    v1  INT IDENTITY,
    v2  INT,
    v3  VARCHAR(64)
)
```

The table has three columns: an integer identity, another integer, and a string. Since it doesn't have any indexes on it yet, this table is a heap. INSERTs will be fast, since they won't require any validations for uniqueness and since the sort order and indexes don't have to be maintained.

Next, let's add a half million rows to the table, so you'll have a decent amount of data to run test queries against:

```
DECLARE @i INT
SET @i = 0
WHILE (@i < 500000)
BEGIN
    INSERT INTO ind
        (v2, v3)
        VALUES
        (@i * 2, 'test')
    SET @i = @i + 1
END
```

The **v1 IDENTITY** column will automatically be filled with integers from 1 to 500,000. The **v2** column will contain even integers from zero to one million, and the **v3** column will contain a fixed string. Of course, this would be faster if you did multiple inserts in a single transaction, as discussed previously, but that's overkill for a one-time-only script like this.

You can have a look at the table's physical characteristics on disk by running the following command:

```
DBCC SHOWCONTIG (ind) WITH ALL_INDEXES
```

Since there are no indexes yet, information is displayed for the table only:

```
Table: 'ind' (101575400); index ID: 0, database ID: 23
TABLE level scan performed.
- Pages Scanned................................: 1624
- Extents Scanned..............................: 204
- Extent Switches..............................: 203
- Avg. Pages per Extent........................: 8.0
- Scan Density [Best Count:Actual Count].......: 99.51% [203:204]
- Extent Scan Fragmentation ...................: 0.98%
- Avg. Bytes Free per Page.....................: 399.0
- Avg. Page Density (full).....................: 95.07%
```

You can see from this that the table occupies 1,624 pages and 204 extents and that the pages are 95.07 percent full on average.

Adding a Clustered Index

Here's the first query that you're going to optimize:

```
SELECT v1, v2, v3
    FROM ind
    WHERE v1 BETWEEN 1001 AND 1100
```

You're retrieving all three columns from a range of rows, based on the **v1 IDENTITY** column.

Before running the query, let's look at how SQL Server will execute it. Do that by selecting it in SSMS, right-clicking, and selecting **Display Estimated Execution Plan**. Here's the result:

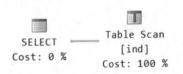

This shows that the query will be executed using a table scan; since the table doesn't have an index yet, the only way to find any specific values in it is to look at each and every row.

Before executing the query, let's flush all buffers from memory:

```
CHECKPOINT
DBCC DROPCLEANBUFFERS
```

The CHECKPOINT command tells SQL Server to write all the dirty buffers it has in memory out to disk. Afterward, all buffers will be clean. The DBCC DROPCLEANBUFFERS command then tells it to let go of all the clean buffers. The two commands together ensure that you're starting from the same place each time: an empty buffer cache.

Next, enable reporting of some performance-related statistics after running each command:

```
SET STATISTICS IO ON
SET STATISTICS TIME ON
```

STATISTICS IO will tell you how much physical disk I/O was needed, and STATISTICS TIME will tell you how much CPU time was used.

Run the query, and click the **Messages** tab to see the reported statistics:

```
Table 'ind'. Scan count 1, logical reads 1624,
physical reads 29, read-ahead reads 1624,
lob logical reads 0, lob physical reads 0, lob read-ahead reads 0.

 SQL Server Execution Times:
   CPU time = 141 ms,  elapsed time = 348 ms.
```

The values you're interested in are 29 physical reads, 1,624 read-ahead reads, 141ms of CPU time, and 348ms of elapsed time. Notice that the number of read-ahead reads is the same as the total size of the table, as reported by DBCC SHOWCONTIG in the previous code listing. Also notice the difference between the CPU time and the elapsed time, which shows that the query spent about half of the total time waiting for the disk reads.

■ **Note** I don't use logical reads as my preferred performance metric because they don't accurately reflect the load that the command generates on the server, so tuning only to reduce that number may not produce any *visible* performance improvements. CPU time and physical reads are much more useful in that way.

The fact that the query is looking for the values of all columns over a range of the values of one of them is an ideal indication for the use of a clustered index on the row that's used in the WHERE clause:

```
CREATE UNIQUE CLUSTERED INDEX IndIX ON ind(v1)
```

Since the v1 column is an IDENTITY, that means it's also UNIQUE, so you include that information in the index. This is almost the same as SQL Server's default definition of a *primary key* from an index perspective, so you can accomplish nearly the same thing as follows:

```
ALTER TABLE ind ADD CONSTRAINT IndIX PRIMARY KEY (v1)
```

The difference between the two is that a primary key does not allow NULLs, where the unique clustered index does, although there can be only one row with a NULL when the index is unique. Repeating the DBCC SHOWCONTIG command now shows the following relevant information:

```
- Pages Scanned...............................: 1548
- Extents Scanned.............................: 194
- Avg. Page Density (full)....................: 99.74%
```

There are a few less pages and extents, with a corresponding increase in page density. After adding the clustered index, here's the resulting query plan:

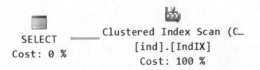

```
    SELECT   ─────    Clustered Index Seek (C...
   Cost: 0 %                [ind].[IndIX]
                            Cost: 100 %
```

The table scan has become a clustered index seek, using the newly created index. After flushing the buffers again and executing the query, here are the relevant statistics:

```
physical reads 3, read-ahead reads 0
CPU time = 0 ms,  elapsed time = 33 ms.
```

The total number of disk reads has dropped from 1,624 to just 3, CPU time has decreased from 141ms to less than 1ms, and elapsed time has decreased from 348ms to 33ms. At this point, our first query is fully optimized.

Adding a Nonclustered Index

Here's the next query:

```
SELECT v1, v2, v3
    FROM ind
    WHERE v2 BETWEEN 1001 AND 1100
```

This is similar to the previous query, except it's using v2 in the WHERE clause instead of v1. Here's the initial query plan:

```
    SELECT   ─────    Clustered Index Scan (C...
   Cost: 0 %                [ind].[IndIX]
                            Cost: 100 %
```

This time, instead of scanning the table, SQL Server will scan the clustered index. However, since each row of the clustered index contains all three columns, this is really the same as scanning the whole table.

Next, flush the buffers again, and execute the query. Here are the results:

```
physical reads 24, read-ahead reads 1549
CPU time = 204 ms,  elapsed time = 334 ms.
```

Sure enough, the total number of disk reads still corresponds to the size of the full table. It's a tiny bit faster than the first query without an index, but only because the number of pages decreased after you added the clustered index.

To speed up this query, add a nonclustered index:

```
CREATE UNIQUE NONCLUSTERED INDEX IndV2IX ON ind(v2)
```

As with the first column, this column is also unique, so you include that information when you create the index.

Running `DBCC SHOWCONTIG` now includes information about the new index:

```
- Pages Scanned.................................: 866
- Extents Scanned..............................: 109
- Avg. Page Density (full).....................: 99.84%
```

You can see that it's a little more than half the size of the clustered index. It's somewhat smaller since it only includes the integer v1 and v2 columns, not the four-character-long strings you put in v3.

Here's the new query plan:

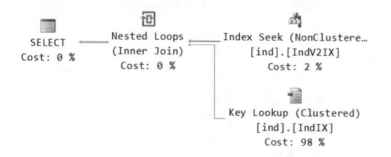

This time, SQL Server will do an inexpensive index seek on the `IndV2IX` nonclustered index you just created. That will allow it to find all the rows with the range of v2 values that you specified. It can also retrieve the value of v1 directly from that index, since the clustered index column is included with all nonclustered indexes. However, to get the value of v3, it needs to execute a key lookup, which finds the matching row using the clustered index. Notice too that the key lookup is 98 percent of the cost of the query.

The two indexes amount to two physically separate tables on disk. The clustered index contains v1, v2, and v3 and is sorted and indexed by v1. The nonclustered index contains only v1 and v2 and is sorted and indexed by v2. After retrieving the desired rows from each index, the inner join in the query plan combines them to form the result.

After flushing the buffers again and executing the query, here are the results:

```
physical reads 4, read-ahead reads 2
CPU time = 0 ms,  elapsed time = 35 ms.
```

The CPU time and elapsed time are comparable to the first query when it was using the clustered index. However, there are more disk reads because of the key lookups.

Creating a Covered Index

Let's see what happens if you don't include v3 in the query:

```
SELECT v1, v2
    FROM ind
    WHERE v2 BETWEEN 1001 AND 1100
```

Here's the query plan:

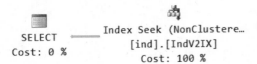

Since you don't need v3 any more, now SQL Server can just use an index seek on the nonclustered index.

After flushing the buffers again, here are the results:

```
physical reads 3, read-ahead reads 0
CPU time = 0 ms,  elapsed time = 12 ms.
```

You've eliminated the extra disk reads, and the elapsed time has dropped significantly too.

You should be able to achieve a similar speedup for the query that uses v3 by adding v3 to the nonclustered index to create a covered index and avoid the key lookups:

```
CREATE UNIQUE NONCLUSTERED INDEX IndV2IX ON ind(v2)
    INCLUDE (v3)
    WITH (DROP_EXISTING = ON)
```

This command will include v3 in the existing index, without having to separately drop it first. Here's the updated DBCC SHOWCONTIG for the nonclustered index:

```
- Pages Scanned................................: 1359
- Extents Scanned..............................: 170
- Avg. Page Density (full).....................: 99.98%
```

The index has grown from 866 pages and 109 extents to 1,359 pages and 170 extents, while the page density remains close to 100 percent. It's still a little smaller than the clustered index because of some extra information that is stored in the clustered index other than just the column data.

The new query plan for the original query with v3 that you're optimizing is exactly the same as the plan shown earlier for the query without v3:

```
   ▦                        ▚
 SELECT  ————— Index Seek (NonClustere…
Cost: 0 %          [ind].[IndV2IX]
                     Cost: 100 %
```

Here are the statistics:

```
physical reads 3, read-ahead reads 0
CPU time = 0 ms,  elapsed time = 12 ms.
```

The results are also the same as the previous test. However, the price for this performance is that you now have two complete copies of the table: one with v1 as the index, and one with v2 as the index. Therefore, while SELECTs of the type you used in the examples here will be fast, INSERTs, UPDATEs, and DELETEs will be slower, because they now have to change two physical tables instead of just one.

Index Fragmentation

Now let's see what happens if you insert 5,000 rows of data that has a random value for v2 that's in the range of the existing values, which is between zero and one million. The initial values were all even numbers, so you can avoid uniqueness collisions by using odd numbers. Here's the T-SQL:

```
DECLARE @i INT
SET @i = 0
WHILE (@i < 5000)
BEGIN
    INSERT INTO ind
        (v2, v3)
        VALUES
        ((CONVERT(INT, RAND() * 500000) * 2) + 1, 'test')
    SET @i = @i + 1
END
```

Those 5,000 rows are 1 percent of the 500,000 rows already in the table. After running the script, here's what DBCC SHOWCONTIG reports for the clustered index:

```
- Pages Scanned...............................: 1564
- Extents Scanned............................: 199
- Avg. Page Density (full)....................: 99.70%
```

For the nonclustered index, it reports the following:

```
- Pages Scanned...............................: 2680
- Extents Scanned............................: 339
- Avg. Page Density (full)....................: 51.19%
```

Notice that the clustered index has just a few more pages and extents, and it remains at close to 100 percent page density. However, the nonclustered index has gone from 1,359 pages and 170 extents at close to 100 percent density to 2,680 pages, 339 extents, and about 50 percent density. Since the clustered index doesn't depend on the value of v2 and since v1 is an IDENTITY value that steadily increases, the new rows can just go at the end of the table.

Rows in the nonclustered index are ordered based on v2. When a new row is inserted, SQL Server places it in the correct page and position to maintain the sort order on v2. If that results in more rows than will fit on the page, then the page is split in two, and half the rows are placed in each page. That's why you see the average page density at close to 50 percent.

Excessive page splits can have a negative impact on performance, since they can mean that many more pages have to be read to access the same amount of data.

Miscellaneous Query Optimization Guidelines

Here are a few high-level guidelines for optimizing your queries:

- If you're writing new queries or code that invokes queries, you should make frequent and regular use of the SQL Profiler to get a feeling for how many round-trips your code is making and how long the queries are taking. For me, it plays an irreplaceable role when I'm doing that kind of work. You might think of SQL Profiler as "Fiddler for SQL Server."

- Avoid cursors. Processing data a row-at-a-time in T-SQL is *very* expensive. Although there are exceptions, 99 percent of the time, it's worth the effort to rewrite your queries to use set-based semantics, if possible. Alternatives include things like table variables, temporary tables, and so on. I've rewritten some cursor-based queries that ran 1,000 times faster as set-based operations. If you can't avoid cursors, identify all read-only queries, and mark the associated cursors as FAST_FORWARD.

- Avoid triggers. Triggers are a powerful tool, but you should think of them as a last resort; use them only if there is no other way. They can introduce massive amounts of overhead, which tends to be of the slow, row-at-a-time type. Because triggers are nominally hidden from the view of developers, what's worse is that the extra overhead is hidden too.

- To avoid performance problems because of deadlocks, make a list of all the stored procedures in your system and the order in which they modify tables, and work to ensure that order is consistent from one stored procedure to another. In cases where consistent order isn't possible, either use an increased transaction isolation level or use locking hints or increased lock granularity.

- Use SET NOCOUNT ON at the top of most of your stored procedures to avoid the extra overhead of returning a result row count. However, when you want to register the results of a stored procedure with SqlDependency or SqlCacheDependency, then you must *not* use SET NOCOUNT ON. Similarly, some of the logic that synchronizes DataSets uses the reported count to check for concurrency collisions.

Data Paging

If you have a large database table and you need to present all or part of it to your users, it can be painfully slow to present a large number of rows on a single page. Imagine a user trying to scroll through a web page with a million rows on it. Not a good idea. A better approach is to display part of the table. While you're doing so, it's also important to avoid reading the entire table at both the web tier and the database tier.

Common Table Expressions

You can use *common table expressions* (CTEs) to address this issue (among many other cool things). Using the PageViews table from the beginning of the chapter as an example, here's a stored procedure that returns only the rows you request, based on a starting row and a page size:

```
CREATE PROC [Traffic].[PageViewRows]
    @startrow INT,
    @pagesize INT
AS
BEGIN
    SET NOCOUNT ON
    ;WITH ViewList ([row], [date], [user], [url]) AS (
        SELECT ROW_NUMBER() OVER (ORDER BY PvId) [row], PvDate, UserId, PvUrl
            FROM [Traffic].[PageViews]
    )
        SELECT [row], [date], [user], [url]
            FROM ViewList
            WHERE [row] BETWEEN @startrow AND @startrow + @pagesize - 1
END
```

The query works by first declaring an outer frame, including a name and an optional list of column names, in this case, ViewList ([row], [date], [user], [url]).

Next, you have a query that appears to retrieve all the rows in the table, while also applying a row number, using the ROW_NUMBER() function, with which you need to specify the column you want to use as the basis for numbering the rows. In this case, you're using OVER (ORDER BY PvId). The columns returned by this query are the same ones listed in the outer frame. It might help to think of this query as returning a temporary result set.

Although the ROW_NUMBER() function is very handy, unfortunately you can't use it directly in a WHERE clause, which is what drives you to using a CTE in the first place, along with the fact that you can't guarantee that the PvId column will always start from one and will never have gaps.

Finally, at the end of the CTE, you have a query that references the outer frame and uses a WHERE clause against the row numbers generated by the initial query to limit the results to the rows that you want to display. SQL Server only reads as many rows as it needs to satisfy the WHERE clause; it doesn't have to read the entire table.

■ **Note** The WITH clause in a CTE should be preceded by a semicolon to ensure that SQL Server sees it as the beginning of a new statement.

Detailed Example of Data Paging

To demonstrate data paging in action, let's build an example that allows you to page through a table and display it in a GridView control. While you're at it, let's take the opportunity to include several of the performance techniques that you have previously covered.

Markup

First, add a new web form to your web site, called paging.aspx, and edit the markup as follows:

```
<%@ Page Language="C#" EnableViewState="false" Async="true" AutoEventWireup="false"
    CodeFile="paging.aspx.cs" Inherits="paging" %>
```

Here you're using several of the best practices discussed earlier: this will be an async page, and both ViewState and AutoEventWireup are disabled.

```
<!DOCTYPE html PUBLIC "-//W3C//DTD XHTML 1.0 Transitional//EN"
   "http://www.w3.org/TR/xhtml1/DTD/xhtml1-transitional.dtd">
<html xmlns="http://www.w3.org/1999/xhtml">
<head runat="server">
    <title></title>
</head>
<body>
    <form id="form1" runat="server">
    <div>
        <asp:GridView ID="pvgrid" runat="server" AllowPaging="true"
            OnPageIndexChanging="PageIndexChanging"
            PageSize="5" DataSourceID="PageViewSource">
            <PagerSettings FirstPageText="First" LastPageText="Last"
                Mode="NumericFirstLast" />
        </asp:GridView>
```

In the GridView control, you enable AllowPaging, assign an OnPageIndexChanging event handler, set the PageSize, and associate the control with a data source. Since you want to use the control's paging mode, using a data source is a requirement. You also use the <PagerSettings> tag to customize the page navigation controls a bit.

```
<asp:ObjectDataSource ID="PageViewSource" runat="server"
    EnablePaging="True" TypeName="Samples.PageViews"
    SelectMethod="GetRows" SelectCountMethod="GetCount">
</asp:ObjectDataSource>
</div>
</form>
</body>
</html>
```

Use an `ObjectDataSource` as the data source, since you want to have programmatic control over the details. You also `EnablePaging` here, associate the control with what will be your new class using `TypeName`, and set a `SelectMethod` and a `SelectCountMethod`, both of which will exist in the new class. The control uses `SelectMethod` to obtain the desired rows and `SelectCountMethod` to determine how many total rows there are so that the `GridView` can correctly render the paging navigation controls.

Stored Procedure

Next, use SSMS to modify the stored procedure that you used in the prior example as follows:

```
ALTER PROC [Traffic].[PageViewRows]
    @startrow INT,
    @pagesize INT,
    @getcount BIT,
    @count    INT OUT
AS
BEGIN
    SET NOCOUNT ON
    SET @count = -1;
    IF @getcount = 1
    BEGIN
        SELECT @count = count(*) FROM [Traffic].[PageViews]
    END
    ;WITH ViewList ([row], [date], [user], [url]) AS (
        SELECT ROW_NUMBER() OVER (ORDER BY PvId) [row], PvDate, UserId, PvUrl
            FROM [Traffic].[PageViews]
    )
    SELECT [row], [date], [user], [url]
        FROM ViewList
        WHERE [row] BETWEEN @startrow AND @startrow + @pagesize - 1
END
```

Rather than requiring a separate round trip to determine the number of rows in the table, what you've done instead is to add a flag to your stored procedure and an output parameter. The T-SQL incurs the overhead of running the `SELECT COUNT(*)` query only if the flag is set.

Code-Behind

Next, edit the code-behind as follows:

```
using System;
using System.Data;
using System.Data.SqlClient;
using System.Threading;
using System.Web;
using System.Web.UI;
using System.Web.UI.WebControls;

public partial class paging : Page
{
    public const string ConnString =
        "Data Source=server;Initial Catalog=Sample;Integrated Security=True;async=true";
    private int _count;

    protected override void OnInit(EventArgs e)
    {
        base.OnInit(e);
        this.RegisterRequiresControlState(this);
    }
```

Since you disabled `AutoEventWireup`, you will override the `OnEvent`-style methods from the base class.

The `ObjectDataSource` control needs to know how many rows there are in the target table. Obtaining the row count is expensive; counting rows is a form of aggregation query that requires reading every row in the table. Since the count might be large and doesn't change often, you should cache the result after you get it the first time to avoid having to repeat that expensive query.

You shouldn't use the `Cache` object unless this is a very frequently accessed page, since in a load-balanced environment, a different server might process the request for the next page, and it wouldn't have the access to the same cache. You could use a cookie, but they are a bit heavyweight for information that's specific to a single page. For data that's specific to a page like this, `ViewState` might be a good choice. However, on this page, you would like to keep `ViewState` disabled because it gets very voluminous for the `GridView` control and therefore has an associated negative effect on page performance. You could enable `ViewState` on the page and just disable it for the `GridView` control, but leaving it enabled for other controls will make the page larger than it has to be. Instead, let's use `ControlState`, which is similar to `ViewState`, except that it can't be disabled.

In `OnInit()`, you call `RegisterRequiresControlState()` to inform the `Page` class that you will be using `ControlState`.

```
    protected override void OnLoad(EventArgs e)
    {
        base.OnLoad(e);
        this.DataReady = new ManualResetEvent(false);
        this.Context.Items["dataready"] = this.DataReady;
        if (!this.IsPostBack)
```

```
        {
            this.Count = -1;
            this.NeedCount = true;
            this.NewPageIndex = 0;
            this.GetPage();
        }
        else
        {
            this.NeedCount = false;
        }
    }
```

In the `OnLoad` method, create a `ManualResetEvent` object that you'll use later to signal an ASP.NET worker thread when the async read is complete. You need this because the `ObjectDataSource` control does its work during the `PreRender` event, which is before the runtime guarantees that any async tasks that you've registered will be complete.

If the current request isn't a postback, that means a user is coming to the page for the first time, and you will need to obtain the row count. After initializing a few instance variables to reflect that initial state, call `GetPage()` to register the async tasks that you'll need. If the request is a postback, then you don't need the row count, since it will be in `ControlState`.

```
    protected override void LoadControlState(object savedState)
    {
        if (savedState != null)
        {
            this.Count = (int)savedState;
        }
    }

    protected override object SaveControlState()
    {
        return this.Count;
    }
```

Unlike with `ViewState`, which uses a `Dictionary` as its primary interface, with `ControlState` you have to override the `LoadControlState()` and `SaveControlState()` methods instead. `LoadControlState()` is called before the `Load` event, and `SaveControlState()` is called after the `PreRender` event. As with `ViewState`, `ControlState` is encoded and stored in the __VIEWSTATE hidden field in your HTML.

```
    public void PageIndexChanging(Object sender, GridViewPageEventArgs e)
    {
        this.NewPageIndex = e.NewPageIndex;
        this.GetPage();
    }
```

You registered the `PageIndexChanging` event handler with the `GridView` control, and it's called after the `Load` event. You use it to capture the `NewPageIndex` that the user clicked to request a new page and then call `GetPage()` to start the async tasks. Since event handlers are called only during a postback, `GetPage()` will be called only once.

In this case, pages are numbered starting at zero.

```
private void GetPage()
{
    PageAsyncTask pat = new PageAsyncTask(BeginAsync, EndAsync, null, null, true);
    this.RegisterAsyncTask(pat);
    this.ExecuteRegisteredAsyncTasks();
}
```

After creating and registering a `PageAsyncTask` object, call `ExecuteRegisteredAsyncTasks()` to start the task immediately. Otherwise, the runtime wouldn't start it until the async point, which is after the `PreRender` event. By that time, the `ObjectDataSource` control will have already started to run, and the worker thread will block waiting for the data. If the async data request hasn't already started by then, the wait will cause the thread to hang.

```
private IAsyncResult BeginAsync(object sender, EventArgs e,
    AsyncCallback cb, object state)
{
    SqlConnection conn = new SqlConnection(ConnString);
    SqlCommand cmd = new SqlCommand("[Traffic].[PageViewRows]", conn);
    cmd.CommandType = CommandType.StoredProcedure;
    SqlParameterCollection p = cmd.Parameters;
    p.Add("startrow", SqlDbType.Int).Value =
        (this.NewPageIndex * this.pvgrid.PageSize) + 1;
    p.Add("pagesize", SqlDbType.Int).Value = this.pvgrid.PageSize;
    p.Add("getcount", SqlDbType.Bit).Value = this.NeedCount;
    p.Add("count", SqlDbType.Int).Direction = ParameterDirection.Output;
    conn.Open();
    IAsyncResult ar = cmd.BeginExecuteReader(cb, cmd);
    return ar;
}
```

The `BeginAsync()` method creates `SqlConnection` and `SqlCommand` objects, sets up the parameters to call our stored procedure, and calls `BeginExecuteReader()` to start the async request. The stored procedure will return a count of the number of rows in the table in the `count` output parameter, but only when `NeedCount` is `true`. Of course, you can't call `Dispose()` or place the `IDisposable` objects here in a `using` block, because you will still need them when the request completes.

```
private void EndAsync(IAsyncResult ar)
{
    using (SqlCommand cmd = (SqlCommand)ar.AsyncState)
    {
        using (cmd.Connection)
        {
            using (SqlDataReader reader = cmd.EndExecuteReader(ar))
            {
                this.Data = new DataTable();
                this.Data.Load(reader);
                this.Context.Items["data"] = this.Data;
```

```
            if (this.NeedCount)
                this.Count = (int)cmd.Parameters["count"].Value;
            this.DataReady.Set();
        }
      }
    }
  }
}
```

As per our async task definition, the EndAsync method is called when the stored procedure is ready for you to retrieve the data. After placing the IDisposable objects in using blocks, create a DataTable and read your data into it using the SqlDataReader returned by EndExecuteReader(). Since you can't easily get a reference to the ObjectDataSource data control object (it may not even exist yet) and since that object can't easily get a reference to our page, you store the results instead in the per-request Items cache. After the results are ready for the ObjectDataSource control object to pick up, call Set() on the ManualResetEvent object to release the worker thread.

```
protected override void OnUnload(EventArgs e)
{
    base.OnUnload(e);
    this.DataReady.Close();
}
```

After the work is done and the page has been rendered and sent to the client, call Close() on the ManualResetEvent object to allow it to quickly release any resources that it might hold. Calling Close() on objects like this that are tightly coupled to the operating system but that aren't IDisposable isn't as imperative as calling Dispose(), but it's still a good habit to get into.

```
public int Count
{
    get
    {
        return this._count;
    }
    set
    {
        this._count = value;
        this.Context.Items["count"] = value;
    }
}

public bool NeedCount { get; set; }
public int NewPageIndex { get; set; }
public ManualResetEvent DataReady { get; set; }
public DataTable Data { get; set; }
}
```

You use the Count accessor to make sure that all sets are reflected in the Items cache.

Object Data Source

Next is the object data source, which is the final class for the example. Add a file for a new class called
`PageViews.cs` to your project in the App_Code folder, and edit it as follows:

```
using System.Data;
using System.Threading;
using System.Web;

namespace Samples
{
    public class PageViews
    {
        public PageViews()
        {
            ManualResetEvent dataReady =
                (ManualResetEvent)HttpContext.Current.Items["dataready"];
            dataReady.WaitOne();
        }
```

In the constructor, get a reference to the `ManualResetEvent` object that the page put in the Items
cache during its Load event. Then call `WaitOne()` to wait until the object is signaled when the `EndAsync()`
method in paging.aspx.cs calls Set().

```
        public int GetCount()
        {
            int count = (int)HttpContext.Current.Items["count"];
            return count;
        }

        public DataTable GetRows(int startRowIndex, int maximumRows)
        {
            DataTable data = (DataTable)HttpContext.Current.Items["data"];
            return data;
        }
    }
}
```

In a similar way, `GetCount()` and `GetRows()` both obtain their return values from the Items cache,
after they are set from the `EndAsync()` method. Notice that you don't use the **startRowIndex** and
maximumRows parameters in `GetRows()`, since your code-behind obtains that information elsewhere.

Results

The resulting web page still needs some work to pretty it up, but it's definitely functional. Equally
important, it's also very scalable, even on extremely large tables. It uses an efficient query for paging, the
row count is cached in `ControlState` so the count query doesn't need to be executed again for every new
page, and you always use only one round-trip to the database. Using an async database call improves
scalability by reducing contention for the ASP.NET thread pool.

Figure 8-2 shows part of page 11 of the output, including the column headers and the navigation links.

row	date	user	
51	6/27/2009 12:59:43 PM	c58f9d4e-2e7b-4337-b09d-209d1b58abc5	http:
52	6/27/2009 12:59:43 PM	c58f9d4e-2e7b-4337-b09d-209d1b58abc5	http:
53	6/27/2009 12:59:43 PM	c58f9d4e-2e7b-4337-b09d-209d1b58abc5	http:
54	6/27/2009 12:59:43 PM	c58f9d4e-2e7b-4337-b09d-209d1b58abc5	http:
55	6/27/2009 12:59:43 PM	c58f9d4e-2e7b-4337-b09d-209d1b58abc5	http:
First ... 11 12 13 14 15 16 17 18 19 20 ... Last			

Figure 8-2. Output from the paging GridView example

Object Relational Models

Language Integrated Query (LINQ) was one of the very cool additions to C# 3.0. It provides a type-safe way to query XML, SQL Server, and even your own objects. LINQ to SQL also provides a mapping from database objects (tables and rows) to .NET objects (classes). That allows you to work with your custom business objects, while delegating much of the work involved with synchronizing those objects to LINQ.

The Entity Framework is a recent alternative to LINQ to SQL, which you can also query with LINQ. NHibernate is an open source system that provides similar functionality.

All of these systems provide an Object Relational Model (ORM), each with its own pros and cons. I have mixed feelings about all ORM systems. I love them because they allow me to develop small, proof-of-concept sites extremely quickly. I can side step much of the SQL and related complexity that I would otherwise need and focus on the objects, business logic and presentation. However, at the same time, I also don't care for them because, unfortunately, their performance and scalability is usually very poor, even when they're integrated with a comprehensive caching system (the reason for that becomes clear when you realize that when properly configured, SQL Server itself is really just a big data cache).

The object orientation of ORM systems very often results in extremely chatty implementations. Because ORM systems tend to make it a little *too* easy to access the database, they often result in making many more round-trips than you really need. I've seen some sites that average more than 150 round-trips to the database per page view!

Although both LINQ and NHibernate's hql do provide some control over the queries that are autogenerated by these systems, in complex applications the queries are often inefficient and difficult or impossible to tune fully. In addition, in their current incarnations, LINQ and the Entity Framework don't provide good support for asynchronous requests, command batching, or multiple result sets, which are all important keys to scalable high-performance databases.

You can also use stored procedures with ORM systems, although you do sacrifice some flexibility in doing so.

Of course, I understand that ORM systems have become extremely popular, largely because of their ease of use. Even so, in their current form I can't recommend any of them in high-performance web sites, in spite of how unpopular that makes me in some circles. LINQ is great for querying XML and custom objects; I just wouldn't use it or the Entity Framework with SQL, except in very limited circumstances, such as the following:

- Rapid prototyping or proofs of concept, where speed of delivery is more important than performance and scalability

- Small-scale projects

- As an alternative to generating dynamic SQL by concatenating strings on the web tier when you can't otherwise avoid it

- As a way of calling stored procedures synchronously with type-safe parameters, such as from a background thread or a Windows service

I'm definitely not saying that working with objects is a bad idea; it's the T-SQL side of things that presents difficulties. You can fill a collection of custom objects yourself very quickly and efficiently by using a `SqlDataReader`; that's what the `SqlDataAdapter` and `DataTable` objects do. If you need change detection, you can use a `DataSet` (which can contain one or more `DataTables`). However, that is a fairly heavyweight solution, so custom objects are usually the most efficient approach.

XML Columns

SQL Server 2005 introduced the ability to store XML data as a native data type. Before that, the alternative was to store it as a blob of text. With XML native columns, you can efficiently query or modify individual nodes in your XML. This feature is useful from a performance perspective in several scenarios:

- As a replacement for sparse columns. Rather than having a very wide table where most of the values are `NULL`, you can have a single XML column instead.

- When you need recursive or nested elements or properties that are difficult to represent relationally.

- When you have existing XML documents that you would like to be able to query or update, while retaining their original structure.

- As an alternative to dynamically adding new columns to your tables. Adding new columns to a table will lock the table while the change is in progress, which can be an issue for very large tables. Adding new columns can also be challenging to track with respect to their impact on existing queries and indexes.

- As an alternative to many-to-many mappings. In cases where a relational solution would include extra tables with name/value pairs and associated mappings and indexes, native XML columns can provide a more flexible solution that avoids the overhead of joining additional tables.

Before going any further, I should say that if your data fits the relational model well, then you should use a relational solution. Only consider XML when relational becomes difficult, awkward, or expensive from a performance perspective, as in the examples I listed earlier. Avoid the temptation to convert your entire schema to XML, or you will be very disappointed when it comes to performance!

XML columns have their own query language, separate from (although integrated with) T-SQL, called XQuery. Rather than diving into its full complexities, let's walk through a couple of examples to give you a sense of what it's like, along with a few performance tips.

XML Schema

Let's build a table of products. The product name is always known, so you'll put that in a relational column. Each product can also have a number of attributes. You expect that the number and variety of attributes will expand over time and that they might have a recursive character to them, so you decide to represent them in XML and include them in an XML column in the products table.

Here's an example of what the initial XML will look like:

```
<info>
    <props width="1.0" depth="3.0" />
    <color part="top">red</color>
    <color part="legs">chrome</color>
</info>
```

SQL Server can associate a collection of XML schemas with an XML column. Although the use of schemas is optional, they do have a positive impact on performance. Without a schema, XML is stored as a string and is parsed for each access. When a schema is present, the XML is converted to binary, which reduces its size and makes it faster to query. In addition, numeric values are stored in their converted form. Without a schema, SQL Server can't tell the difference between an item that should be a string and one that should be a number, so it stores everything as strings.

Since schemas are a good thing, let's create one that describes our XML and create a schema collection to go with it:

```
CREATE XML SCHEMA COLLECTION ProductSchema AS
'<?xml version="1.0"?>
<xs:schema xmlns:xs="http://www.w3.org/2001/XMLSchema">
    <xs:element name="info">
        <xs:complexType>
            <xs:sequence>
                <xs:element name="props" minOccurs="0">
                    <xs:complexType>
                        <xs:attribute name="width" type="xs:decimal" />
                        <xs:attribute name="depth" type="xs:decimal" />
                    </xs:complexType>
                </xs:element>
                <xs:element name="color" minOccurs="0" maxOccurs="unbounded">
                    <xs:complexType>
                        <xs:simpleContent>
                            <xs:extension base="xs:string">
                                <xs:attribute name="part" type="xs:string"
                                    use="required" />
                            </xs:extension>
                        </xs:simpleContent>
                    </xs:complexType>
                </xs:element>
            </xs:sequence>
        </xs:complexType>
    </xs:element>
</xs:schema>'
```

This schema encodes the rules for the structure of your XML: inside an outer `info` element, the optional `<props>` element has optional `width` and `depth` attributes. There can be zero or more `<color>` elements, each of which has a required `part` attribute and a string that describes the `color`. If it's present, the `<props>` element must come before the `<color>` elements (`<xs:sequence>`).

XML schemas can get complex quickly, so I recommend using some software to accelerate the process and to reduce errors. Since the market changes frequently, see my links page at `http://www.12titans.net/p/links.aspx` for current recommendations.

Creating the Example Table

Now you're ready to create the table:

```
CREATE TABLE [Products] (
    [Id]      INT IDENTITY PRIMARY KEY,
    [Name]    VARCHAR(128),
    [Info]    XML (ProductSchema)
)
```

You have an integer `IDENTITY` column as a `PRIMARY KEY`, a string for the product name, and an XML column to hold extra information about the product. You have also associated the `ProductSchema` schema collection with the XML column.

Next, insert a few rows into the table:

```
INSERT INTO [Products]
    ([Name], [Info])
    VALUES
    ('Big Table',
    '<info>
       <props width="1.0" depth="3.0" />
       <color part="top">red</color>
       <color part="legs">chrome</color>
    </info>')
INSERT INTO [Products]
    ([Name], [Info])
    VALUES
    ('Small Table',
    '<info>
       <props width="0.5" depth="1.5" />
       <color part="top">black</color>
       <color part="legs">chrome</color>
    </info>')
INSERT INTO [Products]
    ([Name], [Info])
    VALUES
    ('Desk Chair',
    '<info>
       <color part="top">black</color>
       <color part="legs">chrome</color>
    </info>')
```

You might also try inserting rows that violate the schema to see the error that SQL Server returns.

Basic XML Queries

A simple query against the table will return the Info column as XML:

```
SELECT * FROM Products
```

Now let's make some queries against the XML:

```
SELECT [Id], [Name], [Info].query('/info/props')
    FROM [Products]
    WHERE [Info].exist('/info/props[@width]') = 1
```

The exist() clause is equal to 1 for rows where the XML has a props element with a width attribute. The query() in the selected columns will display the props element and its attributes (and children, if it had any) as XML; it's a way to show a subset of the XML.

Both query() and exist() use XPath expressions, where elements are separated by slashes and attributes are in brackets preceded by an at-sign.

Here's another query:

```
SELECT [Id], [Name], [Info].value('(/info/props/@width)[1]', 'REAL') [Width]
    FROM [Products]
    WHERE [Info].value('(/info/color[@part = "top"])[1]', 'VARCHAR(16)') = 'black'
```

This time, you're looking for all rows where <color part="top"> is set to black. The value() query lets you convert an XQuery/XML value to a T-SQL type so you can compare it against black. In the selected columns, use value() to return the width attribute of the props element. Converting it to a T-SQL type means that the returned row set has the appearance of being completely relational; there won't be any XML, as there was in the previous two queries. Since the XPath expressions might match more than one node in the XML, the [1] in both value() queries says that you're interested in the first match; value() requires you to limit the number of results to just one.

Here's the next query:

```
DECLARE @part VARCHAR(16)
SET @part = 'legs'
SELECT [Id], [Name], [Info].value('(/info/color)[1]', 'VARCHAR(16)') [First Color]
    FROM [Products]
    WHERE [Info].value('(/info/color[@part = sql:variable("@part")])[1]',
        'VARCHAR(16)') = 'chrome'
```

This time, you're using the sql:variable() function to integrate the @part variable into the XQuery. You would use this approach if you wanted to parameterize the query, such as in a stored procedure. On the results side, you're returning the first color in the list.

Modifying the XML Data

In addition to being able to query the XML data, you can also modify it:

```
UPDATE [Products]
    SET [Info].modify('replace value of
        (/info/color[@part = "legs"]/text())[1]
        with "silver"')
    WHERE [Name] = 'Desk Chair'
```

This command will set the value of the `<color part="legs">` element for the `Desk Chair` row to `silver`.

```
UPDATE [Products]
    SET [Info].modify('insert
        <color part="arms">white</color>
        as first
        into (/info)[1]')
    WHERE [Name] = 'Desk Chair'
```

This command inserts a new `color` element at the beginning of the list. Notice that a T-SQL **UPDATE** statement is used to do this type of insert, since you are changing a column and not inserting a new row into the table.

```
UPDATE [Products]
    SET [Info].modify('delete
        (/info/color)[1]')
    WHERE [Name] = 'Desk Chair'
```

This command deletes the first `color` element in the list, which is the same one that you just inserted with the previous command.

XML Indexes

As with relational data, you can significantly improve the performance of queries against XML if you use the right indexes. XML columns use different indexes than relational data, so you will need to create them separately:

```
CREATE PRIMARY XML INDEX ProductIXML
    ON [Products] ([Info])
```

A `PRIMARY XML INDEX` is, as the name implies, the first and most important XML index. It contains one row for every node in your XML, with a clustered index on the node number, which corresponds to the order of the node within the XML. To create this index, the table must already have a primary key. You can't create any of the other XML indexes unless the `PRIMARY XML INDEX` already exists.

■ **Caution** The size of a `PRIMARY XML INDEX` is normally around three times as large as the XML itself (small tags and values will increase the size multiplier, since the index will have more rows). This can be an important sizing consideration if you have a significant amount of data.

```
CREATE XML INDEX ProductPathIXML
    ON [Products] ([Info])
    USING XML INDEX ProductIXML
    FOR PATH
CREATE XML INDEX ProductPropIXML
    ON [Products] ([Info])
    USING XML INDEX ProductIXML
    FOR PROPERTY

CREATE XML INDEX ProductValueIXML
    ON [Products] ([Info])
    USING XML INDEX ProductIXML
    FOR VALUE
```

You create the remaining three indexes in a similar way, using either FOR PATH, FOR PROPERTY, or FOR VALUE. These secondary indexes are actually nonclustered indexes on the node table that comprises the primary index. The PATH index includes the tokenized path of the node and its value. The PROPERTY index includes the original table's primary key plus the same columns as the path index. The VALUE index has the value first, followed by the tokenized path (the inverse of the PATH index).

Each index is useful for different types of queries. Because of the complexity of both the indexes and typical queries, I've found that the best approach for deciding which indexes to generate is to look carefully at your query plans. Of course, if your data is read-only and you have plenty of disk space, then you might just create all four indexes and keep things simple. However, if you need to modify or add to your data, then some analysis and testing is a good idea. XML index maintenance can be particularly expensive; the entire node list for the modified column is regenerated after each change.

Miscellaneous XML Query Tips

Here are a few more tips for querying XML:

- Avoid wildcards, including both the double-slash type (//) and the asterisk type.

- Consider using full-text search, which can find strings *much* more efficiently than XQuery. One limitation is that it doesn't understand the structure of your XML, so it ignores element and attribute names.

- If you search against certain XML values very frequently, consider moving them into a relational column. The move can be either permanent or in the form of a computed column.

- You may be able to reduce the coding effort required to do complex joins by exposing relevant data as relational columns using views.

Data Partitioning

Working with very large tables often presents an interesting set of performance issues. Here's an example:

- Certain T-SQL commands can lock the table. If those commands are issued frequently, they can introduce delays because of blocking.

- Queries can get slower as the table grows, particularly for queries that require table or index scans.

- If the table grows quickly, you will probably want to delete part of it eventually, perhaps after archiving it first. Deleting the data will place a heavy load on the transaction log, since SQL Server will write all the deleted rows to the log.

- If the table dominates the size of your database, it will also drive how long it takes to do backups and restores.

SQL Enterprise and Developer editions have a feature called *table partitioning* that can help address these problems. The way it works is that first you define one or more data value *borders* that are used to determine in which partition to place each row. Partitions are like separate subtables; they can be locked separately and placed on separate filegroups. However, from a query perspective, they look like a single table. You don't have to change your queries at all after partitioning a table; SQL Server will automatically determine which partitions to use.

You can also *switch* a partition from one table to another. After the change, you can truncate the new table instead of deleting it, which is a very fast process that doesn't overwhelm the database log.

Partition Function

Let's walk through a detailed example using the same `PageViews` table that you used earlier. Let's say that the table grows quickly and that you need to keep data for only the last few months online for statistics and reporting purposes. At the beginning of each month, the oldest month should be deleted. If you just used a `DELETE` command to delete the oldest month, it would lock the table and make it inaccessible by the rest of your application until the command completes. If your site requires nonstop 24×7 operations, this type of maintenance action can cause your system to be slow or unresponsive during that time. You will address the issue by partitioning the table by month.

The first step is to create a `PARTITION FUNCTION`:

```
CREATE PARTITION FUNCTION ByMonthPF (DATETIME)
    AS RANGE RIGHT FOR VALUES (
    '20090101', '20090201', '20090301',
    '20090401', '20090501', '20090601',
    '20090701', '20090801', '20090901')
```

The command specifies the data type of the column against which you will be applying the partition function. In this case, that's `DATETIME`. Specifying `RANGE RIGHT` says that the border values will be on the right side of the range.

The values are dates that define the borders. You've specified nine values, which will define ten partitions (N + 1). Since you're using RANGE RIGHT, the first value of 20090101 defines the right side of the border, so the first partition will hold dates less than 01 Jan 2009. The second value of 20090201 says that the second partition will hold dates greater than 01 Jan 2009 and less than 01 Feb 2009. The pattern repeats up to the last value, where an additional partition is created for values greater than 01 Sep 2009.

Partition Scheme

Next, you will create a PARTITION SCHEME, which defines how the PARTITION FUNCTION maps to filegroups:

```
CREATE PARTITION SCHEME ByMonthPS
    AS PARTITION ByMonthPF
    ALL TO ([PRIMARY])
```

In this case, place all the partitions on the PRIMARY filegroup. Multi-filegroup mappings can be appropriate in hardware environments where multiple LUNs or logical drives are available to help spread the I/O load.

At this point, you can use the $partition function along with the name of the PARTITION FUNCTION as defined earlier to test the assignment of partition values to specific partitions:

```
SELECT $partition.ByMonthPF('20090215')
```

That query displays 3, which indicates that a row with a partition value of 20090215 would be assigned to partition number 3.

Now you're ready to create the table:

```
CREATE TABLE [Traffic].[PageViews] (
    [PvId]    BIGINT           IDENTITY,
    [PvDate]  DATETIME         NOT NULL,
    [UserId]  UNIQUEIDENTIFIER NULL,
    [PvUrl]   VARCHAR(256)     NOT NULL
) ON ByMonthPS ([PvDate])
```

Assign the ByMonthPS partition scheme to the table with the ON clause at the end of the definition, along with the column, PvDate, that SQL Server should use with the partition function.

Generating Test Data

At this point, you're ready to generate some test data. For a change of pace, this time you'll use the data generator in Visual Studio Team Database.

Right-click your solution in **Solution Explorer**, select **Add**, then select **New Project**. In the dialog box that comes up, select **Database Projects** in the left panel, and select **SQL Server 2008 Database Project** in the right panel, as in Figure 8-3. Give the project a name, and click **OK**.

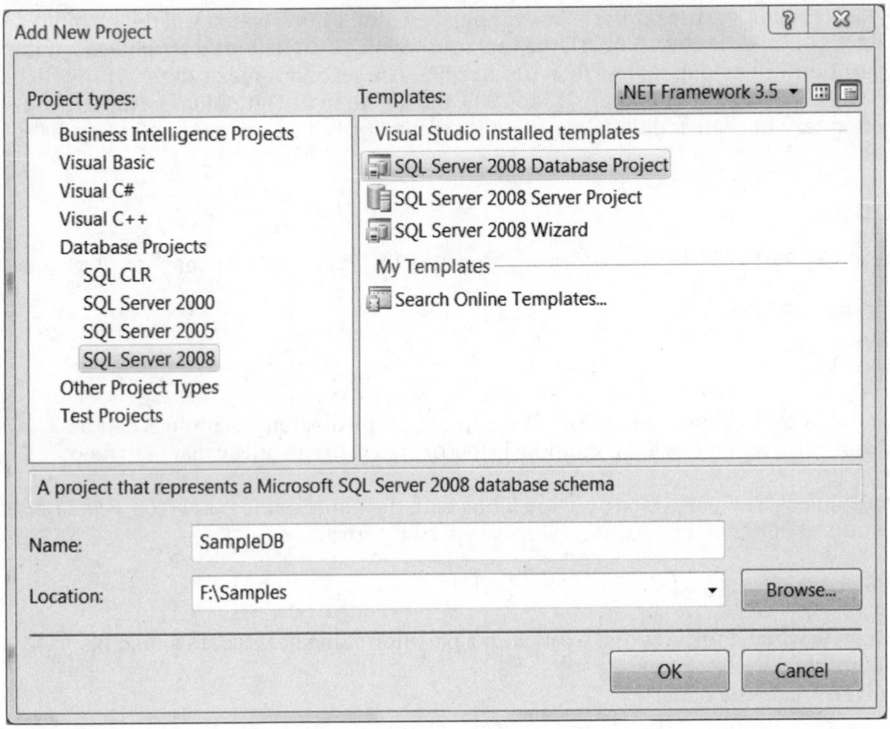

Figure 8-3. Add a new database project in Visual Studio Team Database.

Next, click the new project in **Solution Explorer,** click the **Project** menu at the top of the main window, and select **Import Database Objects and Settings.** Choose or create a connection to your database, and click **Start.** Click **Finish** on the summary page to complete the process. The project will now contain scripts to create tables and other objects in your database.

Next, right-click the database project, select **Add,** and then select **Data Generation Plan.** Make sure the **Data Generation Plan** template is selected in the **Add New Item** dialog box, give the plan a name, and click **OK.** Visual Studio will find all the tables in your database and display them in the top panel of the data generation plan designer.

Uncheck everything except `Traffic.PageViews`, set the number of rows to insert to 50,000, and leave the row selected to bring up its column definitions in the center panel.

In the center panel, change the Generator for `PvUrl` to be **Regular Expression.** The other values can keep their default settings, as in Figure 8-4.

Table (select to include in ...	Rows to Insert	Related Table	Ratio to Related Table
☑ ▦ Traffic.PageViews	50000		

Column (selec...	Key	Data Type	Generator	Generator Output
☐ ▦ PvId		bigint	SQL Computed Value	
☑ ▦ PvDate		datetime	DateTime	Output
☑ ▦ UserId		uniqueidentifier	Guid	Output
☑ ▦ PvUrl		varchar (256)	Regular Expression	Output

Figure 8-4. Selecting the table and configuring the generators in the data generation plan

Scroll to the bottom of the **Property** panel, and set **Expression** to the following:

```
http://www\.[a-zA-Z0-9]{3,12}\.(com|org|net|co\.nz)/
[a-zA-Z0-9]{2,15}\.(htm|html|aspx|php)
```

The data generator will use this regular expression to generate the data in the column. The pattern describes a simple URL.

Next, click the `PvDate` column to select it, and then scroll to the bottom of the **Property** panel and set the **Max** date to **7/5/2009** and the **Min** date to **10/1/2008**. You're using those dates so that they overlap with the partition definition. Also, make sure that **Distribution** is set to **Uniform** and **Unique Values** is set to **False**, as in Figure 8-5.

Properties	▾ ⏛ ✕
PvDate Column	▾
▤ ⏛↓ ▣	
⊟ **Generator**	▲
⊞ Distribution	**Uniform**
Max	**7/5/2009 11:59:59 PM**
Min	**10/1/2008 12:00:00 AM**
Percentage Null	**0**
Seed	**5**
Step	**00:01:00**
Unique Values	**False**

Figure 8-5. Data generator parameters for the date column

Those settings tell the data generator to generate random values within the defined date range.

■ **Note** You can only set **Unique Values** to **False** for columns that are not part of a unique key.

313

Right-click the middle pane, and select **Preview Data Generation**. The **Data Generation Preview** pane should look something like Figure 8-6.

PvId	PvDate	UserId	PvUrl
Computed	1/3/2009 1:36:1...	1a801076-e484-3...	http://www.HGcSv9.co.nz/7yM44T9x5o.html
Computed	12/19/2008 1:3...	9f236be6-a2e4-4...	http://www.4pmBkEm.co.nz/2IJ.htm
Computed	12/13/2008 2:2...	d5d0cfdc-ba5e-1...	http://www.yAmCnL.com/qXC2XdszyFVCGRT...
Computed	3/23/2009 8:30:...	cc2378f5-3287-d...	http://www.hM1U5C3xgV.co.nz/t0uN.htm
Computed	2/6/2009 8:13:0...	41941c25-a649-2...	http://www.Ezhh9273Wnu7.net/LT6y5UkK85q...
Computed	6/16/2009 2:06:...	598d8853-28f4-a...	http://www.o4EboARFR1zD.co.nz/1gG2YyI.php

Data Generation Preview - Traffic.PageViews

Figure 8-6. Data generation preview

Now you're ready to generate the data. Click the **Generate Data** icon button in the toolbar, select the target database in the dialog box that comes up, and click **OK**. Answer **Yes** to the **Do you want to delete existing data?** dialog box, and the generation process will start.

Adding an Index and Configuring Lock Escalation

Back in SSMS, you're ready to add a primary key:

```
ALTER TABLE [Traffic].[PageViews]
    ADD CONSTRAINT [PageViewsPK]
    PRIMARY KEY CLUSTERED ([PvId], [PvDate])
```

Table partitioning requires that the column you use for partitioning must also be present in the clustered key, so you include PvDate in addition to PvId.

Let's also configure the table so that when needed, SQL Server will escalate locks up to the heap or B-tree granularity, rather than to the full table:

```
ALTER TABLE [Traffic].[PageViews]
    SET (LOCK_ESCALATION = AUTO)
```

That can help reduce blocking and associated delays if you're using commands that require table locks.

To see the results of partitioning the test data, run the following query:

```
SELECT partition_number, rows
    FROM sys.partitions
    WHERE object_id = object_id('Traffic.PageViews')
```

The result of the query is shown in Figure 8-7.

	partition_number	rows
1	1	16693
2	2	5558
3	3	4946
4	4	5512
5	5	5286
6	6	5654
7	7	5439
8	8	912
9	9	0
10	10	0

Figure 8-7. Results of data partitioning after test data generation

Partitions 2 through 8 have roughly the same number of rows. Partition 1 has more than the average, because it includes 1 Oct 2008 through 31 Dec 2008, based on the **Min** date that you set for the test data. Partition 8 has less than the average, since the **Max** date didn't include an entire month.

Archiving Old Data

Let's get ready to archive the old data. First, create a table with the same schema and index as the source table:

```
CREATE TABLE [Traffic].[PageViewsArchive] (
    [PvId]   BIGINT              IDENTITY,
    [PvDate] DATETIME            NOT NULL,
    [UserId] UNIQUEIDENTIFIER NULL,
    [PvUrl]  VARCHAR(256)     NOT NULL
) ON ByMonth ([PvDate])

ALTER TABLE [Traffic].[PageViewsArchive]
    ADD CONSTRAINT [PageViewArchivePK]
    PRIMARY KEY CLUSTERED ([PvId], [PvDate])
```

Although it's not a strict requirement, I've also applied the same partitioning scheme.

To move the old data into the new table, you will SWITCH the partition from one table to the other:

```
ALTER TABLE [Traffic].[PageViews]
    SWITCH PARTITION 1
    TO [Traffic].[PageViewsArchive] PARTITION 1
```

Notice that the switch runs very quickly, even for a large table, since it is only changing an internal pointer, rather than moving any data.

Running a SELECT COUNT(*) on both tables shows that the old one now has 33,307 rows, and the new one has 16,693 rows. The total is still 50,000, but you have divided it between two tables.

Now you can truncate the old table to release the associated storage:

```
TRUNCATE TABLE [Traffic].[PageViewsArchive]
```

Once again, notice how that command executes very quickly, since none of the rows in the table has to be written to the database log first, as with a DELETE.

Summary

Data partitioning is a powerful tool for reducing the resources that are consumed by aspects of regular system maintenance, such as deleting old data and rebuilding indexes on very large tables. It can also help reduce blocking by allowing would-be table locks to be moved to the heap or B-tree granularity. The larger your tables are and the more important it is for you to have consistent 24×7 performance, the more useful data partitioning will be.

Full-Text Search

Full-text search has been available in SQL Server for many years. Even so, I've noticed that it is often used only for searching documents and other large files. Although that's certainly an important and valid application, it's also useful for searching relatively short fields that contain text, certain types of encoded binary, or XML.

A common approach to searching text fields is to use a T-SQL LIKE clause with a wildcard. If the column has an index on it and if the wildcard is at the end of the string, that approach can be reasonably fast, provided it doesn't return too many rows. However, if the wildcard comes at the beginning of the LIKE clause, then SQL Server will need to scan every row in the table to determine the result. As you've seen, table and index scans are things you want to avoid. One way to do that is with full-text search.

As an example, let's create a table that contains two text columns and an ID, along with a clustered index:

```
CREATE TABLE TextInfo (
    Id      INT IDENTITY,
    Email   NVARCHAR(256),
    Quote   NVARCHAR(1024)
)

CREATE UNIQUE CLUSTERED INDEX TextInfoIX ON TextInfo (Id)
```

Next, add a few rows to the table:

```
INSERT INTO TextInfo (Email, Quote)
    VALUES (N'joe@gmail.com', N'The less you talk, the more you''re listened to.')
INSERT INTO TextInfo (Email, Quote)
    VALUES (N'bob@yahoo.com', N'Nature cannot be fooled.')
INSERT INTO TextInfo (Email, Quote)
    VALUES (N'mary@gmail.com', N'The truth is not for all men.')
INSERT INTO TextInfo (Email, Quote)
    VALUES (N'alice@12titans.net', N'Delay is preferable to error.')
```

Creating the Full-Text Catalog and Index

To enable full-text search, first create a full-text catalog, and set it to be the default:

```
CREATE FULLTEXT CATALOG [SearchCatalog] AS DEFAULT
```

Next, create the full-text index on the table:

```
CREATE FULLTEXT INDEX
    ON TextInfo (Email, Quote)
    KEY INDEX TextInfoIX
```

That will include both the Email and the Quote columns in the index, so you can search either one. For this command to work, the table must have a clustered index.

■ **Tip** For best performance, the clustered index of the table should be an integer. Wider keys can have a significant negative impact on performance.

For large tables, after running the full-text index command, you will need to wait a while for the index to be populated. Although it should happen very quickly for this trivial example, for a larger table you can determine when the index population is complete with the following query:

```
SELECT FULLTEXTCATALOGPROPERTY('SearchCatalog', 'PopulateStatus')
```

The query will return 0 when the population is done or 1 while it's still in progress.

■ **Caution** When you modify a table that has a full-text search index, there is a delay between when your change completes and when the change appears in the full-text index. High table update rates can introduce significant additional load to update the full-text index. You can configure full-text index updates to happen automatically after a change (the default), manually, or never.

Full-Text Queries

One way of searching the Email column for a particular host name would be like this, with a wildcard at the beginning of a LIKE clause:

```
SELECT * FROM TextInfo t WHERE t.Email LIKE '%12titans%'
```

After creating the full-text index, you can query for an e-mail domain name as follows:

```
SELECT * FROM TextInfo WHERE CONTAINS(Email, N'12titans')
```

One difference between this query and the one using LIKE is that CONTAINS is looking for a full word, whereas LIKE will find the string anywhere in the field, even if it's a subset of a word.

Depending on the size of the table and the amount of text you're searching, using full-text search instead of a `LIKE` clause can improve search times by a factor of 100 to 1,000 or more. A search of millions of rows that might take minutes with a `LIKE` clause can normally be completed in well under a second.

In addition to "direct" matches as in the previous examples, you can also do wildcard searches. Here's an example:

```
SELECT * FROM TextInfo WHERE contains(Quote, N'"nat*"')
```

That query will find all quotes with a word that starts with `nat`, such as `Nature` in the second row. Notice that the search string is enclosed in double quotes within the outer single quotes. If you forget the double quotes, the search will silently fail.

You can also search more than one column at a time, and you can use Booleans and similar commands in the search phrase:

```
SELECT * FROM TextInfo WHERE contains((Email, Quote), N'truth OR bob')
```

That query will find row 3, which contains `truth` in the `Quotes` column, and row 2, which contains `bob` in the `Email` column.

The `FREETEXT` clause will search for words that are very close to the given word, including synonyms and alternate forms:

```
SELECT * FROM TextInfo WHERE freetext(Quote, N'man')
```

That query will match the word `men` in row 3, since it's a plural of `man`.

Obtaining Search Rank Details

The `CONTAINSTABLE` and `FREETEXTTABLE` clauses do the same type of search as `CONTAINS` and `FREETEXT`, except they return a temporary table that includes a `KEY` column to map the results back to the original table and a `RANK` column that describes the quality of the match (higher is better):

```
SELECT ftt.[RANK], t.Id, t.Quote
    FROM TextInfo AS t
    INNER JOIN CONTAINSTABLE([TextInfo], [Quote], 'delay ~ error') ftt
        ON ftt.[KEY] = t.Id
        ORDER BY ftt.[RANK]
```

That query will sort the results by `RANK` and include `RANK` as a column in the results.

Full-Text Search Syntax Summary

Here's a summary of the search syntax that applies to `CONTAINS`, `CONTAINSTABLE`, `FREETEXT`, and `FREETEXTTABLE`:

- Phrase searches must be in double quotes, as in `"word phrase"`.

- Searches are not case sensitive.

- Noise words such as *a, the, and* are not searchable.

- Punctuation is ignored.

- For nearness-related searches, use the `NEAR` keyword or the tilde character [~], which is a synonym, as in `word NEAR other`.

- You can chain multiple nearness searches together, as in `word ~ still ~ more`.

- Inflectional variations are supported: `FORMSOF(inflectional, keyword)`. For example, `FORMSOF(inflectional, swell) AND abdomen` will find rows containing both `swollen` and `abdomen`.

- You can't use the `NEAR` operator with `FORMSOF`.

- Initial search results are sorted by the quality of the resulting match (rank).

- You can influence result ranking using weight factors that are between 0.0 and 1.0, as in `ISABOUT(blue weight(0.8), green weight(0.2))`.

The following additional syntax is available only for `CONTAINS` and `CONTAINSTABLE`:

- You must enclose wildcards in double-quotes, as in `"pram*"`.

- Wildcards are valid only at the end of strings, not the beginning.

- Boolean operators are supported (with synonyms): `AND` (&), `AND NOT` (&!), `OR` (|). `NOT` is applied before `AND`.

- `AND` cannot be used before the first keyword.

- You can use parentheses to group Boolean expressions.

Full-text search has considerable additional depth. Features that I didn't cover here include searching binary-formatted documents, like Word or PDF files, multilingual support, configurable stop words, a configurable thesaurus, various management views, and so on.

Service Broker

As I discussed in the section on thread management in Chapter 5, tasks that take a long time to complete can have a very negative impact on the performance of your site. This includes things like sending an e-mail, executing a long-running database query, generating a lengthy report, or performing a time-consuming calculation. In those cases, you may be able to improve the scalability and performance of your site by offloading those tasks to another server. One way to do that is with *Service Broker*, which is a persistent messaging and queuing system that's built in to SQL Server.

You can also use Service Broker to time-shift long-running tasks. Instead of offloading them to different servers, you might run them from a background thread on your web servers, but only during times when your site isn't busy.

Service Broker has several features that differentiate it from simply running a task in a background thread, as you did earlier:

- Messages are persistent, so they aren't lost if a server goes down.

- Messages are transactional, so if a server goes down after retrieving a message but before completing the task, the message won't be lost.

- Service Broker will maintain the order of your messages.

- You can configure Service Broker to validate your messages against an XML schema, or your messages can contain arbitrary text or binary data, such as serialized .NET objects.

- You can send messages transactionally from one database server to another.

- You can send a sequence of messages in a single *conversation*, and Service Broker guarantees to deliver them all together.

- Service Broker guarantees that it will deliver each message once and only once. That means you can have multiple servers reading from the same queue, without worrying about how to make sure that tasks only get executed once.

To send Service Broker messages on a single database server, you will need four different types of database objects:

- A MESSAGE TYPE defines the validation for your messages.

- A CONTRACT defines which MESSAGE TYPEs can be sent by the INITIATOR of the message (the sender) or the TARGET (the recipient).

- A QUEUE is a specialized table that holds your messages while they're in-transit.

- A SERVICE defines which CONTRACTs can be stored in a particular queue.

When you send or receive messages, you group them into CONVERSATIONs. A CONVERSATION is just an ordered group of messages. In addition to your own messages, your code also needs to handle a few system messages. In particular, Service Broker sends a special message at the end of each conversation.

At a high level, when you send a message, you can think of it as being inserted into a special table called a QUEUE. When you read the message, it's deleted from the table (QUEUE), and assuming the transaction is committed, Service Broker guarantees that no one else will receive the same message. With some effort, you could implement similar functionality yourself with vanilla database tables, but handling things such as multiple readers, being able to wait for new messages to arrive, and so on, can be complex, so why reinvent the wheel when you don't have to do so?

Enabling and Configuring Service Broker

Let's walk through an example. First, before you can use Service Broker, you need to enable it at the database level:

```
ALTER DATABASE [Sample] SET ENABLE_BROKER WITH ROLLBACK IMMEDIATE
```

Next, create a MESSAGE TYPE:

```
CREATE MESSAGE TYPE [//12titans.net/TaskRequest]
    AUTHORIZATION [dbo]
    VALIDATION = NONE
```

In this case, specify no VALIDATION, since you want to send arbitrary text or binary data. If you're sending XML messages, you can have them validated against a schema as part of the send process.

Next, create a CONTRACT:

```
CREATE CONTRACT [//12titans.net/TaskContract/v1.0]
    AUTHORIZATION [dbo]
    ([//12titans.net/TaskRequest] SENT BY INITIATOR)
```

I've specified a version number at the end of the CONTRACT name to simplify the process of adding a new contract later, if needed. You would need a new CONTRACT if you wanted to send a different type of message.

Next, create a QUEUE and an associated SERVICE:

```
CREATE QUEUE [dbo].[TaskRequestQueue]

CREATE SERVICE [//12titans.net/TaskService]
    AUTHORIZATION [dbo]
    ON QUEUE [dbo].[TaskRequestQueue] ([//12titans.net/TaskContract/v1.0])
```

The SERVICE associates the queue with the CONTRACT.

Stored Procedure to Send Messages

Now that the infrastructure is in place, you're ready for a stored procedure to send messages:

```
CREATE PROC [dbo].[SendTaskRequest]
    @msg VARBINARY(MAX)
AS
BEGIN
    SET NOCOUNT ON
    DECLARE @handle UNIQUEIDENTIFIER
    BEGIN TRANSACTION
        BEGIN DIALOG @handle FROM SERVICE [//12titans.net/TaskService]
            TO SERVICE '//12titans.net/TaskService'
            ON CONTRACT [//12titans.net/TaskContract/v1.0]
            WITH ENCRYPTION = OFF
        ;SEND ON CONVERSATION @handle
            MESSAGE TYPE [//12titans.net/TaskRequest] (@msg)
        END CONVERSATION @handle
    COMMIT TRANSACTION
END
```

Within a transaction, the code begins a DIALOG, which is a type of CONVERSATION that provides exactly-once-in-order messaging. The DIALOG connects a sending SERVICE and a receiving SERVICE, although in this case you're using the same service type for both directions. You also specify which CONTRACT you will be using for this CONVERSATION. If you try to SEND MESSAGE TYPEs that you didn't include in the specified CONTRACT, it will produce an error. Although CONVERSATIONs can be encrypted, which can be useful when you're sending messages from one machine to another, you disable encryption in this case.

After starting the DIALOG, the code SENDs the message, ENDs the CONVERSATION, and COMMITs the transaction.

Stored Procedure to Receive Messages

Next, here's a stored procedure to receive the messages:

```
CREATE PROC [dbo].[ReceiveTaskRequest]
    @msg VARBINARY(MAX) OUT
AS
BEGIN
    SET NOCOUNT ON
    DECLARE @handle UNIQUEIDENTIFIER
    DECLARE @msgtable TABLE (
        handle    UNIQUEIDENTIFIER,
        [message] VARBINARY(MAX),
        msgtype   VARCHAR(256)
    );
    SET @handle = NULL
    WAITFOR (
        RECEIVE [conversation_handle], message_body, message_type_name
        FROM [dbo].[TaskRequestQueue]
        INTO @msgtable
    ), TIMEOUT 60000
    SELECT @handle = handle
        FROM @msgtable
        WHERE msgtype = 'http://schemas.microsoft.com/SQL/ServiceBroker/EndDialog'
    IF @handle IS NOT NULL
    BEGIN
        END CONVERSATION @handle
    END
    SELECT @msg = [message]
        FROM @msgtable
        WHERE msgtype = '//12titans.net/TaskRequest'
END
```

When receiving a message, the associated transaction will generally be at an outer scope, so don't create one here. After declaring a few variables, the code calls RECEIVE, specifying the QUEUE that you want to read from and the output data that you're interested in: the CONVERSATION handle, the message body, and the message type. Since you might get more than one row of data (in this case, the data itself and an EndDialog message), use the INTO clause of the RECEIVE statement to put the data into a temporary table.

The RECEIVE is wrapped in a WAITFOR statement, with a timeout set to 60,000ms. If nothing arrives in the QUEUE after 60 seconds, it will time out.

After the data arrives, you check to see whether it contains an EndDialog message. If it does, then end this side of the CONVERSATION. Both the sender and the receiver must separately end their half of the CONVERSATION.

Finally, SELECT the message body from the temporary table, based on the message type that you're looking for, and return that data to the caller using an output variable.

Testing the Example

To test things, first either open two windows from SSMS to your database or start a second instance of SSMS. In one window, run the following commands as a single batch:

```
DECLARE @msg VARBINARY(MAX)
EXEC dbo.ReceiveTaskRequest @msg OUT
SELECT CONVERT(VARCHAR(MAX), @msg)
```

The command should wait and do nothing. After 60 seconds, it should time out. Before it times out, run the following commands in a single batch from another window:

```
DECLARE @msg VARBINARY(MAX)
SET @msg = CONVERT(VARBINARY(MAX), 'abc')
EXEC dbo.SendTaskRequest @msg
```

In this case, you're just sending the text abc after converting it to a VARBINARY(MAX). After the message is sent, you should see the receive window display the same message shortly thereafter.

■ **Note** Although Service Broker's internal message delivery mechanisms are triggered right away when you send a message, on a very busy system the delay before it's received might be several seconds or more; it's fast but not instantaneous.

Avoiding Poisoned Messages

You should be sure to avoid *poisoned* messages. These happen when you pull a message off the QUEUE in a transaction and then ROLLBACK the transaction instead of committing it, usually in response to an error. After that happens five times for the same message, Service Broker will abort the process by disabling the QUEUE.

A good way to avoid poisoned messages is to catch errors or exceptions that probably won't go away if you just repeat the command. You can log the bad messages to another table or to the Windows event log. After that, go ahead and COMMIT the transaction to remove the message that failed, rather than rolling back.

Sending E-mail via Service Broker

Sending large volumes of e-mail from your web site can quickly become a significant issue from a performance and scalability perspective.

A common approach is to connect from a page to an SMTP server synchronously. The SMTP server is often the one that's included with Windows, installed locally on each web server. This approach has several drawbacks:

- The synchronous connection has a negative impact on scalability.

- IIS and your application have to compete with the SMTP server for resources.

- You will need to allow your web servers to make outgoing SMTP connections, which is a bad idea from a security perspective.

- You have no way to get any feedback from the SMTP server regarding whether the message was delivered successfully to its final destination.

- In a load-balanced configuration, web servers are intended to be fully redundant. If one server crashes, no data should be lost. However, with an SMTP server on each web server, if a machine crashes, any queued e-mail messages will be lost.

- The interaction with the SMTP server isn't transactional. You will need considerable additional logic on the web side to handle the case where the SMTP server generates an error or happens to be offline for some reason.

- This approach doesn't respond well to peak loads. If you suddenly have a large number of e-mails to send, it can have an adverse impact on the performance of your site as a whole.

A typical response to the previous realizations is to use a dedicated e-mail server. However, that by itself isn't enough, since it would be a single point of failure. That leads to a load-balanced pair or cluster of servers, with RAID disks so that data isn't lost. By this point, the resulting system is getting reasonably complex, yet it still doesn't address all the drawbacks in previous the list.

A better approach is to use Service Broker. Web pages can use async database calls to queue messages with the details about the e-mail to be sent. A thread running on a dedicated server then reads messages from the queue and sends the requested e-mail directly to the remote SMTP server, bypassing the need for a local one. You can deploy as many servers as you need to handle the workload. They can all be reading from the same queue, without having to worry about getting duplicate messages. Although you still end up with separate servers, the architecture is easier to configure since you don't need load balancing or RAID disks. As with web servers, the servers reading and processing Service Broker messages would be stateless; all the state information is stored in SQL Server.

The reader threads might be located in a Windows service, which simplifies certain aspects of management and deployment. They could also be background threads in a special-purpose web site.

Even if you wanted to connect directly to the destination SMTP server from your web application, you wouldn't normally have the ability to handle remote e-mail servers that aren't available. Handling those connection retries is one reason you need a local SMTP server in the usual scenario.

With a dedicated server that uses Service Broker queuing, an alternative approach makes it possible for the application to track the delivery of each e-mail more accurately. You can look up the IP address of the remote e-mail server based on the MX record of the destination host and send the e-mail directly there if it's accessible; otherwise, queue it for retry using a separate retry queue.

Creating a Background Worker Thread

Let's walk through a detailed example and build on the stored procedures you defined earlier. First, right-click your web site in **Solution Explorer** and select **Add New Item**. Select **Global Application Class**, and click **Add**. Open the newly created Global.asax file, and replace all the template text with the following single line:

```
<%@ Application Language="C#" Inherits="Global" %>
```

The default `<script>`-based approach that Visual Studio uses makes it difficult to use certain features of the code editor, so I prefer to put the source code in a class by itself. To do that, add a new class to the `App_Code` folder in your web site, and call it `Global.cs`. Edit the file as follows:

```
using System;
using System.Threading;
using System.Web;

public class Global : HttpApplication
{
    private static Thread TaskThread { get; set; }

    public Global()
    {
    }

    void Application_Start(object sender, EventArgs e)
    {
        if ((TaskThread == null) || !TaskThread.IsAlive)
        {
            ThreadStart ts = new ThreadStart(BrokerWorker.Work);
            TaskThread = new Thread(ts);
            TaskThread.Start();
        }
    }

    void Application_End(object sender, EventArgs e)
    {
        if ((TaskThread != null) && (TaskThread.IsAlive))
        {
            TaskThread.Abort();
        }
        TaskThread = null;
    }
}
```

The `Application_Start()` method creates and starts our background worker thread when the web app first starts, and `Application_End()` stops it when the app shuts down.

Reading and Processing Messages

Next, create a class file called `BrokerWorker.cs`, and edit it as follows:

```
using System;
using System.Data;
using System.Data.SqlClient;
using System.Diagnostics;
using System.IO;
```

```
using System.Net.Mail;
using System.Runtime.Serialization.Formatters.Binary;
using System.Threading;
using System.Transactions;

public static class BrokerWorker
{
    public const string ConnString =
        "Data Source=server;Initial Catalog=Sample;Integrated Security=True";

    public static void Work()
    {
        DateTime lastLogTime = DateTime.Now;
        string lastMessage = String.Empty;

        for (; ; )
        {
            using (TransactionScope scope = new TransactionScope())
            {
                using (SqlConnection conn = new SqlConnection(ConnString))
                {
                    using (SqlCommand cmd =
                        new SqlCommand("[dbo].[ReceiveTaskRequest]", conn))
                    {
                        cmd.CommandType = CommandType.StoredProcedure;
                        cmd.CommandTimeout = 600;         // seconds
                        cmd.Parameters.Add("msg", SqlDbType.VarBinary, -1).Direction =
                            ParameterDirection.Output;
```

This is the code for the worker thread. It runs in a loop forever. Establish a transaction using `TransactionScope`, and then configure the `SqlConnection` and `SqlCommand` objects to refer to your stored procedure using a synchronous connection. Set the command timeout to 600 seconds and add a single output parameter of type `VARBINARY(MAX)`.

```
                        byte[] msg = null;
                        try
                        {
                            conn.Open();
                            cmd.ExecuteNonQuery();
                            msg = cmd.Parameters["msg"].Value as byte[];
                            if (msg != null)
                            {
                                PerformTask(msg);
                            }
                        }
```

After opening a connection to the database, run the stored procedure. If there aren't any messages in the queue, it will wait for 60 seconds and then return with a `null` result. If a message did arrive, call `PerformTask()` to do the work.

```
                catch (Exception e)
                {
                    if (e is ThreadAbortException)
                    {
                        break;
                    }
                    else
                    {
                        TimeSpan elapsed = DateTime.Now - lastLogTime;
                        if ((lastMessage != e.Message) ||
                            (elapsed.Minutes > 10))
                        {
                            EventLog.WriteEntry("Application", e.Message,
                                EventLogEntryType.Error, 105);
                            lastLogTime = DateTime.Now;
                        }
                        else if (lastMessage == e.Message)
                        {
                            Thread.Sleep(60000);
                        }
                        lastMessage = e.Message;
                    }
                }
                finally
                {
                    if (msg != null)
                    {
                        scope.Complete();
                    }
                }
            }
        }
    }
}
```

Since you're running in a background thread, catch all `Exceptions`. If it's a `ThreadAbortException`, then break from the outer loop and exit gracefully. Otherwise, write an error message to the Windows event log, taking care to make sure that you don't flood the log or go CPU-bound doing nothing but processing errors. Do that by checking for recurring messages in the `Exception`, by tracking the last time that you wrote to the event log, and by sleeping for a minute if there are repeat errors.

Whether there was an exception or not, call `scope.Complete()` to commit the transaction, which avoids the problems associated with poison messages. In a production system, you might want to save the failed message in a table for possible later processing or analysis.

```
private static void PerformTask(byte[] msg)
{
    BinaryFormatter formatter = new BinaryFormatter();
    using (MemoryStream stream = new MemoryStream(msg))
    {
        TaskRequest request = formatter.Deserialize(stream) as TaskRequest;
```

```
        if (request != null)
        {
            switch (request.TaskType)
            {
                case TaskTypeEnum.Email:
                    SmtpClient smtp = new SmtpClient("localhost");
                    smtp.Send("rick@12titans.net", request.EmailToAddress,
                        request.EmailSubject, request.EmailMesssage);
                    break;
            }
        }
    }
}
```

The `PerformTask()` method deserializes the incoming message, transforming it back into a `TaskRequest` object. Then you use those parameters to send the e-mail. In this case, I'm still using a local SMTP server. In a production system, you would look up the MX record of the destination host and send the mail directly there, with a separate queue for retries, as I described earlier.

Next, add another class file called `TaskRequest.cs`:

```
using System;

[Serializable]
public class TaskRequest
{
    public TaskRequest()
    {
    }

    public TaskTypeEnum TaskType { get; set; }
    public string EmailToAddress { get; set; }
    public string EmailSubject { get; set; }
    public string EmailMesssage { get; set; }
}

public enum TaskTypeEnum
{
    None,
    Email
}
```

`TaskRequest` is a `Serializable` class that holds the information that you want to pass from the web tier to the task thread.

Web Form to Queue a Message to Send an E-mail

Next, add a web form called `broker-email.aspx`, and edit the markup as follows:

```
<%@ Page Language="C#" EnableViewState="false" AutoEventWireup="false"
    Async="true" CodeFile="broker-email.aspx.cs" Inherits="broker_email" %>
<!DOCTYPE html PUBLIC "-//W3C//DTD XHTML 1.0 Transitional//EN"
  "http://www.w3.org/TR/xhtml1/DTD/xhtml1-transitional.dtd">
<html xmlns="http://www.w3.org/1999/xhtml">
<head runat="server">
    <title></title>
</head>
<body>
    <form id="form1" runat="server">
    <div>
        Email: <asp:TextBox ID="Email" runat="server" /><br />
        Subject: <asp:TextBox ID="Subject" runat="server" /><br />
        Body: <asp:TextBox ID="Body" runat="server" Width="500" /><br />
        <asp:Button ID="Submit" runat="server" Text="Submit" /><br />
        <asp:Label ID="Status" runat="server" ForeColor="Red" />
    </div>
    </form>
</body>
</html>
```

Notice that ViewState and AutoEventWireup are disabled and Async is enabled. The page has three
<asp:TextBox> controls that you'll use to set the parameters for the e-mail, along with a submit button
and an <asp:Label> control for status information.

Next, edit the code-behind:

```
using System;
using System.Data;
using System.Data.SqlClient;
using System.IO;
using System.Runtime.Serialization.Formatters.Binary;
using System.Web;
using System.Web.UI;

public partial class broker_email : Page
{
    public const string ConnString =
        "Data Source=server;Initial Catalog=Sample;Integrated Security=True;Async=True";

    protected override void OnLoad(EventArgs e)
    {
        base.OnLoad(e);
        if (this.IsPostBack)
        {
            PageAsyncTask pat = new PageAsyncTask(BeginAsync, EndAsync, null, null, true);
            RegisterAsyncTask(pat);
        }
    }
```

You're using what I hope is by now a familiar pattern for an async page, including a connection string with async enabled. Start the `PageAsyncTask` only if the page is a postback, since the `TextBox` controls won't have anything in them otherwise.

```
private IAsyncResult BeginAsync(object sender, EventArgs e,
    AsyncCallback cb, object state)
{
    TaskRequest request = new TaskRequest()
    {
        TaskType = TaskTypeEnum.Email,
        EmailToAddress = this.Email.Text,
        EmailSubject = this.Subject.Text,
        EmailMesssage = this.Body.Text
    };
    SqlConnection conn = new SqlConnection(ConnString);
    SqlCommand cmd = new SqlCommand("[dbo].[SendTaskRequest]", conn);
    cmd.CommandType = CommandType.StoredProcedure;
    BinaryFormatter formatter = new BinaryFormatter();
    using (MemoryStream stream = new MemoryStream())
    {
        formatter.Serialize(stream, request);
        stream.Flush();
        cmd.Parameters.Add("msg", SqlDbType.VarBinary).Value = stream.ToArray();
    }
    conn.Open();
    IAsyncResult ar = cmd.BeginExecuteNonQuery(cb, cmd);
    return ar;
}
```

The `BeginAsync` method creates a `TaskRequest` object and assigns its properties based on the incoming contents of the `TextBoxes`. Then it serializes the object and passes it to the `SendTaskRequest` stored procedure.

```
private void EndAsync(IAsyncResult ar)
{
    using (SqlCommand cmd = (SqlCommand)ar.AsyncState)
    {
        using (cmd.Connection)
        {
            cmd.EndExecuteNonQuery(ar);
            this.Status.Text = "Message sent";
        }
    }
}
```

When the stored procedure completes, call `EndExecuteNonQuery()` and set a message in the `Status` control.

Results

With all of the components in place, when you bring up `broker-email.aspx` in a browser, fill in the form, and click `Submit`, it sends a message via Service Broker to the background thread, which then sends an e-mail. The process happens very quickly.

This architecture also allows a couple of new options that aren't easily possible with the usual approach:

- You can easily restrict the times of day at which e-mails are sent, or you can limit the rate they're sent so that they don't place a disproportionate load on your network.

- As another load-management technique, you can explicitly control how many e-mail requests are processed in parallel at the same time. You might adjust that number based on the time of day or other parameters.

In addition to using Service Broker for e-mail, you can also use it for any long-running tasks that can be executed independently of web pages and that you would like to move out of the web tier, such as reports, long-running relational or MDX queries, data movement or ETL, calling web services, event notification (instant messaging, SMS, and so on), application-specific background tasks, and so on. However, since the queuing process does involve some overhead (including some database writes), you should make sure that the task isn't too small. Otherwise, it may be better to do it inline instead.

Data Change Notifications

To help facilitate caching database query results at the web tier, you can register a subscription with SQL Server so that it will send a notification when the results of a query may have changed. This is a much more efficient and scalable alternative to using some form of timeouts combined with polling.

As you learned in Chapter 3, the `SqlCacheDependency` class uses notifications of this type to remove items from the cache automatically when they change. A related approach is to register a change event handler to be called when the notification arrives, using the `SqlDependency` class.

The notification mechanism relies on Service Broker, so you have to enable it for your database before attempting to use it, as described earlier. As with `SqlCacheDependency`, it also uses a dedicated thread on the .NET side, which you need to start before registering a subscription by calling `SqlDependency.Start()`.

Using a change event handler allows you to take additional action when the data changes. Rather than just removing a cache entry, you might also proactively read the data again, send messages to a log, and so on.

SQL Server is designed to support up to hundreds or perhaps a thousand or so simultaneous notification subscriptions per database server (total for all incoming connections), but not tens or hundreds of thousands or more. On a large system, you may therefore need to ration the number of subscriptions that a single web server is allowed to make.

Query Restrictions

You can register change notification subscriptions for command batches or stored procedures, including cases that return multiple result sets. However, the particular queries that are eligible for subscriptions are heavily restricted; you must compose them according to a strict set of rules. These are the most important things to remember when you're first getting notifications to work correctly:

- Use full two-part table names, such as `[dbo].[MyTable]`.

- Explicitly name every column (asterisks and unnamed columns are not allowed).

- Don't use `SET NOCOUNT ON` in a stored procedure.

- Don't use a `TOP` expression.

- Don't use complex queries or aggregations.

■ **Caution** If you try to subscribe to a command that isn't correctly composed, SQL Server may fire an event immediately after you issue the query. Be sure to check for error conditions in your event handler to avoid overloading your system with many unnecessary queries.

The details of the final bullet in the previous list require a much longer list. First, here are the things that you *must* do:

- The connection options must be set as follows (these are usually system defaults):

  - `ANSI_NULLS ON` (must also be set when a stored procedure is created)

  - `ANSI_PADDING ON`

  - `ANSI_WARNINGS ON`

  - `CONCAT_NULL_YIELDS_NULL ON`

  - `QUOTED_IDENTIFIER ON` (must also be set when a stored procedure is created)

  - `NUMERIC_ROUNDABORT OFF`

  - `ARITHABORT ON`

- Reference a base table.

Here are the things that you *must not* do, use, include, or reference:

- `READ_UNCOMMITTED` or `SNAPSHOT` isolation.

- Computed or duplicate columns.

- Aggregate expressions, unless the statement uses group by. In that case, you can use `COUNT_BIG()` or `SUM()` only.

- Commands that involve symmetric encryption, such as `OPEN SYMMETRIC KEY`, `ENCRYPTBYKEY()`, and so on.

- Any of the following keywords or operators: `HAVING`, `CUBE`, `ROLLUP`, `PIVOT`, `UNPIVOT`, `UNION`, `INTERSECT`, `EXCEPT`, `DISTINCT`, `COMPUTE`, `COMPUTE BY`, `INTO`, `CONTAINS`, `CONTAINSTEXTTABLE`, `FREETEXT`, `FREETEXTTABLE`, `OPENROWSET`, `OPENQUERY`, or `FOR BROWSE`.

- Views.

- Server global variables (that start with @@).

- Derived or temporary tables.

- Table variables.

- Subqueries.

- Outer joins.

- Self joins.

- The NTEXT, TEXT, or IMAGE data types (use VARCHAR(MAX) or VARBINARY(MAX) instead).

- Aggregate functions: AVG, COUNT, MAX, MIN, STDEV, STDEVP, VAR, VARP, or user-defined aggregates.

- Nondeterministic functions, such as RANK() and DENSE_RANK(), or similar functions that use the OVER clause.

- System views, system tables, catalog views, or dynamic management views.

- Service Broker QUEUEs.

- Conditional statements that can't change and that don't return results (such as WHILE(1=0)).

- A READPAST locking hint.

- Synonyms.

- Comparisons based on double or real data types.

Example: A Simple Configuration System

As an example, let's build a simple configuration system. First, create a table to hold the configuration data, and create a primary key for the table:

```
CREATE TABLE [dbo].[ConfigInfo] (
    [Key]      VARCHAR(64)    NOT NULL,
    [Strval]   VARCHAR(256)   NULL
)

ALTER TABLE [dbo].[ConfigInfo]
    ADD CONSTRAINT [ConfigInfoPK]
    PRIMARY KEY CLUSTERED ([Key])
```

■ **Note** Although it's syntactically acceptable to define a primary key in the CREATE TABLE DDL, I've taken to the style of keeping them separate. That approach lets me provide an explicit name for the index, which is sometimes needed, and separating the DDL is a requirement of the Team Database software in order to ease database management and deployment.

Next, insert a couple of rows into the table:

```
INSERT INTO [dbo].[ConfigInfo]
    ([Key], [Strval]) VALUES ('CookieName', 'CC')
INSERT INTO [dbo].[ConfigInfo]
    ([Key], [Strval]) VALUES ('CookiePath', '/p/')
```

Create a stored procedure to read the table:

```
CREATE PROCEDURE [dbo].[GetConfigInfo]
AS
BEGIN
    SELECT [Key], [Strval] FROM [dbo].[ConfigInfo]
END
```

Notice that you are not using SET NOCOUNT ON, that the table has a two-part name, and that you named all the columns explicitly.

Next, add a new class to your project in a file called ConfigInfo.cs:

```
using System.Data;
using System.Data.SqlClient;

public static class ConfigInfo
{
    public const string ConnString =
        "Data Source=server;Initial Catalog=Sample;Integrated Security=True";
    public static DataTable ConfigTable { get; set; }

    public static void Start()
    {
        SqlDependency.Start(ConnString);
        LoadConfig();
    }

    public static void Stop()
    {
        SqlDependency.Stop(ConnString);
    }
```

Expose the configuration data to the rest of the application using the DataTable in ConfigTable.

You will call the `Start()` and `Stop()` methods from the `Global.cs` class (see the code a little later). The methods start and stop the `SqlDependency` notification handling thread, and the `Start()` method also calls `LoadConfig()` to read the configuration data for the first time.

```
private static void LoadConfig()
{
    using (SqlConnection conn = new SqlConnection(ConnString))
    {
        using (SqlCommand cmd = new SqlCommand("[dbo].[GetConfigInfo]", conn))
        {
            cmd.CommandType = CommandType.StoredProcedure;
            SqlDependency depend = new SqlDependency(cmd);
            depend.OnChange += OnConfigChange;
            ConfigTable = new DataTable();
            conn.Open();
            using (SqlDataReader reader = cmd.ExecuteReader())
            {
                ConfigTable.Load(reader);
            }
        }
    }
}
```

This method calls the stored procedure and stores the results in the publically accessible `DataTable`. However, before calling `ExecuteReader()`, create a `SqlDependency` object that's associated with this `SqlCommand` and add `OnConfigChange()` to the list of the object's `OnChange` event handlers.

```
private static void OnConfigChange(object sender, SqlNotificationEventArgs e)
{
    SqlDependency depend = (SqlDependency)sender;
    depend.OnChange -= OnConfigChange;
    if (e.Type == SqlNotificationType.Change)
        LoadConfig();
}
```

The `OnConfigChange()` event handler removes itself from the event handler list and then calls `LoadConfig()` again if the `SqlNotificationType` is `Change`, meaning that the data returned by the subscribed query may have changed. The response might also be `Subscribe`, which would indicate that there was an error in establishing the subscription. In that case, you can look at `e.Info` to determine the reason for the problem.

Next, update the `Global.cs` class (which you created for an earlier example) to call the `Start()` and `Stop()` methods from `Application_Start()` and `Application_End()`, respectively:

```
void Application_Start(object sender, EventArgs e)
{
    . . .

    ConfigInfo.Start();
}
```

```
void Application_End(object sender, EventArgs e)
{
    . . .
    ConfigInfo.Stop();
}
```

After starting the application, executing the following command from SSMS will cause OnConfigChange() to run, and it will read the configuration data again from the ConfigInfo table:

```
UPDATE [dbo].[ConfigInfo]
    SET [Strval] = 'CD'
    WHERE [Key] = 'CookieName'
```

You can see the response happen either with SQL Profiler or by setting an appropriate breakpoint with the debugger.

■ **Note** Since data change notifications use Service Broker, they are subject to the same underlying performance implications. In particular, notifications are sent asynchronously from when you make changes. That means there will be a slight delay from the time you make the change until servers receive and respond to the notification.

Data change notifications are a powerful mechanism that you can use on the web tier to eliminate polling for data changes, while also reducing the latency from when you modify data until your servers know about it and start using it.

Resource Governor

Most web sites have several different kinds of database traffic. For example, in addition to "regular" transactions, you might have logging, back-end reports, and customer order placement. You might also have several classes of users, such as anonymous users, logged-in users, administrative users, and perhaps privileged VIP users. The default configuration is that each database connection receives equal priority. If your database encounters regular resource contention, you can improve the performance of user-visible commands using a SQL Enterprise/Developer-only feature called *Resource Governor*.

Resource Governor allows you to specify the minimum and maximum percentage of CPU time and memory that SQL Server will allocate to a certain group of connections. You determine the grouping programmatically, using a classifier function. You should use Resource Governor to help minimize the impact of background tasks, such as logging, on user-visible foreground tasks. You can also use it to provide different levels of performance for different types of users.

Configuration

As an example, let's say that you would like to make sure that VIP users on your site have better performance than regular users. First, make sure that SQL Auth is enabled. Right-click the top-level database node in **Object Explorer** in SSMS, and select **Properties**. Click **Security** in the panel on the left, and make sure that **SQL Server and Windows Authentication mode** is selected on the right, as in Figure 8-8.

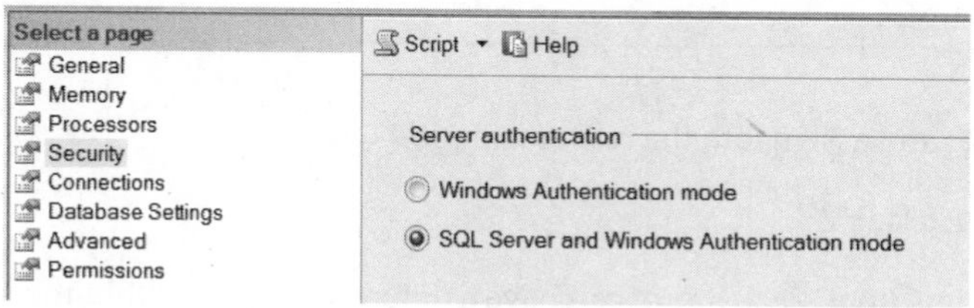

Figure 8-8. Enable SQL Authentication mode

Click **OK** to dismiss the dialog box. Then open a **New Query** window, and select **master** as the destination database. Since Resource Governor settings are applied to all logins, they are configured in the **master** database.

Next, create a new login for the VIP users:

```
CREATE LOGIN vip WITH PASSWORD = 'Pass@Word1'
```

In a live environment, you would also need to create an associated **user** and to assign role membership and permissions, and so on. However, for the purpose of this example, you can skip those steps.

Resource Governor includes two standard resource pools: `DEFAULT` and `INTERNAL`. All connections are assigned to the `DEFAULT` pool, and functions such as the lazy writer, checkpoint, and ghost record cleanup are assigned to the `INTERNAL` pool. Both pools have a minimum and maximum CPU and memory set to 0 percent and 100 percent, which means they effectively aren't constrained. You can modify the settings of the `DEFAULT` pool, but not the `INTERNAL` pool.

You would like to guarantee your VIP users a significant fraction of available CPU time, so you need a new `RESOURCE POOL`:

```
CREATE RESOURCE POOL VipPool
  WITH (MIN_CPU_PERCENT = 80,
  MAX_CPU_PERCENT = 100)
```

This says that for the group of connections assigned to this pool, Resource Governor will guarantee a minimum of 80 percent of the CPU, and the pool can use up to 100 percent. However, *those allocations apply only when CPU uses becomes constrained*. If `VipPool` is using only 5 percent of the CPU and `DEFAULT` connections are using 85 percent, then CPU use is unconstrained, and Resource Governor won't change the way CPU time is allocated. However, if connections assigned to the `VipPool` wanted to increase their usage to 50 percent, then Resource Governor would step in and reduce CPU use by the `DEFAULT` pool from 85 percent to 50 percent so that both pools could operate within their specified parameters.

The sum of all minimum allocations can't exceed 100 percent.

Resource allocation works similarly with the maximum parameters. The resources used by each pool can exceed their specified maximums, as long as there isn't any contention. Resource Governor never limits the total CPU used by SQL Server; it only adjusts the allocations of CPU use to particular pools or groups. If a pool had a maximum allocation of 50 percent CPU and no other pools were active, it would be able to use 100 percent of the CPU if it needed to do so.

■ **Note** Resource Governor resource allocations apply only within a single instance of SQL Server; they do not take other applications or instances on the box into consideration.

Next, create a resource WORKLOAD GROUP, and assign it to the resource pool:

```
CREATE WORKLOAD GROUP VipGroup USING "VipPool"
```

You can have multiple groups in the same pool. Each group can have a different priority within the pool. You can also set limits for each group on things like the maximum CPU time that can be used by a single request or the maximum degree of parallelism.

Next, create a classifier function in the master database. Double-check that your query window in SSMS is set to the master database first (or execute USE master):

```
CREATE FUNCTION classifier()
    RETURNS SYSNAME
    WITH SCHEMABINDING
AS
BEGIN
    DECLARE @group SYSNAME
    SET @group = 'default'
    IF SUSER_NAME() = 'vip'
        SET @group = 'VipGroup'
    RETURN @group
END
```

If the current login is vip, then the function returns VipGroup, which is the name of the WORKLOAD GROUP to which the connection will be assigned.

The classifier function can look at any system parameters you like to determine to which WORKLOAD GROUP the current connection belongs. You return the group name as a SYSNAME (a string). Since the classifier function runs for every login, it should execute quickly to avoid performance issues.

The previous function determines group membership based on the current login name. You might also look at things like the application name, using the APP_NAME() function (you can set its value in your connection string), the user's role, the time of day, and so on.

Next, assign the classifier function to Resource Governor:

```
ALTER RESOURCE GOVERNOR
    WITH (CLASSIFIER_FUNCTION = [dbo].[classifier])
```

Finally, activate the changes:

```
ALTER RESOURCE GOVERNOR RECONFIGURE
```

One handy aspect of Resource Governor is that you can change the resource allocations on the fly, while the server is running. If the usage patterns on your system differ significantly at different times of the day, week, or month, you might run a SQL Agent job to configure Resource Governor appropriately for those times.

If you change the classifier function, keep in mind that connections are assigned to a WORKLOAD GROUP only when they are first created. An existing connection would have to be closed and then reopened in order to use a new classifier function. With standard connection pooling on ASP.NET, that may not happen as soon you might expect.

SSMS also provides a GUI that you can use to manage Resource Governor. To see the changes you just made, open **Management** in **Object Explorer**. Then right-click **Resource Governor** and select **Properties**. SSMS will display a dialog box similar to the one in Figure 8-9.

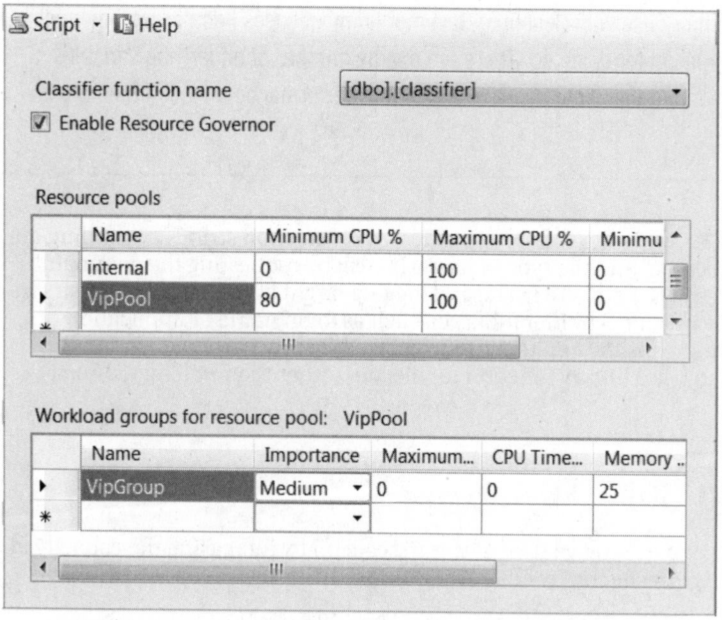

Figure 8-9. Resource Governor management GUI in SQL Management Studio

Testing

To test the changes, open a new instance of SSMS, but connect using the `vip` login and password that you created rather than your usual credentials. Put the following code in both the original window and the new one:

```
DECLARE @count BIGINT
SET @count = 0
DECLARE @start DATETIME
SET @start = GETDATE()
WHILE DATEDIFF(second, @start, GETDATE()) < 30
BEGIN
    SET @count = @count + 1
END
SELECT @count
```

This is a CPU-bound script that just increments a counter as much as it can over a 30-second period. Start the script in the original window, and then as quickly as you can afterward, start it in the `vip` window so that both windows are running at the same time.

When the commands complete, you should see that the final count in the `vip` window is roughly 80 percent of the sum of the two counts. On my local machine, it was about 78 percent, rather than the 50 percent or so that it would be without Resource Governor.

■ **Caution** Although you can restrict memory use with Resource Governor, in most cases I don't recommend it unless you have a compelling technical reason for doing so. There are a large number of underlying variables surrounding memory allocation, and I've found that it's difficult to predict the performance impact if memory is restricted.

To use this feature from ASP.NET, your code should use different connection strings depending on the nature of the command to be executed, and the type of user who will be requesting the command. For example, anonymous users, logged-in users, VIP users, and logging might all use connection strings with differences that you can identify in your classifier function, such as login name or application name, as described earlier. Since that means the connection string used for any particular command might not always be the same, I like to use a library function to select it, rather than pulling it directly from `web.config` or the database.

Scaling Up vs. Scaling Out

As database servers approach their capacity, one way to grow is to scale up by increasing the capacity of your existing servers. The other way is to scale out by adding additional servers. Each approach has its pros and cons.

Scaling Up

In general, scaling up to add capacity to your site is easier and more cost effective, from both a hardware and a software perspective, than scaling out. However, you will of course reach a limit at some point where you can't scale up any more, at which point scaling out becomes your only alternative.

There are also cases where you want to improve performance, rather than to add capacity. In that event, there are times where scaling out is more effective than scaling up.

In deciding which way to go, one of the first things to look at is how busy the CPUs are. If they're close to 100 percent most of the time, then you're CPU bound, and adding more I/O capacity or more memory won't help. You can add more CPU sockets or cores, or switch to CPUs with a larger cache or a higher clock rate. Once your system has reached its capacity in those areas, you will need to upgrade the entire server to continue scaling up. The associated cost factor if often a good motivator for scaling out at that point instead. However, in my experience, there is usually plenty of room for improvement in other areas before you reach this point.

■ **Note** Since SQL Server is licensed per CPU *socket* rather than per *core*, the most cost-effective way to increase CPU capacity is to use as many CPU cores as you can, at the highest clock rate and with the largest cache you can. Fast multicore CPUs are much less expensive than adding a license for an additional CPU socket.

For I/O-bound systems, a common scenario would be to scale up by adding more memory first, up to your system's maximum (or approximately the size of your database, whichever is less) or what your budget allows. Next, add more disks and/or controllers to increase your system's I/O throughput. I/O bound servers can often benefit from a surprisingly large number of drives. Proper disk subsystem design is critical and has a huge impact on performance. See Chapter 10 for additional details.

In the process of architecting a scaling approach, there are a couple of things to keep in mind:

- Adding more I/O capacity in the form of a new server (scale out) is more expensive than adding it to an existing one (scale up).

- You can increase database write performance by first making sure that your database log files are on dedicated volumes and then by adding more drives to those volumes. That's much less expensive than adding more servers.

- Adding I/O capacity won't help if your system is CPU bound.

Scaling Out

When you reach the point where scaling out makes sense, you can partition your data in several different ways:

- *Horizontally.* Place parts of your tables on each server. For example, put users with names starting from A to M on server #1, and put users with names starting from N to Z on server #2. For the boundaries to be adjustable, you may also need some new "directory" tables, so your application can tell which servers have which rows.

- *Vertically.* Place entire tables on one server or another. Ideally, group the tables so that the ones that need to be joined together are on the same server.

- *Read-only servers.* You can place your read-only data onto separate servers. The easiest approach would be to copy all the related tables, rather than trying to divide them in some way. You can keep the machines with read-only copies in sync with a writable copy by using replication and load balance several together for additional scalability, as in Figure 8-10. You can configure the servers as a *scalable shared database*, with a common data store, or as separate servers, each with its own data.

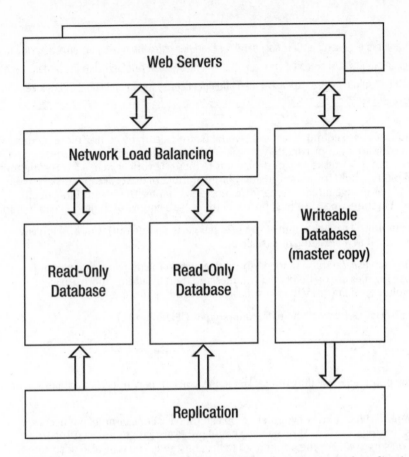

Figure 8-10. Load-balanced read-only databases kept in sync with replication.

- *Write-mostly servers*: If your application does a lot of logging, or other heavy writes, you can partition that work off onto one or more servers dedicated to that purpose. However, as I mentioned, increasing the write performance of an existing server is usually less expensive than using multiple new servers.

If your database contains large amounts of read-only data, you may be able to improve performance by moving it onto a read-only filegroup. That allows SQL Server to make several optimizations, including eliminating all locks.

Another design parameter is the possibility of using SQL Express. For example, the load-balanced array of read-only servers shown in Figure 8-10 could be running SQL Express. That can be particularly effective if the database is small enough to fit in memory so that I/O isn't an issue. However, if I/O *is* an issue, it's better to create a single scaled-up server that's faster and less expensive than an array of cheap servers.

Identifying System Bottlenecks

To determine which type of scaling would be most effective, you can use Windows performance counters to help identify your system's bottlenecks. You can configure and view performance counters using the perfmon tool. There are a staggering number of counters from which to choose. The ones I've found to be most useful for SQL Server scalability analysis are listed next. Ideally, you should make all measurements when your database is under peak load and after the database cache is fully warmed up and populated.

- **PhysicalDisk**, for all active volumes used by the database:

  - **Avg. Disk Queue Length**: For OLTP systems, this should be less than one per active spindle (not including the extra drives needed for your RAID configuration). For example, if you have 20 spindles in RAID 10, that would be 10 active spindles, so the counter value should be less than 10. For staging databases, the value can be as high as 15 to 20 per active spindle.

  - **Avg. Disk sec/Transfer**: Your target should be under 0.020 (20ms).

  - **Disk Transfers/sec**: A properly configured data volume using 15,000rpm drives on a quality hardware RAID controller or SAN should be capable of roughly 400 transfers per second per active spindle. A log volume with the same type of drives should be able to do 12,500 transfers per second per active spindle.

- **Processor**

  - **% Processor Time**: The average use should be below about 75 percent. Brief peaks to 100 percent do not necessarily indicate that your system is underpowered. Since this counter shows the average use over all CPU cores, you should also check Task Manager to make sure you don't have a single process that's consuming all or most of one or more cores.

- **SQLServer:Buffer Manager.**

  - **Buffer cache hit ratio**: This shows how often the data you request is already in memory. If this is below 90 percent, you can probably benefit from additional memory. Ideal values are above 99 percent.

  - **Lazy writes/sec**: This shows how often the lazy writer thread is writing dirty pages to disk. Values greater than 20 indicate that more memory could help performance.

  - **Page life expectancy**: This indicates how long pages are staying in cache, in seconds. Values less than about 350 would be one of the strongest indications that you need more memory.

- **SQLServer:Memory Manager.**

  - **Target Server Memory (KB)**: This indicates how much memory is available for SQL Server.

- **Total Server Memory (KB)**: This indicates how much memory SQL Server is currently using. If **Total Memory** is well under **Target Memory**, that's an indication that you probably have enough memory. However, you shouldn't use these counters to determine whether you *don't* have enough memory. In particular, if they're equal or close to equal, that by itself does *not* mean that you need more memory.

I often prefer to use the report format in perfmon, as in Figure 8-11. You can select report format from the **Change Graph Type** button at the top of the panel.

PhysicalDisk	1 F:	2 E:
Avg. Disk Queue Length	0.000	0.000
Avg. Disk sec/Transfer	0.000	0.000
Disk Transfers/sec	0.000	0.000
Processor	_Total	
% Processor Time	7.272	
SQLServer:Buffer Manager		
Buffer cache hit ratio	100.000	
Lazy writes/sec	0.000	
Page life expectancy	6,655.000	
SQLServer:Memory Manager		
Target Server Memory (KB)	773,664.000	
Total Server Memory (KB)	63,176.000	

Figure 8-11. SQL Server performance counters in perfmon's report format

High Availability

Load-balanced web servers provide resilience against hardware failures at the web tier. High availability technologies such as database clustering and mirroring can provide a similar type of resilience for your database tier.

There are a few important performance-related trade-offs between clustering and mirroring. With clustering, there is very little additional overhead during normal operations. However, if a failure happens, it can take 30 seconds or more for the backup server to come online. Any transactions that were in progress at the time of the failure will have to be rolled back. In addition, the backup server will start with an empty RAM cache, so performance will probably be poor for a while after the switchover, until the cache fills.

With mirroring, the active and backup servers are both always running, so switchover takes only a couple of seconds. However, the trade-off is a slight degradation in performance during normal operation, since the active database has to forward all data modification commands to the backup server. You can minimize the impact of that additional overhead by using asynchronous mirroring. When the backup server comes online, its RAM cache may not be identical to that of the primary server, but it won't be empty either, so the post-switchover performance loss shouldn't be as significant as with a cluster, assuming that the hardware of both mirrors is the same.

Another trade-off between clusters and mirrors is that you can place read-only queries against a mirror but not against the backup server in a cluster. The hardware you use for mirrors can be anything that will run SQL Server; the servers don't even have to be identical (although it's a good idea if they are).

With clustering, you should only use hardware that Microsoft has specifically approved for use in a cluster. Clusters require a multiported disk subsystem, so both the primary server and the backup can access them. Mirrors can use standard single-ported disk controllers. Clusters tend to be more complex to configure and maintain than mirrors.

You can geographically separate the machines in a mirror. You should keep machines in a cluster physically close to each other, ideally in the same rack.

■ **Tip** If you're not using a high availability architecture in your production system yet but there's a good chance that you will in the future, you should do your development, testing, and initial deployment using a named instance rather than a default instance. Since that can require some additional setup (SQL Browser), different management, and different connection strings, it's a good idea to address those issues early in your development process.

Although SQL Standard supports only two-node clusters, with SQL Enterprise you can have up to 16 nodes. In a multi-database-server environment, that means you should need fewer standby (and idle) machines. For example, you might have three active nodes and one standby node, configured so that any of the active machines can failover to the standby.

A so-called active-active configuration is also possible. For example, you might have three active nodes, where each node can fail over to another active node. However, if your servers regularly operate at close to capacity, that configuration can result in one node becoming overloaded in the event of a failure. Having an idle standby node allows much more resilience in the event of a failure.

Miscellaneous Performance Tips

Here are a couple of additional performance tips:

- Database connections are pooled by default by ASP.NET. To minimize the number of simultaneous connections your application needs, you should open a connection right before you use it and then call `Dispose()` as soon as you're done (ideally with a `using` statement).

- Keeping the connection open longer is acceptable, provided that the total execution time can be reduced by using a transaction, command batching, or multiple result sets.

- Minimize filesystem fragmentation and the resulting reduction in disk throughput by setting a large initial file size for your database and log, as well as a large incremental size. Ideally, the file sizes should be large enough that neither the data file nor the log should ever have to grow.

- To minimize fragmentation that might be introduced by the NTFS filesystem, ideally each disk volume should only hold one database data or log file.

- Don't shrink or autoshrink your files, since that can undo the benefits of giving them a large-enough-to-grow size.

- Minimize the number of databases you have; one database is ideal. More than one increases maintenance and deployment effort and complexity and can cost you performance. More than one database log file means that you either need multiple dedicated drives to ensure that all writes will be sequential or need to combine multiple logs on a single drive and therefore lose the ability to do sequential writes (with an associated performance hit). You can achieve all of the partitioning and security benefits of multiple databases with just one instead.

- Consider using SQL CLR for stored procedures or functions that contain a large amount of procedural code. T-SQL is great for set-based operations, but its procedural features are minimal. As with vanilla stored procedures, avoid putting too much business logic in a SQL CLR procedure. However, if a little extra logic in the database can help you avoid some round-trips, then it's worth considering. SQL CLR is also a great way to share constants between your web application and your stored procedures.

- Avoid aggregation queries as much as you can. When you need them, consider caching their results on the web tier or in a small table, which you then recompute periodically. That way, you can easily share the results among multiple web servers, further minimizing the number of times you need to run the queries. Each web server can use `SqlCacheDependency` to watch for changes in the results table. Another option is to use Analysis Services to generate preaggregated results and to make your aggregation queries against that data instead of against the relational store. I'll cover that approach in detail in the next chapter.

Summary

In this chapter, I covered the following:

- Understanding how SQL Server can act like a large cache if it has enough RAM and how using the 64-bit version is an important part of being able to use that memory effectively.

- Understanding the importance of placing database log files on a volume by themselves.

- Using stored procedures instead of dynamic SQL whenever you can.

- Using command batching, table-valued parameters, and multiple result sets to improve performance by reducing the number of database round-trips.

- Using transactions to reduce I/O pressure to the database log, which can significantly improve database write performance.

- Improving the performance of future queries with data precaching. By executing a similar query before the anticipated one, you can read the required data pages into memory before they are needed.

- Using clustered and nonclustered indexes to speed up your queries.

- Choosing indexes to minimize table and index fragmentation.

- Constructing and using efficient data paging queries.

- Integrating data paging with a `GridView` control, an `ObjectDataSource`, async queries, per-request caching, multiple result sets, and `ControlState`.

- Choosing ADO.NET over LINQ or the Entity Framework when you need top performance.

- Using the XML data type, querying and modifying XML columns, and using XML indexes and schemas to improve query performance.

- Partitioning large tables to improve performance and ease maintenance tasks.

- Using full-text search to improve query performance.

- Using Service Broker to move or defer long-running tasks.

- Subscribing to and using data change notifications.

- Using Resource Governor to balance or give priority to workloads on busy servers.

- Choosing between scaling up and scaling out and knowing whether your server needs more RAM, disk, or CPU.

- Understanding the trade-offs between using clustering or mirroring for high-availability.

CHAPTER 9

■ ■ ■

SQL Server Analysis Services

In the previous chapter, you saw how aggregation queries, such as counts and sums, can have a significant adverse impact on the performance of a database. The problems arise partly because of the time it takes the relational database to step through each row in the tables involved and partly because of an increase in memory use. If the aggregation requires scanning a large table or index, the process can displace other buffers from memory so that SQL Server has to read them from disk again the next time another query needs them.

One way to improve the performance of aggregation queries is to cache their results. To make the cached results available to all the servers in your web tier, you can use a small database table for your cache. Imagine that you have many different kinds of aggregations that you would like to cache, over a variety of parameters. If you were to take that concept and expand on it considerably, you would eventually find that you need a way to query the cached data and to update it regularly and that it's possible to gain some powerful insights into your data that way. This realization resulted in the creation of the first multidimensional databases (MDDBs) and eventually an entire industry known as *business intelligence* (BI). SQL Server Analysis Services (SSAS) is Microsoft's BI product. It comes "in the box" with the commercial and developer versions of Microsoft's relational database (not with SQL Express).

Although BI seems to be used most often to support back-end reporting, it can also play an important role in improving the performance of your web tier. You can move aggregation queries to SSAS and eliminate their adverse performance impact on your relational database. Not only should the aggregation queries themselves run faster, but the rest of your RDBMS should run faster too as buffering efficiency improves and the load on your disk subsystem declines.

Communication about BI and data warehousing is unfortunately often made confusing because of a conflicting use of a plethora of industry-specific terms by companies, books, and individuals. To help reduce confusion here, I've listed the terms and definitions *as I use them* in the glossary. Even if you've worked with BI before, I encourage you to review the glossary.

This chapter starts with a summary of how SSAS works and how you can use it in your web site. You then walk through a detailed example that involves building a cube and issuing queries against it from a web page.

Analysis Services Overview

The term *multidimensional* is used when talking about BI because the technology allows you to look at aggregations from several different directions. If you had a table of past order details, you might want to look at things such as the number of orders by date, the number of orders by customer, dollars by customer, or dollars by state the customer lives in. Each of these different views through your data is called a *slice*.

A collection of aggregations is called a *cube*. A cube is the multidimensional equivalent of a single relational database management system (RDBMS); a cube contains facts and dimensions, whereas an RDBMS contains tables. A collection of cubes is called a *multidimensional database* (MDDB). When you add an SSAS project to Visual Studio, you are adding an MDDB.

SSAS retrieves the data that it uses for its calculations from an RDBMS. To do that, first you define a *data source* that contains instructions about how to connect to your database. Then, define a *Data Source View* (DSV) that tells SSAS how the tables in your database are associated with each other. With the DSV in place, you can define and build a cube. When you define a cube, you specify which tables contain *facts*, which are collections of numeric information and foreign keys. You also specify which tables contain *dimensions*, which are collections of primary keys and strings (usually). At first, a cube contains only some high-level precomputed aggregations. As you place queries against the cube, SSAS caches any new aggregations that it has to calculate. You can also configure your cube to precompute a larger number of aggregations up front.

After you've defined a cube in Visual Studio, you need to deploy it to the server before you can place queries against it. After deployment, SSAS may need to reaggregate the associated data through *processing*. Using *proactive caching*, you can automate processing so that it happens either periodically or when data changes. You can also request reprocessing from Visual Studio or SQL Server Integration Services (SSIS).

After you have deployed and processed a cube, you can issue queries against it. Visual Studio contains a data browser that supports an easy drag-and-drop query interface you can use for testing. For reporting, data browsing, or testing purposes, you can also use pivot tables in Excel to browse the data, or you can view its structure with pivot diagrams in Visio. In addition, SQL Server Reporting Services (SSRS) can query the data and generate reports from the results.

You can use SQL Server Management Studio (SSMS) to interface to SSAS; instead of connecting to a relational database, you can connect to SSAS. The primary query language used by SSAS is called *Multidimensional Expressions* (MDX). You can send MDX to SSAS using SSMS and view the results there as you would view rows returned from a table in an RDBMS.

SSAS also supports an XML-based language called XMLA, which is useful mostly for administrative or DDL-like functions such as telling SSAS to reprocess a cube, create a dimension, and so on.

While you're debugging, you can connect to SSAS with SQL Profiler to see queries and other activity, along with query duration measurements.

From your web site, you can send queries to SSAS using the ADOMD.NET library. The structure of the library is similar to ADO.NET, with the addition of a `CellSet` class as an analog of `DataSet` that understands multidimensional results.

In spite of its benefits, SSAS does have some limitations:

- It doesn't support conventional stored procedures, in the same sense as the relational database. Stored procedures in SSAS are more like CLR stored procedures, in that they require a .NET assembly.

- You can't issue native async calls using ADOMD.NET as you can with ADO.NET.

- ADOMD.NET doesn't support command batching of any kind.

- MDX queries are read-only. The only way to update the data is to reprocess the cube.

- There is normally a delay between when your relational data changes and when the data in the cube is reprocessed. You can minimize that latency by using proactive caching. In addition, the smaller the latency is, the higher the load is on your relational database, because SSAS reads the modified data during reprocessing.

Example MDDB

I've found that the best way to understand SSAS is by example. Toward that end, let's walk through one in detail. You start by defining a relational schema and then building a DSV and a cube, along with a few dimensions and a calculated member.

The application in this example might be part of a blog or forum web site. There is a collection of Items, such as blog posts or comments. Each Item has an ItemName and belongs to an ItemCategory such as News, Entertainment, or Sports, and an ItemSubcategory such as Article or Comment. You also have a list of Users, each with a UserId and a UserName. Each User can express how much they like a given Item by voting on it, with a score between 1 and 10. Votes are recorded by date.

The queries you want to move from the relational database to SSAS include things like these:

- What are the most popular Items, based on their average votes?

- How many votes did all the Items in each ItemCategory receive during a particular time period?

- How many total votes have Users cast?

RDBMS Schema

First, you need a table to hold your Users, along with an associated index:

```
CREATE TABLE [Users] (
    UserId      INT IDENTITY,
    UserName    VARCHAR(64)
)

ALTER TABLE [Users]
    ADD CONSTRAINT [UsersPK]
    PRIMARY KEY ([UserId])
```

Next, create a table for the Items and its index:

```
CREATE TABLE [Items] (
    ItemId          INT IDENTITY,
    ItemName        VARCHAR(64),
    ItemCategory    VARCHAR(32),
    ItemSubcategory VARCHAR(32)
)

ALTER TABLE [Items]
    ADD CONSTRAINT [ItemsPK]
    PRIMARY KEY ([ItemId])
```

Next, you need a table for the Votes and its index:

```
CREATE TABLE [Votes] (
    VoteId      INT IDENTITY,
    UserId      INT,
    ItemId      INT,
    VoteValue   INT,
    VoteTime    DATETIME
)

ALTER TABLE [Votes]
    ADD CONSTRAINT [VotesPK]
    PRIMARY KEY ([VoteId])
```

You also need two foreign keys to show how the Votes table is related to the other two tables:

```
ALTER TABLE [Votes]
    ADD CONSTRAINT [VotesUsersFK]
    FOREIGN KEY ([UserId])
    REFERENCES [Users] ([UserId])

ALTER TABLE [Votes]
    ADD CONSTRAINT [VotesItemsFK]
    FOREIGN KEY ([ItemId])
    REFERENCES [Items] ([ItemId])
```

Notice that the names for the corresponding foreign key and primary key columns are the same in each table. This will help simplify the process of creating a cube later.

Also, notice that the values in the Votes table are all either numeric or foreign keys, except VoteTime. Votes is the central fact table.

With the schema in place, let's use the Data Generator again to create some test data, as in the previous chapter. Table 9-1 shows the relevant data-generation patterns. All the columns should be configured with **Unique Values** set to **false**.

Table 9-1. Data Generator Patterns for the SSAS Example

Table	Column	Generator	Expression	Length	Seed
Items	ItemName	RegEx	([A-Z][a-z]{2,10})([A-Z][a-z]*){0,2}	40	15
Items	ItemCategory	RegEx	(News|Entertainment|Business|Sports|Health|Science)	32	17
Items	ItemSubcategory	RegEx	(Articles|Images|Comments)	32	19
Users	UserName	RegEx	[a-zA-Z][a-z0-9]*	24	13
Votes	UserId	Integer	Uniform, Min=1, Max=50000		5
Votes	ItemId	Integer	Uniform, Min=1, Max=2500		9
Votes	VoteValue	Integer	NormalInverse, Min=1, Max=10		11
Votes	VoteTime	DateTime	Uniform, 10/1/2008, 7/31/2009		7

Notice that each item has a different Seed value. That helps prevent unintended correlations between the data that can otherwise happen as a side effect of the random number generator.

Generate 2,500 rows for the Items table, 50,000 rows for Users, and 5,000,000 rows for Votes.

Data Source View

With your schema and data in place, you're ready to start building a cube. To have the correct project type available, you should install SQL Server client tools on your machine first, either as part of installing a local instance of SQL Server or separately, but using the same installer. You can walk through the following example using either Business Intelligence Development Studio (BIDS), which is a special version of Visual Studio that's installed with the SQL Server client tools, or a regular version of Visual Studio:

1. Right-click your solution in **Solution Explorer**, select **Add ➤ New Project**, and then select **Business Intelligence Projects** in the **Project types** panel on the left and **Analysis Services Project** in the **Templates** panel on the right. Call the project SampleCube, and click **OK**.

2. In the new project, right-click **Data Sources** and select **New Data Source** to start the **Data Source Wizard**. Click **Next**. In the **Select how to define the connection** dialog box, configure a connection to the relational database that has the schema and data you created in the previous section.

3. Click **Next** again. In the **Impersonation Information** dialog box, select **Use the Service Account**. SSAS needs to connect directly to the relational store in order to access the relational data. This tells SSAS to use the account under which the SSAS service is running to make that connection. This should work if you kept all the defaults during the installation process. If you've changed any of the security settings, you may need to assign a SQL Server Auth account or add access for the SSAS service account.

4. Click **Next**. In the **Completing the Wizard** dialog box, keep the default name, and click **Finish** to complete the creation of the data source.

5. Right-click **Data Source Views**, and select **New Data Source View** to bring up the **Data Source View Wizard**. Click **Next**, and select the data source you just created.

6. Click **Next** again. In the **Select Tables and Views** dialog box, for each of the three tables from your test schema, click the table name in the left panel, and then click the right-arrow button to move the table name into the right panel, as shown in Figure 9-1.

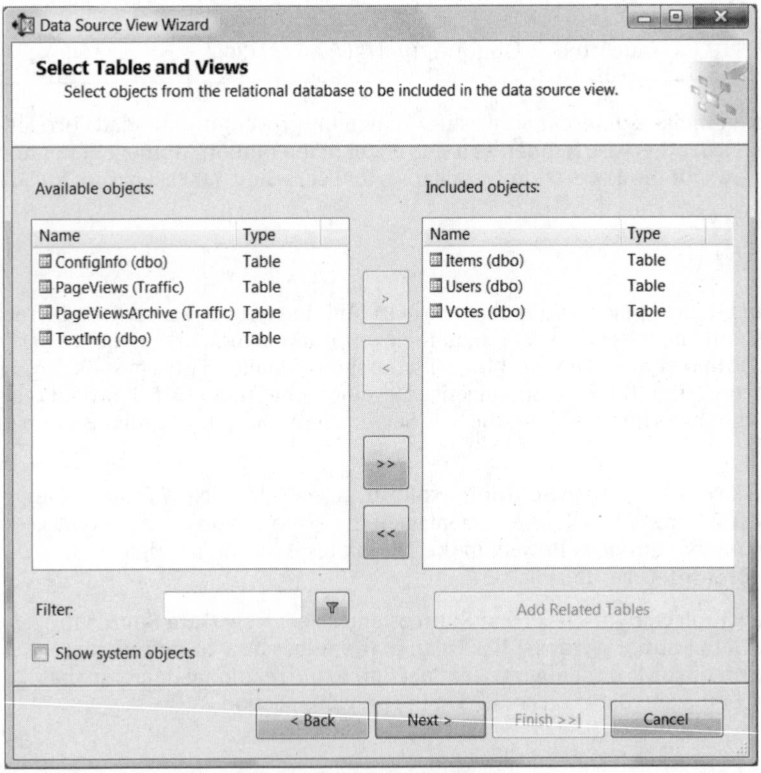

Figure 9-1. Select tables and views for the example cube.

7. Click **Next** to advance to the **Completing the Wizard** dialog box, accept the default name, and click **Finish**. Doing so displays the initial DSV, as in Figure 9-2.

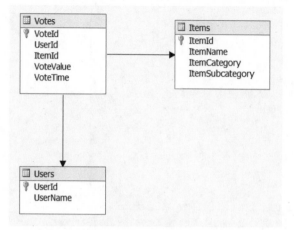

Figure 9-2. Initial data source view

You can see that the DSV shows primary keys with a small key icon. The arrows between the tables show how they're related.

When you build the cube, you want to be able to do analysis based on the date when users placed their votes. For that to work, you need to generate a different version of the VoteTime column that contains a pure date, rather than the mixed date and time created for you by the data generator. That way, the pure date can become a foreign key into a special table (dimension) you create a little later.

You can do this by adding a named calculation to the Votes table. Right-click the header of the Votes table, and select **New Named Calculation**. Call the column VoteDate, and enter CONVERT(DATETIME, CONVERT(DATE, [VoteTime])) for the expression, as shown in Figure 9-3. That converts the combined date and time to a DATE type (introduced in SQL Server 2008) and then back to a DATETIME type.

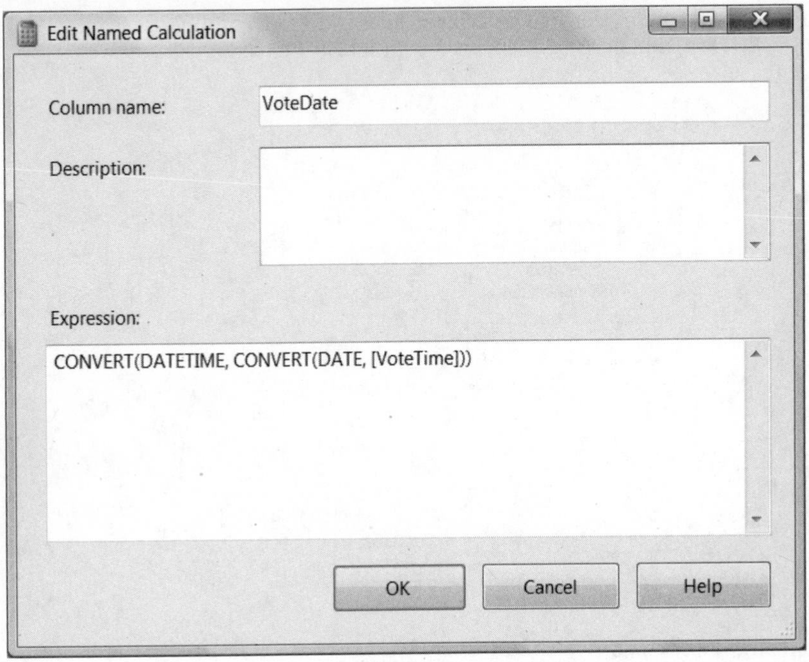

Figure 9-3. Create a named calculation.

Let's double-check that the named calculation is working correctly. Right-click the `Votes` table, and select **Explore Data**. Your results should look something like Figure 9-4, particularly in the sense that the times on the `VoteDate` column are all zero.

Table | Pivot Table | Chart | Pivot Chart

VoteId	UserId	ItemId	VoteValue	VoteTime	VoteDate
1	16920	1072	8	2009-01-25 11:58:35Z	2009-01-25 00:00:00Z
2	14223	1147	2	2009-06-22 20:40:52Z	2009-06-22 00:00:00Z
3	13150	149	10	2009-04-19 22:12:28Z	2009-04-19 00:00:00Z
4	31270	1199	9	2008-10-16 21:18:05Z	2008-10-16 00:00:00Z
5	23175	675	1	2009-01-20 09:29:50Z	2009-01-20 00:00:00Z

Figure 9-4. Using Explore Data to double-check the `VoteDate` named calculation

Cube

To create the cube, follow these steps:

1. Right-click **Cubes** in **Solution Explorer**, and select **New Cube** to open the **Cube Wizard**.

2. Click **Next**. In the **Select Creation Method** dialog box, accept the default of **Use existing tables**, because you want to create a cube based on the tables in your data source.

3. Click **Next**. In the **Select Measure Group Tables** dialog box, select the `Votes` table. That is your fact table, which forms the core of your measure group. Measure groups can contain more than one fact table.

4. Click **Next**. In the **Select Measures** dialog box, keep the default selections, with both **Vote Value** and **Votes Count** selected. *Measures* are numeric quantities (usually aggregations) that are associated with a fact table, such as counts and sums.

5. Click **Next**. In the **Select Dimensions** dialog box, keep the default selections, which include both the `Users` and `Items` tables. *Dimensions* contain primary keys and usually one or more strings that are associated with those keys (such as `UserName`).

6. Click **Next**. In the **Completing the Wizard** dialog box, keep the default name, and click **Finish**. When it completes, you should see a diagram that looks very similar to the DSV in Figure 9-2, except the fact table now has a yellow title and the dimensions have blue titles.

Although it's possible to build and deploy the cube at this point, before you can make any useful queries against it, you must add a time dimension and add the string columns from the `Items` and `Users` tables to the list of fields that are part of those dimensions.

Time Dimension

The time dimension will hold the primary keys for the `VoteDate` calculated member column you added to the DSV, which will be the foreign key.

To add the time dimension, follow these steps:

1. Right-click **Dimension** in Solution Explorer, and select **Add New Dimension** to open the Dimension Wizard.

2. Click **Next**. In the **Select Creation Method** dialog box, select **Generate a time table on the server**. Unlike the other two dimensions, this one will exist in SSAS only; it won't be derived from a relational table.

3. Click **Next**. In the **Define Time Periods** dialog box, set the earliest date for your data as the **First Calendar Day** and the end of 2009 for the **Last Calendar Day**. In the **Time Periods** section, select **Year**, **Half Year**, **Quarter**, **Month**, **Week**, and **Date**, as in Figure 9-5. Those are the periods SSAS will aggregate for you and that you can easily query against.

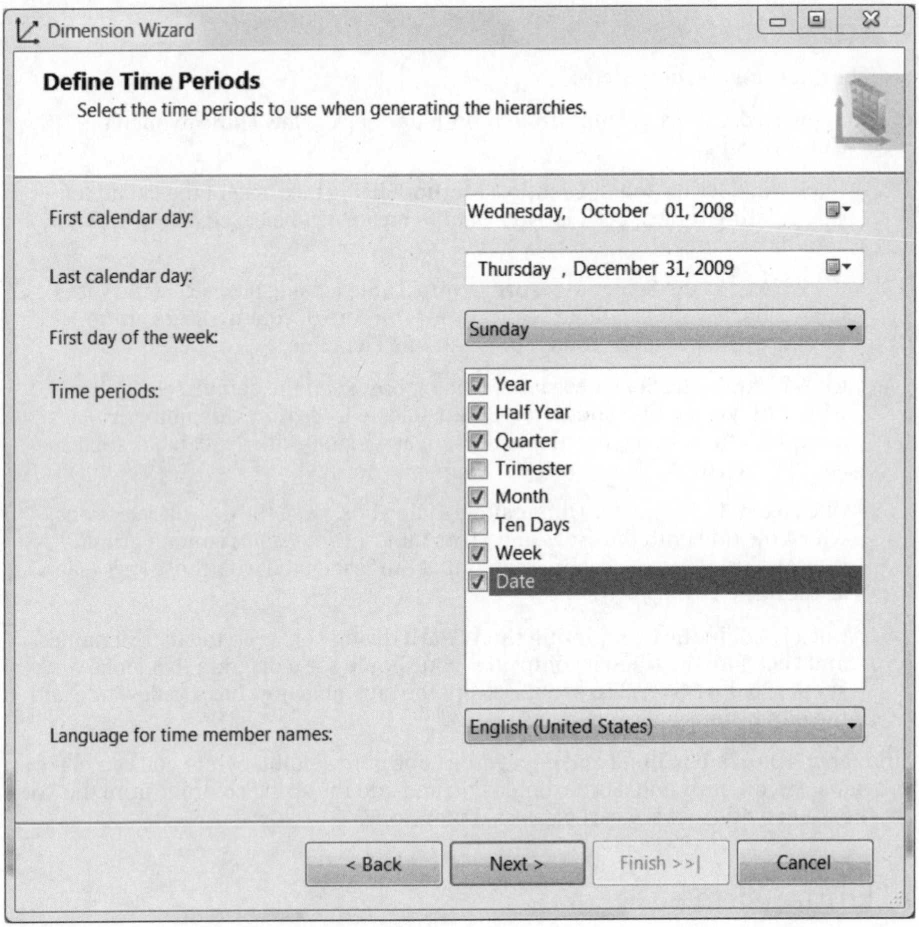

Figure 9-5. Define time periods for the time dimension.

4. Click **Next**. In the **Select Calendars** dialog box, keep the default selection of **Regular calendar**.

5. Click **Next**. In the **Completing the Wizard** dialog box, keep the default name, and click **Finish**. You should see the **Dimension designer** for the new wizard, which you can close.

6. After creating the dimension table, you need to associate it with a column in the **Votes** fact table. To do that, open the cube designer, select the **Dimension Usage** tab, right-click the background of the panel, and select **Add Cube Dimension**. In the dialog box that comes up, select the **Time** dimension, and click **OK**. Doing so adds a **Time** dimension row to the list of dimensions on the left of the **Dimension Usage** panel.

7. Click the box at the intersection of the **Time** row and the **Votes** column, and then click the button on the right side of that box to bring up the **Define Relationship** dialog box. Select a **Regular** relationship type, set the **Granularity attribute** to **Date**, and set the **Measure Group Column** to VoteDate, as in Figure 9-6. That's your new date-only calculated column with the time details removed so that you can use it as a foreign key into to the **Time** dimension.

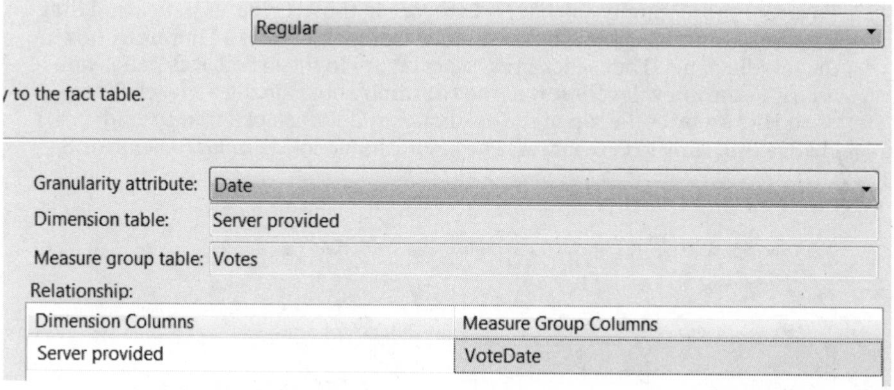

Figure 9-6. Define the relationship between the Time dimension and the VoteDate column.

8. Click **OK**. The **Dimension Usage** panel shows the new relationship, as in Figure 9-7.

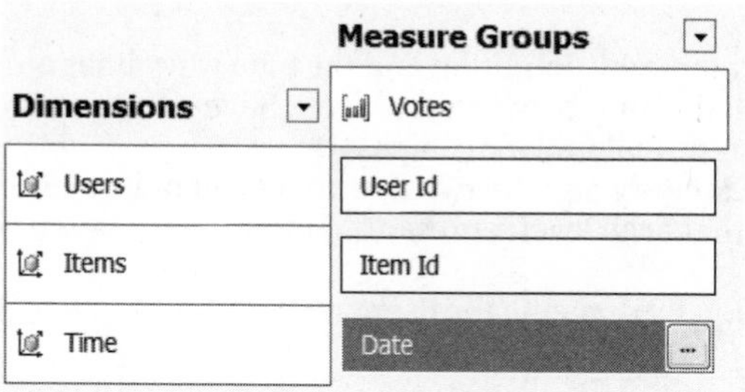

Figure 9-7. The Dimension Usage panel after adding the Time dimension

Items and Users Dimensions

Although the cube-creation wizard added dimensions for the Items and Users tables, they only contain an ID field. To be useful for queries, you need to add the string columns as dimension attributes. For the Items dimension, you also define a hierarchy that shows how ItemSubcategory is related to ItemCategory:

1. Double-click **Items.dim** in **Solution Explorer** to open the dimension designer. Click ItemName in the **Data Source View** panel on the right, and drag it to the **Attributes** panel on the left. Repeat for ItemCategory and ItemSubcategory.

2. To create the hierarchy, click Item Category in the Attributes panel, and drag it to the **Hierarchies** panel in the middle. Doing so creates a **Hierarchy** box in the middle panel. Then, click Item Subcategory in the Attributes panel, and drag it to the **<new level>** row in the **Hierarchy** box. Finally, right-click the word **Hierarchy** at the top of the box in the middle, select **Rename**, and change the name to Categories. The result should look similar to Figure 9-8.

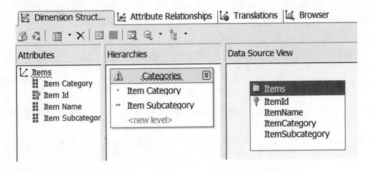

Figure 9-8. Dimension designer for the Items dimension

The warning triangle at upper left in the hierarchy definition and the blue wavy lines are there to remind you that you haven't established a relationship between the levels. Such a relationship could be a self-join in the original table, such as for parent-child relationships.

Notice the single dot to the left of **Item Category** and the two dots to the left of **Item Subcategory**. Those are reminders of the amount of detail that each level represents. Fewer dots means a higher level in the hierarchy and therefore less detail.

Repeat the process for the Users dimension by dragging the UserName column from the **Data Source View** to the **Attributes** panel.

Calculated Member

To determine the most popular Items on your site, one of the things you're interested in is the average vote. You can calculate that by taking the sum of the VoteValues for the period or other slice you're interested in and dividing by the number of votes.

To define the calculation, open the cube designer by double-clicking **Sample.cube**. Select the **Calculations** tab at the top of the designer, and click the **New Calculated Member** icon button (hover over a button to see a tooltip with the button's name). Set the name of the calculation to [`Vote Ave`], and set the expression to the following:

```
[Measures].[Vote Value] / [Measures].[Votes Count]
```

Regardless of whether you query by date or by `ItemCategory` or any other dimension attribute, SSAS uses the corresponding sum and count for just the data you request.

Next, set the **Format string** to `"0.000"` to indicate that the average should include three digits to the right of the decimal place, as in Figure 9-9.

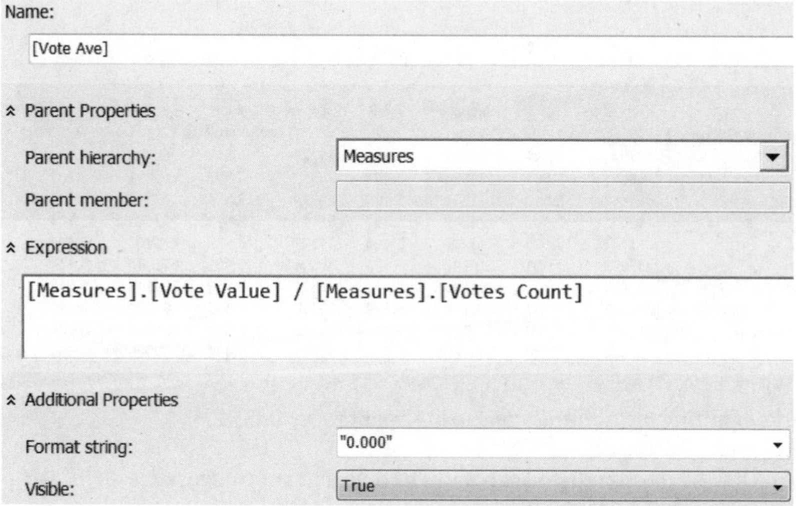

Name:

    [Vote Ave]

⋩ Parent Properties

    Parent hierarchy: Measures

    Parent member:

⋩ Expression

```
[Measures].[Vote Value] / [Measures].[Votes Count]
```

⋩ Additional Properties

    Format string: "0.000"

    Visible: True

Figure 9-9. Define a calculated member for determining the average vote.

Deploy and Test

Now, you're ready to deploy the cube to the server and to do some initial testing:

1. Right-click **SampleCube** in **Solution Explorer**, and select **Deploy**. Doing so sends the cube definition to SSAS and tells it to use the DSV to read the data it needs from the relational database and to process the cube.

2. Back in the cube designer, click the **Browse** tab. You see a list of measures and dimensions on the left and a reporting panel on the right. Notice the areas that say **Drop Column Fields Here**, **Drop Row Fields Here**, and **Drop Totals or Detail Fields Here**.

3. Expand the **Votes** measure in the left panel, and drag **Vote Count** into the center **Detail Fields** area. Doing so shows the total number of rows in the **Votes** table, which is 5 million. Repeat the process with the **Vote Ave** calculated member to see the average value of all votes. Notice that **Vote Ave** has three digits to the right of the decimal point, as you specified in the **Format String**.

4. Expand the **Items** dimension, and drag **Item Category** to the **Row Fields** area. Notice how the counts and averages expand to show details based on the row values. Repeat the process for Item **Subcategory**, drop it to the right of the **Category** column, and expand the **Business** category to see its subcategories.

5. Expand the **Time** dimension, and drag **Half Year** to the **Column Fields** area. The final results are shown in Figure 9-10.

Item Category ▾	Item Subcategory ▾	Half Year ▾							
		Semester 2, 2008		Semester 1, 2009		Semester 2, 2009		Grand Total	
		Votes Count	Vote Ave	Votes Count	Vote Ave	Votes Count	Vote Ave	Votes Count	Vote Ave
⊟ Business	Articles	75759	5.509	148482	5.512	25779	5.517	250020	5.512
	Comments	78806	5.509	154878	5.499	26337	5.505	260021	5.503
	Images	86986	5.500	171452	5.495	29329	5.514	287767	5.498
	Total	241551	5.506	474812	5.502	81445	5.512	797808	5.504
⊞ Entertainment		251657	5.505	493539	5.496	84507	5.489	829703	5.498
⊞ Health		263932	5.481	518448	5.503	88646	5.481	871026	5.494
⊞ News		245039	5.507	481593	5.500	82511	5.483	809143	5.500
⊞ Science		271908	5.501	532669	5.499	90959	5.485	895536	5.498
⊞ Sports		241694	5.502	473747	5.506	81343	5.502	796784	5.504
Grand Total		1515781	5.500	2974808	5.501	509411	5.492	5000000	5.500

Figure 9-10. Results of testing the example cube using the Browser in SSAS

Notice how the calculations for the intermediate aggregates of date and subcategory are all calculated automatically without any additional coding.

Example MDX Queries

Here's a T-SQL query to determine the total number of rows in the **Votes** table in the relational database:

```
select
    COUNT(*) [Votes Count]
    FROM [Votes]
```

The result is

	Votes Count
1	5000000

After running `CHECKPOINT` and `DBCC DROPCLEANBUFFERS` on my desktop machine, that takes about 18 seconds to run and has about 20,000 disk reads.

To use the cube from your web site, you query it using MDX. Use SSMS to test your queries.

After connecting to the relational database as you have before, click **Connect** in **Object Explorer**, select **Analysis Services**, provide the appropriate credentials, and click the **Connect** button. After it connects, expand the **Databases** menu, right-click **SampleCube**, and select **New Query ➤ MDX**.

Now you can execute the following MDX query, which is equivalent to the earlier T-SQL query:

```
SELECT
    [Measures].[Votes Count] ON COLUMNS
    FROM [Sample]
```

Votes Count
5000000

This says to use the `Votes Count` measure on the columns with the `Sample` cube. You can't use SSMS to get time information from SSAS as you can with the relational database, but you can use SQL Profiler. It shows that the query takes about 2ms.

Next, let's look at the number of votes for the month of January 2009, grouped by `ItemCategory`. Here's the T-SQL query and its result:

```
SELECT i.ItemCategory, COUNT(*) [Votes Count]
    FROM [Votes] v
    INNER JOIN [Items] i ON i.ItemId = v.ItemId
    WHERE v.VoteTime BETWEEN '20090101' AND '20090201'
    GROUP BY ROLLUP(i.ItemCategory)
    ORDER BY i.ItemCategory
```

	ItemCategory	Votes Count
1	NULL	508692
2	Business	81054
3	Entertainment	84360
4	Health	88659
5	News	82645
6	Science	91122
7	Sports	80852

With an empty cache, that takes about 6.8 seconds to execute, still with about 20,000 disk reads. However, recall from the previous chapter that columns used to select a group of rows are good candidates for indexes. The estimated query plan tells you that you're missing an index, so let's create it:

```
CREATE NONCLUSTERED INDEX [VotesTimeIX]
    ON [Votes] ([VoteTime])
    INCLUDE ([ItemId])
```

Repeating the query with an empty cache shows that the execution time is now only 0.7 seconds, with about 1,400 disk reads. Let's see how SSAS compares.

Here's the equivalent MDX query and its result:

```
SELECT
        [Measures].[Votes Count] ON COLUMNS,
        [Items].[Item Category].Members ON ROWS
        FROM [Sample]
        WHERE [Time].[Month].[January 2009]
```

	Votes Count
All	508692
Business	81054
Entertainment	84360
Health	88659
News	82645
Science	91122
Sports	80852
Unknown	(null)

You are specifying Votes Count for the columns again, but this time the Members of the Item Category dimension are the rows. The Members include the children, such as Business, Entertainment, and so on, along with the special All member, which refers to the total.

You use the WHERE clause to specify a filter for the data that appears in the middle of the result table. In this case, you want the data for January 2009. The result is the intersection of ROWS, COLUMNS, and the WHERE clause: Votes Counts for Item Categories in January 2009.

SQL Profiler tells me that this query takes 3ms or 4ms to execute, which is well below the 700ms for its relational equivalent. This also avoids the 1,400 disk reads on the relational side and the associated reduction in memory available for other queries.

Next, let's filter those results to show the Health row only. Here's the relational query and its result:

```
SELECT
    COUNT(*) Health
    FROM [Votes] v
    INNER JOIN [Items] i ON i.ItemId = v.ItemId
    WHERE v.VoteTime BETWEEN '20090101' AND '20090201'
    AND i.ItemCategory = 'Health'
```

	Health
1	88659

You just check for the Health category in the WHERE clause.

Here's the MDX equivalent and its result:

```
SELECT
    [Measures].[Votes Count] ON COLUMNS,
    [Items].[Item Category].&[Health] ON ROWS
    FROM [Sample]
    WHERE [Time].[Month].[January 2009]
```

	Votes Count
Health	88659

Instead of including all the Item Category members on the rows, you include only the Health row by specifying its name, preceded by an ampersand. The WHERE clause is unchanged.

Rather than getting too distracted with T-SQL, let's focus on the MDX only from now on. You can apply the same pattern from earlier to look at average vote values for each Item:

```
SELECT
    [Measures].[Vote Ave] ON COLUMNS,
    [Items].[Item Name].Children ON ROWS
    FROM [Sample]
    WHERE [Time].[Month].[January 2009]
```

	Vote Ave
Aajglbp Gvg	5.597
Abie Pydlvt Ochqsq	5.486
Abxn Epgtxfyy	5.206
Acdzl	5.437
Acoxphmanc	5.263
Actuwazeys Im Cdrxbabzk	5.024
Acyjmknu Rstnqansa Fvbzmjrmua	5.648

Vote Ave is the calculated member you defined earlier. For this query, you're using Children instead of Members, which excludes the total from the All member. This query returns one row for each of the 2,500 Items. Let's filter the results to return only the Items with the top five highest average vote values:

```
SELECT
    [Measures].[Vote Ave] ON COLUMNS,
    TOPCOUNT(
        [Items].[Item Name].Children,
        5,
        [Measures].[Vote Avg]
        ) ON ROWS
    FROM [Sample]
    WHERE [Time].[Month].[January 2009]
```

	Vote Ave
Ajozyjqbhl	6.505
Pdobipinkma	6.392
Oohaumgq V	6.344
Rpsodvlu Ddfbwtwdelo	6.288
Itdsnrl Weaglawp Ghmsqgkyfz	6.258

You use the TOPCOUNT() function to select the top five.

So far, your query results have had only a single column. Let's look at the number of votes by Item Category, split out by Quarter:

```
SELECT
    [Time].[Quarter].Children ON COLUMNS,
    [Items].[Item Category].Children ON ROWS
    FROM [Sample]
    WHERE [Measures].[Votes Count]
```

	Quarter 4, 2008	Quarter 1, 2009	Quarter 2, 2009	Quarter 3, 2009	Quarter 4, 2009
Business	241551	235704	239108	81445	(null)
Entertainment	251657	245650	247889	84507	(null)
Health	263932	257582	260866	88646	(null)
News	245039	239363	242230	82511	(null)
Science	271908	265088	267581	90959	(null)
Sports	241694	235086	238661	81343	(null)
Unknown	(null)	(null)	(null)	(null)	(null)

To do that, you specify the Children of the Quarter dimension as the columns. However, that result includes some null rows and columns, because you don't have any Unknown items (Unknown is another default Member) and because you don't have any Votes in Quarter 4, 2009.

Let's filter out the null rows and columns:

```
SELECT
    NONEMPTY([Time].[Quarter].Children,
        [Items].[Item Category].Children) ON COLUMNS,
    NONEMPTY([Items].[Item Category].Children,
        [Time].[Quarter].Children) ON ROWS
    FROM [Sample]
    WHERE [Measures].[Votes Count]
```

	Quarter 4, 2008	Quarter 1, 2009	Quarter 2, 2009	Quarter 3, 2009
Business	241551	235704	239108	81445
Entertainment	251657	245650	247889	84507
Health	263932	257582	260866	88646
News	245039	239363	242230	82511
Science	271908	265088	267581	90959
Sports	241694	235086	238661	81343

The NONEMPTY() function selects non-null entries with respect to its second argument and the WHERE clause. For example, the first call says to return only Children of the Quarter dimension that have a non-null Votes Count for all of the Item Category Children.

Let's show just the results for the Health Category and include a breakdown by Subcategory:

```
SELECT
    NONEMPTY([Time].[Quarter].Children,
        [Items].[Item Category].Children) ON COLUMNS,
    ([Items].[Item Category].&[Health],
            [Items].[Item Subcategory].Children) ON ROWS
    FROM [Sample]
    WHERE [Measures].[Votes Count]
```

		Quarter 4, 2008	Quarter 1, 2009	Quarter 2, 2009	Quarter 3, 2009
Health	Articles	79419	77668	78716	26953
Health	Comments	90801	88117	89518	30378
Health	Images	93712	91797	92632	31315

Including the Health Category and the Subcategory Children together inside parentheses is an MDX syntax that indicates they are a *tuple*. That's how you specify that you want to show the Subcategories of the Health Category. In the results, notice that each row has two labels, one for each member of the tuple.

Next, let's say that you want to see the Votes Count totals for the Health Category for the three days ending on March 7, 2009:

```
SELECT
    LASTPERIODs(
        3,
        [Time].[Date].[Saturday, March 07 2009]
        ) ON COLUMNS,
    [Items].[Item Category].&[Health] ON ROWS
    FROM [Sample]
    WHERE [Measures].[Votes Count]
```

	Thursday, March 05 2009	Friday, March 06 2009	Saturday, March 07 2009
Health	2813	2824	2881

The LASTPERIODS() function uses the position of the specified date in its dimension and includes the requested number of periods by using sibling nodes in the dimension. If you replaced the date in the query with a Quarter, the query results would show three quarters instead of three days.

Next, let's take the sum of those three days:

```
WITH
    MEMBER [Measures].[Last3Days]
            AS 'SUM(LASTPERIODS(3, [Time].[Date].[Saturday, March 07 2009]),
                    [Measures].[Votes Count])'
        SELECT
                [Measures].[Last3Days] ON COLUMNS,
                [Items].[Item Category].&[Health] ON ROWS
                FROM [Sample]
```

	Last3Days
Health	8518

You don't have a dimension for those three days together, like you do for full weeks, months, quarters, and so on, so you have to calculate the result using the SUM() function. You use the WITH MEMBER clause to define a temporary calculated member, which you then use in the associated SELECT statement. The arguments to the SUM() function are the date range and the measure that you want to sum over those dates.

Next, let's extend that query further by including a sum of the Vote Values for those three days, as well as the average Vote Value. Let's also look at those values for the top five Items, based on their average vote value:

```
WITH
    MEMBER [Measures].[Last3DaysCount]
        AS 'SUM(LASTPERIODS(3, [Time].[Date].[Saturday, March 07 2009]),
            ([Measures].[Votes Count]))'
    MEMBER [Measures].[Last3DaysSum]
        AS 'SUM(LASTPERIODS(3, [Time].[Date].[Saturday, March 07 2009]),
            ([Measures].[Vote Value]))'
    MEMBER [Measures].[Last3DaysAvg]
        AS '[Measures].[Last3DaysSum] / [Measures].[Last3DaysCount]',
            FORMAT_STRING = '0.000'
SELECT
    {[Measures].[Last3DaysCount],
        [Measures].[Last3DaysSum],
        [Measures].[Last3DaysAvg]
        } ON COLUMNS,
    TOPCOUNT(
        [Items].[Item Name].Children,
        5,
        [Measures].[Last3DaysAvg]) ON ROWS
    FROM [Sample]
```

	Last3DaysCount	Last3DaysSum	Last3DaysAvg
Wiocjljjb Rque	14	120	8.571
Kpjjyluiu Daonpovc Pgmxqlhv	19	161	8.474
Vlvlj	18	145	8.056
Mrhnfdgmm Tfcnsfl Wm	18	144	8.000
Gzrkf Dejwmabayn	16	126	7.875

To include the three different calculated members in the columns, you specify them as a *set* using curly braces. Notice too that you specify a format string for `Last3DaysAvg`, as you did for `Vote Ave` when you were building the cube.

MDX is a powerful language that's capable of much more than I've outlined here. Even so, the syntax and capabilities covered in this section should be enough for you to offload a number of aggregation queries from your relational database, including sums, counts, averages, topcount, lastperiods, and summaries by multiple dates or periods.

ADOMD.NET

Before you can query SSAS from your web application, you need to download and install the ADOMD.NET library, because it's not included with the standard .NET distribution. It's part of the Microsoft SQL Server Feature Pack. You can download the October 2008 version for SQL Server 2008 from the following URL:

```
http://www.microsoft.com/downloads/
    details.aspx?displaylang=en&FamilyID=228de03f-3b5a-428a-923f-58a033d316e1
```

After completing the installation, right-click your web site in **Solution Explorer**, and select **Add Reference**. On the **.NET** tab of the dialog box, select the latest version of **Microsoft.AnalysisServices.AdomdClient**, and click **OK**. See Figure 9-11.

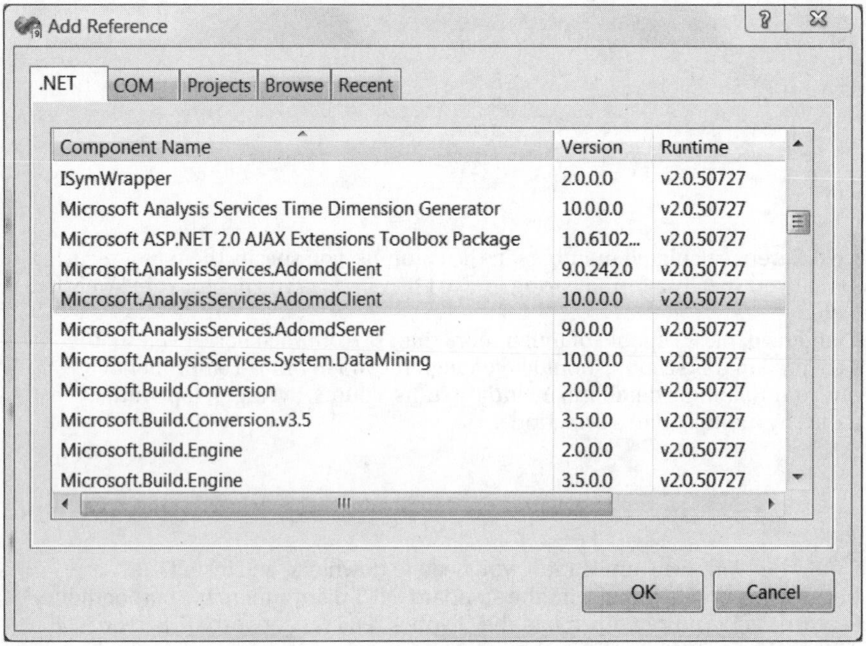

Figure 9-11. *Add a reference to the ADOMD.NET library.*

Example with a Single-Cell Result

For the first example, let's make a web page that displays a single result from an MDX query. In particular, the query retrieves the total number of votes for the Health Category for January 2009.

First, create a new web form called mdx1.aspx, and edit the markup as follows:

```
<%@ Page Language="C#" EnableViewState="false" AutoEventWireup="false"
    CodeFile="mdx1.aspx.cs" Inherits="mdx1" %>
<!DOCTYPE html PUBLIC "-//W3C//DTD XHTML 1.0 Transitional//EN"
    "http://www.w3.org/TR/xhtml1/DTD/xhtml1-transitional.dtd">
<html xmlns="http://www.w3.org/1999/xhtml">
<body>
Total
<asp:Label ID="RowName" runat="server" />
votes for January 2009:
<asp:Label ID="TotHealthVotes" runat="server" />
</body>
</html>
```

The markup mainly has two `<asp:Label>` controls, which you use to display the results. Here's the code-behind:

```
using System;
using System.Web.UI;
using Microsoft.AnalysisServices.AdomdClient;

public partial class mdx1 : Page
{
    private const string connStr = "data source=.;initial catalog=SampleCube";

    protected override void OnLoad(EventArgs e)
    {
        base.OnLoad(e);
        using (AdomdConnection conn = new AdomdConnection(connStr))
        {
            const string mdx = "SELECT " +
                    "[Measures].[Votes Count] ON COLUMNS, " +
                    "[Items].[Item Category].&[Health] ON ROWS " +
                    "FROM [Sample] " +
                    "WHERE [Time].[Month].[January 2009]";
            using (AdomdCommand cmd = new AdomdCommand(mdx, conn))
            {
                conn.Open();
                var reader = cmd.ExecuteReader();
                if (reader.Read())
                {
                    this.RowName.Text = reader[0].ToString();
                    this.TotHealthVotes.Text = reader[1].ToString();
                }
            }
        }
    }
}
```

You can see that the code pattern for using ADOMD.NET is analogous to standard ADO.NET. You are mainly just replacing `SqlConnection` with `AdomdConnection`, and `SqlCommand` with `AdomdCommand`. The library doesn't have a native asynchronous interface like ADO.NET, so you're using a synchronous page.

One difference compared with the relational database is that you have to include the full text of the MDX query, because SSAS doesn't support stored procedures in the same way. The result set is also somewhat different, because each row can have labels, in addition to each column. The difference isn't too noticeable here, because the result has only one row, with a label in column 0 and the result in column 1. It is more apparent in the next example.

When you run the page, it displays the following:

```
Total Health votes for January 2009: 88659
```

You can use a query like this to avoid executing the equivalent aggregation query on the relational side. In a production system, you may want to cache the result at your web tier to avoid executing the query more often than necessary.

Displaying a Multiple-Row Result Using a GridView

For the next example, let's display the results of an MDX query that returns a number of rows. Let's look at the number of votes for each Category for January 2009.

Here's the markup for mdx2.aspx:

```
<%@ Page Language="C#" EnableViewState="false" AutoEventWireup="false"
    CodeFile="mdx2.aspx.cs" Inherits="mdx2" %>
<!DOCTYPE html PUBLIC "-//W3C//DTD XHTML 1.0 Transitional//EN"
    "http://www.w3.org/TR/xhtml1/DTD/xhtml1-transitional.dtd">
<html xmlns="http://www.w3.org/1999/xhtml">
<head runat="server">
    <title></title>
</head>
<body>
    <form id="form1" runat="server">
    <div>
        <asp:GridView ID="MdxGrid" runat="server" />
    </div>
    </form>
</body>
</html>
```

You have an <asp:GridView> control that holds the results.

Here's the code-behind:

```
using System;
using System.Data;
using System.Web.UI;
using Microsoft.AnalysisServices.AdomdClient;

public partial class mdx2 : Page
{
    private const string connStr = "data source=.;initial catalog=SampleCube";

    protected override void OnLoad(EventArgs e)
    {
        base.OnLoad(e);
        using (AdomdConnection conn = new AdomdConnection(connStr))
        {
            const string mdx = "SELECT " +
                            "[Measures].[Votes Count] ON COLUMNS, " +
                            "[Items].[Item Category].Members ON ROWS " +
                            "FROM [Sample] " +
                            "WHERE [Time].[Month].[January 2009]";
            using (AdomdCommand cmd = new AdomdCommand(mdx, conn))
            {
                conn.Open();
                CellSet cs = cmd.ExecuteCellSet();
                DataTable dt = new DataTable();
                dt.Columns.Add(" ");
```

```
        Axis columns = cs.Axes[0];
        TupleCollection columnTuples = columns.Set.Tuples;
        for (int i = 0; i < columnTuples.Count; i++)
        {
            dt.Columns.Add(columnTuples[i].Members[0].Caption);
        }
        Axis rows = cs.Axes[1];
        TupleCollection rowTuples = rows.Set.Tuples;
        int rowNum = 0;
        foreach (Position rowPos in rows.Positions)
        {
            DataRow dtRow = dt.NewRow();
            int colNum = 0;
            dtRow[colNum++] = rowTuples[rowNum].Members[0].Caption;
            foreach (Position colPos in columns.Positions)
            {
                dtRow[colNum++] =
                    cs.Cells[colPos.Ordinal, rowPos.Ordinal].FormattedValue;
            }
            dt.Rows.Add(dtRow);
            rowNum++;
        }
        this.MdxGrid.DataSource = dt;
        this.MdxGrid.DataBind();
    }
  }
 }
}
```

The outer structure of the code is the same as the first example, with AdomdConnection and AdomdCommand. However, this time you're using ExecuteCellSet() to run the query. It returns a CellSet object, which is the multidimensional equivalent of a DataTable. Unfortunately, you can't bind a CellSet directly to the GridView control, so you have to do some work to transform it into a DataTable, which you can then bind to the grid.

See Figure 9-12 for the results.

	Votes Count
All	508692
Business	81054
Entertainment	84360
Health	88659
News	82645
Science	91122
Sports	80852
Unknown	

Figure 9-12. Web page containing a multirow MDX query result

Updating Your Cube with SSIS

As you've been developing your example cube, you are only pulling over new data from the relational engine when you manually reprocess the cube. SSAS retrieves data from the relational engine through the DSV you created along with the cube.

In a production environment, you would of course want to automate that process. One approach is to use SQL Server Integration Services (SSIS) to run a task that tells SSAS to process the cube in the same way as previously. You can then create a job in SQL Agent to run that task once a day or as often as you need it.

Let's walk through the process:

1. Right-click your solution in **Solution Explorer**, and select **Add ➤ Add New Project**. In the dialog box, select **Business Intelligence Projects** in the left panel and **Integration Services Project** on the right. Call the project SampleSSIS, and click **OK**.

2. Right-click SampleSSIS, and select **Add ➤ New Item**. Select **New SSIS Project**, call it ProcessCube.dtsx, and click **Add**. Doing so opens the SSIS package designer with the **Control Flow** tab selected by default.

3. Click the **Toolbox** panel, and drag **Analysis Services Processing Task** from the **Toolbox** to the surface of the SSIS package designer. See Figure 9-13.

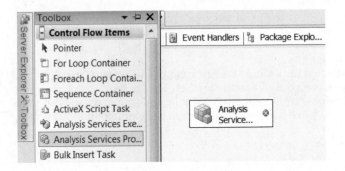

Figure 9-13. Adding the Analysis Services Processing task to the SSIS package

4. Double-click the task to open its task editor. Select **Processing Settings** in the left panel, and click **New** in the right panel to add a new connection manager. In the **Add Analysis Services Connection Manager** dialog box, click **Edit**. In the **Connection Manager** dialog box, define your connection parameters, and set the **Initial Catalog** to SampleCube. Click **Test Connection**, and then click **OK**. See Figure 9-14.

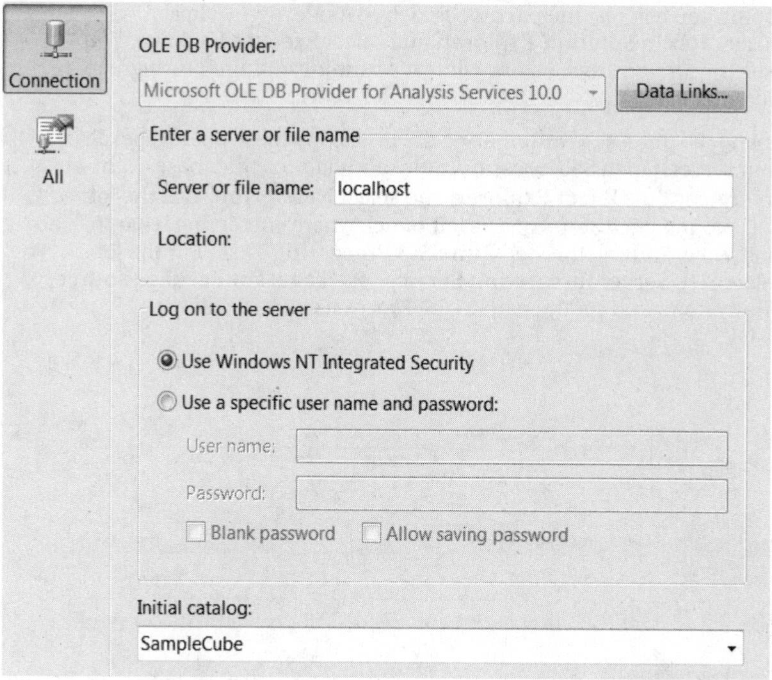

Figure 9-14. Adding a connection manager for the example cube

5.   Click **OK** again to get back to the **Analysis Services Processing Task Editor**.
     To specify the cube that you want to process, click **Add**, select **SampleCube**,
     and click **OK**. See Figure 9-15. Notice that by default **Process Options** is set to
     Process Full, which tells SSAS to re-create the data in the cube from scratch
     using the DSV you configured earlier. Click **OK** again to dismiss the editor.

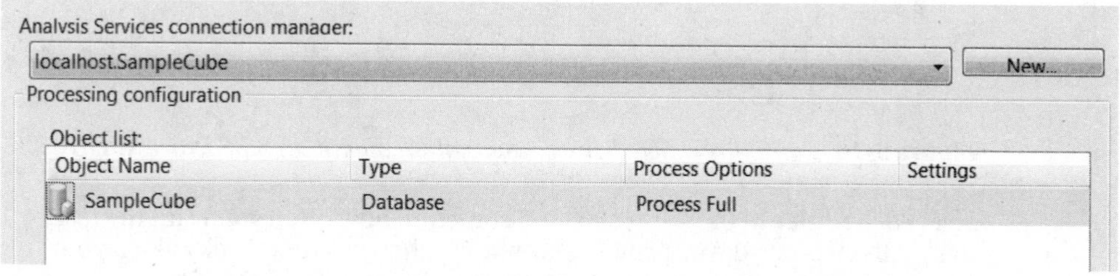

Figure 9-15. Configure the cube in the Analysis Services Processing Task Editor.

6. At this point, you can test the package in debug mode. Right-click
    `ProcessCube.dtsx` in **Solution Explorer**, and select **Execute Package**. You
    should see the task box turn yellow while it's running and then turn green
    when it completes.

7. To complete the process of automating the task, copy the `ProcessCube.dtsx`
    file to your server. Open SSMS, connect to your relational database, right-click
    SQL Server Agent in **Object Explorer**, and select **New ➤ Job**. Call the job
    `Process Cube`, and click **Steps** on the left panel, where you define what this job
    does. Click **New**, and call the step **Run SSIS Processing Task**. For the job
    Type, select **SQL Server Integration Services Package**. For **Package source**,
    select **File system**, and set the path to the `ProcessCube.dtsx` file. See Figure 9-
    16. Click **OK**.

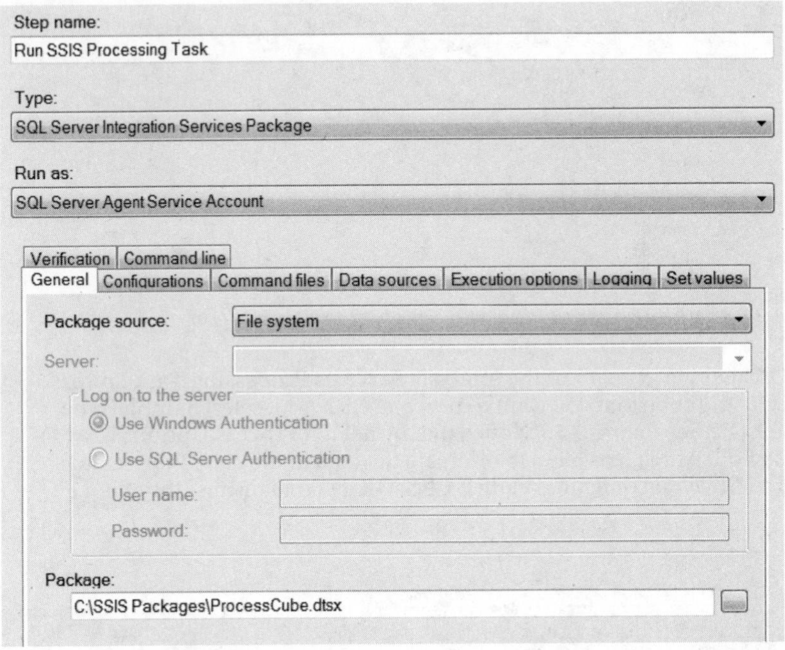

Figure 9-16. Configure a SQL Server Agent job step with an SSIS Processing Task.

8. Select **Schedules** in the left panel, and configure how often you want the task
    to run. If once-per-day processing is enough, choose a time of day when your
    site isn't busy to reduce the impact on your live site. Click **OK** to finish
    configuring the job.

After configuring the job, you can test it by right-clicking the job name in **Object Explorer** and selecting **Start job at step**.

The approaches to cube processing discussed so far have involved SSAS pulling data from the relational store. It is also possible to push data into SSAS using a different type of SSIS task. Pushing data is useful in cases where you also need to manipulate or transform your data in some way before importing it into a cube, although a staging database is preferable from a performance perspective (see the section on staging databases later in this chapter).

Proactive Caching

A much more efficient way to automate cube updates in your production environment is with a SQL Server Enterprise and Developer-only feature called *proactive caching*.

Data Storage Options

SSAS maintains two different types of data. One is measure group data, which includes your fact and dimension tables, also known as *leaf data*. The other is precalculated aggregations. You can configure SSAS to store each type of data either in a native SSAS-specific format or in the relational database. You have three options:

- Multidimensional OLAP, or *MOLAP* mode, stores both the measure group data and the aggregation data in SSAS. Aggregates and leaf data are stored in a set of files in the local filesystem. SSAS runs queries against those local files.

- Relational OLAP, or *ROLAP* mode, stores both the measure group data and the aggregation data in the relational database.

- Hybrid OLAP, or *HOLAP* mode, stores aggregations in local files and stores the leaf data in the relational database.

MOLAP mode generally provides the best query performance. However, it requires an import phase, which can be time-consuming with large datasets. ROLAP is generally the slowest. You can think of both ROLAP and HOLAP as being "real time" in the sense that OLAP queries reflect the current state of the relational data. Because those modes make direct use of your relational database during query processing, they also have an adverse effect on the performance of your database, effectively defeating one of your main motivations for using SSAS in the first place.

You can configure the storage mode from the **Partitions** tab in the cube designer. Right-click the default partition, and select **Storage Settings**. See Figure 9-17.

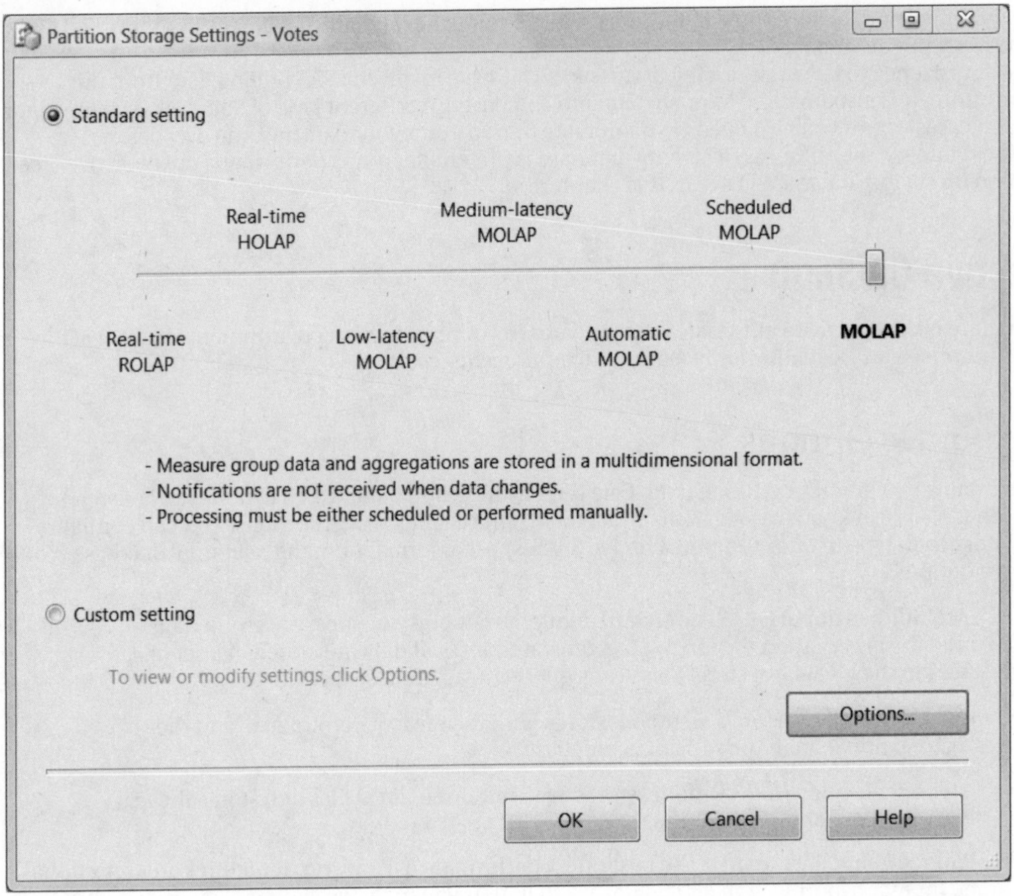

Figure 9-17. Partition storage settings

Caching Modes

SSAS supports several different processing-related settings for proactive caching. Click the **Options** button in the dialog box in Figure 9-17. See Figure 9-18.

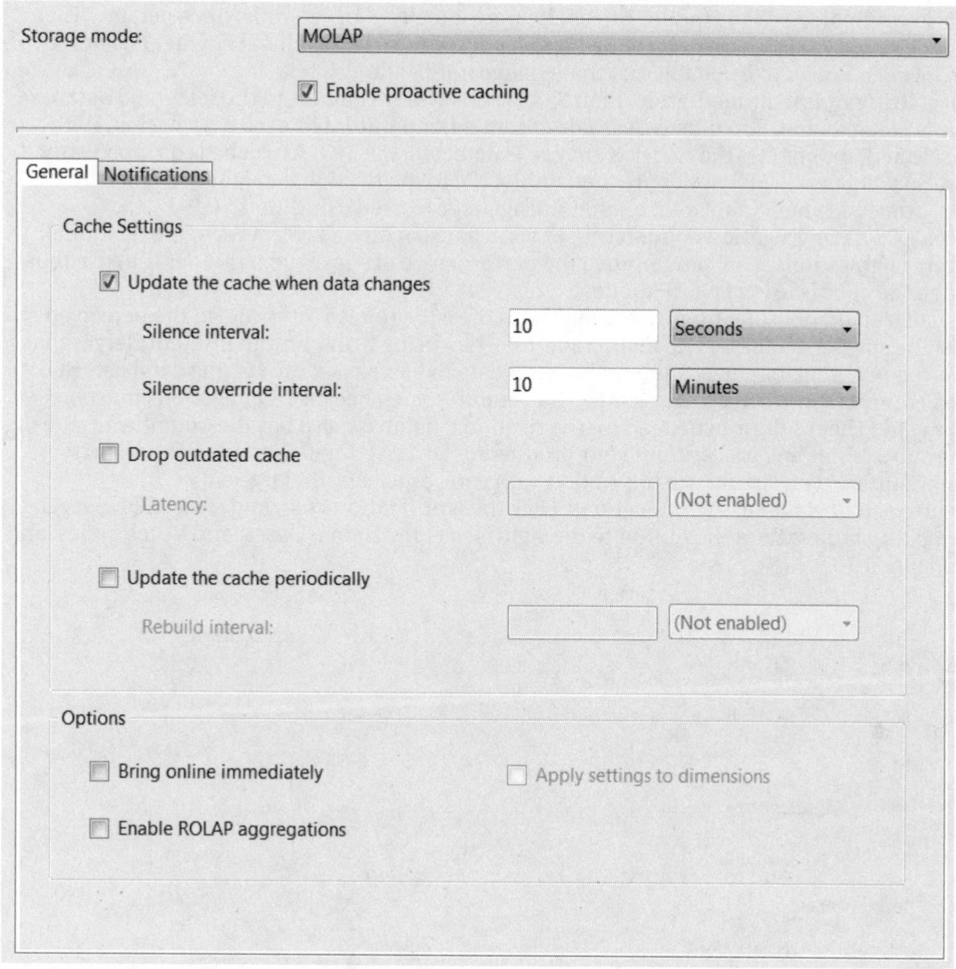

Figure 9-18. Proactive caching options

Select the **Enable proactive caching** check box to enable the options.

One option is to process the cube, also known as *updating the cache*, when SSAS receives a notification from the relational database that the data has changed. There are two parameters: the **silence interval** is how long SSAS should try to wait after the last change notification before processing the cube. **Silence override interval** is how long SSAS waits after receiving the first change notification, but without the silence interval being satisfied. The net effect is that if there is a short burst of activity on the staging database, SSAS processes the cube after the silence interval. If the activity goes on for a long time, then it delays processing until the silence override interval has passed.

The next option is whether SSAS should **Drop outdated cache** (the imported and processed data). The **Latency** parameter is the time from when it starts rebuilding the cube until when it drops the cache.

You can also configure SSAS to **Update the cache periodically**—for example, once per day. That mode does not depend on SSAS receiving change notifications from the relational engine. The other modes require Service Broker to be enabled so that change notifications work.

If you select **Bring online immediately**, then SSAS sends ROLAP queries to the relational database while the cube is being rebuilt. You must select this option if **Drop outdated cache** is selected. With both options selected, the effect is that when a change is detected, the MOLAP cache is dropped after the latency period. Subsequent OLAP queries are then redirected to the relational database using ROLAP. When the cube processing has completed, queries are again processed using MOLAP.

The **Enable ROLAP aggregations** option causes SSAS to use materialized views in the relational database to store aggregations. This can improve the performance of subsequent queries that use those aggregates when the cube is using ROLAP mode.

Together, you can use these settings to manage both the cube refresh interval and the perceived latency against the staging database. The main trade-off when using **Bring online immediately** is that although it has the potential to reduce latency after new data has arrived in the staging database, ROLAP queries may be considerably slower than their MOLAP counterparts, because aggregations must be computed on the fly. The resulting extra load on the relational database also has the potential of slowing down both the cube-rebuilding process and your production OLTP system. Therefore, although it's appealing on the surface, you should use this option with care, especially for large cubes.

To configure relational database notifications, click the **Notifications** tab, and select **SQL Server** and **Specify tracking tables**. Click the button to the right, select the **Items**, **Users**, and **Votes** tables, and click **OK**. See Figure 9-19.

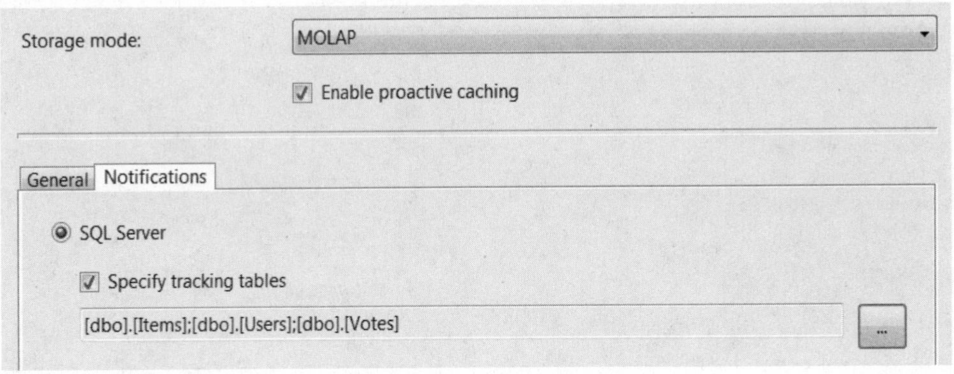

Figure 9-19. Specify SQL Server notifications for proactive caching.

■ **Note** Only tables are allowed for SQL Server notifications. The use of views or stored procedures is not supported.

After making the configuration changes, deploy the cube to the server so that the changes take effect.

You can test your proactive caching settings as follows. First, issue the following MDX query from SSMS, which shows the number of rows in the fact table:

```
SELECT
    [Measures].[Votes Count] ON COLUMNS
    FROM [Sample]
```

Next, make a change to the relational data by inserting a row into the Votes table:

```
INSERT INTO Votes
    (UserId, ItemId, VoteValue, VoteTime)
    OUTPUT INSERTED.VoteId
    VALUES
    (2, 2, 1, GETDATE())
```

After allowing enough time for your configured silence interval to pass, along with time to reprocess the cube, issue the MDX query again; you should see that the reported count has increased by one.

The achievable cube-refresh interval ultimately depends on factors such as the following:

- The amount of new data at each refresh

- Available hardware on both the relational database and the SSAS machines: CPU count and speed, amount of RAM, speed of disks and number of available LUNs or channels, and speed of the network between the machines

- Speed of the relational database, including both how fast it can deliver data to SSAS and how fast it can process aggregation queries in ROLAP mode

- If you're using SSIS for data import: how fast it can pull data from the production databases (query complexity, production database machine speed, and load during the ETL process)

- Amount of preaggregation done in each partition in the cube (additional preaggregation can improve the performance of some queries but requires more time during cube processing)

- Total number of dimension attributes

- Other performance-related parameters and settings in SSAS, such as partition configurations, hierarchies, and so on

Using a Staging Database

Although allowing SSAS to import data directly from your production relational database/OLTP system can be acceptable in some scenarios, it is often better from a performance and scalability perspective to use a staging database instead.

A *staging database* is another relational database that sits between your OLTP store and SSAS. It differs from your OLTP store in the following ways:

- It is organized structurally with a star snowflake schema that's similar to your cubes, with one or more central fact tables and associated dimension tables.

- It contains more historical data, leaving only reasonably current data on your OLTP system.

- You should configure the hardware to support bulk I/O, optimized for queries that return many more rows on average than your OLTP system.

Such a system is sometimes also called a *data warehouse*, although I prefer to use that term to refer to a collection of *data marts*, where each data mart contains an OLTP system, a staging database, and SSAS.

A staging database has the following benefits:

- You can run queries against the staging database without affecting the performance of your OLTP system.

- SSAS can import data from the staging database so the process doesn't burden your production OLTP system (although you still need to import data into the staging database).

- You can offload (partition) your OLTP database by moving older archival data into the staging database and keeping transaction tables relatively short.

- The staging database provides a solid base that you can use to rebuild cubes from scratch if needed, without adversely affecting the performance of your OLTP system.

A typical architecture involves using SSIS to create a database snapshot on your OLTP system and then pulling data from the snapshot (which helps keep it consistent), transforming it, and storing it in the staging database. SSAS then uses proactive caching to receive notifications when the staging database changes, and pulls data from there for processing your cubes. See Figure 9-20.

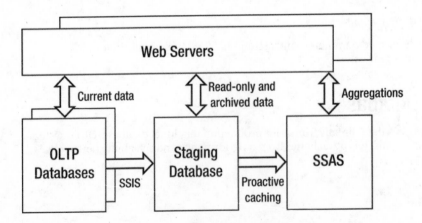

Figure 9-20. Data tier architecture with a staging database and SSAS

You can run production queries against all three data stores: the OLTP system for current data, the staging database for read-only and archived data, and SSAS for aggregation queries. You can run back-end reports from either the staging database or SSAS, or both.

During the ETL process, SSIS can perform functions such as the following:

- Data cleansing

- Ensuring fact table foreign keys are present as primary keys in the corresponding dimensions

- Removing unused columns

- Data denormalization (joins across multiple tables)

- Creating new columns that are derived from existing columns

- Replacing production keys with surrogate keys (optional, but recommended)

- Split tables into facts and dimensions (which should result in much smaller dimensions)

- Handling incremental updates so the entire staging database doesn't need to be rebuilt each time

While designing the SSIS packages to move data from your OLTP system to a staging database, you should also analyze each dimension and fact table:

- Which columns should be included? You should only include columns needed in the cube.

- Can rows in the table ever change? If so, a *slowly changing dimension* (SCD) will probably be required.

- How should changes be managed? Updated or historical?

- Are there any data transformations that should be done during the export, transform, and load (ETL) process, such as converting `DATETIME` values to date-only as in the example?

- Review the business keys on the relational side to make sure new ones are always increasing and to verify that there aren't any unexpected values (negative numbers, nulls, and so on).

- For fact tables that are also dimensions, fact columns should be extracted and placed into a separate table from the dimension columns.

- Look for optimizations that may be possible for the resulting dimension tables, such as removing duplicates.

As the amount of data that you are processing increases, there may eventually be a time when the structure of some queries should change for performance reasons. For example, if a multitable join for the fact tables gets too slow or puts too much of a load on the source database, you can replace it with a sequence of **Lookup** steps in the data flow.

Summary

In this chapter, I covered the following:

- Using SSAS to offload aggregation queries from your relational database and why that's important from a performance and scalability perspective

- Understanding SSAS and multidimensional databases

- Understanding some of the limitations of SSAS and ADOMD.NET

- Building an example cube

- Using example MDX queries against the sample cube

- Using ADOMD.NET to programmatically send MDX queries to SSAS and display the results on a web page

- Using SSIS and SQL Server Agent to update your cube

- Using proactive caching to reduce the latency between changes in your relational data and corresponding updates to your cubes

- Using a staging database to reduce the load on your OLTP server during cube processing

■ ■ ■

Infrastructure and Operations

Creating fast and scalable software is of course central to building an ultra-fast web site. However, the design of your production hardware and network environment, the process of deploying your software into production, and the process you follow to keep everything running smoothly are also vitally important factors.

Most web sites are evolving entities; their performance and character change over time as you add and remove code and pages, as your traffic increases, and as the amount of data you are managing increases. Even if your end-to-end system is fast to begin with, it may not stay that way unless you plan ahead.

Establishing the right hardware infrastructure and being able to deploy new releases quickly and to detect and respond to performance problems quickly are key aspects of the ultra-fast approach.

In this chapter, I will cover the following:

- Instrumentation

- Capacity planning

- Disk subsystems

- Network design

- Firewalls and routers

- Load balancers

- DNS

- Staging environments

- Deployment

- Server monitoring

Instrumentation

I have seen many web sites that look fast during development but rapidly slow down when they get to production. Another common scenario is a site that runs well most of the time but suffers from occasional dramatic slowdowns. Without the proper infrastructure and operations process, debugging those types of problems can be extremely challenging and time-consuming. One tool that can be immensely helpful is instrumentation in the form of *performance counters* (or just *counters* for short).

Counters are extremely lightweight objects that you can use to record not only counts of various events (as the name implies) but also timing-related information. You can track averages as well as current values. The operating system supports counters directly. You can view all counters on your system using perfmon. You can see them as a graph or in chart form in real time, or you can collect them into a file for later processing. You can also view them from a remote machine, given the appropriate permissions. Even for an application that is very rich in counters, the incremental CPU overhead is well under 1 percent.

All of Microsoft's server products include custom counters. Your applications should use them for the same reason Microsoft does: to aid performance tuning, to help diagnose problems, and to help identify issues before they become problems.

Here are some guidelines on the kinds of things that you should consider counting or measuring with counters:

- All off-box requests, such as web service calls and database calls, both in general (total number of calls) and specifically (such as the number of site login calls).

- Page-load times for pages that are particularly performance sensitive.

- Number of pages processed, based on type, category, and so on. The built-in ASP.NET and IIS counters provide top-level, per-web-site numbers.

- Queue lengths (such as for background threads).

- Handled and unhandled exceptions.

- Number of times an operation exceeds a performance threshold.

For the last point, the idea is to establish performance thresholds for certain tasks, such as database calls. You can determine the thresholds based on testing or on reports from your production site under load. Then, your code measures how long those operations actually take, compares the measurements against the predetermined thresholds, and increments a counter if the threshold is exceeded. Your goal is to establish an early warning system that alerts you if your site's performance starts to degrade unexpectedly.

You can also set counters conditionally based on things such as a particular username, browser type, and so on. If one user contacts you and reports that the site is slow but most people say it's OK, having some appropriate counters in place lets you get a breakdown of exactly which parts of that user's requests are having performance problems.

There are several types of counters:

- `NumberOfItems32`

- `NumberOfItems64`

- `NumberOfItemsHEX32`

- `NumberOfItemsHEX64`

- `RateOfCountsPerSecond32`

- `RateOfCountsPerSecond64`

- `CountPerTimeInterval32`

- CountPerTimeInterval64

- RawFraction

- RawBase

- AverageTimer32

- AverageBase

- AverageCount64

- SampleFraction

- SampleCounter

- SampleBase

- CounterTimer

- CounterTimerInverse

- Timer100Ns

- Timer100NsInverse

- ElapsedTime

- CounterMultiTimer

- CounterMultiTimerInverse

- CounterMultiTimer100Ns

- CounterMultiTimer100NsInverse

- CounterMultiBase

- CounterDelta32

- CounterDelta64

Counters are organized into named categories. You can have one category for each major area of your application, with a number of counters in each category.

Here's an example of creating several counters in a single category (see **App_Code\PerfCounters.cs**):

```
using System.Diagnostics;

if (!PerformanceCounterCategory.Exists("Membership"))
{
    var ccd = new CounterCreationData("Logins", "Number of logins",
        PerformanceCounterType.NumberOfItems32);
    var ccdc = new CounterCreationDataCollection();
    ccdc.Add(ccd);
    ccd = new CounterCreationData("Ave Users", "Average number of users",
        PerformanceCounterType.AverageCount64);
    ccdc.Add(ccd);
```

```
    ccd = new CounterCreationData("Ave Users base", "Average number of users base",
        PerformanceCounterType.AverageBase);
    ccdc.Add(ccd);
    PerformanceCounterCategory.Create("Membership", "Website Membership system",
        PerformanceCounterCategoryType.MultiInstance, ccdc);
}
```

That creates a new 32-bit integer counter called Logins and a 64-bit average counter called Ave Users in a new category called Membership. Base counters must always immediately follow average counters. The reported value is the first counter divided by the base.

You can also create counters on your local machine from **Server Explorer** in Visual Studio. Click your machine name, right-click **Performance Counters**, and select **Create New Category**. See Figure 10-1.

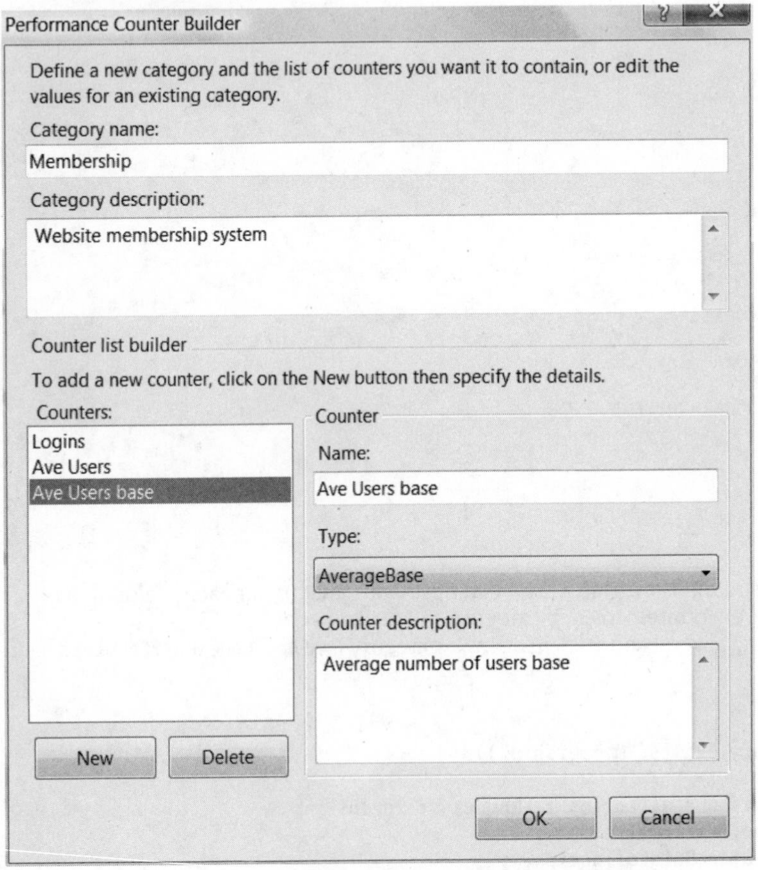

Figure 10-1. Adding new performance counters from Server Explorer in Visual Studio

To create new counters programmatically, your application needs either to have administrative privileges or to be a member of the Performance Monitor Users group. For web applications, that means you should usually use a separate program to install them to avoid having to elevate the privileges of the identity you use for your AppPools.

Using a counter is even easier than creating one:

```
using System.Diagnostics;

var numLogins = new PerformanceCounter("Membership", "Logins", false);
numLogins.Increment();
```

This example increments the value in the Logins counter you created previously. You can also IncrementBy() an integer value or set the counter to a specific RawValue.

■ **Note** Performance counters are read-only by default. Be sure to set the ReadOnly flag to false before setting a value, either implicitly with the third argument to the PerformanceCounter constructor or explicitly after obtaining an instance.

After you have created your counters and your web site is running, you can select and view them using perfmon, as you did in Chapter 8 for SQL Server. See Figure 10-2.

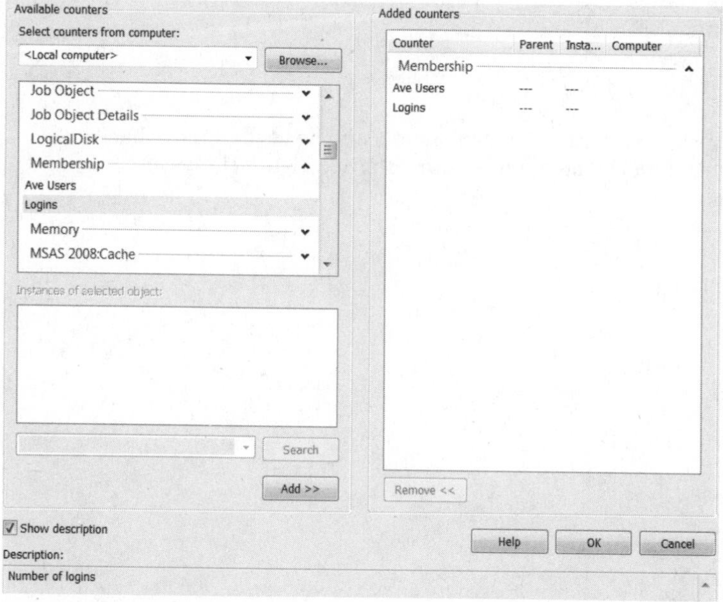

Figure 10-2. Viewing custom performance counters with perfmon

Capacity Planning

As your site grows, in order to avoid unexpected surprises with regard to performance, it's important to be able to anticipate the future performance of your site under load. You should be able to track the current load on your servers and use that to predict when you will need additional capacity. However, in order for your capacity planning process to be effective, it's important to follow several guidelines.

During development, you should place a maximum load on your servers and observe how they behave. As you learned earlier, if you're using synchronous threads, it may not be possible to bring your servers anywhere close to 100 percent CPU use. Even so, whatever that limit is on your system, you should understand it. Another argument for using async threads is that because they allow increased CPU use, they improve not only overall hardware utilization but capacity planning as well.

Next, it's important to minimize the different *types* of servers you deploy in your web tier. If you have one type of server to handle membership, another for profiles, another for content, and so on, then each one will behave differently under load. One type of server may overload while the others are close to idle. As your site grows, it becomes increasingly difficult to predict which servers will overload before others. In addition, it's generally more cost effective to allow multiple applications to share the same hardware. That way, heavily loaded applications can distribute their load among a larger number of servers. That arrangement also smoothes the load on all the servers and makes it easier to do capacity planning by forecasting the future load on the basis of current load.

If necessary, you can use WSRM to help balance the load among different AppPools or to provide priority to some over others, as discussed in Chapter 4.

You should track performance at all the tiers in your system: network: web, data, disk, and so on. The CPU on your database server may be lightly loaded, whereas its disk subsystem becomes a bottleneck. You can track that by collecting a standard set of counters regularly when your system is under load. You can use perfmon, or you can write an application that reads the counters and publishes them for later analysis.

Disk Subsystems

Disks are mechanical devices. They contain rotating magnetic media and heads that move back and forth across that media, where they eventually read or write your data. See Figure 10-3.

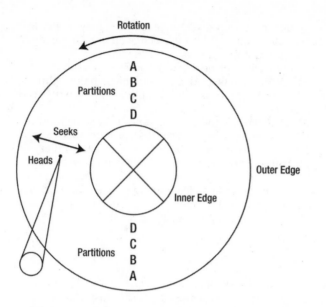

Figure 10-3. Physical disk platter and heads

Most modern drives support *Native Command Queuing* (NCQ), which can queue multiple requests and service them in an order that is potentially different than the order in which you submitted them. The drives also have some RAM, which is used to buffer data from reads and which can optionally be used to buffer write data. Data on the media is organized into physical 512-byte blocks, which is the minimum amount of data that the drive can read or write at a time.

You need to consider a number of disk-related topics when taking an ultra-fast approach, so let's take a look.

■ **Note** Both on-drive and on-controller write caches can significantly improve burst disk-write performance. However, in order to ensure the integrity of your data, you should enable them only if your system has a battery backup. Otherwise, data on your disks can be lost or corrupted in a power failure.

Random vs. Sequential I/Os per Second

One way to measure disk performance is in terms of I/Os per second (IOPS) at a given buffer size.

As an example, let's look at a typical 15,000rpm SAS disk. At that speed, it takes 4ms for the media to complete one rotation. That means to go from one random rotational position to another takes on average half that time, or 2ms. Let's say the average time for the heads to move (average seek) is 2.9ms for reads and that the average time to read 8KB (SQL Server's page size) is 0.12ms. That makes the total 5.02ms. Over one second, the drive can make about 199 of those 8KB random reads, or 199IOPS. That's only 1.6MB/sec. In other words, when disks operate in random mode, they can be extremely slow.

If the disk is reading sequentially, then the average maximum sustainable read rate may be about 70MBps. That's 8,750IOPS, or 44 times faster than random mode. With such a large difference, clearly anything you can do to encourage sequential access is very important for performance.

This aspect of disk performance is why it's so important to place database log files on a volume of their own. Because writes to the log file are sequential, they can take advantage of the high throughput the disks have in that mode. If the log files are on the same volume as your data files, then the writes can become random, and performance declines accordingly.

One cause of random disk accesses is using different parts of the same volume at the same time. If the disk heads have to move back and forth between two or more areas of the disk, performance can collapse compared to what it would be if the accesses were sequential or mostly sequential. For that reason, if your application needs to access large files on a local disk, it's a good idea to manage those accesses through a single thread.

This issue often shows up when you copy files. If you copy a huge file from one place to another on the same volume, the copy progresses at a fraction of the rate that it can if you copy from one physical spindle to another. That's also why multithreaded copies from the same disk can be so slow.

NTFS Fragmentation

The NTFS filesystem stores files as collections of contiguous disk blocks called *clusters*. The default cluster size is 4KB, although you can change it when you first create a filesystem. The cluster size is the smallest size unit that the operating system allocates when it grows a file. As you create, grow, and delete files, the space NTFS allocates for them can become *fragmented*; it is no longer contiguous. To access the clusters in a fragmented file, the disk heads have to move. The more fragments a file has, the more the heads move, and the slower the file access.

One way to limit file fragmentation is to regularly run a defragmentation utility. If your servers tend to be not busy at a particular time of the day or week, you can schedule defragmentation during those times. However, if you require consistent 24 × 7 performance, then it's often better to take one or a few servers offline while defragmentation is running, because the process completely saturates your disk subsystem.

To schedule regular disk defragmentation, right-click the drive name in **Windows Explorer**, and select **Properties**. Click the **Tools** tab, and then click **Defragment Now**, as shown in Figure 10-4.

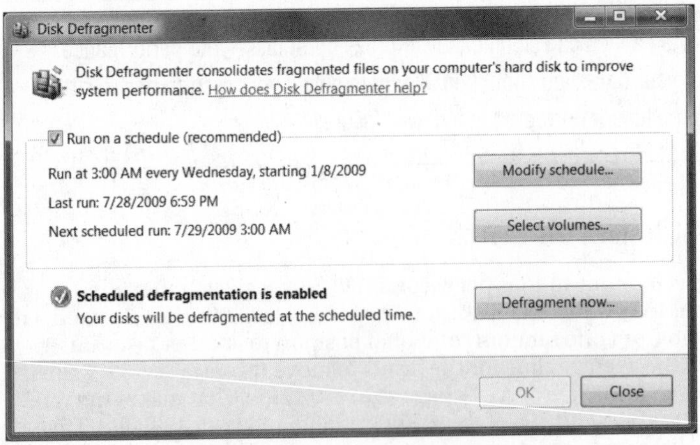

Figure 10-4. Scheduling periodic disk defragmentation

If your system regularly creates and deletes a large number of files at the web tier, then periodic defragmentation can play an extremely important role in helping to maintain the performance of your system.

You may also encounter cases where you have a few files that regularly become fragmented. In that case, instead of defragmenting your entire drive, you may want to defragment just those files. Alternatively, you may want to check to see how many fragments certain files have. For both of those scenarios, you can use the `Contig` utility. It's available as a free download:

`http://technet.microsoft.com/en-us/sysinternals/bb897428.aspx`

For example, you can use `Contig` as follows to see how many fragments a file has:

```
C:\>contig -a file.zip

Contig v1.55 - Makes files contiguous
Copyright (C) 1998-2007 Mark Russinovich
Sysinternals - www.sysinternals.com

C:\file.zip is in 17 fragments

Summary:
     Number of files processed   : 1
     Average fragmentation       : 17 frags/file
```

You defragment the file like this:

```
C:\>contig file.zip

Contig v1.55 - Makes files contiguous
Copyright (C) 1998-2007 Mark Russinovich
Sysinternals - www.sysinternals.com

Summary:
     Number of files processed   : 1
     Number of files defragmented: 1
     Average fragmentation before: 17 frags/file
     Average fragmentation after : 1 frags/file
```

When you create a large file on an empty filesystem, it is contiguous. Because of that, to ensure that your database data and log files are contiguous, you can put them on an empty, freshly created filesystem and set their size at or near the maximum they will need. You also shouldn't shrink the files, because they can become fragmented if they grow again after shrinking.

If you need to regularly create and delete files in a filesystem and your files average more than 4KB in size, you can minimize fragmentation by choosing an NTFS cluster size larger than that. Although the NTFS cluster size doesn't matter for volumes that contain only one file, if your application requires mixing regular files with database data or log files, you should consider using a 64KB NTFS cluster size to match the size of SQL Server extents.

Before your application begins to write a file to disk, you can help the operating system minimize fragmentation by calling `FileStream.SetLength()` with the total size of the file. Doing so provides the OS with a hint that allows it to minimize the number of fragments it uses to hold the file. If you don't know the size of the file when you begin writing it, you can extend it in 64KB or 128KB increments as you go (equal to one or two SQL Server extents) and then set it back to the final size when you're done.

You can help maximize the performance of NTFS by not putting too many files in a single folder. Although the only NTFS-imposed limit on the number of files one folder holds is disk space, I've found that limiting each folder to no more than about 1,000 files helps maintain optimal performance. If your application needs significantly more files than that, you can partition them into several different folders. You can organize the folders by something like the first part of file name to help simplify your partitioning logic.

Disk Partition Design

You can improve the throughput of your disks by taking advantage of the fact that the outer edge of the disk media moves at a faster linear speed than the inner edge. That means the maximum sustainable data transfer rate is higher at the outer edge.

Figure 10-5 shows example transfer rates for a 15,000rpm 73GB SAS drive from one of my servers. The left side of the chart shows the transfer rate at the outer edge, and the right side is the inner edge.

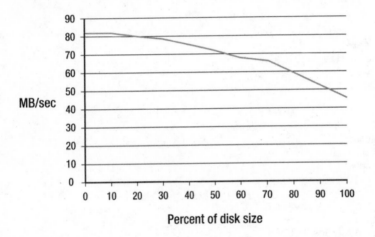

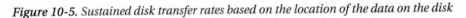

Figure 10-5. Sustained disk transfer rates based on the location of the data on the disk

You can see that the maximum transfer rate only holds over about the first 30 percent of the drive. After that, performance declines steadily. At the inner edge of the drive, the maximum transfer rate is only about 55 percent of the rate at the outer edge.

In addition, you can reduce average seek times by placing your data only in a narrow section of the disk. The narrower the area, the less distance the heads have to travel on average.

For random access, minimizing seek times is much more important than higher data rates. For sequential access, the reverse is true.

Extending the previous example, let's say you have a 73GB drive. You can make a partition covering the first 30 percent of the drive, which is about 20GB. The first partitions you create on a drive are at the outer edge of the media, as shown in Figure 10-3. The rotational latency in that partition is still 2ms, but the average seek is reduced to about 1.2ms. (Seek times aren't linear; the heads accelerate when they start and then decelerate as they approach the destination.) The data-transfer time is a tiny bit better, at

0.1ms. The total is 3.3ms, which is about 303IOPS. That's about a 50 percent improvement in random disk I/O throughput, simply by limiting the size of the partition. You can improve throughput even more by further reducing the partition's size.

For an equal partition size, you can increase disk performance further by using drives with more platters, because doing so lets you use physically narrower partitions for the same amount of space. The drives electronically switch between different heads to access the additional platters. That switching time doesn't affect latency; so, for example, the average seek for the example 20GB partition may drop to around 0.44ms, which increases throughput to about 394IOPS, or roughly twice the original value.

Of course, that's still a far cry from sequential throughput. The next step in increasing disk performance is to use several disks together as a RAID volume.

RAID Options

The most common types of RAID are 0, 1, 5, and 10. RAID 3 and 6 are less common but are still useful in certain environments. In my experience, the others are rarely used.

RAID 0 and Stripe Size

RAID 0, also known as *disk striping*, puts one small chunk of data on one drive, the next logical chunk on the next drive, and so on. It doesn't use any redundancy, so if one drive in a volume fails, the rest of the data in the volume is also lost. As such, it is not an appropriate configuration to use in production.

The size of the chunk of data on each drive is sometimes known as the *strip size*. The strip size times the number of drives is the *stripe size*. If your application reads that many bytes at once, all of the drives are active at the same time.

Let's say you have four drives configured as a RAID 0 volume. With a 64KB stripe size, the strip size is 16KB. If you read 16KB from the beginning of the volume, only the first drive is active. If you read 32KB, the first two drives are active at the same time. With 64KB, the controller requests 16KB from all four drives at once. With individual 16KB requests, your I/O throughput is still limited to the speed of a single drive. With 64KB per read, it is four times as high. What you see in practice is somewhere in between, with the details depending not only on your application but also on the particular disk controller hardware you're using. There is quite a bit of variation from one vendor to another in terms of how efficiently controllers are able to distribute disk I/O requests among multiple drives, as well as how they handle things like read-ahead and caching.

RAID 1

RAID 1 is also known as *mirroring*. The controller manages two disks so that they contain exactly the same data. The advantage compared to RAID 0 is that if one of the drives fails, your data is still available. Read throughput can in theory be faster than with a single drive, because the controller can send requests to both drives at the same.

RAID 5

RAID 5 is similar to RAID 0, except each stripe also includes block-level parity data. The parity information moves from one drive to the next for each stripe. Unlike with RAID 0, if one of the drives fails, your data is safe because the controller can reconstruct it from the remaining data and the parity information. Reads can be as almost as fast as with RAID 0, because the controller doesn't need to read the parity unless there's a failure. Writes that are less than a full stripe size need to read the old parity first, then compute the new parity, and write it back. Because the controller writes the new parity to the same physical location on the disk as the old parity, the controller has to wait a full rotation time before the parity write completes. A battery-backed cache on the controller can help.

If the controller receives a write request for the full stripe size on a RAID 5 volume, it can write the parity block without having to read it first. In that case, the performance impact is minimal.

When several RAID 5 volumes are striped together, it's known as RAID 50.

RAID 10

RAID 10 is a combination of RAID 1 and RAID 0. It uses mirroring instead of parity, so it performs better with small block writes.

RAID 3

RAID 3 is like RAID 5, except it uses byte-level instead of block-level parity, and the parity information is written on a single drive instead of being distributed among all drives. RAID 3 is slow for random or multithreaded reads or writes, but can be faster than RAID 5 for sequential I/O.

RAID 6

RAID 6 is like RAID 5, except that instead of one parity block per stripe, it uses two. Unfortunately, as disk drive sizes have increased, unrecoverable bit error rates haven't kept pace, at about 1 in 10^{14} bits (that's 10TB) for consumer drives, up to about 1 in 10^{16} bits for Enterprise drives. With arrays that are 10TB or larger, it begins to be not just *possible* but *likely* that in the event of a single drive failure, you can also have an unrecoverable error during the process of recovering the array. Some controllers help reduce the risk of a double-failure by periodically reading the entire array. RAID 6 can help mitigate the risk even further by maintaining a second copy of the parity data.

RAID 5 with a hot spare is a common alternative to RAID 6. Which approach is best depends heavily on the implementation of the controller and its supporting software.

RAID Recommendations

Although the exact results differ considerably by controller vendor, Table 10-1 shows how the most common RAID technologies roughly compare to one another, assuming the same number of drives for each.

Table 10-1. Relative RAID Performance

RAID Type	Small Reads	Large Reads	Small Writes	Large Writes
0	Good	Excellent	Excellent	Excellent
5	Good	Excellent	Poor	Excellent
10	Excellent	Good	Good	Good

I've left off RAID 1 because it can have only two drives; and in that configuration, it's the same thing as a two-drive RAID 10. Also keep in mind that although I've included RAID 0 for comparative purposes, it isn't suitable for production environments, because it doesn't have any redundancy.

Although SQL Server's disk-access patterns vary, as a rule of thumb for data files it tends to read 64KB extents (large reads) and write 8KB pages (small writes). Because RAID 5 does poorly with small writes and very well for large reads, it's a good choice for databases that either are read-only or are not written very much. Either RAID 5 or 10 can work well for databases with typical read/write access patterns, depending on the details of your system, including both hardware and software. RAID 10 is usually the best option for the write-heavy database log and tempdb. See Table 10-2.

Table 10-2. RAID Recommendations by Database Type

Database Type	RAID Level
Read-heavy	5
Read-write	5 or 10
Write-heavy (logs, tempdb)	10

If you're using RAID 5, depending on your specific controller hardware, it's generally a good idea to use a stripe size of 64KB if you can, so that it's the same as the SQL Server extent size. That should enable better performance for large writes. For RAID 10, the stripe size isn't as important. In theory, a smaller stripe size should be more efficient. Unfortunately, in practice, it doesn't seem to work out that way because of controller quirks. Even so, if you have enough drives that you can spread out a stripe so that one 8KB SQL Server page is split between at least two drives, that should help.

■ **Note** Some RAID controllers use the strip size for the definition of the array, instead of the stripe size. Even worse, some vendors confuse or mix the terms.

Although the technology is always evolving, I've found that SAS or SCSI drives work best in high-performance arrays. One reason is that their implementations of NCQ seem to be more effective than those in SATA drives. NCQ can help minimize latency as the disk-queue depth increases. It works by sorting the requests in the queue by their proximity to the current location of the disk heads, using a so-called *elevator* algorithm. The heads move in one direction until there are no more requests to service, before reversing and moving in the other direction. SAS drives support bidirectional communication with the drive, which is helpful during heavy use. They also tend to have better MTBF and bit error rates than SATA drives.

When you are designing high-performance disk arrays, you should apply the same partitioning strategy that you used for the single-drive case: one small, high-speed partition at the beginning of the drive. You can follow that with a second smaller partition to hold tempdb, a third small partition for the system databases (master, model, and msdb), and a fourth for backups, which occupies most of the volume.

You should also consider controller throughput. A PCIe 1.1 x4 controller may be capable of roughly 800MBps of throughput. At 400IOPS per drive, a single drive can read only 3.2MBps in random access mode, or around 75MBps in sequential mode. On an OLTP system, where the workload is a mix of random and sequential, you can estimate that total throughput may peak at around 25MBps per drive. That means a maximum of about 32 drives per controller for the data files and up to about 10 drive pairs (20 drives) per controller for the log files.

As your system grows, you can put a new SQL Server filegroup on each new volume.

The requirements for a staging database are somewhat different. Because the tables are larger and because you should design the system to handle table and index scans as it exports data to SSAS, more of the I/O is sequential, so the sustainable maximum I/O rate is higher. You may want only half as many drives per controller compared to the OLTP case. I would expect the disk-queue length to be substantially higher on a staging database under load than on an OLTP system.

Storage Array Networks

Another alternative is to use a *storage array network* (SAN). SANs are great for environments where reliability is more important than performance, or where you prefer to rely on an outside vendor to help set up, tune, and configure your disk subsystem. It can be very handy to be able to delegate that work to an outside firm so that you have someone to call if things break. The disadvantage is cost.

Using the information I've presented here, you can readily build an array that outperforms a SAN for a fraction of the price. However, in many shops, do-it-yourself configurations are discouraged, and that's where SANs come in.

You must be cautious about two things with SANs. First, having a huge RAM cache in the SAN doesn't always help. It can mask performance issues with the drives themselves for a while, but the maximum *sustained* performance is ultimately determined by the drives, not by how much cache the system has. Second, when it comes to SQL Server in particular, recall from the earlier discussion about how it manages memory that it is basically a huge cache. That makes it difficult for a SAN to cache something useful that SQL Server hasn't already cached.

Another issue is focusing only on random IOPS. I've seen some SANs that don't allow you to differentiate between random and sequential IOPS when you configure them. One solution in that case is to put a few extra drives in the CPU chassis and to use those for your log files instead of the SAN.

Controller Cache

The issue with cache memory also applies to controllers. The cache on controllers can be helpful for short-duration issues such as rotational latency during RAID 5 writes. However, having a huge cache can be counterproductive. I encourage you to performance-test your system with the disk controller cache disabled. I've done that myself and have found multiple cases where the system performs better with the cache turned off.

The reasons vary from one controller to another, but in some cases, disabling the cache also disables controller read-ahead. Because SQL Server does its own read-ahead, when the controller tries to do it too, it can become competitive rather than complementary.

Solid State Disks

Solid state disks (SSDs) built with flash memory are starting to become price-competitive with rotating magnetic media on a per-GB basis when you take into account that the fastest part of conventional disks is the first 25 to 30 percent.

SSDs have a huge performance and power advantage over disks, because they don't have any moving parts. Rotational delay and seek times are eliminated, so the performance impact is extremely significant. Random access can be nearly as fast as sequential access, and issues such as fragmentation are no longer a concern from a performance perspective.

Flash-based SSDs have some unique characteristics compared to rotating magnetic media:

- They use two different underlying device technologies: multilevel cell (MLC) and single-level cell (SLC) NAND memory.

- You can only write them between roughly 10,000 (MLC) and 100,000 (SLC) times before they wear out (even so, they should last more than 5 years in normal use).

- Write speeds with SLC are more than twice as fast as MLC.

- SLC has nearly twice the mean time between failure (MTBF) of MLC (typically 1.2M hours for MLC and 2.0M hours for SLC).

- MLC-based devices have about twice the bit density of SLC.

SSDs are organized internally as a mini-RAID array, with multiple channels that access multiple arrays of NAND memory cells in parallel. The memory consists of sectors that are grouped into pages. The details vary by manufacturer, but an example is something like 4KB sectors and 64KB pages.

With disks, you can read and write individual 512-byte sectors. With SSDs, you can read an individual sector, but you can only write at the page level and only when the page is empty. If a page already contains data, the controller has to erase it before it can be written again.

SSDs have sophisticated vendor-specific controllers that transparently manage the page-erase process. The controllers also map block addresses from logical to physical, which helps even out the wear on the memory cells (*wear leveling*).

The current generation of SSDs is available in two broad flavors. One has the same form factor and electrical interface as a 2.5-inch SATA disk. The other sits on a PCIe card that plugs directly into the bus. The former are easy to integrate into existing systems, and you can readily boot from them. The latter in theory have a performance advantage, but they require special support in order to be bootable.

Typical performance of a single SSD is close to the limit of the SATA 3.0 Gbps interface specification, at 250MBps for sequential reads. An MLC device may have sequential write speeds of roughly 70MBps, with SLC at around 150MBps. At those speeds, you can see how a single SSD could have faster random-access reads than an array of 50 or more disks.

SSDs with SATA interfaces are compatible with standard RAID controllers. By grouping several SSDs in RAID, you can easily reach the limit of PCIe bus bandwidth (although you hit the controller's limit first). PCIe 1.1 throughput is limited to about 300MBps per channel; that's about 1.2GBps for an x4 slot, or 2.4GBps for an x8 slot. Fortunately, PCIe 2.0 doubles those numbers, as does SATA 6.0 Gbps for the disk interface.

I fully expect to see flash-based SSDs completely replace rotating magnetic disks in high-performance production environments over the next few years.

Network Design

One source of latency in your data center is the network that connects your servers. For example, a 100Mbps network has an effective data-transfer rate of up to roughly 10MBps. That means a 100KB response from your database takes 10ms to transfer. Recall from the earlier discussion of threading in ASP.NET that long request latency can have a significant adverse impact on the scalability of your site and that the issue is compounded if you are making synchronous requests. If you were to increase the speed of the network connection to 1Gbps, with effective throughput of roughly 100MBps, that would reduce the latency for a 100KB response from 10ms to just 1ms.

The issue isn't performance; reducing the time that it takes to process a single request by 9ms won't visibly improve the time it takes to load a page. The issue is scalability. A limited number of worker threads are available at the web tier. In synchronous mode, if they are all waiting for data from the data tier, then any additional requests that arrive during that time are queued. Even in async mode, a limited number of requests can be outstanding at the same time; and the longer each request takes, the fewer total requests per second each server can process.

The importance of minimizing latency means that network speeds higher than 1Gbps are generally worthwhile. 10Gbps networking hardware is starting to be widely available, and I recommend using it if you can.

For similar reasons, it's a good idea to put your front-end network on one port and your back-end data network on a separate port, as shown later in Figure 10-7. Most commercial servers have at least two network ports, and partitioning your network in that way helps to minimize latency.

Jumbo Frames

Another way to increase throughput on the network that connects your web servers to your database is to enable jumbo frames. The maximum size of a standard Ethernet packet, called the *maximum transmission unit* (MTU), is 1,518 bytes. Most gigabit interfaces, drivers, and switches (although not all) support the ability to increase the maximum packet size to as much as 9,000 bytes. Maximum packet sizes larger than the standard 1,518 bytes are called *jumbo frames*. They are available only at gigabit speeds or higher; they aren't available on slower 100Mbps networks.

Each packet your servers send or receive has a certain amount of fixed overhead. By increasing the packet size, you reduce the number of packets required for a given conversation. That, in turn, reduces interrupts and other overhead. The result is usually a reduction in CPU use, an increase in achievable throughput, and a reduction in latency.

An important caveat with jumbo frames is that not only do the servers involved need to support them, but so does all intermediate hardware. That includes routers, switches, load balancers, firewalls, and so on. Because of that, you should not enable jumbo frames for ports that also talk to the Internet. If you do, either the server has to take time to negotiate a smaller MTU, or the larger packets are fragmented into smaller ones, which has an adverse impact on performance. However, jumbo frames can be very useful on the private network segments that connect your web and database servers.

To enable jumbo frames, follow these steps:

1. Start **Server Manager**, select **Diagnostics** in the left panel, and then choose **Device Manager**.

2. Under **Network Adapters** in the center panel, right-click a gigabit interface, and select **Properties**.

3. Click the **Advanced** tab, select **Jumbo Frame** (or something similar like **Jumbo MTU**), and set the MTU size, as shown in Figure 10-6.

Repeat the process for all servers that will communicate with each other, setting them all to the same MTU size.

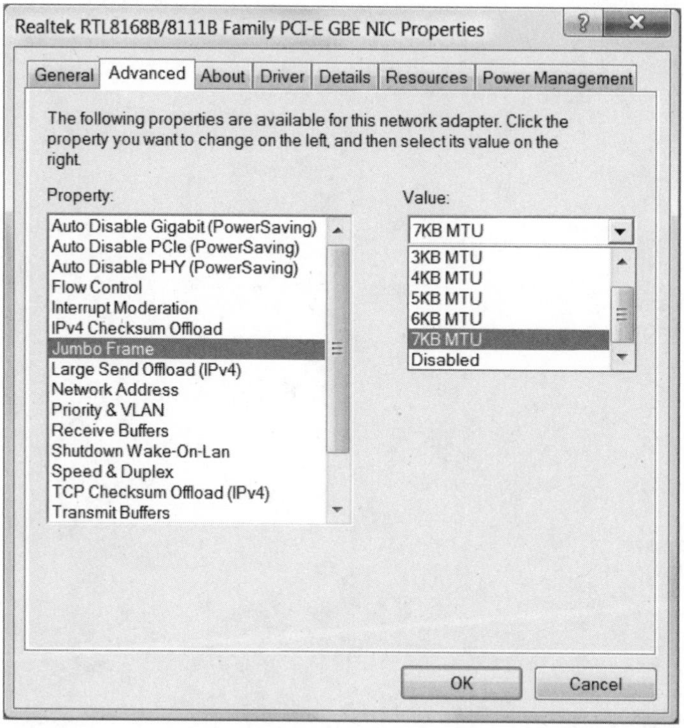

Figure 10-6. Enabling jumbo frames on your network interface

Link Aggregation

If you have more than one web server, then another technique for increasing throughput and decreasing latency for your database servers is to group two network ports together so they act as a single link. The technology is called *link aggregation* and is also known as *port trunking* or *NIC teaming*. It is managed using the Link Aggregation Control Protocol (LACP), which is part of IEEE specification 802.3ad. Unfortunately, this isn't yet a standard feature in Windows, so the instructions on how to enable it vary from one network interface manufacturer to another. You need to enable it both on your server and on the switch or router to which the server is connected.

When it is enabled, link aggregation lets your server send and receive data at twice the rate it would be able to otherwise. Particularly in cases where multiple web servers are sharing a single database, this can help increase overall throughput. See Figure 10-7.

If you have only one web server, you should have one network port for connections to the Internet and one for the database. Link aggregation won't help in that case, unless your web server happens to have three network ports instead of the usual two.

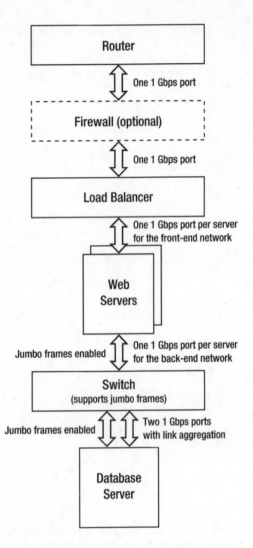

Figure 10-7. Optimized network design with jumbo frames and link aggregation

Firewalls and Routers

When you are considering whether a server-side firewall would be appropriate for your environment, it's important to take your full security threat assessment into account. The biggest threats that most web sites face are from application vulnerabilities such as SQL injection or cross-site scripting, rather than from the kinds of things that firewalls protect against.

From a performance and scalability perspective, you should be aware that a firewall may introduce additional latency and other bottlenecks, such as limiting the number of simultaneous connections.

It's my view that most vanilla web sites don't need hardware firewalls. They can be a wonderful tool for protecting against things such as downloading malicious files or accidentally introducing a virus by connecting an unprotected laptop to your network. However, in a production environment, you should prohibit arbitrary downloads onto production servers and connecting client-type hardware to the production network, which dramatically reduces the risk of introducing viruses or other malware. A large fraction of the remaining types of external attacks can be prevented by simply filtering out all requests for connections to ports other than 80 (HTTP) or 443 (SSL).

Another service that hardware firewalls can provide is protection against network transport layer attacks, such as denial of service. If those are a concern for you, and if you don't have access to your router, then a hardware firewall may be worth considering.

If you do use a hardware firewall, you should place it between your router and your load balancer, as shown in Figure 10-7, so that it can filter all traffic for your site.

Another valid use for firewalls is as a virtual private network (VPN) endpoint. You should not have a direct path from the public Internet to your back-end database servers. To bypass port filtering and to gain access to those back-end servers, you should connect to your remote servers over VPN. Ideally, the VPN should connect to a separate management network, so the VPN endpoint doesn't have to handle the full traffic load of your site.

Windows Firewall and Antivirus Software

You can apply port-filtering functions using Windows Firewall, which you should enable on all production servers. Using a software firewall also helps protect you against a variety of threats that hardware firewalls can't address, such as application bugs that may allow an attacker to connect from one server to another. Because those attacks don't normally go through the hardware firewall on their way from one server to another, they can't be filtered that way, whereas a software firewall running on each machine can catch and filter that type of network traffic.

On smaller sites where your users can upload files onto your servers, you should consider using server-side antivirus software as an alternative to a hardware firewall.

Using Your Router as an Alternative to a Hardware Firewall

In most hosted environments, you don't need a router of your own; your ISP provides it for you. However, your site grows, at some point you will want to take over management of your network connection, including having a router. Having access to your router also means you can use it to help improve the performance and security of your site. For example, you can use it to do port filtering. Many routers, including those that run Cisco IOS, also support protection against things like SYN floods and other denial-of-service attacks. Being able to offload that type of work onto your router, and thereby avoid the need for a hardware firewall, can help minimize latency while also reducing hardware and ongoing maintenance costs.

Load Balancers

As your site grows and as resilience in the event of hardware failures becomes more important, you will need to use some form of load balancing to distribute incoming HTTP requests among your servers.

Although a hardware solution is certainly possible, another option is *network load balancing* (NLB), which is a standard feature with Windows Server.

NLB works by having all incoming network traffic for your virtual IP addresses (normally, those are the ones public users connect to) delivered to all your servers and then filtering that traffic in software. It does therefore consume CPU cycles on your servers. The most recent scalability tests I've seen show that NLB can be a reasonable option up to no more than about eight servers. Beyond that, the server-to-server overhead is excessive, and hardware is a better choice.

As with hardware load balancers, keep in mind that NLB works at the link protocol level, so you can use it with any TCP- or UDP-based application, not just IIS or HTTP. For example, you can use it to load-balance DNS servers.

To configure NLB, follow these steps:

1. Install the Network Load Balancing feature from Server Manager.

2. Open the Network Load Balancing Manager from Administrative Tools.

3. Right-click **Network Load Balancing Clusters** in the left pane, select **New Cluster**, and walk through the wizard.

When you are selecting load balancing hardware, pay particular attention to network latency. As with the other infrastructure components, minimizing latency is important for optimal performance.

In addition to its usual use in front of web servers, another application for load balancing is to support certain configurations in the data tier. For example, you may distribute the load over two or more identical read-only database servers using NLB.

You can also use *reverse load balancing* (RLB) to facilitate calls from one type of web server to another from within your production environment, such as for web services. As with public-facing load balancing, RLB lets you distribute the internal load among multiple servers and to compensate in the event of a server failure.

DNS

Before a client's browser can talk to your web site for the first time, it must use DNS to resolve your hostname into an IP address. If your site uses a number of subdomains, as I suggested in Chapter 2, then the client's browser needs to look up each of those addresses. The time it takes for name resolution has a direct impact on how quickly that first page loads.

DNS data is cached in many places: in the browser, in the client operating system, in the user's modem or router, and in their ISP's DNS server. Eventually, though, in spite of all the caches, your DNS server must deliver the authoritative results for the client's query.

There's a whole art and science to making DNS fast and efficient, particularly in global load balancing and disaster failover scenarios. However, for many sites, it's enough to know that the performance of the server that hosts your DNS records is important to the performance of your site. Even relatively small sites can often benefit from hosting their own DNS servers, because some shared servers can be terribly slow.

For larger sites, it usually makes sense to have at least two load-balanced DNS servers. That helps with performance and provides a backup in case one of them fails. The DNS protocol also allows you to specify one or more additional backup servers at different IP addresses, although you can't specify the order in which clients access the listed DNS servers.

The main requirement for DNS servers is low latency. That is sometimes compatible with running other applications on the same hardware, depending on the amount of traffic at your site.

You may also consider a commercial service that specializes in robust high-speed DNS, such as UltraDNS (see `www.ultradns.com`).

When you are entering records for your domains and subdomains into your DNS zones, be sure to use A records whenever possible and avoid CNAME records. Depending on the DNS server software you're using and where the names are defined, it can take an extra round-trip to resolve CNAMEs, whereas A records are fully resolved on the initial query.

You should also set the DNS *time to live* (TTL) value for your site, which determines how long the various DNS caches should hold onto the resolved values. Some sites use a short TTL as part of a site failover scheme. If the primary site fails, the DNS server provides the IP address of the backup site instead of the primary. If sites were using the primary address, when their cache times out, DNS returns the secondary address, and they begin using the backup site. However, if you are not using DNS as part of your failover scheme, then in general a longer TTL time helps improve your site's performance by limiting how often clients need to reissue the DNS lookups. Because server IP addresses occasionally change, such as if you move to a new data center, you shouldn't set the value to be huge. Usually, something around 24 hours or so is about right.

Staging Environments

To minimize the time it takes to deploy a new release into production and to reduce the risk of post-deployment issues, it helps tremendously if you can establish a staging environment. Larger systems often warrant multiple staging environments.

As an example, you can have one server that you use for nightly builds. Developers and Quality Assurance (QA) can use that server for testing. QA may have a second staging environment for performance testing or other testing that can interfere with developers. When a new release is ready for exposure to public users, you can deploy it into a beta test environment, using servers in your data center. You may even have two beta environments, sometimes called early and late, beta-1 and beta-2, alpha and beta, or beta and preproduction. After the beta test phase, you finally move the release into your production environment.

The organization of your staging environments can vary considerably, depending on the scale of your project. You can separate them by AppPool on a single machine, you might use several virtual servers, or they can be physically separate machines.

In addition to giving you a chance to catch bugs before they enter production, this approach also provides an opportunity to double-check your site's performance for each release. It's a good idea to track the performance of various aspects of your site over time and make sure things don't degrade or regress beyond a certain tolerance.

Staging environments also provide a mechanism that lets you respond quickly to site bugs or urgent changes in business requirements. I've worked with many companies that skip this phase, and it's shocking how much time they seem to spend doing firefighting when new releases don't behave as expected. Another observation I can offer is that large sites that don't use staging environments also tend to be the ones with the largest performance problems, in part no doubt because they don't have a good preproduction test environment.

A common argument against using staging environments is that it's too costly to reproduce the entire production environment multiple times. This is another good reason to minimize the different types of servers you need. Your system architecture should make it possible to run your entire site on one or two servers at most, regardless of how big or complex it is. Even if your production web farm has hundreds of machines, being able to run and test everything functionally in a controlled environment is invaluable. I'm not saying there aren't exceptions; but even when there are, try to isolate those components that you can separately stage, test, and deploy.

Deployment

Deploying your site to a single server is normally straightforward:

1. Copy your latest release to the production machine.

2. Create an `AppOffline.htm` file in the root of the existing site to take it offline. The contents of that file are displayed to users who visit your site while you're working on it. This standard ASP.NET feature doesn't require any code.

3. Copy or unzip the new code into place.

4. Make any required OS, IIS, or database schema changes.

5. Remove (or rename) `AppOffline.htm`.

However, this seemingly simple process quickly gets very complex and error prone as your site increases in size and begins to include multiple servers. Constant 24 × 7 uptime and avoiding significant performance hiccups both add significant wrinkles. How do you upgrade without taking the whole site offline? How do you reliably get the exact same settings and files on a large number of servers?

For a small number of servers—up to roughly four or five or so—if you can take your site offline for an extended period, you should be able to use the single-server deployment process and make it work. However, beyond that, or as soon as you introduce a requirement for uninterrupted uptime or consistent site performance during upgrades, then you need to take a different approach.

To address the uninterrupted uptime requirement, the best solution is to use rolling upgrades. For example, if you have two load-balanced web servers, you take one offline first, upgrade it, and bring it back online; then, you repeat the process for the second one. With a larger number of servers, you can of course take more of them offline at a time. Hardware load balancers can be very helpful in orchestrating switching the load quickly from one group of servers to another.

Data Tier Upgrades

Complications with deployment often arise when you also need to make changes to the data tier. The solution requires support in your software architecture as well as in the deployment process. Some of the techniques you may use include the following:

- When changing your schema, also change existing stored procedures or create new views that use the new schema to the extent possible. New SPs that use the new schema can exist side by side with the old ones. During the upgrade, servers running the previous version can use the old SPs, while the new version uses the new code.

- Design your DAL to support new and old modes, and provide a mechanism to switch between the two. You can initially deploy using the old mode, upgrade the data tier, and then command all the servers to switch to the new mode at the same time, or fall back to the old mode if there's a problem.

- If your site can't go offline completely during upgrades, perhaps it can run in a read-only mode for a short time. If so, first create a database snapshot. Then, send a command to your web servers, telling them to use a new connection string that references the snapshot instead of the main DB, so that they are isolated from the changes, and to restrict access to read-only mode. When the upgrade is done, reverse the process.

In a clustered environment, for operating system changes and updates, you can modify the standby node first, then make it the active node, update and reboot the primary node, and then switch back.

I don't mean to trivialize the process; there is of course much more to it than I've outlined here, and the details tend to be application-specific. The point I'm trying to make is that this is an important problem; and if it affects your application, it's much easier to address sooner than later.

Improving Deployment Speed

Another aspect of deployment is getting it done quickly. If it takes you a week to deploy a new release, that means you can't make new releases often, you have that much less time available to work on your site's features and performance, and site bugs become extremely expensive to fix.

I've worked with several very large sites that can roll out an entire new release to many dozens of servers in under an hour. It's possible to be efficient enough that you can afford to deploy a new release every few weeks.

In my experience, being able to deploy rapidly is a critical prerequisite to building a fast and scalable site. An inability to respond to user feedback and your own observations quickly inevitably leads to problems.

I have also worked with companies that are only able to roll out new versions once every 10 to 12 months or more. Not surprisingly, they also tend to be the ones with the largest performance problems. Many small releases are infinitely easier to manage than a few huge ones.

In a multiserver environment, you can simplify and speed up the deployment process by using image-based deployment. Instead of copying your code to each server separately, you copy it to a single master server. In addition to your application, you can also make OS and IIS changes to that machine. You can apply the latest OS updates, for example. Then, when you're sure everything is correct on that machine, you multicast a copy of it to your production servers. The application that handles this process is called *Windows Deployment Services* (WDS), and it's included as a standard role with Windows Server Standard and above.

Using image-based deployment helps you guarantee that all your servers are exactly the same, by eliminating per-machine manual updates. It's also very fast; you should be able to reimage a server completely in around 20 minutes. Even better, you can reimage many servers in the time it takes to do one, because the data is multicast. This approach also lets you handle server failure or data corruption efficiently. Instead of trying to figure out which files may have been damaged if a server fails, just reimage the server. If it fails again, then the hardware is bad. Easy.

Page Compilation

After deploying a new release to your web tier, with the default ASP.NET dynamic compilation mechanism, the runtime compiles your pages on a folder-by-folder basis when they are first accessed. The larger your site is, the more time this can take. I've seen sites that take many minutes to recompile when they first start, which is definitely not an ideal user experience.

You can address this problem in a couple of ways. My preference is to build a precompiled site using a web deployment project, as I described in Chapter 2. That way, you can generate a single DLL for your whole site. The deployment files include .aspx pages as placeholders, but not the code-behind. When the web site first starts, the runtime doesn't need to do any additional compilation, so your site can be active right away.

Another approach is to keep dynamic compilation but run a script against your site before you enable public access. The script causes the runtime to compile everything by requesting one page from each folder. If you're using image-based deployment, you should invoke the script and the compilation before creating your deployment image. Of course, the larger your site is, the more error-prone and time-consuming this sort of process is, and the more appealing precompilation becomes.

Cache Warm-Up

The larger your database is, and the more RAM you have available on your database server, the longer it takes for the RAM cache to be refilled from disk after a restart. Recall the earlier discussions about how SQL Server uses memory: when your data is in RAM, the database acts like a big cache. Let's say you have 32GB of RAM and a disk subsystem that can deliver 60MB per second from the SQL Server data files. There may be enough room for up to 30GB of cached data, which takes more than 8 minutes to read from disk. During that time, your site may be much slower than it is after the cache is full.

You can address this issue by using a stored procedure to precache the tables your site is likely to need. You can run the SP from a web page, or maybe from SSMS, when you reboot the server. Although minimizing the use of aggregate functions in production is a sound practice, they can be a very good tool in this case. The SP can do a SELECT COUNT(*) to bring in a whole table. Of course, you can limit or optimize as needed using the same principle. The goal is to read the data so that it's available in RAM before your web pages need it.

To help decide which objects to bring into memory, it may help to know how large they are. You can see that with the sp_spaceused command:

```
EXEC sp_spaceused N'dbo.Votes'
```

You can use a similar approach to warm up the cache on your web servers when they first start. You might do that from a background thread, rather than writing specialized web pages, so the process is automatic when the sites first start.

Server Monitoring

After you build and deploy a high-performance web site, in order to make sure that it performs as you designed it and that performance doesn't unexpectedly degrade under load or over time, it is important to monitor the performance of your servers.

Having an ultra-fast site means having not only fast pages but also fast response and resolution times in the event of problems. Minimizing your mean time to resolution (MTTR) should be one of your design goals.

Monitoring your servers for failures and other problems is relatively straightforward when you have only a couple of them. For example, you may capture the output from a perfmon trace a few times a week and then analyze it offline. You should also regularly check the Windows error logs.

However, as your site grows to include more servers, monitoring becomes increasingly challenging. On a small site, the outright failure of a server is usually obvious. On a large site, although a load balancer should stop sending requests to a web server that has completely failed, it can mean a reduction in capacity if you don't notice it quickly. Partial or intermittent failures can be much more difficult to detect without good instrumentation and monitoring.

Certain types of problems produce symptoms that you can detect early, before an outright failure happens. *Proactive monitoring* allows you to detect failures that either make things very slow or return erroneous results in a way that a vanilla load balancer may not be able to detect. Accurate load forecasting, capacity planning, and trend analysis also rely on being able to monitor all your servers regularly and to track those results over time.

Proactive monitoring lets your operations staff more effectively isolate and fix errors without involving your development team. This, in turn, helps improve the long-term performance and scalability of your site by allowing developers to remain focused on development, rather than getting distracted with debugging operations-related problems in production. Using proactive monitoring to minimize your MTTR also helps keep your end users happy in the event of failures.

You should consider monitoring from four different perspectives:

- **User perspective.** Make sure web pages return the correct content, without errors.

- **Database perspective.** Make sure performance-sensitive queries are running without errors and within their design thresholds, including connect time, query execution time, and data transfer time.

- **Performance counters.** Use both custom counters from your application and counters from IIS, SQL Server, and Windows to identify resource use and various internal metrics and trends.

- **Windows event logs.** Continuously monitor the logs for errors and other unexpected events.

Several commercial tools collect this type of data from your servers into a central repository and then allow you to generate reports, raise events, or define actions based on the results. For example, such a tool may send an e-mail to you if CPU use on a particular server exceeds 95 percent for more than 10 minutes, or page you if a certain database query takes more than 10 seconds to execute.

Microsoft calls its offering in this area System Center Operations Manager (SCOM). SCOM uses *Agents* installed on each server to collect monitoring data and send it back to a central console. You can also configure Agents to issue web or database requests and to raise alerts if the response doesn't conform to your expectations.

Most of Microsoft's server products, including IIS and SQL Server, have SCOM management packs that include various heuristics to help you monitor and manage those applications.

Third-party plug-ins are also available for SCOM from companies such as AVIcode; these can provide even more detail in the events and reports that SCOM generates.

Summary

In this chapter, I covered the following:

- Instrumenting your application using performance counters to simplify performance tuning and problem diagnosis

- Improving your ability to do capacity planning

- Improving the throughput of your disk subsystem by optimizing partition design to maximize IOPS and by encouraging sequential I/O over random I/O

- Defragmenting whole filesystems and specific files

- Comparing RAID levels and choosing between them

- Understanding why network latency is important and how you can use faster network speeds, jumbo frames, and link aggregation to minimize it

- Understanding how hardware firewalls can influence scalability, where they fit into your network architecture when you need them, and how you may be able to use Windows Firewall, antivirus software, and router-configuration changes as alternatives

- Using NLB as an alternative to a hardware load balancer

- Configuring DNS for optimum performance

- Using staging environments to decrease the time that it takes to deploy a new release

- Developing a sound deployment strategy and knowing when to use WDS to deploy your application quickly

- Using a precompiled site to eliminate the slow site issues that otherwise accompany dynamic page compilation after a new release

- Warming up the caches at your web and data tiers after a restart

- Using proactive monitoring to check your servers for intermittent or soon-to-be problems, to monitor current performance and trends, and to minimize the time it takes you to respond to problems when they occur

■ ■ ■

Putting It All Together

Writing software has some interesting similarities to building a skyscraper. The architecture of a building defines its style, aesthetics, structure, and mechanics. Software architecture includes the same things; there's a definite flow and texture to it. There's an art to both, and software can be just as beautiful as a building.

With a good architecture, the pieces fit together smoothly. The relationships between building blocks are clear. The system can be more easily developed, maintained, deployed, expanded, and managed. You can tell you're working with a good architecture during the development phase because the hiccups tend to be small; forward progress tends to be consistent, you can fix bugs readily when they're found, and there are no big surprises.

A good architecture is a key prerequisite for an ultra-fast web site. You might be able to make a few fast pages without one, in the same way that you might be able to build a few rooms of a skyscraper without one. However, in order to build a large site, you need a cohesive plan.

This chapter covers the following:

- Where to start

- How to choose and tune your software development process

- How to establish a rough sense of the target performance of your site (your *league*) and how to use that to establish some architectural guidelines

- Tools to aid the development process

- How to approach your architectural design

- Detailed checklists that summarize recommendations from earlier chapters

Where to Start

Although every project has unique requirements, I can offer some guidelines that I've found helpful in kicking off new projects that incorporate the ultra-fast principles:

- Establish the software development process that you're going to use. In my experience, choosing the wrong process, or not having a formal process at all, is one of the most common reasons projects get off track.

- Define your project's requirements in detail, and determine your league. This process helps establish the foundation and motivation for many aspects of the project.

- Establish a solid infrastructure to support your development, including software tools and build, test, and staging environments.

- Define your system architecture. Start with a high-level block diagram, and work down to functional building blocks. Spend more time in this phase than you think you need.

- The design phase is a key part of your development process. However, be careful not to over-design. One of the most important insights about software development that I've gained in my 30+ years in the business is this: *the software **is** the design*. In other words, the only way to specify a software design *completely* is to actually build it.

- Software development projects are driven by cost, schedule, features, and quality (performance and security are aspects of quality). With careful planning, you can choose which three of those four attributes you want to constrain. Although trade-offs are possible, you can't constrain all of them at the same time. It reminds me of the Heisenberg Uncertainty Principle in physics, which says that you can determine either position or momentum to arbitrary precision, but that the more accurately you know one, the less accurately you know the other. Most projects start out trying to control cost. Features are next, because that's what management thinks they are paying for. Then, the projects inevitably have business requirements that force delivery by a certain date. With cost, schedule, and features heavily constrained, projects end up sacrificing quality. When they find the quality is unacceptable, they lose control of cost and schedule, and the next result is huge cost overruns and delays. The solution is straightforward: let features be the aspect that you allow to change; maintain the cost, schedule, and quality constraints, and cut features if you must.

- Project staffing is of course a crucial element. Good people are at the heart of any successful project. However, it's also true that having too many people, or people with the wrong skills, can significantly delay your project.

Development Process

As I mentioned, using the right development process is an important cornerstone to the success of any complex software project. Surprisingly, most companies I've worked with use an ad hoc process that is often based around what they're comfortable with or an approach they find to be intuitive, rather than on what the industry has found to be effective.

I am keenly aware that the choice of development process is often a near-religious one and that there is no one-size-fits-all solution. However, given the importance of choosing and using a good process to building an ultra-fast site, let's review one way of doing things in detail.

After working with dozens of companies that create software, some as the core of their business and others because they are forced into it, I've seen just about every different type of software development process you can imagine. My experience also includes working at Microsoft for several years on a development team. In addition, I've done a considerable amount of development in my own company, where I've been able to choose and customize the process.

The conclusion I've reached is that the process Microsoft uses is an excellent starting point. The company's ability to deliver regularly such a broad array of immensely complex products is a testament to its success.

For example, the Developer Division at Microsoft employs more than 2,000 people. They create more than 30 different products for software developers, including Visual Studio, the .NET Framework, and Team Foundation. Their code base consists of more than 8 million lines of code, and they are able to regularly release substantial new versions and feature enhancements that are used by tens of thousands of developers all over the world.

Microsoft used its internal experience as the foundation for the MSF Agile process, which it has incorporated into Team Foundation. I have an ultra-fast spin on this approach, which includes several additional techniques that can improve team effectiveness even more, particularly when it comes to quality and performance.

Organization

The team at Microsoft that builds an individual software product is called a *Product Group*. Table 11-1 shows the number of people in each role in a typical medium-sized Product Group of 40 people.

Table 11-1. Product Group Team Member Roles

Role	Number of People
Group management	1
Developers	10
Quality Assurance (QA)/test	18
Program management	4
Documentation, education, localization	4
Marketing	3

■ **Note** The number of people involved with testing is almost twice the number of developers.

Program managers drive features. They own the customer experience and are responsible for managing the Product Group and for helping team members make decisions regarding priorities. They are also responsible for writing a design specification for each feature.

Project Phases and Milestones

Microsoft breaks down a project into phases, with a milestone or deliverable at the end of each phase, as indicated in Table 11-2.

Table 11-2. Project Phases and Milestone

Phase	Milestones
Planning (M0)	Vision statement
M1	Technology preview
M2	Zero bug bounce (ZBB) and feature complete
Beta 1	ZBB and Beta 2
Beta 2	ZBB and Release Candidate 1 (RC1)
RC1	Release to Manufacturing/Release to Web (RTM/RTW)

All milestones include quality-based exit criteria. Each phase is finished only when the milestones are complete. Features that don't meet the exit criteria on time can be dropped. There may be additional beta test and release candidate phases if they are needed.

In the planning phase, most of the developers, testers, and documentation or localization staff aren't yet involved. The marketing team gathers requirements based on product concepts that upper management provides.

Marketing then works with engineering and program management to create a *vision statement* along with an initial schedule, including estimates of which features will go into which release, and their priorities. The vision statement adds details to the initial concept and the requirements and becomes the input to the system architecture design. Coding for new features is typically broken down into eight- to ten-week periods.

The M2 and beta-test phases end with a milestone called *zero bug bounce* (ZBB). The idea is to help ensure application stability by delaying exit from the project phase until there have been no new bugs for 48 hours. Features that are still generating new bugs at the end of the project phase may be cut or deferred to the next release to help ensure quality.

After the end of M2, the team no longer starts development on any new features. Instead, they focus all remaining time on testing, fixing bugs, and improving stability and quality.

Coding

In addition to the code for the features they're working on, developers are also responsible for writing unit tests. The tests should exercise the new feature with a goal of at least 70 percent code coverage. All unit tests must run correctly before a developer checks in their changes.

After check-in, other team members are notified about the nature of the changes, either by e-mail or through the source control system or a central management web site.

The full product is built and released every evening, using an automated build system that's managed by the build team. They deploy the nightly builds to a dedicated staging environment the next day, where the builds are used to test the previous day's changes.

Testing

The QA team is responsible for writing and executing test plans and for building and maintaining test-specific infrastructure, as well as performing tests and reporting the results.

Testing includes functional, performance, load (scalability), deployment, operations, monitoring, and regression tests. It is the testing team's responsibility to make sure the software is ready both for end users and for deployment and operations.

To give you an idea of the scale of testing that goes into an enterprise-class product, Visual Studio has more than 10 million functional test cases. Microsoft uses about 9,000 servers to run the tests, and a full test pass takes about three weeks to run. That's more than one test case per line of code and roughly one test server for every thousand test cases.

Bug Tracking

Program managers triage bugs and assign them a priority from zero to four. Priority zero (P0) means developers should stop whatever else they were doing and fix the bug immediately. That may happen if the production site is having urgent problems or if the developer broke the build somehow. P1 and P2 bugs are for the most important features. P3 bugs are "if you have time," and P4 bugs are "if you feel like it."

Bugs are tracked in a central location, such as Team Foundation, which facilitates reporting and change-history tracking. The tool that Microsoft used internally for many years to track bugs, called Product Studio, inspired the bug-tracking part of Team Foundation.

When team members check in a fix for a bug, they mark the bug *resolved*. The person who entered it originally is then responsible for verifying the fix before they close it.

After the project gets to the feature-complete milestone at the end of M2, all development efforts focus on testing and bug fixing. The goal is either to fix bugs or to defer them (and possibly the related feature) to the next release. By the time they release the product, there should be no bugs outstanding that they haven't consciously deferred.

Beginning in the Beta 2 phase, the team locks down the design more and more as the release date approaches. The bug triage team establishes a priority and importance threshold, or *bug bar*, to decide between bugs that will be fixed in the current release and bugs that will be deferred. They then raise the bar as time goes on. The goal is to maximize stability by minimizing changes. With a good architecture and a sound software development process, the number of must-fix *showstopper* bugs naturally drops to zero as the ship date approaches.

After bugs stop coming in, the build goes into *escrow* for a few days to be sure the system remains stable while testing continues. If everything is still OK after that, the build is released to manufacturing or to an operations team and the Web.

User Feedback

User feedback, including the response to beta tests and release candidates, forms an important pillar of the development process. From a performance perspective, you should confirm that your users think the parts of the site they are interested in are fast. You should also provide an easy way for them to let you know if they have problems. There's no better monitor for quality problems than your users.

Microsoft solicits feedback from many different sources, including its Connect site, forums, newsgroups, the Technical Assistance Program (TAP), and Community Technology Previews (CTPs). The company analyzes that feedback continuously and uses it to drive product features and priorities.

The Ultra-fast Spin

Here are a few variations on Microsoft's process that I've found can further reduce risk and that help to deliver a scalable, high-performance, high-quality site.

Depth-First Development

The most powerful technique is something I call *depth-first development* (DFD). The idea flows from an additional project requirement, which is that instead of trying to target artificial delivery dates, you should build your site in such a way that you could deploy it into production at almost any time in the development process, not just at the very end. Projects that use DFD are never late.

Implementing DFD involves building the software infrastructure that you need to deploy and operate your site before building more user-visible features. That includes things such as how you handle software updates in production, custom performance counters, logging, capacity planning, using data access and business logic layers, how you handle caching, deployment, and so on.

With this approach, I've found that although developing the first few pages on a site goes very slowly, things are also dramatically easier as the site grows.

With a more conventional approach, the "deep" aspects of your system, such as deployment and operations, are often left to the end as developers focus on features. In many companies, the features are what earn pats on the back from management, so they naturally receive first priority. The deep components are also sometimes forgotten in the original development plan and schedule, because they relate to *all* features rather than to one particular feature. What's often missed is the fact that those components aid development, too. You can use the same system that your operations team will use to identify bugs quickly after the site goes live to help you find and fix problems during development.

Imagine building a race car. When the car is in a race, you know you will need to be able to fill it with fuel quickly. However, you will also be doing a lot of testing with the car before the race. Think about how much time you could save at the test track if you had the ability to quick-fill early on.

DFD also helps you iron out deployment and operations issues early, when they are usually orders of magnitude less expensive to fix. For a large site, it allows the hardware infrastructure to be built up incrementally, alongside the software.

You might think of DFD as *narrow but deep*: build everything you need but *only* what you need, and nothing more. The idea is to focus on what the site could use immediately if it was in production, rather than what it might need many months from now.

DFD helps minimize code rework by establishing important patterns early. If you don't add things like logging to your system early, then when you do add them, they end up touching nearly your entire system. A large number of changes like that can easily introduce instabilities, as well as being costly and time-consuming. It's much better to establish the coding pattern early and then use it as you go.

Unit Testing

Another area where I like to do things a little differently involves unit tests. First, I appreciate the concept behind test-first development very much, and I've used it at length. Unfortunately, I can't endorse its use in real-world environments. My experience has been that it doesn't produce better code or reduce development time compared to other alternatives. However, unit tests *are* extremely important.

In addition to developers coding their own tests, I also like to have developers write unit tests for each other's code. In some shops, having QA write unit tests can also be useful. The idea is that developers (myself included) sometimes become stuck thinking about their code in a certain way, and they miss code paths and bugs that others may see. Having developers write tests for each other's code is a wonderful prelude to code reviews.

I also like to include performance-specific unit tests that verify not just functionality but also quality. Those tests can help to identify regressions. If someone introduces a change that slows down another part of the system, it's much better to catch it when the change is first made than after the code is running in production.

Unit tests should include your stored procedures as well as your .NET code. You can use a data generator, as you did in several examples earlier in the book, to create a realistic number of rows for your tests. Visual Studio Team Database includes support for autogenerating unit test stubs for stored procedures. You can also easily add checks to ensure that the calls execute within a certain amount of time. Combined with the data generator, that provides a great way to help avoid performance surprises when your code goes into production.

Other Tips

Here are a few more tips:

- Establish formal coding standards. The larger your team is, the more important it becomes for everyone to use a consistent style. Humans are very good at processing familiar patterns. An experienced developer can quickly tell a lot about how code works just by how it looks when it's formatted in a consistent and familiar way. I suggest starting with the Visual Studio standard code-formatting rules, because that makes it easy for everyone on the team to be consistent. Then, add rules for items such as comments, order of objects within a file, mapping between file names and their contents, object naming, and so on. The whole thing shouldn't be more than a couple of pages long.

- Store your schema definitions and other database scripts and code in source code control along with the rest of your site. It's a good idea for the same reason that using source control for the rest of your site is. To make it easier to track changes, separate your scripts at the database object level (table, stored procedures, and so on) rather than having a single do-all file.

- Tightly couple your source control system and your bug-tracking system. Doing so provides a valuable synergy that allows you see not only what changed in your system from one check-in to another, but why.

- Schedule regular code reviews to look at the code your team is developing. In addition to checking the code for functional accuracy, also look at it from a quality perspective, including maintainability, performance, security, and so on. I've also found regular *brown bag* talks to be useful, where team members give a presentation about the details of their design and implementation.

- Refactor your code frequently. Make sure it's readable, remove dead code, make sure names adhere to your coding standards, improve the code's maintainability, factor out duplicate code, refine your class design, and so on. I'm not saying to focus on refactoring to the point of distraction, but if you see something that's not structured correctly that you can fix easily, you should fix it. Similarly, if you make changes that cause other code to not be needed any more or that introduces redundant code, it's better to fix those issues sooner than later.

- Leverage code analysis tools to help identify static code patterns that can be a problem. One option is FxCop, which is available as a free download:

  ```
  http://www.microsoft.com/downloads/
              details.aspx?FamilyID=9aeaa970-f281-4fb0-aba1-d59d7ed09772
  ```

  FxCop has rules that look at library design, globalization, naming conventions, performance, interoperability, portability, security, and usage. Similar functionality is also built in to some editions of Visual Studio.

League

To help focus your efforts on the tasks that are most likely to improve the performance and scalability of your site, I've found that it's useful to establish a rough sense of your site's target performance and scalability.

I've never seen a formal partitioning along these lines, so I came up with my own system that I call *leagues*. See Table 11-3.

Table 11-3. League Definitions

League	Description
LG-1	Shared hosting. You don't have direct control of the server, and you share it with other sites.
LG-2	Dedicated server, single machine. You have full control over the server. The web site, database, and optionally SSAS run on the same machine, possibly along with other applications.
LG-3	Two servers. Your web site runs on one, and your database and SSAS run on the other.
LG-4	Two or more web servers, with one database server. The web servers run in a load-balanced configuration, using either NLB or a hardware load balancer.
LG-5	Two or more web servers, with one high-availability database, using either clustering or mirroring.
LG-6	Two or more web servers, with multiple partitioned databases, some or all of which are highly available. The partitioned databases may include support for things like logging or read-only databases.
LG-7	Two or more web servers, with multiple partitioned high-availability databases and multiple physical locations that you manage. The multiple locations may be for disaster failover, global load balancing, and so on.

These definitions don't include secondary hardware or software that may be attached to your system, nor do they say anything about how big your servers are or even how much traffic they serve.

Knowing the league you're playing in helps simplify many decisions during your site development process. Certain architectural options may be reasonable for one league that would be very unreasonable at another. For example, even though I don't recommend in-proc session state, if you're targeting LG-1, where your site is always on a hosted server, then it may be an option for you because it works in a single-server environment. On the other hand, if you're targeting LG-4, you can quickly rule out in-proc session state, because it doesn't work correctly in a true load-balanced environment.

Similar decisions and analysis are possible across many dimensions of web site development. For example, the requirements for logging, staging environments, monitoring, and deployment vary from one league to another.

Establish your league by determining where your site will be within three to five years. Keep in mind that higher leagues cost more to build and operate. Overestimating your league will result in unnecessary costs; underestimating will result in rework down the road and potential performance and operations issues in the meantime.

When you know your league, use it as a focal point in your architectural analysis and decision making. For example, in LG-5, adding a high-availability database also means that having a Windows domain in your production environment would be a good idea to help manage the cluster. With that in mind, you may need to allocate additional resources for primary and secondary domain controllers.

Tools

Using good tools can make a huge difference in both developer productivity and code quality. I'm always shocked when I see companies with large software teams and poor tools. The time saved with good tools invariably reduces labor costs through productivity improvements, which allows smaller teams. Then costs decline even more because smaller teams are more efficient and because high-quality code doesn't take as much effort to maintain.

Imagine a carpenter with hand tools compared to power tools, or carrying firewood in your backpack instead of in the back of a truck, or making changes to a book you've written with pencil and paper instead of a word processor. It's the same idea for software development.

Of course, exactly which tools to use is often a matter of debate. Visual Studio is at the heart of ASP.NET development, and I'm partial to the Microsoft tools because they are seamlessly integrated. I find the overhead of using tools that aren't integrated into Visual Studio to be time-consuming and error-prone. There are also open source options and third-party vendors of integrated tools that can be very good alternatives.

When you have the tools, it's important to know how to use them well, so a little training can go a long way—even just a webcast or two. Visual Studio includes a number of productivity-enhancing features, some of which aren't very visible unless you know they're there (things like code snippets).

Some of the more important tools that ultra-fast developers should have available include the following:

- Code analysis

- Code coverage

- Code profiler

- Memory profiler

- SQL Server profiler

- Source code control

- Bug tracking

- SQL data generator

- Web load test generator

- Unit test framework for .NET and T-SQL

- Web debugger (such as Fiddler)

Architecture

Whether you're working on a new site or modifying an existing one, it's a good idea to spend some time putting together an architectural block diagram. It may sound simple and obvious, but it's a useful exercise. Figure 11-1 shows an example architectural diagram for high-end LG-6 system.

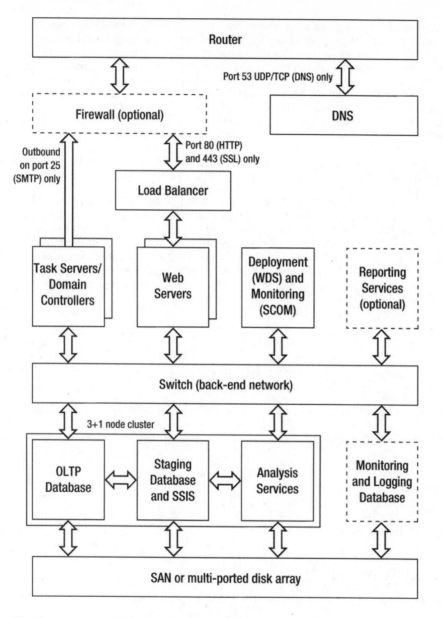

Figure 11-1. Example architectural block diagram

Include all the main components of your system, and break them out both logically and physically. Include third-party resources that your site relies on.

With a draft diagram in hand (or, even better, on a whiteboard), think about the issues discussed earlier in the book: minimizing round-trips, minimizing latency, caching, deployment, monitoring, upgrading, partitioning, AppPools, minimizing the number of different server types, and so on. You may find that a slight reorganization of your production environment can result in significant improvements.

Something else to consider in the area of architecture is the number of tiers in your system. By *tiers*, I mean software layers that are separated by out-of-process calls, such as web services or database calls (a DAL or a business logic layer is not a tier). Keeping the core principles in mind, it should come as no surprise that I favor flat architectures, because they tend to minimize round-trips. In general, a two-tier server architecture, where your web tier talks directly to your data tier, can perform much better than three-tier or *N*-tier systems.

Architects often introduce additional tiers as a way to reduce the load on the database. However, as I discussed at length earlier in the book, you can usually do better by offloading the database in other ways, such as by caching, partitioning, read-only databases, Service Broker, and SSAS.

Allowing the web tier to connect directly to the database also facilitates `SqlDependency` type caching, where SQL Server can send notifications to the web tier when the results of a prior query have changed.

Another goal of additional middle tiers is often to provide a larger cache of some kind. However, recall from the earlier discussion that the way SQL Server uses memory means it can become a large cache itself. Because SQL Server can process queries very quickly when the data it needs is already in memory, it is difficult to improve that performance by adding more cache in another tier. The reverse is often true: the additional latency introduced by a middle tier can have an adverse impact on performance and scalability.

Checklists

Here are a few checklists that summarize recommendations from earlier chapters:

Principles and Method (Chapter 1)

- ❑ Focus on perceived performance.
- ❑ Minimize blocking calls.
- ❑ Reduce round-trips.
- ❑ Cache at all tiers.
- ❑ Optimize disk I/O management.

Client Performance (Chapter 2)

- ❑ Put one or more requests for resources in the first 500 bytes of your HTML.
- ❑ Move requests for resources from the <head> section into the <body> of your HTML, subject to rendering restrictions.
- ❑ Make the position of objects on the page independent of download order, with early- and late-loading techniques (load large objects as late as you can).
- ❑ Use lowercase for all your URLs.

❑ Use a single, consistent URL for each resource, with matched case and a single domain name.

❑ Use from two to four subdomains to optimize parallel loading of your static files.

❑ Try to start a request for one image or CSS file before loading a script file from the same domain so that the requests happen in parallel.

❑ Minimize the number of different script files you're using. If you can't avoid having multiple files, combine them into a small number of files on the server.

❑ If you need multiple script files because they call `document.write()`, use `innerHTML` or direct DOM manipulation instead.

❑ If you can't avoid `document.write()`, use absolute positioning to invoke the script late in the file or use the hidden `<div>` technique.

❑ Create browser-specific pages on the server rather than with script.

❑ Use the page `onload` handler to request objects that aren't needed until after everything else on the page, such as rollover images or images below the fold.

❑ Replace spacer GIFs and text images with CSS.

❑ Merge multiple CSS files into one.

❑ Hide, remove, or filter comments from your HTML, CSS, and JavaScript.

❑ Install the Web Deployment Projects add-in for Visual Studio, and use it to run a JavaScript minifier such as `jsmin` to reduce the size of your JavaScript and to build a precompiled site for easy and fast deployment.

❑ Use lowercase HTML tags and property names.

❑ Consider using CSS instead of images for transparency, borders, color, and so on.

❑ Consider varying CSS transparency instead of using separate rollover images.

❑ Use image tiling to keep your images sizes to the bare minimum, such as for backgrounds.

❑ Crop or resize images to the minimum size.

❑ Use the smaller of GIF or PNG format for lossless images, and use JPEG for complex images without sharp edges in them (such as photos).

❑ Enable progressive rendering on large PNG and JPEG images, to improve perceived performance.

❑ Increase the level of compression on JPEG images to the maximum that's reasonable for your application.

❑ Use the lowest bit depth on your images that you can (8-bit images are smaller than 24-bit images).

❑ Use image slicing to improve the perceived performance of large images.

❑ Consider using image maps instead of multiple images for things like menus (although a text and CSS-based menu is even better).

❑ Specify an image's native size or larger in an `<img>` tag. If you need to use a size that's smaller than native, you should resize the source image instead.

❑ Instead of modifying image sizes to adjust fill and spacing on a page, use CSS.

❑ Set a relatively near-term expiration date on your `favicon.ico` file (such as 30 days).

❑ Consider running your HTML and CSS through an optimizer, such as the one available in Expression Web.

❑ Remove unused and duplicate CSS classes.

❑ Remove unused JavaScript.

❑ Move `style` definitions into your CSS file.

❑ Consider generating inline CSS the first time a user requests a page on your site, followed by precaching the CSS file to reduce the load time for subsequent pages.

❑ Validate form fields on the client before submitting them to the server.

❑ Don't enable submit buttons until all form fields are valid.

❑ Use script to avoid or delay submitting a form if the new parameters are the same as the ones that were used to generate the current page.

❑ Use script or Silverlight to generate repetitive HTML, which reduces HTML size.

❑ Use script or Silverlight to add repetitive strings to property values in your HTML.

❑ Minimize the total size of your cookies by using short names, optimized encoding, merging multiple cookies into one, and so on.

❑ Set an explicit `path` for all cookies, and avoid using the root path (/) as much as possible.

❑ Group pages and other content that need cookies into a common folder hierarchy, to help optimize the cookie `path` setting.

❑ Reference your static content from subdomains that never use cookies.

❑ Optimize your CSS by merging and sharing class definitions, leveraging property inheritance, eliminating whitespace, using short specifiers, property cascading, and so on.

❑ Combine multiple images used on one page into a single file, and use CSS image sprites to display them.

❑ Leverage DHTML to avoid a server round-trip for things like showing and hiding part of the page, updating the current time, changing fonts and colors, and event-based actions.

❑ Use Ajax to make partial-page updates.

❑ Use Silverlight as a supplement to JavaScript for things like cross-domain web services and for more complex logic, because it uses type-safe .NET languages.

❑ Consider Silverlight as an alternative to HTML for forms, charts, graphs, animation, grids or tables with client-side sorting, and so on.

❑ Use Silverlight to manage data in isolated storage that can be used by the client from one page to another.

❑ Prefer CSS to `<table>`.

❑ When you can't avoid `<table>`, consider using `<col>`, and make sure to set the size properties of any images the `<table>` contains.

❑ Include a `<!DOCTYPE>` tag at the top of your HTML.

❑ If you can anticipate the next page that a user will request, use script to precache the content and DNS entries that page will use.

❑ Optimize the performance of your JavaScript.

Caching (Chapter 3)

❑ Enable `Cache-Control: max-age` for your static content, with a far-future expiration date.

❑ Review all pages of your dynamic content, and establish an appropriate caching location and duration for them: client-only, proxies, server-side, cache disabled, and so on.

❑ Use cache profiles in `web.config` to help ensure consistent policies.

❑ Disable `ViewState` by default at the page level. Only enable it on pages that post back and where you explicitly need the functionality it provides.

❑ Create and use a custom template in Visual Studio that disables `ViewState`, disables `AutoEventWireup`, and sets a base class for your page, if you're using one.

❑ Use `ViewState` or `ControlState` to cache page-specific state.

❑ Prefer using cookies or Silverlight isolated storage to cache state that's referenced by multiple pages, subject to size and security constraints.

❑ Send a privacy policy HTTP header (`P3P`) whenever you set cookies.

❑ Use `Cache.SetVaryByCustom()` for pages that vary their content based on HTTP headers such as `Accept-Language`.

❑ If your site has a large quantity of static content, consider using a CDN to offload some of it.

❑ Change the name of your static files (or the folders they're in) when you version them, instead of using query strings, so that they remain cacheable by `http.sys`.

❑ Enable output caching for your user controls, where appropriate.

❑ If you have pages that you can't configure to use the output cache, consider either moving some of the code on the pages into a cacheable user control or using substitution caching.

❑ Avoid caching content that is unique per user.

❑ Avoid caching content that is accessed infrequently.

❑ Configure cached pages that depend on certain database queries to drop themselves from the cache based on a notification that the data has changed.

❑ Use the `VaryByCustom` function to cache multiple versions of a page based on customizable aspects of the request such as cookies, role, theme, browser, and so on.

❑ Use a cache validation callback if you need to determine programmatically whether a cached page is still valid.

❑ Use `HttpApplicationState`, `Cache`, and `Context.Items` to cache objects that have permanent, temporary, and per-request lifetimes, respectively.

❑ Associate data that you store in `Cache` with a dependency object to receive a notification that flushes the cache entry if the source data changes.

❑ Consider using a `WeakReference` object to cache objects temporarily in a lightweight way compared the `Cache` object, but with less control over cache lifetime and related events.

❑ Use the 64-bit versions of Windows Server and SQL Server.

❑ Make sure your database server has plenty of RAM, which can help improve caching.

❑ Consider precaching SQL Server data pages into RAM by issuing appropriate queries from a background thread when you can anticipate the user's next request.

❑ For dynamic content that changes frequently, consider using a short cache-expiration time rather than disabling caching.

IIS 7 (Chapter 5)

❑ Partition your application into one or more AppPools, using the Integrated pipeline mode.

❑ Configure AppPool recycling to happen at a specific time each day when your servers aren't busy.

❑ Consider using a web garden (particularly if your site is LG-3+ but you are temporarily using LG-2).

❑ If you're using multiple AppPools, consider using WSRM to help ensure optimal resource allocation between them when your system is under load.

❑ Use Log Parser to check your IIS logs for HTTP `404 Not Found` errors and other similar errors that may be wasting server resources.

❑ Configure IIS to remove the `X-Powered-By` HTTP header.

❑ Install an `HttpModule` to remove the `Server` and `ETag` HTTP headers.

❑ Modify your `web.config` to remove the `X-Aspnet-Version` HTTP header.

❑ Enable site-wide static file compression.

❑ Add support for the `deflate` compression option to `applicationHost.config`.

❑ Specify `staticCompressionLevel="10"` and `dynamicCompressionLevel="5"` in `applicationHost.config`.

❑ Turn off the feature that disables compression if the server's CPU use exceeds a certain threshold.

❑ Modify `applicationHost.config` to allow the `<urlCompression>` tag to be specified in `web.config`.

❑ Use the `<urlCompression>` tag in `web.config` to selectively enable dynamic compression.

❑ Enable `dynamicCompressionBeforeCache` so that your content is cached after it's compressed rather than before.

❑ Keep your URLs short and your folder hierarchies flat, rather than deep.

❑ Consider using virtual directories to help flatten existing hierarchies.

❑ Consider using URL rewriting to help shorten URLs and make them more meaningful for search engines.

❑ Use Failed Request Tracing to validate caching behavior and to find pages that fail or run too slowly.

❑ Consider using IIS bandwidth throttling to help smooth the load on your servers, particularly during peak periods.

ASP.NET Threads and Sessions (Chapter 5)

❑ Use asynchronous pages for all pages that do I/O, including accessing the database, web service calls, filesystem access, and so on.

❑ Modify the `<applicationPool>` section in your `Aspnet.config` file to reflect the load you anticipate on your servers.

❑ Use code rather than the runtime to enforce concurrency limits where the load on a remote system is an issue, such as with some web services.

❑ If you have an existing site that uses synchronous calls, you're seeing low CPU use and high request latencies, and your code is compatible with load balancing, consider temporarily using multiple worker processes while you migrate to async pages.

❑ Add a background worker thread to your application, and use it for tasks that don't have to be executed in-line with page requests, such as logging.

❑ Avoid session state if you can; use cookies or Silverlight isolated storage instead whenever possible.

❑ If you do need session state, configure the runtime to store it in SQL Server.

❑ When using session state, disable it by default in `web.config`, and enable it only on the pages that need it.

❑ Configure `ReadOnly` session state for pages that don't need to write it.

❑ If your site makes heavy use of session state, maximize the performance of the supporting hardware, and consider using partitioning for added scalability.

❑ When you choose which objects to store in the `Session` dictionary, prefer basic data types to custom objects.

Using ASP.NET to Implement and Manage Optimization Techniques (Chapter 6)

❑ Use master pages as a dynamic page template system.

❑ Use custom user controls to factor out code that you use on several different pages.

❑ Consider applying output caching to your user controls.

❑ Use short strings for control IDs, because the strings can appear in your HTML.

❑ Use IDs only when you need to reference an object from your code-behind.

❑ Use ASP.NET themes to help group and manage your style-related assets. Prefer `styleSheetThemes` to standard themes.

❑ Use ASP.NET skins to help define default or often-used user control properties.

❑ If you need in-depth support for mobile devices, download and install the Mobile Device Browser File.

❑ Use the `Request.Browser` object and browser prefixes to specify browser-specific logic.

❑ Use an optimized `GetVaryByCustomString()` to limit the number of different versions of browser-specific pages or controls that the runtime caches.

❑ Consider using control adapters to help optimize generated HTML.

❑ Consider generating CSS and JavaScript dynamically, particularly for things like browser dependencies.

❑ Use custom user controls or control adapters to automatically assign your static files to multiple subdomains and to implement other techniques from Chapter 2.

❑ If you have many images that are larger on the server than the client needs them to be, consider using a dynamic image-resizing control that resizes and caches them on the server before sending the smaller files to the client.

Managing ASP.NET Application Policies (Chapter 7)

❑ Consider using one or more `HttpModules` to enforce things like site-wide cookie policies, centralized monitoring and logging, custom session handling, and custom authorization and authentication.

❑ Because `HttpModules` run in-line with every request, try to offload long-running tasks (such as logging to a database) onto a background worker thread when you can.

❑ Consider using a custom `HttpHandler` for dynamic content that doesn't include a markup file, such as dynamic images and charts.

❑ Use an async `HttpModule` or `HttpHandler` if your code needs to access the database or do any other I/O.

❑ Create a page base class, and use it with all your pages.

❑ Disable `AutoEventWireup` in the `Page` directive, and override the `OnLoad()` style methods instead of using the default `Page_Load()` style.

❑ Consider using a page adapter to implement site-wide page-specific policies, such as custom `ViewState` handling.

❑ Identify client requests that are page refreshes, and limit or minimize the processing to create a new page when appropriate.

❑ Consider using programmatic URL rewriting to help shorten the URLs of your dynamic content.

❑ Minimize the use of redirects. Use `Server.Transfer()` instead when you can.

❑ When you use redirects, be sure to end page processing after issuing the redirect.

❑ Regularly review the HTTP requests and responses that your pages make, using the Fiddler web proxy debugger.

❑ For pages with long-running tasks and where Ajax wouldn't be appropriate, consider flushing the response buffer early to help improve perceived page-load time.

❑ Use whitespace filtering to minimize the size of your HTML (although you must disable `dynamicCompressionBeforeCache` if you do).

❑ Check `Page.IsPostBack` to see whether you can avoid repeating work that is already reflected on the page or stored in `ViewState`.

❑ Before performing any time-consuming operations on a page, check the `Response.IsClientConnected` flag to make sure the client still has an active network connection.

❑ Disable debug mode for the version of your site that runs in production.

SQL Server Relational Database (Chapter 8)

❑ Make sure your database data and log files are on separate disks from one another.

❑ To increase database write performance, add more spindles to your log volumes.

❑ Optimize your data volumes for read performance (IOPS) by adding more spindles.

❑ Make sure you have enough RAM, and add more if you don't (helps improve read performance).

❑ Use stored procedures as your primary interface to the database.

❑ Use dynamic SQL, triggers, or cursors *only* when there is no other way to solve a particular problem.

❑ When you have to use dynamic SQL, always use it with parameterized queries.

❑ Structure your stored procedures to help minimize database round-trips.

❑ Use command batching, table-valued parameters, and multiple result sets to help minimize database round-trips.

❑ Group multiple `INSERT`, `UPDATE`, and `DELETE` operations into transactions to help minimize database log I/O pressure.

❑ If you can anticipate the next database-related action a user will take, consider using a background thread to issue a query that precaches the data you need at the database tier.

❑ Optimize the data types you choose for your tables; prefer narrow, always-increasing keys to wide or randomly ordered ones.

❑ Optimize the indexes for your tables, including clustered vs. nonclustered indexes and including extra columns to allow the indexes to cover queries.

❑ Try to structure your queries and indexes to avoid table and index scans.

❑ Make frequent use of SQL Profiler to observe the activity on your database, including the queries that your application is issuing and how long they take to run.

❑ To prevent deadlocks, ensure that you access lockable database objects consistently in the same order.

❑ Use `SET NOCOUNT ON` at the top of your stored procedures, except in cases where the results are associated with `SqlDependency`.

❑ Use data paging to help limit rows displayed on a page to a reasonable number.

❑ Due to its support for native async commands, command batching, multiple result sets, and table-valued parameters, you should prefer ADO.NET to ORM systems such as LINQ to SQL and the Entity Framework or NHibernate, particularly for large projects.

❑ ORM systems may be acceptable for LG-1 or LG-2 sites or for rapid prototyping that won't evolve into production code.

❑ Consider using XML columns as an alternative to having many sparse columns when you have properties that are difficult to represent in relational form, when you have XML documents that you need to query, as an alternative to adding new columns dynamically to your tables, or as an alternative to many-to-many mappings.

❑ Avoid using wildcards in your XML queries.

❑ For sites that require consistent performance and 24 × 7 uptime, consider using table partitioning to ease ongoing maintenance issues; doing so requires SQL Server Enterprise (LG-5+).

❑ Prefer full-text search to wildcard searches using the T-SQL `LIKE` clause.

❑ Enable Service Broker in your database.

❑ Use Service Broker to offload or time-shift long-running tasks to a background thread (LG-1 to LG-3) or to a Windows Service (LG-3+).

❑ Use Service Broker to queue requests to send e-mails, rather than sending them in-line.

❑ Associate `SqlDependency` or `SqlCacheDependency` objects with database queries that return cacheable results (requires Service Broker).

❑ Use Resource Governor to help maintain the relative priorities of certain types of database traffic, such as low-priority logging compared to your VIP users or purchase transactions; this requires SQL Server Enterprise (LG-5+).

❑ Prefer scaling up your database servers first, before scaling out.

❑ For read-heavy workloads, consider using several load-balanced read-only database servers (LG-6+).

❑ Monitor the relevant Windows and SQL Server performance counters to help identify bottlenecks early and for long-term trend analysis and capacity planning.

❑ Be sure to take into account the time for a failover to happen when designing your high-availability architecture. Prefer clustering when a fail-over time of 30 seconds or more is acceptable, and prefer mirroring when a shorter time is required (LG-5+).

❑ Set a large enough file size for your database data and log files that they should never have to autogrow.

❑ Don't shrink or autoshrink your database files.

❑ Minimize the number of different databases you need.

❑ Consider SQL CLR for functions, types, or stored procedures that contain a large amount of procedural code or to share constants or code between your web and data tiers.

SQL Server Analysis Services (Chapter 9)

❑ Avoid using the relational database for aggregation queries such as sums and counts; whenever possible, use SSAS for that instead (LG-2+).

❑ Download and install ADOMD.NET so that you can query your cubes from your web site (LG-2+).

❑ Use SSMS to test your MDX queries.

❑ Use both Visual Studio and Excel to peruse your cube and to make sure the data is organized as you intended.

❑ As with relational queries, be sure to cache the results of MDX queries when it makes sense to do so. Keep in mind that cubes are updated less often than your tables.

❑ For sites with SQL Server Standard, use SSIS and SQL Agent to automate the process of updating your cubes (LG-2+).

❑ For sites with SQL Server Enterprise, configure proactive caching to update your cubes when the relational data changes (LG-5+).

❑ Consider using a staging database in between your OLTP database and SSAS. Populate the staging database with SSIS, and allow it to be used for certain types of read-only queries (LG-6+).

Infrastructure and Operations (Chapter 10)

❑ Use custom performance counters to instrument and monitor your application.

❑ Minimize the different types of web and application servers that you use in your production environment. If necessary, use WSRM to help balance the load among different AppPools.

❑ Test your servers to determine how they behave under heavy load, including determining their maximum CPU use. Use that information in your capacity planning analysis.

❑ Optimize your disk subsystem by using disks with a high rotation speed, narrow partitions, an appropriate RAID type, matching controller capacities with the achievable throughput, having enough drives, using a battery-backed write cache, and so on.

❑ Minimize NTFS fragmentation by putting your database files on fresh filesystems by themselves.

❑ For filesystems where you add and delete files regularly, periodically run a disk or file defragmentation tool and use a cluster size that reflects your average file size.

❑ Prefer SAS or SCSI drives to SATA when maximizing throughput or data reliability are important.

❑ Keep an eye on SSD technology; SSDs are much faster than rotating disks and may soon be stable enough to deploy in production environments.

❑ Consider using a SAN in environments where building and maintaining your own disk arrays isn't practical, or where data reliability is paramount.

❑ Use a high-speed back-end network: at least 1Gbps, and 10Gbps if you can (LG-3+).

❑ Configure the network that connects your web tier with your data tier to use jumbo frames (LG-3+).

❑ Configure the network from your database servers to the local switch to use link aggregation (LACP) (LG-4+).

❑ Enable Windows Firewall on all your servers.

❑ For LG-1 to LG-3 sites where users can upload files onto your web server, consider using server-side antivirus software as an alternative to a hardware firewall (LG-4+ sites shouldn't store any uploaded files on the web servers).

❑ If you have access to your router, configure it to do port filtering and to protect against things like SYN floods and other DDOS attacks (LG-4+).

❑ For sites with up to eight web servers, consider using NLB for load balancing. For more than eight servers, use a hardware load balancer (LG-4+).

❑ Consider running your own DNS server or subscribing to a commercial service that provides high-speed DNS.

❑ Prefer DNS `A` records to `CNAME` records whenever possible.

❑ If you aren't using DNS as part of a failover scheme (LG-7), set your default TTL to around 24 hours.

❑ Establish staging environments for testing both in development and in preproduction.

❑ Establish a deployment procedure that allows you to complete deployments quickly. It may be manual for smaller sites or automated using WDS for larger sites.

❑ Establish a procedure for upgrading your data tier.

❑ Deploy your web site in precompiled form.

❑ Warm up the cache after a restart on both your web and database servers.

❑ Consider deploying a system to monitor your servers proactively, such as System Center Operations Manager (LG-4+).

Summary

In this chapter, I covered the following:

- The steps to follow to kick off a new project that incorporates ultra-fast principles, as well as the importance of developing a good architecture

- An overview of Microsoft's internal software development process

- The ultra-fast spin on the software development process, including how you can use Depth-first Development to improve the quality and predictability of your project

- The importance of unit testing, including testing for quality-oriented metrics such as execution time

- How determining the league of your system can help provide a focal point for many architectural decisions

- The importance of good software tools, as well as a list of the more important ones to have available

- An example architectural block diagram

- Why two-tier server architectures are generally preferable to three-tier or N-tier

- Detailed checklists with recommendations from earlier chapters

Glossary

Business Intelligence Terminology

cube

Multidimensional data processed by a single MDDB.

data mart

Often used to refer to the staging database, OLAP Services, and report server related to a particular set of business processes, such as Sales or Marketing. Companies often have multiple data marts.

data mining

Statistical analysis of data, usually with a predictive orientation. You can do data mining against either relational or multidimensional data. However, the required analysis is often much more efficient when multidimensional data is used. The results of data-mining analysis are stored in separate structures and are queried separately from the source MDDB. Analysis Services includes a data-mining component.

data warehouse

The collection of all data marts in a company. Some business intelligence (BI) vendors also use the term to refer to certain pieces of the overall architecture, such as just the staging database or just OLAP Services. In SQL Server, for example, the AdventureWorks sample refers to the staging database as the data warehouse.

dimension

The peripheral tables of either a star schema or a snowflake schema, when the central table is a fact table. Dimension tables normally contain mostly strings in their non-key columns. Some architectures require that all original keys be replaced with *surrogate* keys, which simplifies certain types of updates.

DMX

Data Mining Extensions. The language used to query data-mining structures.

ETL

Export, Transform and Load. The process of exporting (reading) data from a source database; transforming it through a series of steps that may include cleaning, duplicate removal, schema modifications, and so on; and loading the data in a destination database. SQL Server Integration Services (SSIS) is an example of an ETL tool.

fact table

The central table of a star or snowflake schema, with columns that are all either numeric or foreign keys to the dimensions. Examples of numeric columns include price, quantity, weight, extended price, and discount. You can represent dates as foreign keys in the fact table that refer to a date dimension. The date dimension provides a breakdown of the date by week, month, quarter, year, and so on.

HOLAP

Hybrid OLAP. A mode in which some data, such as aggregations, is stored locally, and detailed data is stored in a remote RDBMS.

KPI

Key Performance Indicator. In the generic sense, a high-level calculated value that gives an idea about the performance of some aspect of a business. For example, total revenue is a typical KPI. KPIs in Microsoft products have a more specific definition that includes icons to represent *good, caution,* and *bad* (such green, yellow, and red stoplights), along with optional additional icons to represent trends—up, down, and sideways.

MDDBS

Multidimensional Database System. Also called an MDDB. A database that is optimized for working with multidimensional data (sometimes called OLAP Services). SQL Server Analysis Services (SSAS) is an example of an MDDB. Also refers to a collection of cubes.

MDX

Multidimensional Expressions. The language used to query OLAP Services. Microsoft provides support for MDX both directly in Business Intelligence Developer Studio (BIDS) and programmatically with ADOMD.NET.

measure

A numeric column in a fact table. Measures are sometimes used to refer to individual non-key cells in a fact table.

measure group

A single fact table and its related dimensions. There can be multiple measure groups per cube in Analysis Services in SQL Server 2005 and later. SQL Server 2000 supports only one measure group per cube.

MOLAP

Multidimensional OLAP. A mode in which OLAP queries are run against a data store that's local to the MDDB. When a cube is processed by SSAS, data files are created in the local filesystem in MOLAP mode. Because the cube can be re-created from the source database, this is also sometimes called a *MOLAP cache*; but it contains preprocessed aggregates and other metadata, so strictly speaking it is more a transformation of the source data than a cache.

multidimensional data

One fact table or more and the associated dimensions, transformed and optimized for processing, including aggregation (sums, totals, counts, and so on) and grouping by hierarchies or time. Multidimensional data is no longer relational. After transformation, multidimensional data is called a *cube*.

OLAP

Online Analytic Processing. The primary type of processing done by an MDDB.

OLTP

Online Transactional Processing. The primary type of processing done by an RDBMS.

RDBMS

Relational Database Management System. What most users consider to be their central data store, often referred to as just a *database*. SQL Server's Relational Database is an example.

report server

A dedicated server to handle creation and distribution of reports that are based on queries to either an MDDB or an RDBMS. Some architectures also use queries to the staging database for certain types of reports. Queries against production databases for reporting purposes only are strongly discouraged, due to their generally negative impact on performance and scalability.

ROLAP

Relational OLAP. A mode in which OLAP queries are run against a remote RDBMS. Rather than precomputing aggregates as in MOLAP, they are computed on the fly using SQL queries against the source RDBMS. As a result, this mode tends to be much slower than MOLAP.

staging database

An RDBMS that sits between production database servers and an MDDB. Production databases have a number of attributes, such as a high degree of normalization, that tend to make them an inefficient source for an MDDB.

A common solution to this problem is the creation of one or more staging databases. An ETL process reads data from the production databases and stores it in a star or snowflake schema in the staging database. The MDDB is then loaded and refreshed from the staging database. This also helps minimize the load impact on production servers.

The amount of history retained in the staging database is typically much larger than in the production databases. Using a staging database for historical queries often helps improve the scalability of the production servers. Some architects don't allow queries against the staging database, and others do (I'm in the latter camp).

star schema

A relational schema that consists of a single central table and multiple peripheral tables. The peripheral tables contain primary keys that are referenced by foreign keys in the central table. A fully connected set of relational tables can be transformed into a star schema using denormalization, where parts of multiple tables are joined together to form the central table.

star snowflake schema

A star schema that includes additional tables that are referenced by keys in the peripheral tables. At most one level of indirection exists between the outermost tables and the central table. Also called a *snowflake schema*.

Index

Special Characters

$ (dollar sign), 206
~ (tilde character), 319
<% %> code block, 28

Numerics

/3GB flag, 264
32-bit systems, memory organization, 264
64-bit systems, memory organization, 264
64KB extents, 264
302 Found redirects, 249
304 Not Modified message, 74
404 Not Found errors, 134

■A

absolute positioning, 64, 423
Accept header, 44
Accept-Language header, 103
accessors, 266
ACK packets, 15–16
AcquireReaderLock( ) method, 187
AcquireRequestState event, 197
ActionType enum, 181
active-active configuration, 345
ActiveViewIndex property, 215
ADAL abstract class, 284
adapterType property, 218
Add Cache Rule dialog, IIS Manager, 106
Add Custom HTTP Response Header dialog, IIS Manager, 38
Add New Project dialog box, Visual Studio, 311–312
Add or Edit Resource Allocation dialog box, WSRM, 132
Add Rule dialog box, WSRM, 131

Add rule(s) dialog box, IIS Manager, 146
Add Virtual Directory option, IIS Manager, 145
Add Web Deployment Project option, Visual Studio, 29
Add Web Reference dialog, Visual Studio, 174
AddBrowser( ) method, 219
AddBrowserBegin( ) method, 284
AddBrowserEnd( ) method, 284
AddCacheDependency( ) method, 113–114
AddCacheItemDependency( ) method, 113
AddMachine stored procedure, 238
Address Windowing Extensions (AWE), 264
AddValidationCallback, 116
Adobe Photoshop
    compression, 32–33
    cost of, 10
    image slicing, 34
AdomdCommand object, 371
AdomdConnection object, 371
ADOMD.NET library
    multiple-row results, 372–373
    overview, 350–351, 369–370
    single-cell results, 370–371
ADO.NET, command batching for, 267
Advanced Output Cache Rule Settings dialog box, IIS Manager, 109–110
Advanced Settings dialog, IIS Manager, 128
agents, SCOM, 409
aggregation queries
    avoiding, 346
    caching results, 349
    performance impact, 265, 286
agility goal, 3
Ajax
    avoiding full page loads, 9
    client performance, 52–55
    precaching, 62
    search engines, 251